CORRECTING
the
C U L T S

CORRECTING
the
CULTS

Expert Responses to
Their Scripture Twisting

Norman L. Geisler
and Ron Rhodes

BakerBooks
Grand Rapids, Michigan

© 1997 by Norman L. Geisler and Ron Rhodes

Published by Baker Books
a division of Baker Publishing Group
P.O. Box 6287, Grand Rapids, MI 49516-6287
www.bakerbooks.com

Second printing, August 2005

Paperback edition published 2005
ISBN 0-8010-6550-X

Previously published in 1997 under the title When Cultists Ask

Printed in the United States of America

The Library of Congress has cataloged the hardcover edition as follows:
Geisler, Norman L.
    When cultists ask : a popular handbook on cultic misinterpretations / Norman L. Geisler and Ron Rhodes.
        p. cm.
    ISBN 0-8010-1149-3 (cloth)
    1. Cults—Controversial literature—Handbooks, manuals, etc. 2. Sects—Controversial literature—Handbooks, manuals, etc. 3. Apologetics—Handbooks, manuals, etc. 4. Bible—Criticism, interpretation, etc.—Handbooks, manuals, etc. I. Rhodes, Ron. II. Title.
BP603.G45   1997
220.6—dc21   97-23217

CONTENTS

ACKNOWLEDGMENTS

I wish to thank Kenny Hood, David Johnson, Trevor Mander, Douglas Potter, Steve Puryear, and especially my wife, Barbara, who helped me in the preparation of this manuscript. Without their able assistance I would not have been able to produce my part of the book.

—*Norman L. Geisler*

In addition to those mentioned above, I wish to thank my wife, Kerri, whose assistance and encouragement are always much appreciated, and our two children, David and Kylie (my personal cheering squad).

—*Ron Rhodes*

INTRODUCTION

Understanding the Cults

Cults and new religions are exploding in unprecedented proportions on the American horizon. As the light of Christianity fades, darkness is flooding in from every side. Jehovah's Witnesses, Mormons, and New Age religions galore are all seeking the souls of human beings. Each professes to have the latest way to enlightenment, the prophet for our time, or the sure way to universal peace.

Some experts say there are about 700 cults, while others say there are as many as 3,000. Cults of one form or another involve more than 20 million people in the United States, and they are multiplying at an alarming rate. Worldwide there are now over 5 million Jehovah's Witnesses (who spend over one billion man–hours per year proselytizing), almost 9 million Mormons (presently growing at a rate of 1,500 new members per day), and tens of millions of New Agers.

World religions that are diametrically opposed to Christianity are also growing at a frightening rate. For example, there are nearly one billion Muslims in the world. That is about one out of every 5 persons on earth! In North America alone it is estimated that there are between 4 and 8 million Muslims. And there are more than 1,100 Muslim mosques in the United States.

Clearly, Christians must take the cultic threat seriously and learn to defend Christianity in the face of the onslaught. This book will help you accomplish that goal. But first, it is important that we understand some of the common traits of the cults.

What Is a Cult?

There is no universally agreed–upon definition of a cult; there are only some generally recognizable traits. Actually, there are three different dimensions of a cult—*doctrinal, sociological,* and *moral.* Below we take a brief look at these. Keep in mind, though, that not every cult manifests every single trait we discuss.

Doctrinal Characteristics of a Cult

There are a number of doctrinal characteristics of cults. One will typically find an emphasis on new revelation from God, a denial of the sole authority of the Bible, a denial of the Trinity, a distorted view of God and Jesus, or a denial of salvation by grace.

New Revelation. Many cult leaders claim to have a direct pipeline to God. The teachings of the cult often change and, hence, they need new "revelations" to justify such changes. Mormons, for example, once excluded African Americans from the priesthood. When social pressure was exerted against the Mormon church for this blatant form of racism, the Mormon president received a new "revelation" reversing the previous decree. Jehovah's Witnesses engaged in the same kind of change regarding the earlier Watchtower teaching that vaccinations and organ transplants were prohibited by Jehovah.

Denial of the Sole Authority of the Bible. Many cults deny the sole authority of the Bible. The Mormons, for example, believe the Book of Mormon is higher Scripture than the Bible. Jim Jones, founder and leader of Jonestown, placed himself in authority over the Bible. Christian Scientists elevate Mary Baker Eddy's book *Science and Health* to supreme authority. Reverend Moon placed his book *The Divine Principle* in authority over all his followers. New Agers believe in many modern forms of authoritative revelation, such as *The Aquarian Gospel of Jesus the Christ.*

A Distorted View of God and Jesus. Many cults set forth a distorted view of God and Jesus. The "Jesus Only" Oneness Pentecostals, for example, deny the Trinity and hold to a form of modalism, claiming that Jesus is God, and that "Father," "Son," and "Holy Spirit" are simply singular names for Jesus. The Jehovah's Witnesses deny both the Trinity and the absolute deity of Christ, saying that Christ is a lesser god than the Father (who is God Almighty). The Mormons say Jesus was "procreated" (by a heavenly father and a heavenly mother) at a point in time, and was the spirit–brother of Lucifer. Mormons do speak of a "Trinity," but redefine it into Tritheism (i.e., three gods). The Baha'is say Jesus was just one of many prophets of God. The Jesus of the spiritists is just an advanced medium. The Jesus of the Theosophists is a mere reincarnation of the so–called World Teacher (who is said to periodically reincarnate in the body of a human disciple). The Jesus of psychic Edgar Cayce is a being who in his first incarnation was Adam and in his thirtieth reincarnation was "the Christ."

Related to the above, cults also typically deny the bodily resurrection of Jesus Christ. The Jehovah's Witnesses, for example, say that Jesus was raised from the dead as an invisible spirit creature. Herbert W. Armstrong, founder of the Worldwide Church of God, also denied the physical, bodily resurrection of Christ. (Note that in recent years the Worldwide Church of God has repudiated many of Armstrong's teachings and has taken significant steps toward orthodoxy.)

Denial of Salvation by Grace. Cults typically deny salvation by grace, thus distorting the purity of the gospel. The Mormons, for example, emphasize the necessity of becoming more and more perfect in this life. The Jehovah's Witnesses emphasize the importance of distributing Watchtower literature door–to–door as a part of "working out" their salvation. Herbert W. Armstrong said that the idea that works are not required for salvation is rooted in Satan.

From the brief survey above, it is clear that all cults deny one or more of the fundamental, essential doctrines of Christianity.

Sociological Characteristics of a Cult

In addition to the doctrinal characteristics of cults, many (not all) cults also have sociological traits. These include authoritarianism, exclusivism, dogmatism, close–mindedness, susceptibility, compartmentalization, isolation, and even antagonism. Let us take a brief look at these.

Authoritarianism. Authoritarianism involves the acceptance of an authority figure who often uses mind–control techniques on group members. As prophet and/or founder, this leader's word is considered ultimate. The late David Koresh of the Branch Davidian cult in Waco, Texas, is a tragic example. Other cults that involve authoritarianism include the Children of God (now called "The Family"), the Unification Church, and Jonestown (headed by Jim Jones).

Cult prophets/founders should not be confused with legitimate reformers/revivalists, such as Martin Luther and John Wesley. The differences are significant. A reformer, in contrast to a cult founder, leads people by love, not by fear. He influences by love, not by hate. He tries to motivate the heart but makes no attempt to control the mind. He leads his followers like a shepherd leads sheep; he does not drive them like goats.

Exclusivism. Another characteristic of cults is an exclusivism that says, "We alone have the truth." The Mormons believe they are the exclusive community of the saved on earth. The Jehovah's Witnesses believe they are the exclusive community of the saved.

Some groups manifest exclusivism in their practice of communal living. Under such conditions it is easier to maintain control over cult members.

Examples of this kind of cult include the Children of God and the Branch Davidians.

It is important to note that there are some religious groups that practice communal living that are not cults. The Jesus People USA in Chicago are an example of a good Christian group that lives communally.

Dogmatism. Closely related to the above, many cults are dogmatic—and this dogmatism is often expressed institutionally. For example, Mormons claim to be the only true church on earth. The Jehovah's Witnesses claim that the Watchtower Society is the sole voice of Jehovah on earth. David Koresh said he alone could interpret the Bible. Many cults believe they have the truth in a suitcase, as it were. They alone are in possession of the divine oracles.

Close–mindedness. Hand in hand with dogmatism is the characteristic of close–mindedness. This unwillingness to even consider any other point of view often has radical manifestations. One educated Mormon we encountered said he did not care if it could be proved that Joseph Smith was a false prophet; he still would remain a Mormon. A Jehovah's Witness we met once refused to finish reading an article that proved the deity of Christ because, said he, "It is disturbing my faith."

Susceptibility. The psychological profile of many individuals who are sucked into cults is not flattering. All too often, though not always, people who join cults are highly gullible. Sometimes they are even psychologically vulnerable. But above all, the cultic mentality is characterized by an unhealthy compartmentalization (that is, they "compartmentalize" conflicting facts and ignore anything that contradicts their claims). Many Mormons have a "burning in the bosom" which makes it nearly impossible to reason with them about their faith. Cultists often accept teachings by a kind of blind faith that is impervious to sound reasoning. One Mormon missionary said he would believe the Book of Mormon even if it said there were square circles!

Isolationism. The more extreme cults sometimes create fortified boundaries, often precipitating tragic endings, such as the disaster in Waco, Texas, with the Branch Davidian cult. Deserters are considered traitors, and their lives are sometimes put in jeopardy by more zealous members of the cult. In many cases cult members are told that if they leave the group, they will be attacked and destroyed by Satan. The erection of such barriers, whether physical or psychological, creates an environment of isolation, which in turn often leads to antagonism.

Antagonism. In a context of isolation, both fear and antagonism toward the outside world is often generated. All other groups are considered apostate. They are considered "the enemy" and "tools of Satan." In extreme cases this may lead to an armed conflict, as in Jonestown and Waco.

Moral Characteristics of a Cult

On top of the doctrinal and sociological traits of cults, there are also some moral dimensions to be considered. Among those that crop up most often are legalism, sexual perversion, intolerance, and psychological or even physical abuse. Again, though, not every cult manifests every one of these traits.

Legalism. Setting down a rigid set of rules by which the devotees must live is common to many cults. These standards are usually extrabiblical. The Mormon teaching forbidding the use of coffee, tea, or any drink with caffeine is a case in point. The requirement of the Watchtower Society for Jehovah's Witnesses to distribute literature door to door is another example. Monastic-type asceticism, with its rigorous rule–keeping, is often seen as a means of gaining favor with God. As such, it is a manifestation of the common cultic rejection of God's grace.

Sexual Perversion. Along with legalism, the twin vice of moral perversion is often found in the cults. Joseph Smith (and other Mormon leaders) had many wives. David Koresh claimed to own all the women in his group, even the young girls. According to a 1989 revelation, this reportedly included girls as young as ten. The Children of God cult throughout its history has used "flirty fishing" techniques to sexually lure people into the cult. Sex between adults and children has been reported in this cult.

Physical Abuse. Tragically, some cults engage in forms of physical abuse. Ex–cult members often accuse their former leaders of engaging in beatings, sleep deprivation, severe food deprivation, and beating children until they are bruised and bleeding. Sometimes there are charges of satanic ritualistic abuse, though these seem to be much more rare than advertised. However, psychological abuse, such as fear, intimidation, and isolation, is more common. The ultimate physical abuse is illustrated in the person of cult leader Jim Jones, who led all the members of Jonestown to drink poisoned punch.

Intolerance toward Others. Toleration is not one of the virtues of the cultic mentality. Intolerance is often manifest in antagonism and sometimes culminates in killings. Both Mormon and Branch Davidian history have examples of this kind of violent intolerance. Of course, other religious groups, such as radical Muslims, are known for the same. Closer to home, the Spanish Inquisition is a manifestation of Christian cultic zeal.

Cultic Methodology

Cults are well known for their questionable methods. For example, cults often engage in moral deception and aggressive proselytizing. Let's take a brief look at these.

Moral Deception. Moonies are known for their so–called heavenly deception. Duplicity and lies are used to win converts into the movement. Mormon founder Joseph Smith also engaged in fraudulent tactics which, on occasion, even landed him in court, where he was once found guilty and fined. Modern leaders of Transcendental Meditation have also been deceptive in trying to further their cause.

Far more common is the cults' use of Christian terms infused with new meanings, thus deceiving untrained Christians into believing the cult is Christian. For example, New Age cults sometimes use the Christian terms "resurrection" and "ascension" when they really mean the "rise" of Christ–consciousness in the world. The familiar Christian term "born again" is often employed by New Agers to support the doctrine of reincarnation. The term "the Christ" is used by New Agers to seek Christian approval when to them it actually means an occult office held by various gurus throughout history.

Aggressive Proselytizing. There is, of course, a good sense in which every missionary religion proselytizes. That is, they attempt to win converts for their faith. Christianity, Judaism, Islam, and even forms of Hinduism and Buddhism attempt to convert people to their beliefs.

Cults, however, carry proselytizing activities to an extreme. Often their excessive proselytizing is an attempt to gain God's approval. They work *for* grace rather than *from* grace as the Bible teaches (2 Cor. 5:14). Sometimes their efforts are exerted in satisfaction of their own egos. Many times their overzealous proselytizing involves impersonal evangelism or button-holing people. Followers of the Boston Church of Christ are known for overzealous attempts to make converts on college campuses throughout the United States. Both Mormons and Jehovah's Witnesses have extensive door–to–door programs of proselytizing, though they are usually less obnoxious in their approach.

Of course, it is important to note that while almost all cults are aggressive evangelizers, not all aggressive evangelizers are cults. Campus Crusade for Christ and Jews for Jesus are ministries that are zealous in evangelism, but they are not cults. Indeed, if the Christian church were more zealous in true evangelism, the world would have less cultic proselytizing.

Why Are the Cults Growing?

One noted cult researcher observed that the cults are "the unpaid bills of the church." The church has failed to doctrinally train its members; it has failed to make a real moral difference in the lives of its members; it has failed to meet people's deepest needs; and it has failed to provide people with a sense of belonging. The failure of the church is wide and deep, and this has made it easy for the cults to flourish.

But, of course, the growth of the cults is attributable to many other factors as well. Among other things, the cults are multiplying because of the growth of relativism, selfism, subjectivism, and mysticism. Further, moral rebellion and the breakdown of families have contributed to the increase in cults worldwide. Consider the following:

Doctrinal Failure. Walter Martin once said that the rise of the cults is "directly proportional to the fluctuating emphasis which the Christian church has placed on the teaching of biblical doctrine to Christian laymen. To be sure, a few pastors, teachers, and evangelists defend adequately their beliefs, but most of them—and most of the average Christian laymen—are hard put to confront and refute a well–trained cultist of almost any variety" (*The Rise of the Cults*, 24). The failure of the church to teach sound doctrine leads to the acceptance of false doctrine. One cannot recognize error unless one first understands the truth. Counterfeits are known only by comparison with the genuine.

Increase in Relativism. The growth of relativism in our culture has also contributed to the rise of cults. The statements, "That may be true for you but not for me" and "Everything is relative to the situation," are almost proverbial today. This plague of relativism has nearly inundated the land. Along with the "Do your own thing" mentality has come the "Have your own religion" syndrome. Secular humanism's denial of all God–given absolutes has led to a God–sized vacuum in our society into which Eastern mysticism has rapidly moved.

Mystical Turn East. "The Turn East," as Harvey Cox of Harvard University titled his book, has been as natural as it is phenomenal. Once American society rejected its Judeo–Christian roots for secular humanism, which cannot satisfy the heart–desires of people, the only major force left was Eastern mysticism. Christian theism affirms that God created all. Secularistic atheism declares there is no God at all. Both of these being found unsatisfactory, our culture has now turned to Eastern cults that proclaim that God is all and all is God.

This turn Eastward has been accompanied by a turn inward. The mystical cults, stressing as they do subjective experience and inner feeling, have grown rapidly in the wake of mysticism. We have turned as a culture from exploring the universe out there to exploring the universe *in here*—inside of us. The focus is not so much on *outer space* as on *inner space*. This, of course, is what the Eastern mystics have always taught, and it plays right into the hands of New Age cults.

Emphasis on Self. The growth of selfishness has also contributed to the proliferation of the cults. The "Do your own thing" mentality leads naturally to the "Start your own cult" movement. We might say the cults are religious freedom gone to seed. The humanistic "Every man for himself" philosophy is a perfect fertilizer for the growth of new religions that cater to the felt needs, rather than the real needs, of the individual.

Stress on Feelings. Another factor leading to the rise of cults is the growth of subjectivism and existentialism. Granted the seemingly insatiable appetite for religion, the "If it feels good, do it" syndrome leads naturally to seeking out religions that feel good. While some still seek the psychedelic shortcut to Nirvana through mind–expanding drugs, others seek a subjective mystical experience that transcends the routines of daily life. This accounts in large part for the growth of New Age cults, such as Transcendental Meditation.

Moral Rebellion. Beneath all the sociological and psychological factors giving rise to cults is moral depravity. The Bible makes it very clear that human beings are in rebellion against the God who is there (Rom. 1:18f.). One dimension of this rebellion is moral. People turn to more comfortable religions when their chosen lifestyle is contrary to the moral imperatives of a transcendent and sovereign God. The moral perversion existing in many cults is ample testimony to the depravity found in the world of the cults. The followers of the Hindu guru Rajneesh engaged in orgies in Oregon. David Berg's Children of God cult is well known for its sexual perversions. In fact, moral perversion is characteristic of many cults. This moral rebelliousness was manifest in the antiestablishment, antigovernment, and antifamily movement growing out of the 60s, and its inertia has carried it into the 90s.

Social Breakdown of Families. Walter Martin once said, "We see a generation without a sense of history—cut off from the past, alienated from the present, and having a fragmented concept of the future. The 'now' generation is in reality a lost generation" (*The New Cults,* 28). Many cults have capitalized on the breakdown of families in our society and have become surrogate families for the "lost generation."

It is not without significance that many cult members address the leaders of their cult in parental terms. For example, New Ager Elizabeth Clare Prophet, who heads the Church Universal and Triumphant, is affectionately known among her followers as "Guru Ma." David "Moses" Berg, founder of the Children of God, was often called "Father David" by cult members. Likewise, Reverend Moon is often called "Father Moon" by members of the Unification Church.

What Makes Cults Dangerous?

Cults present many dangers both to the church and to individuals. These dangers are spiritual, psychological, and even physical. Consider the following:

Spiritual Dangers of Cults

Cults are involved in serious error, and error is always dangerous because it misleads people. The Bible declares that the devil is the father of lies: "He was a murderer from the beginning, and has not stood in the truth, because there is no truth in him. When he speaks falsehood, he speaks of what is his own; for he is a liar and its father" (John 8:44). Ultimately all error is inspired of the devil. As the apostle Paul put it, "Now the Spirit speaks expressly, that in the latter times some shall depart from the faith, giving heed to seducing spirits, and doctrines of demons" (1 Tim. 4:1).

Those who believe lies are already deceived. And if they act on these lies they are in danger. Some everyday examples make the point well. If you believe a railroad flashing sign is just stuck when it isn't, you are in serious danger of being hit by a train. If you believe ice on a lake is very thick when it is thin, you are in danger of drowning. If you think you are on a two–way street when it is one–way, you are in dire danger of a head–on collision.

The spiritual danger of believing a lie is even more serious—it has eternal consequences! To die while believing in the Jesus of the Jehovah's Witnesses or the Jesus of Mormonism is to die believing in a counterfeit Jesus who preaches a counterfeit gospel which yields a counterfeit salvation (which, in fact, is no salvation at all).

Psychological Dangers of Cults

The psychological damage done by cults can be immense. Cults often prey on vulnerable people. Many cults seek out "loners" and lavish affection upon them (sometimes called "love bombings") until they become "hooked." Cult leaders become the absolute authority for weak individuals who have had little or no authority in their family background. In some cases this authority can extend to every area of life—how long you sleep, what you eat, what kinds of clothes you wear, and so forth. Such individuals become psychologically enslaved to the whims of the cult leader.

Physical Dangers of Cults

In view of recent occurrences, every cult should have a warning label: "WARNING: This religion may be dangerous to your health and life." In 1983, Hobart Freeman, leader of the Faith Assembly in Fort Wayne, Indiana, died having thrown away his heart medicine. Some 52 other members of his group died, many of them babies and children. Jim Jones led 900 of his followers in an alleged suicide pact. Likewise David Koresh led some 80 of his followers in a fiery suicide in Waco, Texas, in 1992.

Little wonder the Bible constantly warns against false doctrine. Jesus said, "Beware of false prophets, which come to you in sheep's clothing, but inwardly they are ravening wolves" (Matt. 7:15).

Scripture–Twisting and the Cults

In view of this deluge of counterfeits, believers have an unparalleled need for a deeper understanding of authentic Christianity. For it is impossible to recognize a fraud unless we have an understanding of the genuine. Error can only be correctly measured over against the truth of God's inerrant Word.

The fact is, the cults are notorious *Scripture–twisters.* When dealing with cults, one must keep in mind that they are always built not upon what the Bible teaches but upon what the founders or leaders of the respective cults say the Bible teaches.

The present book was written to help you, the reader, lovingly turn the tables on the cultist and "untwist" the Scriptures so the cultist can see what the Scriptures really teach. Remember—Jesus said his words lead to eternal life (John 6:63). But for us to receive eternal life through his words, they must be taken as he intended them to be taken. A cultic reinterpretation of Scripture that yields another Jesus and another gospel (2 Cor. 11:3–4; Gal. 1:6–9) will yield only eternal death (Rev. 20:11–15).

This book was also written to help you "untwist" the faulty interpretations of *aberrant* groups that fall short of the definition of a cult. The Roman Catholic Church is an example. Though it is essentially a Christian church and *not* technically a cult (at least not in its official teachings), there are nevertheless many aberrant doctrines that are taught within Roman Catholicism. These doctrinal aberrations are so serious that aspects of orthodoxy are undermined, thus warranting the Protestant Reformation of the sixteenth century and the continued separation of present–day Protestantism from Catholicism. You will find that this book will help you answer Roman Catholic aberrations from Scripture.

We must remember that one way we can shine as lights in our world (Matt. 5:16) is to set a consistent example before others of what it means to correctly handle the word of truth (2 Tim. 2:15). By so doing, others may come to imitate us in this regard. And as others learn to imitate us in correctly handling Scripture, so they too can be used of God to set an example before still others.

The process begins with a single person—you! *Together* we can curb the growth of the cults and aberrant groups.

GENESIS

GENESIS 1:1–2—Is the Holy Spirit a person, or is the Holy Spirit "God's active force"?

MISINTERPRETATION: Jehovah's Witnesses think this verse implies that the Holy Spirit is not a person but, rather, God's active force. God allegedly used this "force" in creating the universe. They believe that, since the Hebrew word for "spirit" also can be translated "wind," they are justified in translating the term as "active force" in Genesis 1:2 (*Should You Believe in the Trinity?* 1989, 20).

CORRECTING THE MISINTERPRETATION: The Hebrew word *ruach* can have a variety of meanings—including "breath," "wind," and "Spirit (i.e., the Holy Spirit)." However, since references to the Holy Spirit, both here and elsewhere throughout Scripture, consistently provide evidences for the *personality* of the Holy Spirit, the translation "active force" should be ruled out.

First of all, even here the Holy Spirit is engaged in the act of creation, which involves intelligent action in forming the world. The very act of "hovering" over the waters implies an intelligent purpose.

Elsewhere in the Old Testament, the Holy Spirit manifests the attributes of personality. He can anoint for a preaching ministry (Isa. 61:1) and even be grieved by our sin (Isa. 63:10; cf. Eph. 4:30). In fact, all the essential characteristics of personality are attributed to the Holy Spirit in Scripture—he has a mind (Rom. 8:27; 1 Cor. 2:10; Eph. 1:17), emotions (Eph. 4:30), and will (1 Cor. 12:11). A mere "force" does not have these attributes.

Furthermore, the Holy Spirit does things only a person could do. For example, he teaches (John 14:26), guides (Rom. 8:14), issues commands (Acts 8:29), prays (Rom. 8:26), and speaks to people (John 15:26; 2 Peter 1:21).

Finally, the Holy Spirit is consistently treated as a person. For example, he can be lied to (Acts 5:3). One cannot lie to a force (say, electricity) or to any impersonal thing. Only *a person* can be lied to. In view of such factors, one cannot translate *ruach* as "active force" when used of the Holy Spirit, for the Holy Spirit is quite clearly a person. See comments on Acts 2:4.

GENESIS 1:26—Does this verse indicate that there is more than one god?

MISINTERPRETATION: If there is only one God, why does this verse in Genesis use the word *us* in reference to God? Mormons often note that the Hebrew word usually translated God, *Elohim,* is in the plural, and the plural pronoun *us* is used. To them this indicates that there is more than one God: "In the very beginning the Bible shows there is a plurality of Gods beyond the power of refutation. . . . The word *Elohim* ought to be in the plural all the way through—Gods" (Smith, 1976, 372).

CORRECTING THE MISINTERPRETATION: Several explanations for the use of the pronoun *us* have been offered throughout history. Some commentators have claimed that God is addressing the angels. But this is unlikely since in verse 26 God says, "Let us make man in *our* image," while verse 27 makes it clear that "God created man in *his own* image; in the image of *God* he created him," and not in the image of the angels.

Others have claimed that the plural pronoun refers to the Trinity. It is true that the New Testament (e.g., John 1:1) teaches that the Son was involved in the creation of the heavens and the earth. Also, Genesis 1:2 indicates that the Holy Spirit was involved in the creation process. However, students of Hebrew grammar point out that the plural pronoun *us* is simply required by the plural Hebrew noun *Elohim,* which is translated "God" ("Then God [*Elohim,* plural] said, 'Let *us* [plural] make man in *our* [plural] image'"). Consequently, they claim that this statement should not be used to prove the doctrine of the Trinity.

Still others have asserted that the plural is used as a figure of speech called a *majestic plural.* Indeed, the Qur'an, which denies that there is more than one person in God, uses *us* of God. In this use, God is speaking to himself in such a manner as to indicate that all of his majestic power and wisdom were involved in the creation of humanity. As has been noted, the plural pronoun *us* corresponds to the plural Hebrew word *Elohim,* which is translated God. The fact that the name *God* is plural in Hebrew does not indicate that there is more than one God. (Queen Victoria used a plural of majesty when referring only to herself. She once commented, "We are not amused.") A number of passages in the New Testament refer to God with the singular Greek noun *theos*, which is also translated "God" (for example John 1:1; Mark 13:19; Eph. 3:9). The plural nature of the Hebrew word is designed to give a fuller, more majestic sense to God's name.

It should be noted, however, that the New Testament clearly teaches that God is a Trinity (Matt. 3:16–17; 2 Cor. 13:14; 1 Peter 1:2), and, although the doctrine of the Trinity is not fully developed in the Old Testament, it is foreshadowed (cf. Ps. 110:1; Prov. 30:4; Isa. 63:7, 9–10).

GENESIS 1:26—Does the fact that we are created in God's image mean that we are "little gods," as Word-Faith leaders say?

MISINTERPRETATION: Word-Faith teachers suggest that the Hebrew word for "likeness" in this verse literally means "an exact duplication in kind" (Savelle, 1990, 141). Indeed, humanity "was created on terms of equality with God, and he could stand in God's presence without any consciousness of inferiority. . . . God has made us as much like Himself as possible. . . . He made us the same class of being that He is Himself" (Hagin, 1989, 35–36, 41).

CORRECTING THE MISINTERPRETATION: All Genesis 1:26–27 is teaching is that humanity was created in God's image or likeness in the sense that a human being is a finite reflection of God in rational nature (Col. 3:10), in moral nature (Eph. 4:24), and in dominion over creation (Gen. 1:27–28). In the same way that the moon reflects the brilliant light of the sun, so finite humanity (as created in God's image) is a limited reflection of God in these aspects. This verse has nothing to do with human beings becoming God or being in God's "class."

If it were true that human beings are "little gods," then one would expect them to display qualities similar to those known to be true of God. However, when one compares the attributes of humankind with those of God, we find ample testimony for the truth of Paul's statement in Romans 3:23 that human beings "fall short of the glory of God." Consider:

1. God is *all-knowing* (Isa. 40:13–14), but a human being is limited in knowledge (Job 38:4);
2. God is *all-powerful* (Rev. 19:6), but a human being is weak (Heb. 4:15);

3. God is *everywhere-present* (Ps. 139:7–12), but a human being is confined to a single space at a time (John 1:50);
4. God is *holy* (1 John 1:5), but even human "righteous" deeds are as filthy garments before God (Isa. 64:6);
5. God is *eternal* (Ps. 90:2), but humanity was created at a point in time (Gen. 1:1, 26–27);
6. God is *truth* (John 14:6), but a human heart (since the Fall) is deceitful above all else (Jer. 17:9);
7. God is characterized by *justice* (Acts 17:31), but humankind is lawless (1 John 3:4; see also Rom. 3:23);
8. God is *love* (Eph. 2:4–5), but human relationships are plagued with numerous vices like jealousy and strife (1 Cor. 3:3).

GENESIS 1:26–27—Does this passage support the idea that God has a physical body?

MISINTERPRETATION: Mormons argue that, because humans were created with a body of flesh and bones, God the Father must have a physical body, since humanity was created in God's image (Smith, 1975, 1:3).

CORRECTING THE MISINTERPRETATION: A fundamental interpretive principle is that Scripture interprets Scripture. When other Scriptures about God's nature are consulted, the Mormon understanding of Genesis 1:26–27 becomes impossible. John 4:24 indicates that God is spirit. Luke 24:39 tells us that a spirit does not have flesh and bones. Conclusion: Since God is spirit, he does not have flesh and bones. Moreover, contrary to Mormonism, God is not (and never has been) a man (Num. 23:19; Isa. 45:12; Hosea 11:9; Rom. 1:22–23).

GENESIS 1:26–27—Does the fact that a human being is made in the image of God support the Christian Science claim that humanity is co-eternal with God?

MISINTERPRETATION: These verses assert that God created humanity in his own image. Christian Science founder Mary Baker Eddy urges that this means that "man and woman—as coexistent and eternal with God—forever reflect, in glorified quality, the infinite Father-Mother God" (Eddy, 516).

CORRECTING THE MISINTERPRETATION: Eddy completely misunderstands this passage of Scripture. Several mistakes will be briefly noted.

It is contrary to the meaning of the words "image" and "likeness" to insist that humankind is like God in all respects. Even an "image" in this context is not the same as the original, as is clear from the use of this same Hebrew word (*tzehlem*) of an idol (e.g., Num. 33:52; 2 Chron. 23:17; Ezek. 7:20) as only a *representation* of the god, not the god itself.

The word *create* reveals that the text is not speaking of something that is eternal but of something that came to be. This word *(bara)* is never used in the Old Testament of something that is eternal. Indeed, in this context it means something that is brought into being. The same is true of the New Testament use of the word for "create" (cf. Col. 1:15–16; Rev. 4:11).

Also, it is a fallacy to assume, as Eddy does, that because we are like God, God must be like us. For example, she speaks of God as male and female ("Father-Mother God"). This is known in logic as an *illicit conversion.* Just because all horses have four legs does not mean that all four-legged things are horses. And just because God made male and female does not mean he is male and female. "God is spirit" (John 4:24), yet he made people with bodies (Gen. 2:7). Just because we have a physical body does not mean that God has one too.

The Old Testament was first written as a Jewish book, and Judaism is uncompromisingly a monotheistic religion. But Christian Science is pantheistic, and Eddy is reading her pantheistic view into this Jewish document. A human being is neither eternal with God nor identical with God. Each person is a finite creature who was brought into existence by an infinite God and who resembles God *morally* and *personally,* but is not the same *metaphysically.*

GENESIS 2:7—Does this verse prove that human beings do not have a soul that survives death?

MISINTERPRETATION: Jehovah's Witnesses cite this verse to prove that man does not have a soul that is distinct from the body. "Bible usage shows the soul to be a person or an animal or the life that a person or an animal enjoys" (*Mankind's Search for God,* 1990, 125). Hence, people are souls in the sense that they are living beings, not in the sense that they have an immaterial nature that survives death.

CORRECTING THE MISINTERPRETATION: In Genesis 2:7 the Hebrew word for "soul" *(nephesh)* means "living being." However, this Hebrew word is a rich one, carrying various nuances of meaning in different contexts. A fundamental mistake beginning Hebrew and Greek students sometimes make is to assume that, if a Hebrew or Greek word is used in a particular way in one verse, it must mean the same thing in all its other uses. But this is simply wrong. The fact is, Hebrew and Greek words can have different nuances of meaning in different contexts. The word *nephesh* is an example. While the word means "living being" in Genesis 2:7, the word refers to a soul or spirit as distinct from the body in Genesis 35:18.

Moreover, when we examine what the whole of Scripture teaches about the soul, it is clear that the Watchtower Society (Jehovah's Witnesses) position is wrong. For example, Revelation 6:9–10 refers to disembodied souls under God's altar (it would be nonsense to interpret the reference to "soul" in this verse as "living being"—"I saw underneath the altar the *living beings* of those who had been slain"). First Thessalonians 4:13–17 says Christ will bring with him the souls and spirits of those who are now with him in heaven and will reunite their spirits to resurrection bodies. In Philippians 1:21–23 Paul says it's better to depart and be with Christ. In 2 Corinthians 5:6–8 Paul says that to be absent from the body is to be at home with the Lord. Clearly, the whole of Scripture teaches that each person has a soul that survives death.

GENESIS 2:7—Is Christian Science correct in claiming that God did not create matter?

MISINTERPRETATION: Christian Science teaches that God did not create any matter, and that matter is not a real thing that was ever created by anyone. Though Genesis 2:7 says God "formed the man from the dust of the ground," Christian Scientists conclude "it must be a lie, for God presently curses the ground," according to Genesis 3:17 (Eddy, 524).

CORRECTING THE MISINTERPRETATION: The Bible clearly affirms that God created human beings with a physical body. To draw any inference to the contrary from any text is to contradict the plain teaching of the Word of God.

The Bible declares that "the LORD God formed the man from the dust of the ground and breathed into his nostrils the breath of life, and the man became a living being" (Gen. 2:7). The "dust of the ground" is an obvious reference to physical, material stuff.

Further, God said to Adam and Eve, "By the sweat of your brow you will eat your food until you return to the ground, since from it you were taken; for dust you are and to dust you will return" (Gen. 3:19). Here, too, the reference is to the physical "ground" and "dust." Further, it says we will *return* to dust, which implies that we *came* from it to begin with, which is what the Bible says elsewhere (cf. Eccl. 12:7).

GENESIS 3:7—Does this verse mark the beginning of Freemasonry, as masons sometimes argue?

MISINTERPRETATION: In Genesis 3:7 we read of Adam and Eve following their sin, "Then the eyes of both of them were opened, and they realized they were naked; so they sewed fig leaves together and made coverings for themselves." Freemasons sometimes try to argue that freemasonry dates back to the time of Adam and Eve, since the fig leaves were actually the first masonic "aprons" (Mather and Nichols, 1993, 7). In freemasonry such aprons are used in various initiatory rituals. Is this interpretation correct?

CORRECTING THE MISINTERPRETATION: The Freemasons are here practicing *eisogesis* (reading a meaning *into* the text) instead of *exegesis* (drawing the meaning *out of* the text). This is evident from the context.

Masonic rituals are nowhere to be found in the context of Genesis 3, not to mention in the rest of the Bible. The fig leaves in Genesis 3 had the sole purpose of covering Adam and Eve's nakedness; they were not utilized in any rituals or initiatory ceremonies.

It should be noted that freemasonry is a religion that is incompatible with Christianity. Among other things, freemasonry teaches that the Bible is one among many "symbols" of God's will. (Other "symbols" of God's will include the Hindu Vedas and the Muslim Qur'an.) Further, Jesus is said to be one among many holy men who set forth a way to God. Also, the various world religions are said to worship the same God with different names (Jehovah, Allah, etc.). Salvation is not based on faith in Christ but is works-oriented. Moreover, freemasons are made to swear oaths that Christians should never even think of uttering—for example, that one is in spiritual darkness and has thus come to freemasonry to find the light.

GENESIS 3:15a—Does this verse teach that the Virgin Mary was sinless?

MISINTERPRETATION: Many Catholic scholars claim that "the seed of the woman was understood as referring to the Redeemer, . . . and thus the Mother of the Redeemer came to be seen in the woman" (Ott, 1960, 200). Even the infallible pronouncement of the immaculate conception "approves of this messianic-marian interpretation" (Ibid.).

CORRECTING THE MISINTERPRETATION: This verse contains no reference to Mary or her alleged immaculate conception. One of the best evidences of this outside the text itself is the fact that even Catholic authorities such as Ott acknowledge that the "literal sense" of this text means that "between Satan and his followers on the one hand, and Eve and her posterity on the other hand, there is to be constant moral warfare. . . . The posterity of Eve includes the Messiah, in whose power humanity will win a victory over Satan" (Ibid.).

Even if by extension Mary could be connected in some indirect way to this text, it is still a gigantic leap to her immaculate conception, which is nowhere stated or implied in this passage. The literal sense is that Eve (not Mary) and her posterity are in moral warfare against Satan and his offspring, culminating in the crushing victory of the Messiah over Satan and his hosts. The "woman" is obviously Eve, and the "seed of the woman" is clearly the literal offspring of Eve (see Gen. 4:1, 25), leading up to and culminating in the victory of Christ over Satan (cf. Rom. 16:20).

Catholics argue that, just as the Messiah is found by extension in the phrase "seed of the woman," Mary, the mother of the Messiah, is implied too. But even if this were so, there is no necessary or logical connection between Mary being mother of the Messiah and her being conceived without sin.

GENESIS 9:4—Does this verse prohibit blood transfusions?

MISINTERPRETATION: The Jehovah's Witnesses believe this verse forbids blood transfusions. They argue that a blood transfusion is the same as eating blood because it is so similar to intravenous feeding (*Reasoning from the Scriptures*, 1989, 73).

CORRECTING THE MISINTERPRETATION: While it is true that Genesis 9:4 prohibits the "eating" of blood, a transfusion does not constitute "eating" blood. Though a doctor might give food to a patient intravenously and call this "feeding," it is simply not the case that giving *blood* intravenously is "feeding." The blood is not received into the body as "food." Eating is the literal taking in of food in the normal manner through the mouth and into the digestive system. Intravenous injections are referred to as "feeding" because the ultimate result is that, through intravenous injection, the body receives the nutrients that it would normally receive by eating. In view of this, Genesis 9:4 and other passages dealing with this prohibition against eating blood cannot be used to support a prohibition of blood transfusions. A transfusion simply replenishes essential, life-sustaining fluid in the body. See also comments on Leviticus 7:26–27; 17:11–12.

GENESIS 14:18—Does this verse give support for the Mormon "Melchizedek priesthood" today?

MISINTERPRETATION: Genesis 14:18 says, "Then Melchizedek king of Salem brought out bread and wine. He was priest of God Most High." Mormons believe the Melchizedek priesthood is an eternal priesthood. Though it was lost from the earth in the early centuries of Christianity, it was restored through Joseph Smith (Smith, 1835, 107:2–4).

CORRECTING THE MISINTERPRETATION: Melchizedek in Genesis 14:18 is a historical person who was a *type* of Christ. A type is a figure pointing forward to something or someone to come. By divine design it foreshadows something or someone yet to be revealed. How did Melchizedek foreshadow Christ? Melchizedek's name gives us the answer. The word *Melchizedek* is made up of two Hebrew words meaning "king" and "righteous." Melchizedek was also a priest. Thus, Melchizedek foreshadowed Christ as a righteous king-priest. These things were true of Melchizedek only in a finite sense, whereas in Christ they are true in an infinite sense.

Can Mormons participate in the Melchizedek priesthood? Hebrews 7:23–24 tells us, "And the former priests, on the one hand, existed in greater numbers, because they were prevented by death from continuing, but He [Jesus], on the other hand, because He abides forever, *holds His priesthood permanently*" (NASB, emphasis added). Christ's priesthood is eternal because he is an eternal being. Unlike humans who perish and die, Christ exists eternally, and therefore his priesthood, by its very nature, is different than anything humans could offer. He is our eternal High Priest who lives forever.

The Greek word for "permanently" in Hebrews 7:24, according to Joseph Thayer, means "priesthood unchangeable and therefore not liable to pass to a successor" (Thayer, 1985, 649). Gerhard Kittel's *Theological Dictionary of the New Testament* likewise tells us, "In the New Testament Hebrews 7:24 says that Christ has an eternal and imperishable priesthood, not just in the sense that it cannot be transferred to anyone else, but in the sense of 'unchangeable'" (Kittel, 1985, 772). Hence, there is no biblical justification for Mormons to think they can participate in the Melchizedek priesthood. This priesthood belongs to Christ alone.

This is further emphasized in Hebrews 7:26: "For it was fitting that we should have such a high priest, holy, innocent, undefiled, separated from sinners and exalted above the heavens" (NASB). What Mormon (or any human) dare claim to be "holy, innocent, undefiled, separated from sinners and exalted above the heavens"?

GENESIS 18:2—Does the Oriental custom of bowing before a person of position justify the Roman Catholic practice of bowing before images?

MISINTERPRETATION: Genesis 18:2b informs us that "Abraham looked up and saw three men standing nearby. When he saw them, he hurried from the entrance of his tent to meet them and bowed low to the ground." Does this justify the Roman Catholic practice of bowing before images?

CORRECTING THE MISINTERPRETATION: The Catholic argument that religiously bowing down before an image is not wrong because there are many cases in the Bible where such bowing down is approved, as in Genesis 18:2, confuses two very different contexts.

First, they were bowing out of *respect,* not out of *reverence.*

Second, bowing was understood as a *social* practice, not a *religious rite.*

Third, the Bible condemns even bowing before an angel in the worship of God (Rev. 22:8–9).

Fourth, the Bible clearly condemns bowing before any image in religious veneration (see, for example, Exod. 20:4).

Finally, God acted at one point to avoid this very practice. Knowing that devout Israelites might be tempted to venerate the remains of Moses, God buried him where no one knows (Deut. 34:6). His apparent aim was to prevent idolatry that the devil desires to encourage (Jude 9).

GENESIS 19:8—Was the sin of Sodom homosexuality or inhospitality?

MISINTERPRETATION: Some have argued that the sin of Sodom and Gomorrah was inhospitality, not homosexuality. They base this on the

Canaanite custom that guarantees protection of those coming under one's roof. Lot is alleged to have referred to it when he said, "Don't do anything to these men, for they have come under the protection of my roof" (Gen. 19:8b). So Lot offered his daughter to satisfy the angry crowd in order to protect the lives of the visitors who had come under his roof. And the request of the men of the city to "know" simply means "to get acquainted" (Gen. 19:7), since the Hebrew word *know (yadha)* generally has no sexual connotations whatsoever (cf. Ps. 139:1). It is important to understand what Scripture says on this because certain New Agers such as Matthew Fox believe homosexuality is just as acceptable to the "cosmic Christ" as heterosexuality (see his book, *The Coming of the Cosmic Christ*).

CORRECTING THE MISINTERPRETATION: (See comments on Ezekiel 16:49.) While it is true that the Hebrew word *know (yadha)* does not necessarily mean "to have sex with," nonetheless in the context of the text on Sodom and Gomorrah it clearly has this meaning. This is evident for several reasons. First of all, ten of the twelve times this word is used in Genesis it refers to sexual intercourse (for example, Gen. 4:1, 25).

Second, it is used to refer to sexual intercourse in this very chapter. For Lot refers to his two virgin daughters as not having "known a man" (19:8) which is an obvious sexual use of the word.

Third, the meaning of a word is discovered by the context in which it is used. And the context here is definitely sexual, as is indicated by the reference to the wickedness of the city (18:20) and the virgins offered to appease their passions (19:8).

Fourth, "know" cannot mean simply "get acquainted with," because it is equated with a "wicked thing" (19:7).

Fifth, why offer the virgin daughters to appease them if their intent was not sexual? If the men had asked to "know" the virgin daughters no one would have mistaken their sexual intentions.

GENESIS 32:30—Can God's face be seen?

MISINTERPRETATION: Jacob said, "I saw God face to face, and yet my life was spared" (Gen. 32:30). Mormons claim that God the Father has a physical body with a face that can be seen (Richards, 1978, 16).

CORRECTING THE MISINTERPRETATION: First, it is possible for a blind person to speak "face to face" with someone without seeing their face. The phrase *face to face* in Hebrew usage means personally, directly, or intimately. Moses had this kind of unmediated relationship with God. But he, like all other mortals, never saw the "face" (essence) of God directly.

The Bible is clear that "God is a spirit" (John 4:24). And "a spirit does not have flesh and bones" (Luke 24:39). So, God does not have a physical face.

GENESIS 40:20–22—Does this passage indicate that we should not celebrate birthdays?

MISINTERPRETATION: This passage indicates that on pharaoh's birthday he had the chief baker killed. The Jehovah's Witnesses say that since the Bible presents birthdays in an unfavorable light, Christians should avoid them (*Reasoning from the Scriptures*, 1989, 68–69).

CORRECTING THE MISINTERPRETATION: This is "guilt by association." Genesis 40:20–22 proves only that the Pharaoh was evil, not that birthdays are evil.

Pharaoh also did something good on his birthday—he declared amnesty for the chief cupbearer (Gen. 40:21). But it would be just as foolish to argue that birthdays are good based on pharaoh's good deed as it would be to argue that birthdays are bad because of pharaoh's bad deed.

What is more, while there are no scriptural commands to celebrate birthdays, neither are there commandments against it. There is no reason it cannot be celebrated, like everything else, "to the glory of God" who created us (1 Cor. 10:31).

There is nothing wrong with giving proper honor to another human being. The Bible says: "Render to all what is due them: . . . honor to whom honor [is due]" (Rom. 13:7 NASB). Since a typical birthday does not worship another human being, there is no reason we cannot honor them on this occasion.

EXODUS

EXODUS 7:11—How could the wise men and sorcerers of pharaoh perform the same feats of power that God told Moses to perform? Does this give credence to occultism?

MISINTERPRETATION: Several passages in Exodus (7:11, 22; 8:7) seem to say that the wise men, sorcerers, and magicians of pharaoh did some of the same works with their "secret arts" (NIV, NASB) or "enchantments" (KJV) that God commanded Moses and Aaron to perform. However, Moses and Aaron claimed to have been sent from the Lord God. How could these men perform the same feats of power as Moses and Aaron did by the power of God? Does this indicate that occultists have supernatural powers?

CORRECTING THE MISINTERPRETATION: The Bible indicates that one of Satan's tactics in his effort to deceive humankind is to employ counterfeit miracles (see 2 Thess. 2:9 and comments on Rev. 16:14). Exodus 7:11 states, "Then pharaoh also called the wise men and the sorcerers; now the magicians of Egypt, they also did in like manner with *their enchantments*" (KJV). Each of the other verses makes a similar claim. The passage states that the feats of pharaoh's magicians were performed "by their [magical] enchantments."

Some commentators assert that the feats of the magicians were merely tricks. Perhaps the magicians had enchanted snakes so that they became stiff and appeared to be rods. When cast down upon the floor, they came out of their trance and began to move as snakes. Some say these were acts of Satan who actually turned the rods of the magicians into snakes. This, however, is not plausible in view of the fact that only God can create life, as even the magicians later recognized (Exod. 8:18–19).

Whatever explanation one might take regarding how these feats were accomplished, one common point holds for every explanation and is found in the text itself. It is clear that by whatever power they performed these feats, they were not accomplished by the power of God. Rather, they were performed "by their enchantments."

The purpose of these acts was to convince pharaoh that his magicians possessed as much power as Moses and Aaron, and it was not necessary for pharaoh to yield to their request to let Israel go. It worked, at least for the first three encounters (Aaron's rod, the plague of blood, and the plague of frogs). However, when Moses and Aaron, by the power of God, brought forth lice from the sand, the magicians were not able to counterfeit this miracle. They could only exclaim, "This is the finger of God" (Exod. 8:19).

There are several points by which one can discern the differences between a satanic sign and a divine miracle.

Divine Miracle	Satanic Sign
Supernatural	Supernormal
Connected with truth	Connected with error
Associated with good	Associated with evil
Never associated with the Occult	Often associated with the Occult
Always successful	Not always successful

These differences can be seen in these passages in Exodus. Although the magicians could turn their rods into snakes, their rods were swallowed up by Aaron's rod, indicating superiority. Although the magicians could turn water to blood, they could not reverse the process. Although the magicians could bring forth frogs, they could not get rid of them. Their acts were supernormal, but not supernatural.

Although the magicians could copy some of the miracles of Moses and Aaron, their message was connected with error. Basically they tried to copy the miracles of God's chosen men in order to convince pharaoh that the God of the Hebrews was no more powerful than the gods of Egypt. Although pharaoh's magicians were able to simulate the first three miracles performed by God through Moses and Aaron, there came a point at which their enchantments were no longer able to counterfeit the power of God.

EXODUS 13:19—Does the preservation of Joseph's bones support the Roman Catholic belief in the veneration of relics?

MISINTERPRETATION: In Exodus 13:19 "Moses took the bones of Joseph with him [out of Egypt] because Joseph had made the sons of

Israel swear an oath" (see Gen. 50:25). Roman Catholic scholars use this verse to support their dogma that "it is permissible and profitable to venerate the relics of saints" (Ott, 1960, 319). The Council of Trent declared: "Also the holy bodies of the holy martyrs and of the others who dwell with Christ . . . are to be honored by the faithful" (Denzinger, 1957, no. 985). Ott says that "the reason for the veneration of relics lies in this, that the bodies of the saints were living members of Christ and Temples of the Holy Ghost; that they will again be awakened and glorified and that through them God bestows many benefits on mankind" (Ibid.).

CORRECTING THE MISINTERPRETATION: The Catholic dogma of venerating relics and images is without foundation in this Scripture or any other.

The Exodus passage states clearly the purpose for taking Joseph's bones out of Egypt and it was not to venerate them. We read, "Moses took the bones of Joseph with him because Joseph had made the sons of Israel swear an oath." He had said, "God will surely come to your aid, and then you must carry my bones up with you from this place" (Exod. 13:19).

Even noted Catholic authority Ludwig Ott admits that "Holy Writ does not mention the veneration of relics" (Ibid.). And the so-called "precedents" in Scripture do not prove the Catholic point. For the bones of Joseph were not *venerated;* they were simply *preserved* (Exod. 13:19). Hence, to use this as a biblical proof for venerating relics is to jerk the verse out of context.

Moreover, God condemned the veneration of sacred objects. When the brazen serpent, which God had ordained for the salvation of the Israelites in the wilderness, was later venerated, it was considered idolatry (2 Kings 18:4).

God clearly commanded his people not to make graven *images* or to *bow* down to them in an act of religious devotion (Exod. 20:4, 5). This is the same error of the pagans who "revered and worshiped the creature rather than the Creator" (Rom. 1:25). The Bible forbids us ever to make or even to "bow" down before an "image" of any creature in an act of religious devotion: "You shall not make for yourselves any *carved image,* or *any likeness* of anything that is in heaven above, or that is in the earth beneath, or that is in the waters under the earth; you *shall not bow down nor serve them*" (Exod. 20:4–5 NKJV, emphasis added).

EXODUS 20:4–5—Does this text forbid the wearing of a cross?

MISINTERPRETATION: Jehovah's Witnesses believe the command in this verse not to make an idol forbids people from wearing a cross (*Let God Be True,* 1946, 146).

CORRECTING THE MISINTERPRETATION: Pagans of ancient times engaged in idolatry by bowing down in worship before material objects. Wearing a cross *is not* idolatry because the cross itself is not worshiped or venerated. Christians wear a cross because they worship and venerate Christ. It is merely an *outward* symbol for an *inner* worshipful attitude toward Christ. If anyone did worship a cross (or any other symbol), or bow down before it, then it would be a form of idolatry (Exod. 20:4).

EXODUS 20:8–11—Why do Christians worship on Sunday when the commandment sets apart Saturday as the day of worship?

MISINTERPRETATION: This commandment states that the seventh day of the week, Saturday, is the day the Lord selected for rest and worship. However, in the New Testament the Christian church began to worship and rest on the first day of the week, Sunday. Are Christians violating the Sabbath commandment by worshiping on the first day of the week rather than the seventh day? Some sabbatarian groups, such as Seventh-Day Adventists, think so.

CORRECTING THE MISINTERPRETATION: The basis for the command to observe the Sabbath, as stated in Exodus 20:11, is that God rested on the seventh day after six days of work, and that God blessed the seventh day and sanctified it. The Sabbath day was instituted as a day of rest and worship. The people of God were to follow God's example in his pattern of work and rest. However, as Jesus said in correcting the distorted view of the Pharisees, "The Sabbath was made for man, and not man for the Sabbath" (Mark 2:27). The point Jesus made is that the Sabbath was not instituted to enslave people, but to benefit them. The spirit of Sabbath observance is continued in the New Testament observance of rest and worship on the first day of the week (Acts 20:7; 1 Cor. 16:2).

It must be remembered that, according to Colossians 2:17, the Sabbath was "a shadow of things to come, but the substance is of Christ" (NKJV). The Sabbath observance was associated with redemption in Deuteronomy 5:15 where Moses stated, "Remember that you were a slave in the land of Egypt, and that the Lord your God brought you out from there by a mighty hand and by an outstretched arm; therefore the Lord your God commanded you to keep the Sabbath day." The Sabbath was a shadow of the redemption that would be provided in Christ. It symbolized the rest from our works and an entrance into the rest of God provided by his finished work.

Although the moral principles expressed in the commandments are reaffirmed in the New Testament, the command to set Saturday apart as a day of rest and worship is the only commandment not repeated. There are very good reasons for this. New Testament believers are not under the Old Testament law (Rom. 6:14; 2 Cor. 3:7, 11, 13; Gal. 3:24–25; Heb. 7:12). By his resurrection on the first day of the week (Matt. 28:1), his continued appearances on succeeding Sundays (John 20:26), and the descent of the Holy Spirit on Sunday (Acts 2:1), the early church was given the pattern of Sunday worship. This they did regularly. Sunday worship was further hallowed by our Lord, who appeared to John in that last great vision on "the Lord's day" (Rev. 1:10). It is for these reasons that Christians worship on Sunday, rather than on the Jewish Sabbath. See comments on Acts 17:1–3.

EXODUS 20:14—How could there still be polygamy among God's people after the commandment to have only one spouse?

MISINTERPRETATION: The commandments explicitly state, "You shall not commit adultery" (Exod. 20:14) and "You shall not covet your neighbor's *wife*" (singular, Exod. 20:17). Although it may be possible to excuse the polygamy of those who lived before the giving of the Ten Commandments, this is not the case for the people of God who lived after this time, such as King David and King Solomon. How could God bless these men when, according to these commandments, they were living in adultery? This is an important question, for the Mormons say that prophet Joseph Smith received a "revelation" from the Lord that plural marriage was God's will for his followers (Smith, 1835, 132:61–62).

CORRECTING THE MISINTERPRETATION: The Bible speaks emphatically against polygamy (see comments on 1 Kings 11:1). Jesus made it clear in Matthew 19:9 that the original plan of God from the creation was monogamous marriage. This is evident from the fact that God created only one wife for Adam. Deuteronomy 17:17 prohibits polygamy among kings, who normally were the ones to practice it in international alliances: "Neither shall he multiply wives." In each case of polygamy we find a failure to live up to God's ideal. It was not God's ideal that a man should divorce his wife (Matt. 19:9), yet, because of the hardness of the hearts of the people, Moses allowed divorce under certain conditions. Similarly, polygamous marriage was not God's ideal for marriage, but because of the hardness of hearts, it was tolerated. However, the fact that God tolerated polygamy does not prove that he prescribed or approved of it.

The Bible records many things of which it does not approve. Genesis 3:4 records the lie of Satan, but nowhere is his lie approved of. There is no instance in the Scriptures where God blesses a man because he has many wives. In fact, we find that the polygamist paid bitterly for his sin. First Kings 11:4 states that Solomon's wives "turned his heart after other gods; and his heart was not loyal to the Lord his God." God blesses his people despite the fact that they often fall short of his ideal. God blessed David and Solomon, not because of their polygamy, but despite their sin.

EXODUS 24:9–11—How could these people see God when God said in Exodus 33:20, "No man may see me and live?"

MISINTERPRETATION: Exodus 24:9–11 records that Moses, Aaron, Nadab, Abihu, and seventy of the elders of Israel ascended the mountain of God and "saw the God of Israel." Mormons believe that God has a physical body and hence can be seen by men (McConkie, 1966, 278). Can people really see God?

CORRECTING THE MISINTERPRETATION: It should be noted that God invited them to "see" him. In Exodus 19:12–13 God told Moses to set the boundaries around the mountain so that no one should even touch its base without the punishment of death. However, God specifically invited these people to ascend the mountain in order to consecrate them for the service to which they had been appointed, and to seal the covenant which had been established between God and the nation of Israel.

It is clear from the description and from other passages of Scripture (Exod. 33:19–20; Num. 12:8), that what these people saw was not the *essence* of God, but rather a visual *representation* of the glory of God. Even when Moses asked to see God's glory (Exod. 33:18–23), it was only a likeness of God which Moses saw (cf. Num. 12:8 where the Hebrew word *temunah* "form," "likeness," is used), and not the very essence of God.

The Bible is very emphatic that "No man has seen God at any time" (John 1:18). Only in heaven "they shall see His face, and His name shall be on their foreheads" (Rev. 22:4). For "now we see in a mirror, dimly, but then face to face" (1 Cor. 13:12).

EXODUS 25:18—Does the use of cherubim over the ark justify the Roman Catholic view that images can be venerated?

MISINTERPRETATION: According to this verse, Moses was commanded by God to "make two cherubim out of hammered gold at the ends of the cover." Obviously this is a sacred image. Roman Catholic scholars argue that this verse justifies their veneration of sacred images.

CORRECTING THE MISINTERPRETATION: This verse does not justify the veneration of sacred images. For one thing, the context makes it clear that the image of the cherubim was not to be venerated or worshiped in any way. Indeed, the position of the cherubim in the most holy place where only the high priest could go once a year on the Day of Atonement (Lev. 16) made it inaccessible to the possibility of worship or veneration by the people.

Note also that these cherubim were not given to Israel as images *of God;* they are representations *of angels.* They were not given for the purpose of worship or veneration; they were given for decorative purposes—as religious art. Roman Catholics are reading something into this verse that is not there.

EXODUS 32:30–32—Does Moses' mediation for Israel support the Roman Catholic belief in a Treasury of Merit from which we may draw?

MISINTERPRETATION: In this passage Moses tells Israel, "I will go up to the Lord, then: perhaps I may be able to make atonement for your sin." Then he prays to God, "If you will only forgive their sin! If not, then strike me out of the book that you have written." Catholic scholars cite this passage to substantiate their claim of a "treasury of the church," that is, a "Treasury of Merit" stored in heaven from which those in need can draw by indulgences. Ludwig Ott claims that "as Christ, the Head, in His expiatory suffering, took the place of the members, so also one member can take the place of another. The doctrine of indulgences is based on the possibility and reality of vicarious atonement" (Ott, 1960, 317).

CORRECTING THE MISINTERPRETATION: There is absolutely nothing in this text about any storehouse of merit in heaven—literal or figurative—to which one can contribute by good deeds and from which others can draw. At best, the passage merely reveals that highly commendable desire of one person who is willing to suffer for another.

Nowhere does the passage say that God accepted Moses' offer to be blotted out of God's book for Israel. In fact, God did not blot him out of his book. What God did accept was Moses' sacrificial desire as an indication of the sincerity of his heart, as God did in the case of Abraham (cf. Gen. 22). But God did not accept any offer to give up a place in God's book for the sins of Israel. God did not accept Moses' life as an atonement for Israel; he merely accepted Moses' *willingness* to be sacrificed for them. Moses never suffered having his name taken out of God's book, to say nothing of any temporal suffering for Israel's sins. Likewise, the apostle Paul expressed a willingness to go to hell if Israel could be saved (Rom. 9:3). This too was an admirable but unfulfillable desire. God never accepted Paul's offer. It was a commendable offer, not actually possible, but nonetheless indicative of Paul's passion for his people.

The concept of a Treasury of Merit to which saints can contribute by their good works is contrary to the all-sufficiency of the meritorious death of Christ on our behalf (cf. John 19:30; Heb. 1:3; 2:14–15).

EXODUS 33:11—Does the fact that Moses spoke to God "face to face" prove that God has a physical body?

See comments on Genesis 32:30.

LEVITICUS

LEVITICUS 7:26–27—Does this verse prohibit blood transfusions?

MISINTERPRETATION: Leviticus 7:26–27 says, "And wherever you live, you must not eat the blood of any bird or animal. If anyone eats blood, that person must be cut off from his people" (NIV). Jehovah's Witnesses say this passage absolutely prohibits blood transfusions (*Aid to Bible Understanding*, 1971, 244).

CORRECTING THE MISINTERPRETATION: Leviticus 7:26–27 forbids the eating of blood. It has nothing to do with blood transfusions. More specifically, the text prohibits *eating animal blood*, not the *transfusion of human blood*. (See comments on Gen. 9:4 for information regarding why eating blood is not the same as a blood transfusion.) It is noteworthy that even orthodox Jews—to whom the law was originally given and who painstakingly drain blood from their kosher food—accept blood transfusions.

LEVITICUS 17:11–12—Does this passage prohibit having a blood transfusion?

MISINTERPRETATION: Leviticus 17:11–12 says, "For the life of the flesh is in the blood, and I have given it to you on the altar to make atonement for your souls; for it is the blood by reason of the life that makes atonement. Therefore I said to the sons of Israel, 'No person among you may eat blood, nor may any alien who sojourns among you eat blood'" (NKJV). Jehovah's Witnesses believe this is another verse that prohibits blood transfusions (*Reasoning from the Scriptures*, 1989, 70).

CORRECTING THE MISINTERPRETATION: The prohibition here is primarily directed at eating flesh that was still pulsating with life because the lifeblood was still in it. The transfusion of blood does not involve eating flesh with the lifeblood still in it. Hence, blood transfusions do not violate Leviticus 17.

LEVITICUS 18:22–24—Haven't the laws against homosexuality been abolished along with laws against eating pork? Weren't those laws attached to the fear of the curse of barrenness anyway?

MISINTERPRETATION: The law against homosexuality is found in Leviticus 18:22, alongside ceremonial and dietary laws. These laws have been done away with (Acts 10:15). This being so, it would seem logical that the laws prohibiting homosexual activity are no longer binding either. Also, according to Jewish belief, barrenness was a curse (Gen. 16:1; 1 Sam. 1:3–8). Children were considered God's blessing (Ps. 127:3). The blessing of the land was connected with the children (Gen. 15:5). It would then be unsurprising that Old Testament law in such a culture would frown on homosexual activity from which no children came. Perhaps what is being condemned is not homosexual activity so much as the refusal to have children.

CORRECTING THE MISINTERPRETATION: Simply because the Mosaic prohibition against homosexuality is in Leviticus does not make it part of the passing ceremonial law. If that were true, the same could be said about rape, incest, and bestiality in the same chapter (Lev. 18:6–14, 22–23). And nowhere are sexual laws connected with the procreation of children. If homosexuals were put to death because they were barren, that would hardly solve the problem of producing more children. Heterosexual marriage would have been a more appropriate punishment.

Laws against homosexuality extend beyond the covenant nation to Gentiles at any rate (Rom. 1:26). Gentiles do not have the ceremonial law (Rom. 2:12–15), nor was there a covenant stake in producing a new generation. It was for this very reason that God brought judgment on the Canaanites (Lev. 18:1–3, 24–25). A Jew caught in homosexuality was destroyed brutally. Yet violators of the dietary laws were considered unclean and had to live outside the camp for a brief time.

If barrenness was a divine curse, then singleness would be sinful. But both our Lord (Matt. 19:11–12) and the apostle Paul (1 Cor. 7:8) sanctioned singlehood by both precept and practice. Yet prohibitions against homosexual practice continue to be promulgated throughout the Epistles (Rom. 1:26–27; 1 Cor. 6:9; 1 Tim. 1:10; and Jude 7).

DEUTERONOMY

DEUTERONOMY 6:4—Does this verse disprove the doctrine of the Trinity?

MISINTERPRETATION: Deuteronomy 6:4 is the Hebrew *Shema:* "Hear, O Israel! The LORD is our God, the LORD is one!" Jehovah's Witnesses say that because God is "one," he cannot possibly be triune. "The *Shema* excludes the Trinity of the Christian creed as a violation of the unity of God" (*Mankind's Search for God,* 1990, 219). Oneness Pentecostals also cite this verse against the doctrine of the Trinity. Oneness Pentecostal leader Robert Sabin says the doctrine of the Trinity "violates the Shema" and "denies . . . the sole and supreme Deity of Jesus" (*Oneness News,* vol. 4.4; and "Irrefutable Reasons Why the Theory of the Trinity Cannot Stand," Oneness Ministries handout, n.d.). Is this a correct understanding of this text?

CORRECTING THE MISINTERPRETATION: Deuteronomy 6:4 does not deny the Trinity but rather establishes one of the planks of the Trinity: *there is one God.* It is important to understand that Scripture interprets Scripture. By interpreting Deuteronomy 6:4 in conjunction with other verses, we learn that the one true God is triune in personality (2 Cor. 13:14), i.e., there are three persons in this one nature.

Each of the three persons of the Trinity is called *God* in Scripture: the Father (1 Peter 1:2), the Son (John 20:28), and the Holy Spirit (Acts 5:3–4). Moreover, each possesses the attributes of deity—including *omnipresence* (Ps. 139:7; Matt. 28:20; Heb. 4:13), *omniscience* (Matt. 9:4; Rom. 11:33; 1 Cor. 2:10), and *omnipotence* (Matt. 28:18; Rom. 15:19; 1 Peter 1:5).

Three-in-oneness within the Godhead is clear in such passages as Matthew 28:19: "Therefore go and make disciples of all nations, baptizing them in the *name* of *the* Father and of *the* Son and of *the* Holy Spirit" (NIV). The word *name* is singular in the Greek, indicating that there is one God. But there are three distinct persons within the God-head, as indicated by the three definite articles in the Greek—*the* Father, *the* Son, and *the* Holy Spirit. This three-in-oneness is also reflected in 2 Corinthians 13:14. So, there is only one God, but there is a plurality within this unity—a plurality of persons within the unity of nature.

DEUTERONOMY 18:10–22—How can false prophets be distinguished from true prophets?

MISINTERPRETATION: The Bible contains many prophecies which it calls upon us to believe because they come from God. However, the Bible also acknowledges the existence of false prophets (Matt. 7:15). Indeed, many religions and cults—including the Jehovah's Witnesses and the Mormons—claim to have prophets. Hence, the Bible exhorts believers to "test" those who claim to be prophets (1 John 4:1f.). What is the difference between a false prophet and a true prophet of God, according to Deuteronomy 18:10–22?

CORRECTING THE MISINTERPRETATION: There are many tests for a false prophet. Several of them are listed in this very passage. Put in question form, the tests are:

1. Do they ever give false prophecies? Do 100 percent of their predictions of future events come true? (Deut. 18:21–22)
2. Do they contact departed spirits? (Deut. 18:11)
3. Do they use means of divination? (Deut. 18:11)
4. Do they involve mediums or witches? (Deut. 18:1)
5. Do they follow false gods or idols? (Exod. 20:3–4; Deut. 13:1–3)
6. Do they deny the deity of Jesus Christ? (Col. 2:8–9)
7. Do they deny the humanity of Jesus Christ? (1 John 4:1–2)
8. Do their prophecies shift the focus off Jesus Christ? (Rev. 19:10)
9. Do they advocate abstaining from certain foods and meats for spiritual reasons? (1 Tim. 4:3–4)
10. Do they deprecate or deny the need for marriage? (1 Tim. 4:3)
11. Do they promote immorality? (Jude 4, 7)
12. Do they encourage legalistic self-denial? (Col. 2:16–23)

A positive answer to any of the above questions is an indication that the prophet is not speaking for God. God does not speak or encourage anything that is contrary to his character and commands as recorded in Scripture. And most certainly the God of truth does not give false prophecies (Deut. 18:21–23).

DEUTERONOMY 18:15–18—Is this a prophecy about the prophet Muhammad?

MISINTERPRETATION: God promised Moses here, "I will raise them up a Prophet from among their brethren [Israel], like unto thee, and will put my words in his mouth, and he shall speak unto them all that I shall command him" (v. 18 KJV). Muslims believe this prophecy is fulfilled in Muhammad, as the Qur'an claims when it refers to "the unlettered Prophet [Muhammad], Whom they find mentioned in their own (Scriptures), in the Law and the Gospels" (Sura 7:157).

CORRECTING THE MISINTERPRETATION: This prophecy could not be a reference to Muhammad. The term *brethren* refers to Israel, not to their Arabian antagonists. Why would God raise up for Israel a prophet from among their enemies. In the surrounding text, the term *brethren* means fellow Israelites. The Levites were told "they shall have no inheritance among their brethren" (v. 2).

Elsewhere in Deuteronomy the term *brethren* also means fellow Israelites, not a foreigner. God told them to choose a king "from among your brethren," not a "foreigner." Israel has never chosen a non-Jewish king.

Further, Muhammad came from Ishmael, as even Muslims admit, and heirs to the Jewish throne came from Isaac. When Abraham prayed "Oh that Ishmael might live before You!" God answered emphatically: "My covenant I will establish with Isaac" (Gen. 17:21). Later God repeated: "It is through Isaac that your offspring will be reckoned" (Gen. 21:12 NIV).

The Qur'an itself states that the prophetic line came through Isaac, not Ishmael: "And We bestowed on him Isaac and Jacob, and We established the Prophethood and the Scripture among his seed" (Sura 29:27). The Muslim scholar Yusuf Ali adds the word *Abraham* and changes the meaning as follows, "We gave (Abraham) Isaac and Jacob, and ordained Among his progeny Prophethood and Revelation." By adding Abraham, the father of Ishmael, he can include Muhammad, a descendent of Ishmael, in the prophetic line. But Abraham's name is not found in the original text.

Jesus perfectly fulfilled this verse, since he was from among his Jewish brethren (cf. Gal. 4:4). He fulfilled Deuteronomy 18:18 perfectly: "He shall speak to them all that I [God] command Him." Jesus said, "I do nothing of myself; but as my Father taught me, I speak these things" (John 8:28 KJV). And, "I have not spoken on My own authority; but the

Father who sent Me gave Me a command, what I should say and what I should speak" (John 12:49). He called himself a "prophet" (Luke 13:33), and the people considered him a prophet (Matt. 21:11; Luke 7:16; 24:19; John 4:19; 6:14; 7:40; 9:17). As the Son of God, Jesus was *prophet* (speaking to men for God), *priest* (Hebrews 7–10, speaking to God for men), and *king* (reigning over men for God, Revelation 19–20).

Other characteristics of the "Prophet" fit only Jesus, not Muhammad. For example, Jesus spoke with God "face to face" and he performed "signs and wonders" (see comments on Deut. 34:10).

DEUTERONOMY 23:17—Was homosexuality condemned merely because it was connected with idolatry?

MISINTERPRETATION: Some argue that the biblical condemnations against homosexuality resulted from the fact that the temple cult-prostitute was associated with these idolatrous practices (Deut. 23:17). They insist that homosexuality as such is not thereby condemned but only homosexual acts that are associated with idolatry, such as the shrine prostitute (cf. 1 Kings 14:24). (As noted in comments for Gen. 19:8, some New Agers believe homosexuality is just as acceptable to the "cosmic Christ" as heterosexuality.)

CORRECTING THE MISINTERPRETATION: Homosexual practices are not condemned in the Bible simply because they were connected with idolatry. This is made evident by several things. Condemnation of homosexual practices is apart from reference to explicit idolatrous practice (Lev. 18:22; Rom. 1:26–27).

When homosexuality is associated with idolatry (such as in temple cult prostitution) it is not essentially connected. It is a concomitant sin but not an equivalent one.

Sexual unfaithfulness is often used metaphorically of idolatry (e.g., Hosea 3:1; 4:12), but it has no necessary connection with it. Idolatry is a spiritual form of immorality, but immorality is not wrong only if it is done in connection with idol worship.

Also, idolatry may lead to immorality (cf. Rom. 1:22–27), but they are different sins. Even the Ten Commandments distinguish between idolatry in the first table of the law, Exod. 20:3–4, and sexual sins in the second table, Exod. 20:14, 17.

DEUTERONOMY 33:2—Is this a prediction of the Prophet Muhammad?

MISINTERPRETATION: Many Islamic scholars believe this verse predicts three separate visitations of God—one on Sinai to Moses, another to Seir (a region near the Dead Sea and the Arabian Desert) through Jesus, and a third in "Paran" (Arabia) through Muhammad who came to Mecca with an army of "ten thousand."

CORRECTING THE MISINTERPRETATION: This contention can be easily answered by looking at a Bible map. Paran is near Egypt in the Sinai peninsula and Seir is in Old Testament Edom (cf. Gen. 14:6; Num. 10:12; 12:16–13:3; Deut. 1:1). Neither are in Palestine where Jesus ministered. Nor was Paran near Mecca, but hundreds of miles away in near southern Palestine in the northeastern Sinai.

Further, this verse is speaking of the "LORD" (Yahweh, not Muhammad) coming. And he is coming with "ten thousand *saints*," not ten thousand *soldiers*, as Muhammad did. There is absolutely no basis in this text for the Muslim contention.

Finally, this prophecy is said to be one "with which Moses the man of God blessed *the children of Israel* before his death" (v. 1). If it were a prediction about Islam, which has been a constant enemy of Israel, it could scarcely have been a blessing to Israel. In fact, the chapter goes on to pronounce a blessing on each of the tribes of Israel by God, who "will thrust out the enemy" (v. 27).

DEUTERONOMY 34:10—Does this verse support the Muslim claim that Jesus could not be the predicted prophet of Deuteronomy 18:18?

MISINTERPRETATION: This verse claims "there arose not a prophet since in Israel like unto Moses" (KJV). Muslims argue that this proves that the predicted prophet could not be an Israelite but was Muhammad instead.

CORRECTING THE MISINTERPRETATION: The "since" means since Moses' death to the time this last chapter was written, probably by Joshua. Even if Deuteronomy or this section of Deuteronomy was written much later, as some critics believe, it still was composed centuries before the time of Christ and, therefore, would not eliminate him.

Note that Jesus was the perfect fulfillment of this prediction of the prophet to come, not Muhammad (see comments on Deut. 18:15–18). This could not refer to Muhammad, since the prophet to come was like Moses who did "all the signs and wonders which the LORD sent" (Deut.

34:11). Muhammad by his own confession did not perform signs and wonders like Moses and Jesus did (see Sura 17:90–93).

The prophet to come was like Moses who spoke to God "face to face" (Deut. 34:10). Muhammad never even claimed to speak to God directly but got his revelations through angels (cf. Sura 2:97). Jesus, on the other hand, like Moses, was a direct Mediator (1 Tim. 2:5; Heb. 9:15) who communicated directly with God (cf. John 1:18; 12:49; 17).

JOSHUA

JOSHUA 1:8—Is this verse a key to financial prosperity, as Word-Faith teachers suggest?

MISINTERPRETATION: Joshua 1:8 says, "This book of the law shall not depart from your mouth, but you shall meditate on it day and night, so that you may be careful to do according to all that is written in it; for then you will make your way prosperous, and then you will have success" (NASB). Word-Faith teachers say this verse is a key to financial prosperity.

CORRECTING THE MISINTERPRETATION: Word-Faith teachers are reading a meaning into this verse that is not there. The context of this verse is *military*, not *financial*. In fact, finances are nowhere in sight in this entire chapter of Joshua.

In the conquest of the Promised Land, God promised Joshua that his military efforts would prosper if he maintained his commitment to meditate upon and obey God's Word. The prospering also no doubt includes the full outworking of the land promises that were given unconditionally by God in the Abrahamic Covenant (Gen. 12:1–3). Later, just before his death, Joshua urged the people to continue living in submission to the Scriptures (Josh. 23:6).

1 SAMUEL

1 SAMUEL 18:1–4—Were David and Jonathan homosexuals?

MISINTERPRETATION: This Scripture records the intense love David and Jonathan had for each other. Some see this as an indication that they were homosexual. They infer this from the fact that Jonathan "loved" David (18:3); that Jonathan stripped in David's presence (18:4); that they "kissed" each other and "exceeded" (1 Sam. 20:41)—a term taken to mean ejaculation. They point also to David's lack of successful relations with women as an indication of his homosexual tendencies.

CORRECTING THE MISINTERPRETATION: There is no indication in Scripture that David and Jonathan were homosexuals. On the contrary, there is strong evidence that they were not. David's attraction to Bathsheba (2 Sam. 11) reveals that his sexual orientation was heterosexual, not homosexual. In fact, judging by the number of wives he had, David seemed to give in to too strong heterosexual desires.

David's love for Jonathan was not sexual *(erotic)* but a friendship *(philic)* love. It is common in Eastern cultures for heterosexual men openly and fervently to express love and affection toward one another.

The "kiss" was a common cultural greeting for men in that day. Furthermore, the kiss did not occur until some time after Jonathan gave David his clothes (1 Sam. 20:41). The emotion they expressed was weeping, not orgasm. The text says, "they kissed each other and wept together—but David wept the most" (1 Sam. 20:41).

Also, Jonathan did not strip himself of all his clothes in David's presence. He only stripped off his armor and royal robe (1 Sam. 18:3) as a symbol of his deep respect for David and commitment to him.

1 SAMUEL 26:19—Does this verse say that we should hate our enemies, as the Children of God cult teaches?

MISINTERPRETATION: Moses David, leader of the Children of God cult, appealed to this verse to justify hating his enemies. He wrote: "I'm sorry, I guess I'm not so loving as Jesus—I'm more like King David (1 Sam. 26:19). Jesus could forgive His enemies, but I curse my enemies. But God said David was a man after his own heart, so maybe I'm more like God, 'cause I want to curse them for hurting my little ones!" (David, 1977, GP No. 577, pp. 1, 2).

CORRECTING THE MISINTERPRETATION: Such a conclusion is farfetched and needs little response. Even in this passage David manifested his love for his enemy (Saul) by not killing him when he could have. David did not hate his enemies. Even in the so-called "cursing" Psalms he speaks of loving his enemies and praying for them. He wrote, "In return for my friendship they accuse me, but I am a man of prayer. They repay me evil for good, and hatred for my friendship" (Ps. 109:4–5).

Rather than take revenge on them, David committed his enemies to the justice of God, who renders to each according to his deeds.

1 SAMUEL 28:7–20—How could God allow the witch of Endor to raise Samuel from the dead when God condemned witchcraft?

MISINTERPRETATION: The Bible severely condemns witchcraft and communication with the dead (Exod. 22:18; Lev. 20:6, 27; Deut. 18:9–12; Isa. 8:19). In the Old Testament, those who practiced it were to receive capital punishment. King Saul knew this and even put all witches out of the land (1 Sam. 28:3). Nevertheless, in disobedience to God, he went to the witch of Endor, asking her to contact the dead prophet Samuel (1 Sam. 28:11–19). The problem here is that she appears to be successful in contacting Samuel, which seems to lend validity to the powers of witchcraft, which the Bible so severely condemns. Those who practice witchcraft, such as Wicca, sometimes cite this verse in support of their religion (Mather and Nichols, 1993, 313).

CORRECTING THE MISINTERPRETATION: Some believe that the witch worked a miracle by demonic powers and actually brought Samuel back from the dead. In support of this they cite passages which indicate that demons have the power to perform miracles (Matt. 7:22; 2 Cor. 11:14; 2 Thess. 2:9, 10; Rev. 16:14). The objections to this view include the fact that death is final (Heb. 9:27). The dead cannot return (2 Sam. 12:23) because there is a great gulf fixed by God (Luke

16:24–26), and demons cannot usurp God's authority over life and death (Job 1:10–12).

Others have suggested that the witch did not really bring up Samuel from the dead, but simply faked doing so. They support this by reference to demons who deceive people who try to contact the dead (Lev. 19:31; Deut. 18:11; 1 Chron. 10:13) and by the contention that demons sometimes utter what is true (cf. Acts 16:17). The objections to this view include the fact that the passage seems to say Samuel did return from the dead, that he provided a prophecy from Samuel that actually came to pass, and that it is unlikely that demons would have uttered truth of God, since the devil is the father of lies (John 8:44).

Another view is that the witch did not bring up Samuel from the dead, but God himself intervened to rebuke Saul for his sin: (a) Samuel seemed to actually return from the dead (vv. 14, 20), but (b) neither humans nor demons have the power to bring people back from the dead (Luke 16:24–31; Heb. 9:27). (c) The witch herself seemed to be surprised by the appearance of Samuel from the dead (v. 12). (d) There is a direct condemnation of witchcraft in verse 9. It is highly unlikely that the same text would give credence to witchcraft by claiming that witches can actually bring people back from the dead. (e) God sometimes speaks in unexpected places through unusual means (cf. Baalam's donkey, Num. 22).

The major objections to this view are that the text does not explicitly say that God performed the miracle, and that a witch's dwelling is a strange place to do it. God is sovereign in regard to when and where he intervenes, however, and not all miracles are labeled as such (cf. Matt. 3:17; 17:1–9). A miraculous act can speak for itself.

2 SAMUEL

2 SAMUEL 6:7—Does reverence for the ark of the covenant support the Roman Catholic view of venerating relics?

MISINTERPRETATION: According to this verse, "The LORD's anger burned against Uzzah because of his irreverent act; therefore God struck him down and he died there beside the ark of God." Does this give credence to the Catholic dogma of venerating religious relics?

CORRECTING THE MISINTERPRETATION: Uzzah was not stricken for failing to venerate the ark but for *disobedience to the law of God* that forbade anyone but a priest to touch it (Num. 4:15; cf. 2 Sam. 6:7).

Showing respect for the ark, in which the very presence of God and his glory was manifested, is far different from venerating the relics of human creatures. For one thing, the ark was a divinely appointed symbol, not the mere remains and adornment of men. For another, it was a special symbol in a unique theocracy, where God personally and visibly (in the cloud of his glory) dwelt among his specially chosen people, Israel. Finally, even granting the special place the ark had, the people were not to venerate it (Exod. 20:4–5) but were simply to obey God's laws with regard to its use.

God clearly commanded his people not to make graven *images* or to *bow* down to them in an act of religious devotion. This is the same error of the pagans who "revered and worshiped the creature rather than the Creator" (Rom. 1:25). The Bible forbids us ever to make or "bow" before an "image" of any creature in an act of religious devotion: "You shall not make for yourselves any carved image, or any likeness of anything that is in heaven above, or that is in the earth beneath, or that is in the waters under the earth; you shall not bow down nor serve them" (Exod. 20:4–5 NKJV, emphasis added).

1 KINGS

1 KINGS 11:1—Do the Scriptures approve of polygamy?

MISINTERPRETATION: Mormons say that prophet Joseph Smith claimed he received a "revelation" from the Lord that plural marriage was God's will for his followers (*Doctrine and Covenants,* 132:61–62). The Scriptures, though, repeatedly warn against having multiple wives (Deut. 17:17) and violating the principle of monogamy—one man for one wife (cf. 1 Cor. 7:2). What, then, are we to make of 1 Kings 11:3 where we are told that Solomon had 700 wives and 300 concubines?

CORRECTING THE MISINTERPRETATION: Monogamy is God's standard for the human race. This is clear since, (1) from the very beginning, God set the pattern by creating a monogamous marriage relationship with one man and one woman, Adam and Eve (Gen. 1:27; 2:21–25). (2) This God-established example was the general practice of the human race until interrupted by sin (Gen. 4:23). (3) The Law of Moses clearly commands even the kings, "You shall not multiply wives" (Deut. 17:17). (4) The warning against polygamy is repeated in the very passage where it numbers Solomon's many wives (1 Kings 11:2), warning "You must not intermarry with them." (5) Our Lord reaffirmed God's original intention by citing this passage (Matt. 19:4) and noting that God created one "male and [one] female" and joined them in marriage. (6) The New Testament stresses that "Each man should have his own wife, and each woman her own husband" (1 Cor. 7:2 NIV). (7) Likewise, Paul insisted that a church leader should be "the husband of one wife" (1 Tim. 3:2, 12). (8) Indeed, monogamous marriage represents the relation between Christ and his bride, the church (Eph. 5:31–32).

Polygamy was never established by God for any people under any circumstances. In fact, the Bible reveals that God severely punished those who practiced it. (1) Polygamy is first mentioned in the context of a sinful society in rebellion against God where the murderer "Lamech took for himself two wives" (Gen. 4:19, 23). (2) God repeatedly warned polygamists of the consequences of their actions "lest his heart turn away" from God (Deut. 17:17; cf. 1 Kings 11:2). (3) God never *commanded* polygamy—like divorce, he only permitted it because of the hardness of their hearts (Deut. 24:1; Matt. 19:8). (4) Every polygamist in the Bible, including David and Solomon (1 Chron. 14:3), paid dearly for his sins. (5) God hates polygamy, as he hates divorce, since it destroys his ideal for the family (cf. Mal. 2:16).

In brief, monogamy is taught in the Bible (1) by *precedent,* since God gave the first man only one wife; (2) by *proportion,* since the numbers of males and females God brings into the world are about equal; (3) by *precept,* since both Old and New Testaments command it; (4) by *punishment,* since God punished those who violated his standard (1 Kings 11:2); and, (5) by *type,* since marriage is a type of Christ and his bride, the church (Eph. 5:31–32). Simply because the Bible records Solomon's sin of polygamy does not mean that God approved of it.

2 KINGS

2 KINGS 13:21—Does the fact that God performed a miracle through Elijah's bones justify venerating relics of the saints as Roman Catholics claim?

MISINTERPRETATION: The text says that "once while some Israelites were burying a man, suddenly they saw a band of raiders; so they threw the man's body into Elisha's tomb. When the body touched Elisha's bones, the man came to life and stood up on his feet" (1 Kings 13:21 NIV). Roman Catholics cite this verse in support of their practice of venerating relics (Ott, 1960, 319).

CORRECTING THE MISINTERPRETATION: This Scripture does not justify venerating relics any more than it would justify venerating other physical means that God has used to convey miracles—such as the rod of Moses, the brazen serpent in the wilderness, the clay Jesus used to heal the blind man, or the hands the apostles used to cure diseases.

As a matter of fact, the Bible condemns the use of the brazen serpent for idolatrous purposes. In Hezekiah's campaign against Judah's idolatry, "he removed the high places, smashed the sacred stones and cut down the Asherah poles. He broke into pieces the bronze snake Moses had made, for up to that time the Israelites had been burning incense to it" (2 Kings 18:4 NIV).

God clearly commanded his people not to make graven *images* or to *bow* down to them in an act of religious devotion (Exod. 20:4, 5). This is the same error of the pagans who "revered and worshiped the creature rather than the Creator" (Rom. 1:25).

2 KINGS 14:29—Are the dead asleep or conscious?

MISINTERPRETATION: As in this passage, the Bible often speaks of death as the time when one "sleeps with his fathers" (e.g., 1 Kings 2:10;

11:21, 43; 14:20 KJV). Jesus said, "Lazarus sleeps" (John 11:11) when he was "dead" (v. 14). Paul speaks of believers who have "fallen asleep" in the Lord (1 Thess. 4:13; cf. 1 Cor. 15:51). The Jehovah's Witnesses believe such verses indicate that "when a person is dead he is completely out of existence. He is not conscious of anything" (*You Can Live Forever in Paradise on Earth*, 1982, 88). Yet, in other places the Bible speaks of persons being conscious in the presence of God after they die (cf. 2 Cor. 5:8; Phil. 1:23; Rev. 6:9).

CORRECTING THE MISINTERPRETATION: The first set of verses refers to the *body*, and the second set to the *soul*. "Sleep" is an appropriate figure of speech for the death of the body, since death is only temporary, awaiting the resurrection when the body will be "awakened." Further, both sleep and death have the same posture—lying down.

The Bible is very clear that the believer's soul (spirit) survives death (Luke 12:4). It is consciously present with the Lord (2 Cor. 5:8) in a better place (Phil. 1:23) where other souls are talking (Matt. 17:3) and even praying (Rev. 6:9–10). Likewise, the unbeliever's soul is in a place of conscious torment (Matt. 25:41; Luke 16:22–26; Rev. 19:20–20:15; see comments on 2 Cor. 5:8).

2 CHRONICLES

2 CHRONICLES 16:12—Does this text teach that king Asa's death resulted from seeking physicians rather than the Lord?

MISINTERPRETATION: According to Christian Science, this passage teaches that King Asa's death was a consequence of his seeking the aid of physicians, rather than from the Lord (Eddy, 245). From this they infer that we too should refrain from drugs and medical assistance, even in time of serious illness.

CORRECTING THE MISINTERPRETATION: Such an inference is not necessary in this context, and it is contrary to other passages of Scripture. Several considerations make this apparent.

The verse does not say it is wrong to seek the aid of a physician but to do this *instead of* seeking the Lord. God wants to be put first (cf. Matt. 6:33; Col. 1:18). As Jeremiah put it, "Cursed is the one who trusts in man, who depends on flesh for his strength and whose heart turns away from the LORD" (Jer. 17:5).

Both the Old and New Testaments recommend the use of medicine. Isaiah the prophet was commanded to "prepare a poultice of figs" for a boil. This poultice was applied to the boil, and he recovered (2 Kings 20:7). And Paul told Timothy, "Stop drinking only water, and use a little wine because of your stomach and your frequent illnesses" (1 Tim. 5:23 NIV).

Finally, the fact that the apostle Paul was afflicted with an infirmity (Gal. 4:13; cf. 2 Cor. 12:7) may be the reason he often traveled with Dr. Luke (see Col. 4:14; 2 Tim. 4:11). Nowhere does the Bible condemn going to a physician or taking medicine. Even Jesus said, "It is not the healthy who need a doctor, but the sick" (Matt. 9:12 NIV). The Bible simply insists that we should seek God first to determine whether the sickness is sent by him.

JOB

JOB 1:5—Does Job's offering of sacrifices for his children support the Roman Catholic teaching about indulgences?

MISINTERPRETATION: Job 1:5 declares that Job offered sacrifices for his children for, he said, "It may be that my sons have sinned and blasphemed God in their hearts." Roman Catholic scholars cite this in support of the "Treasury of Merit" teaching by which one person can atone for the temporal consequences for another's sins in purgatory (Ott, 1960, 317).

CORRECTING THE MISINTERPRETATION: This passage falls far short of supporting the Catholic doctrine of the Treasury of Merit in heaven. A look at the context reveals why.

There is no mention of any such treasury in the text. Nowhere does the passage say that God actually *accepted* such a solicitous act of Job on behalf of his children. The passage is descriptive, not prescriptive, informing us only about what Job *did*, but not whether this is what *ought* to be done. This is true of the record of Job's friends, being only descriptive of what they said, not really of what God thought (Job 42:7).

A careful study of the context reveals that the intent of the passage is to show us how righteous Job was (cf. 1:1), not whether atonement can be made for someone else's sins. Certainly God hears the prayers of a righteous person (Job 42:8; James 5:16). But this in no way implies that they can help atone for the sins of another. The virtue of one human being is not transferable to another. Scripture declares that "the righteousness of the righteous man will be upon himself" (Ezek. 18:20 NASB).

Even if the acts of one righteous person like Job were in some way efficacious for his family or friends on earth, it in no way supports the Catholic belief that this is effective for the departed. Job did it for the living, not for the dead!

Hence, Catholic appeal to this text to support the treasury of merit is groundless.

JOB 1:20–21—Does this verse teach reincarnation?

MISINTERPRETATION: The Bible speaks against the belief in reincarnation (John 9:3; Heb. 9:27). But here Job speaks of a person returning again after he dies. Some reincarnationists have appealed to this verse in support of their doctrine.

CORRECTING THE MISINTERPRETATION: Job is not speaking about the "return" of the soul to another body to live again, but of the return of the body to the grave. God told Adam he would "return to the ground" for "dust you are and to dust you shall return" (Gen. 3:19). And the Hebrew word for "womb" *(shammah)* is used figuratively in Job's poetic expression of the "earth." The ideas of "earth" and "womb" are used in Psalm 139, saying, God formed us in our "mother's womb" in "the lowest parts of the earth" (vv. 13, 15 NKJV). Like the ancient Hebrew book of wisdom, Job believed that people labor "from the day they come forth from their mother's womb, till the day they return to the Mother of all [i.e., the womb of the earth]" (Ecclus. 40:1). Likewise, Job used the poetic expression, "return there [i.e., to my mother's womb]," to refer to the earth from which we all come and to which we all return (cf. Eccles. 12:7).

Even if one insisted on a literal understanding of this figure of speech, it would not prove reincarnation. It would only show that the person returns to his mother's womb after he dies, which is absurd.

Finally, Job did not believe in reincarnation into another mortal body; he believed in resurrection in an immortal body. He declared, "I know that my redeemer lives, and in the end he will stand upon the earth; and after my skin has been destroyed, yet *in my flesh* I will see God" (Job 19:25–26 NIV, emphasis added). He realized that this corruptible flesh would put on incorruptible flesh (cf. 1 Cor. 15:42–44). Reincarnation, by contrast, does not hold that we will be raised once in an immortal physical body; it is the belief that the soul will be reincarnated many times into mortal bodies that will die again. So there is no basis for claiming that Job believed in reincarnation.

JOB 7:9—Does this verse contradict the Bible's teaching about resurrection?

MISINTERPRETATION: The Scriptures teach that all men will be raised bodily from the tomb (cf. Dan. 12:2; 1 Cor. 15:22; Rev. 20:4–6). Indeed, Jesus said that one day "all who are in their graves will hear his voice and come out" (John 5:28–29). However, Job seems to say just the opposite, when he writes, "He who goes down to the grave does not return" (NIV; see also Job 14:12; Isa. 26:14; Amos 8:14). Job 7:9 may come up in discussions with the Jehovah's Witnesses.

CORRECTING THE MISINTERPRETATION: As the first set of passages clearly reveals, there will be a resurrection of all the dead, both the just and the unjust (Acts 24:15; cf. John 5:28, 29). Job himself expressed belief in the resurrection, declaring, "After my skin has been destroyed, yet in my flesh I will see God" (Job 19:26). What he meant when he spoke of someone going down to the grave and not coming up (7:9) is explained in the very next verse: "He will never come to his house again" (v. 10). In other words, those who die do not return to their mortal lives again. Indeed, the resurrection is to an immortal life (1 Cor. 15:53), not to the same mortal life one had before.

Job 14:12 does not deny there will be any resurrection, but simply that there will be none until "the heavens are no more," that is, until the end of the age. But, that is precisely when the resurrection will take place, namely "at the time of the end" (Dan. 11:40; cf. 12:1–2; John 11:24). In fact, the passage actually teaches resurrection. For Job simply spoke of being hidden in the grave by God until an appointed time when God would again remember him (14:13) in the resurrection.

Neither does Isaiah 26:14 deny the resurrection. Here too the resurrection is affirmed in the succeeding verse which states clearly, "Your dead shall live; Together with my dead body they shall arise" (v. 19 NKJV). Obviously, then, verse 14 means they will not live *until the resurrection*. The memory of the wicked will perish from the earthly scene. Not until the heavenly scene dawns will they be raised again.

Some texts that may appear to deny the resurrection (e.g., Amos 8:14) simply refer to the enemies of God falling, never to rise to oppose him again. They will never resume their former sway over God's people. God overthrew them irretrievably.

JOB 14:12—Does this contradict the Bible's teaching on the Resurrection?

See comments on Job 7:9.

JOB 19:26—Does this verse indicate that the resurrection body will be a body of flesh?

MISINTERPRETATION: Satan had afflicted Job's body, and his flesh was rotting away. However, Job expressed his faith in God by saying, "Yet from my flesh I shall see God" (Job 19:26 NASB). Cults, including New Agers and Jehovah's Witnesses, deny a fleshly resurrection.

CORRECTING THE MISINTERPRETATION: The Bible often refers to a resurrection in the flesh (cf. Luke 24:26–27; Acts 2:31). That Job also held to the same is clear for several reasons. First, though the preposition *from (min)* may be translated "without," it is a characteristic of this preposition that when it is used with the verb "to see," it has the meaning "from the vantage point of."

This idea is strengthened by the use of contrasting parallelism employed in this verse. Hebrew poetry often employs two parallel lines of poetic expression which sometimes express contrasting words or ideas (called antithetic parallelism). Here the losing of Job's flesh is contrasted with his trust in God to restore the body that is decaying before his eyes, so that in his own flesh, he would see God. This is a most sublime expression of Job's faith in a literal, physical resurrection.

A physical resurrection is affirmed elsewhere in the Old Testament (Isa. 26:19; Dan. 12:2) and in the New Testament (Luke 24:39; John 5:28–29; Acts 2:31–32). So Job's understanding of a resurrection in the flesh is in accord with the rest of Scripture.

Psalms

PSALM 1:2—Should Christians meditate, or is this a Buddhist and Hindu practice?

MISINTERPRETATION: David declared here that we should "meditate day and night." However, transcendental meditation is associated with Eastern religions, such as Buddhism, Hinduism, and New Age philosophy—which are contrary to Christianity (Ferguson, 1980, 315–16). Should Christians engage in meditation?

CORRECTING THE MISINTERPRETATION: There is a significant difference between Christian meditation and mystical meditation found in many Eastern religions, popularly those known in Western forms as New Age religions. The differences are brought out in this contrast:

	CHRISTIAN	EASTERN RELIGIONS
OBJECT	Something (God)	Nothing (void)
PURPOSE	Worship of God	Merge with God
MEANS	Divine revelation	Human intuition
SPHERE	Through reason	Beyond reason
POWER	By God's grace	By human effort
EXPERIENCE	Objective reality	Purely subjective
IMMEDIATE STATE	Concentration	Relaxation

(See Geisler and Amano, p. 135)

There is a big difference between emptying one's mind to meditate on nothing and filling one's mind with the Word of God to meditate on the Living God. David said he meditated on God's "law"—the Word, not on the void. His purpose was spiritual fellowship with Yahweh, not a mystical union with Brahman or the Tao of Eastern religions.

PSALM 2:7—Does this verse mean that Jesus was born as a spirit child of heavenly parents?

MISINTERPRETATION: Psalm 2:7 says, "I will surely tell of the decree of the LORD: He said to Me, 'Thou art My Son, Today I have begotten Thee'" (NASB). Mormons think this verse supports the idea that Jesus was born a spirit child (by procreation), the offspring of heavenly parents (*Gospel Principles,* 1986, 9).

CORRECTING THE MISINTERPRETATION: The Mormon view on this text is not supported by it or the rest of Scripture. Two things should be kept in mind.

First, the context here is not speaking about a spirit being born in the spirit world but of the "kings of the earth" who "plot" against God's "Anointed" (the Messiah) to rid themselves of him (i.e., kill him). Hence, the most natural sense of his being "begotten" of God to reign over the nations (vv. 7–8) is that he was resurrected from the dead.

Second, a basic principle of biblical interpretation is that the Old Testament should be interpreted according to the greater light of the New Testament. Acts 13:33–34 indicates that the Father's resurrection of Jesus from the dead is a fulfillment of the statement in Psalm 2:7, "Thou art My Son, Today I have begotten Thee." The verse thus has nothing to do with the alleged procreation of Christ.

Other Scriptures make it clear that Christ never came into existence at a point in time but is rather an eternal being. Jesus is as eternal as God the Father (John 1:1) and existed as the eternal "I AM" (cf. Exod. 3:14) before Abraham (John 8:58). He was not "born" as a spirit being at any time. He was only born as a man in Bethlehem, even though he had been eternal (cf. Micah 5:2).

PSALM 37:9, 34—When the wicked are cut off, are they annihilated?

MISINTERPRETATION: The psalmist affirms that "evildoers shall be cut off." Elsewhere (Ps. 73:27; Prov. 21:28), Scripture says they will perish (see comments on 2 Thess. 1:9). Does being "cut off forever" mean the wicked will be annihilated, as many cults (such as the Jehovah's Witnesses) and aberrant groups believe (*Reasoning from the Scriptures,* 1989, 162)?

CORRECTING THE MISINTERPRETATION: Being "cut off" does not mean to be annihilated. If it did, then the Messiah would have been annihilated when he died, since the same Hebrew word *(karath)* is used of the death of the Messiah (Dan. 9:26). But we know that Christ was not annihilated; he lives on forever after his death (cf. Rev. 1:18). Also see comments on 2 Thessalonians 1:9.

PSALM 37:9, 11, 29—Do these verses prove that some of God's people will not go to heaven but will rather live forever on earth?

MISINTERPRETATION: Psalm 37:9 says, "For evildoers will be cut off, But those who wait for the LORD, they will inherit the land." Verse 11 says, "But the humble will inherit the land, And will delight themselves in abundant prosperity." Verse 29 says, "The righteous will inherit the land, And dwell in it forever." The Jehovah's Witnesses think these verses mean that not all good people go to heaven. Some will live for all eternity on earth (*Reasoning from the Scriptures*, 1989, 163).

CORRECTING THE MISINTERPRETATION: This passage is not dealing with a distant eschatological future in which God will destroy the wicked and create a paradise earth for the righteous. Rather, it is dealing with present and near-future circumstances of the Israelites *living at that time* in the promised land.

We note that the Hebrew word translated "land" is often used of the promised land in the Old Testament (see, for example, Deut. 4:38). This seems to be the case here.

The Hebrew word *forever* has a wide range of meanings from "a long period of time" to "for eternity" (Eccles. 3:11). In this context it seems to carry the meaning of "unforeseeable future." The psalmist appears to be saying that future generations of righteous Israelites would continue to dwell in the land into the unforeseeable future. If this is so, then the gist of this passage is that evil people *in the psalmist's lifetime* would be destroyed, while the righteous of his time would experience blessing.

Even if the text is referring to the eternal state, it does not justify the Jehovah's Witness conclusion that not all good people go to heaven. All who believe in Jesus Christ can look forward to a heavenly destiny, not just some select group of 144,000 (see Eph. 2:19; Phil. 3:20; Col. 3:1; Heb. 3:1; 12:22; 2 Peter 1:10–11). Jesus affirmed that all believers will be together in "one flock" under "one shepherd" (John 10:16). There will not be two "flocks"—one on earth and one in heaven.

PSALM 37:20—Does the fact that the wicked will perish mean they will lose consciousness, as annihilationists claim?

MISINTERPRETATION: Repeatedly, the Old Testament speaks of the wicked perishing. The psalmist wrote, "But the wicked will perish: The LORD's enemies will be like the beauty of the fields, they will vanish—vanish like smoke" (Ps. 37:20; cf. 68:2; 112:10; Prov. 11:10). Annihilationists insist that to perish implies one goes to a state of nothingness. The Jehovah's Witnesses believe so (*Mankind's Search for God*, 1990, 128).

CORRECTING THE MISINTERPRETATION: When properly understood in its context, the word *perish* does not support annihilationism.

First, the same word used to describe the wicked perishing in the Old Testament *(abad)* is used to describe the righteous perishing (see Isa. 57:1; Micah 7:2). But even the annihilationists admit that the righteous are not snuffed out of existence. That being the case, there is no reason they should conclude that of the wicked either. *Abad* is used to describe things that are merely lost, but then later found (Deut. 22:3). This proves that "perish" does not mean "go out of existence."

The Bible makes clear references to the lost being in conscious torment and punishment after their death. This is true of human beings (Luke 16:19–31; Rev. 19:20) as well as the devil (Rev. 20:10).

PSALM 45:3–5—Is this a prediction of Muhammad?

MISINTERPRETATION: Since these verses speak of one coming with the "sword" to subdue his enemies, Muslims sometimes cite it as a prediction of their prophet Muhammad, who was known as "the prophet of the sword." They insist it could not refer to Jesus, since he never came with a sword (Matt. 26:52).

CORRECTING THE MISINTERPRETATION: The very next verse (v. 6) identifies the person spoken of as "God," whom Jesus claimed to be (John 8:58; 10:30). Muhammad denied he was God, saying he was only a human prophet. The New Testament affirms that this passage refers to Christ (Heb. 1:8). And, although Jesus did not come the first time with a sword, he will at his Second Coming (cf. Rev. 19:11–16).

PSALM 46:10—Does this verse indicate that human beings can become God, as Maharishi Mahesh Yogi argues?

MISINTERPRETATION: In Psalm 46:10 God says: "Cease striving and know that I am God." Maharishi Mahesh Yogi, the founder of Transcendental Meditation, interprets this verse: "'Be still and know that I am God.' Be still and know that *you* are God and when you know that you are God you will begin to live Godhood, and living Godhood there is no reason to suffer" (*Meditations of Maharishi Mahesh Yogi*, 178). Can this verse be properly understood to mean that human beings can become God?

CORRECTING THE MISINTERPRETATION: This is a *Hebrew* Psalm, and among the Jews the idea that a human being can become a god is the very height of blasphemy. Such an idea is nowhere in this Psalm, not to mention the rest of the Bible.

Even a cursory look at the rest of the psalm indicates that the one true God is portrayed as *distinct from* and *exalted above* the created earth (and man). For example, in verses 10–11 we read, "'Cease striving and know that I am God; I will be exalted among the nations, I will be exalted in the earth.' The LORD of hosts is with us; the God of Jacob is our stronghold" (NASB).

It is the consistent testimony of Scripture that there is only one true God and that humanity is not now, and never will become, God (see Deut. 6:4; 32:39; 2 Sam. 7:22; 1 Kings 8:60; Ps. 86:10; Isa. 44:6; Joel 2:27; 1 Tim. 2:5; James 2:19). See the discussion of Genesis 1:26 for biblical argumentation against the idea that a human can become a god.

PSALM 82:6—Does this verse mean that human beings can become gods?

MISINTERPRETATION: Psalm 82:6 says, "I said, 'You are gods, And all of you are sons of the Most High'" (NASB). Mormons believe this verse supports the idea that human beings may become gods (McConkie, 1966, 321).

CORRECTING THE MISINTERPRETATION: There is no evidence for the Mormon polytheistic belief that men are gods in this text. Unlike the word LORD *(Yahweh)* which always means God, the word "gods" *(elohim)* can be used of God (Gen. 1:1), angels (Ps. 8:4–6; cf. Heb. 2:7), or human beings (as here).

This psalm focuses on a group of Israelite judges who, because they exercised life and death decisions over people, were loosely called "gods." But these judges became corrupted and were unjust. So Asaph, the author of this psalm, said that, even though these judges were called gods, they would *die* like the men they really were (see v. 7).

Asaph may have been speaking in irony in calling these evil judges "gods." If so, then there is no justification for calling them "gods" in any serious sense. In any event, the polytheistic claim is without justification, since this verse is uttered in the context of Jewish monotheism, in which it is blasphemous for any mere human being to be called God in a divine sense (see comments on John 10:34).

Besides, in Isaiah 44:8, God himself asks, "Is there any God besides Me, Or is there any other Rock? I know of none" (NASB). Similarly, Isaiah 43:10 portrays God as saying, "Before Me there was no God formed, And there will be none after Me." Clearly human beings can't become gods.

PSALM 88:11—Do the dead have remembrance of anything?

See comments under Ecclesiastes 9:5.

PSALM 97:7—Doesn't this verse imply there are many gods?

MISINTERPRETATION: The psalmist commands, "Worship Him, all you gods." Yet the Bible elsewhere insists there is only one God (Deut. 6:4). Does Psalm 97:7 indicate there is more than one God, as Mormons believe (Smith, 1977, 370)?

CORRECTING THE MISINTERPRETATION: There is no other *God*, but there are many *gods*. There is only one *true* God, but there are many *false* gods. Indeed, Paul declares that there are demons behind false gods (1 Cor. 10:20). And one day even the demons will bow before the true and living God and confess that he is Lord (Phil. 2:10).

Further, good angels are sometimes called "gods" *(elohim)* in the Bible (Ps. 8:5; cf. Heb. 2:7). This verse (Ps. 97:7) could be a command for the angels to worship God, as they are so commanded in Psalm 148:2: "Praise Him, all His angels."

PSALM 99:10—Does the fact that the wicked will perish mean they will be annihilated?

See comments on Psalm 37:20; 2 Thessalonians 1:9.

PSALM 102:20–21—Is this a prayer to the dead, as some Roman Catholic scholars claim?

MISINTERPRETATION: Roman Catholics appeal to this text to support the dogma of praying to the dead. It says, "Bless the LORD, all you angels. . . . Bless the LORD, all you hosts."

CORRECTING THE MISINTERPRETATION: This is not an actual prayer to angels and saints but is a poetic appeal like the doxology sung by Protestants: "Praise him above, ye heavenly host." Both the poetic nature of the Psalms and the context indicate that the psalmist is merely using a literary device to appeal to all of creation to praise God.

The point of the passage is to exalt God. Its use as a proof text for the doctrine of praying to angels or dead saints is totally foreign to the clearly expressed meaning of this passage.

The Bible speaks strongly against praying to any creatures by insisting that *God* alone should be the object of any religious devotion of prayer (Exod. 20:2–4; Deut. 6:13). There is not a single undisputed instance of any prayer in all of Scripture being addressed to anyone but God.

PSALM 103:3—Does this verse teach that all physical therapies are useless, as Christian Science claims?

MISINTERPRETATION: Christian Scientists point to this promise of the Lord to "heal all your diseases" to support their belief that "drugs, hygiene, and medical therapeutics" are useless (Eddy, 4).

CORRECTING THE MISINTERPRETATION: Nothing is said in the text about the uselessness of medicine. It simply says that God heals all our sicknesses.

It is literally true that God is the one who heals us, even if we take medicine. For the best medicine can do is to help the natural processes of the healing that God created in the body. And when the healing is a special act of God's providence or the result of a direct intervention, it too is of God. Even legitimate psychosomatic healings (where one's beliefs and/or attitudes affect bodily functions) are part of the marvelous process that God has created. So whether a healing is natural, psychological, providential, or supernatural, it is of God.

Not only does the Bible not pronounce all medicine useless, it recommends the use of medicine (see comments on 2 Chron. 16:12).

PSALM 105:15—Does this verse indicate that certain men called by God are beyond criticism and accountability, as Word-Faith teachers suggest?

MISINTERPRETATION: Psalm 105:15 says, "Do not touch My anointed ones, And do My prophets no harm" (NASB). Some Word-Faith teachers cite this verse in arguing that they have been specially anointed by God and should not be criticized for their teachings. They indicate in their words and actions a belief that challenging their teachings amounts to challenging God himself.

CORRECTING THE MISINTERPRETATION: The phrase "the Lord's anointed" is used in Old Testament Scripture to refer to Israel's kings (see 1 Sam. 12:3, 5; 24:6, 10; 26:9, 11, 16, 23; 2 Sam. 1:14, 16; 19:21; Ps. 20:6; Lam. 4:20). In this context the word cannot be interpreted to refer to modern teachers in the church. Further, the word *prophets* in context can only refer to Old Testament prophets, not to modern church leaders. Neither of these designations can be interpreted with reference to teachers in the modern church.

Even if we allowed that this verse could loosely refer to modern church leaders, the warning is against *physically* harming them. It has nothing to do with testing their teachings. In Old Testament times prophets and kings were very much in danger of physical harm—and hence the warning.

Scripture itself instructs us to test all teachings by the Word of God (1 Thess. 5:21). Like the Bereans of old, we must make the Scriptures our measuring stick for truth (Acts 17:11). The Bereans were *commended* for testing the apostle Paul's teachings against Scripture. Paul affirmed elsewhere, "All Scripture is inspired by God and profitable for teaching, *for reproof, for correction,* for training in righteousness; that the man of God may be adequate, equipped for every good work" (2 Tim. 3:16–17 NASB, emphasis added). All of us are to be constantly on guard against false teachings (Rom. 16:17–18; cf. 1 Tim. 1:3–4; 4:16; 2 Tim. 1:13–14; Titus 1:9; 2:1).

There is a sense in which *every* believer in Christ is "anointed" (see 1 John 2:20). In view of this, no Christian leader can lay claim to being special or above others and beyond doctrinal criticism.

PSALM 110:1—Does this verse prove that everyone will be saved, as universalists claim?

MISINTERPRETATION: David said (and Christ repeated): "The LORD says to my Lord: 'Sit at my right hand until I make your enemies a footstool for your feet'" (Ps. 110:1 NIV; cf. Matt. 22:44). Some liberals and universalists cite this verse to support their belief that in the end all people will be saved. Is this a proper use of this text?

CORRECTING THE MISINTERPRETATION: The same objections to universalism apply here as those cited in the discussion of 1 Corinthians 15:25–28. In addition to the individuals here being described as "enemies" who are "subjugated" *(not saved)*, they are called God's "footstool"—hardly an appropriate description of saints who are joint heirs with Christ and have all blessings in heavenly places in Christ (Rom. 8:17; Eph. 1:3).

In the context, David is not speaking of the salvation of the lost. Rather, he is referring explicitly to God's wrath on his enemies (Ps. 110:1, 5), not his blessings on his people.

PSALM 115:16—Does this verse mean many of God's people will live forever on a paradise earth and not in heaven?

MISINTERPRETATION: Psalm 115:16 says, "The heavens are the heavens of the LORD; But the earth He has given to the sons of men" (NASB). Jehovah's Witnesses believe this verse means that God's "other sheep" have a destiny of living forever on a paradise earth (*Let Your Name Be Sanctified*, 1961, 34).

CORRECTING THE MISINTERPRETATION: This verse indicates not that God has given the earth to a limited group of "other sheep" but rather that God has given the earth *to all humankind*. God created the earth, and then he created people to dwell upon it and subdue it (see Gen. 1:28; cf. Ps. 8:6–8).

Scripture elsewhere teaches that all true believers look forward to a heavenly destiny where they will live in the direct presence of God. Indeed, all who believe in Christ are heirs of the eternal kingdom (Matt. 5:5; Gal. 3:29; 4:28–31; Titus 3:7; James 2:5).

PSALM 115:17—Can the dead praise God, or are they unconscious?

See comments on Ecclesiastes 9:5 and 2 Corinthians 5:8.

PSALM 131:8—Does this verse foreshadow the bodily assumption of Mary, as some Catholic scholars claim?

MISINTERPRETATION: It is claimed by some Catholic scholars that passages such as this psalm refer "in a typical sense to the mystery of the bodily assumption; 'Arise, O Lord, into thy resting place; thou and the ark which thou hast sanctified.'" They argue that "the Ark of the Covenant made from incorruptible wood, [was] . . . a type of the incorruptible body of Mary" (Ott, 1960, 209; see also Madrid, 1991, 9f.).

CORRECTING THE MISINTERPRETATION: Using passages such as this to argue for the bodily assumption of Mary only confirms the impression that Roman Catholics are grasping for proof texts.

First, they admit that this is not a literal interpretation of the text but only an alleged "typical" one which, in this case, boils down to an invalid argument from analogy. Even proponents of this view have to admit that none of this "proves" the immaculate conception (Madrid, 12).

Second, the analogy between the Ark and Mary is far-fetched. One Catholic apologist calls this the "most compelling type of Mary's immaculate conception" (Ibid.). But it is only compelling if one makes the unbiblical and unjustified assumption that it is a valid analogy. The fact that there are some similarities proves nothing. There are many similarities between good counterfeit currency and genuine bills. The ineptness of these kinds of analogies surface in Madrid's question: "If you could have created your own mother [as God did in Mary], wouldn't you have made her the most beautiful, virtuous, perfect woman possible?" (Ibid.). No doubt most of us would have done a lot of things differently than God did. If I were God and could have created the most beautiful and perfect place my son would be born, then it certainly would not have been a stinky, dirty animal stable!

Third, nowhere is any such comparison stated or implied in Scripture. Creating analogies like these proves nothing, except that one has no real biblical support for the dogma. Indeed, by the same kind of arguments one could prove almost anything.

Fourth, the argument is based on another baseless belief that Mary's body was incorruptible after her death and before her alleged assumption. The Bible says this was true of Christ (Acts 2:30–31), but it nowhere affirms this of Mary. Even if, as some argue, this text (via David's anticipation of his deliverance in Ps. 16:10) includes Mary's bodily resurrection, nevertheless it does not apply to her in any more special sense than it does to the resurrection of the whole human race in the end times (cf. John 5:28–29; 11:24; 1 Cor. 15:20–21).

Finally, the Bible equates death with the corruption of all human beings except Christ (cf. 1 Cor. 15:42, 53). Yet most Fathers and theologians of the Catholic church believe that "Mary suffered a temporal death" (Ott, 1960, 207) like other mortals. Why then should we believe she was exempted from physical corruption any more than she was exempted from physical death entailed by the fall (Rom. 5:12)?

PSALM 146:3–4—Does this verse prove there is no conscious existence after death?

MISINTERPRETATION: Psalm 146:3–4 says, "Do not trust in princes, In mortal man, in whom there is no salvation. His spirit departs, he returns to the earth; In that very day his thoughts perish" (NASB). The Jehovah's Witnesses believe this passage means there is no conscious existence after death (*Reasoning from the Scriptures,* 1989, 383).

CORRECTING THE MISINTERPRETATION: This verse does not mean that people think no thoughts following death. Rather it means that peoples' plans, ambitions, purposes, and ideas for the future cease and come to naught at the moment of death. This is what the Hebrew word for "thoughts" communicates in Psalm 146:3–4. A person's plans and ideas for the future die with him or her. Hence, instead of trusting in mortal princes, this verse says our trust should be in God.

PROVERBS

PROVERBS 8:22–31—Was Jesus created by God?

MISINTERPRETATION: The Jehovah's Witnesses claim that the person identified as "wisdom" in Proverbs 8:22–31 is Jesus. Since wisdom is said to be created (v. 24), this means Jesus was a created being. "He was a very special person because he was created by God before all other things. . . . For countless billions of years, before even the physical universe was created, Jesus lived as a spirit person in heaven and enjoyed intimate fellowship with his Father, Jehovah God, the Grand Creator.— Proverbs 8:22" (*The Greatest Man Who Ever Lived*, 1991, 11).

CORRECTING THE MISINTERPRETATION: This passage has been the subject of much dispute by both friends and foes of the deity of Christ. It seems best in view of the context and the poetic nature of Proverbs not to take this passage as a direct reference to any person. Poetic expression often speaks of an abstract idea as if it were a person. This "personification" is a common feature of Hebrew wisdom literature. The wisdom referred to in Proverbs 8 is not Jesus. Rather, it is a personification of the virtue or character of wisdom for the purpose of emphasis and impact.

Further, the first nine chapters of Proverbs personify wisdom. And it wouldn't make much sense to say any of these chapters refers directly to Jesus. After all, wisdom is portrayed as a woman who cries out in the streets (1:20–21) and is said to "dwell" with prudence (8:12). It is noteworthy that no New Testament writer applies Proverbs 8 to Jesus Christ.

Apart from the issue of whether this verse relates to Jesus, common sense tells us that wisdom must be as eternal as God himself, who is the ultimate source of all wisdom. In this sense, we cannot allow that Proverbs 8 even supports the idea that wisdom was created. Rather, the Hebrew word here simply indicates that wisdom was *brought forth* to play a role in the creation of the universe. As Proverbs 3:19 put it, "By wisdom the LORD laid the earth's foundations, by understanding he set the heavens in place" (NIV). Thus, some commentators have seen a parallel between this and Jesus, the wisdom of God (1 Cor. 1:24; Col. 2:3), who was the instrumental cause through whom the universe was created (cf. John 1:3; Col. 1:16).

PROVERBS 23:7—Does this verse teach that reality can be shaped by our thoughts, as Christian Scientists claim?

MISINTERPRETATION: Solomon said that as a man "thinks in his heart, so is he" (NKJV). Christian Scientists cite this verse in support of their belief that one can shape reality by his thoughts (Eddy, 70). So anyone who is sick can be healed by simply disbelieving in it.

CORRECTING THE MISINTERPRETATION: There is nothing in this text to justify the so-called mind sciences. In fact, the New International Version translates this phrase, "He is the kind of man who is always thinking about the cost." The whole context of this passage (vv. 6–8) is warning about eating "the bread of a miser" (v. 6). Speaking of the miser, the last verse says, "'Eat and drink,' he says to you, but his heart is not with you." This fits with the idea that the miser's heart is not there because "he is always thinking about the costs," as the NIV translates it.

Even if this verse is translated "as he thinks in his heart, so is he," it does not follow that it supports the Christian Science view. It says nothing about changing reality by our thoughts. The text simply says that we are the way we think. Our thoughts depict the way we really are.

This, of course, does not mean that there is anything wrong with a good positive mental attitude (cf. Phil. 4:8). Nor does it mean that our attitude does not affect our health. For "a happy heart makes the face cheerful, but heartache crushes the spirit" (Prov. 15:13 NIV). But this falls far short of the Christian Science claim that we can create our own reality by the power of thought. For example, one cannot avoid death by thinking it away (Heb. 9:27).

Moreover, one must recognize that man, including his mind and imagination, is fallen (Gen. 6:5). Christian Scientists are blinded to the reality that they are using faulty equipment that can lead them astray. How much better it is to trust in the sure promises of a loving God for provisions in life, rather than having to depend on your visualizing prowess (see Matt. 6:30).

ECCLESIASTES

ECCLESIASTES 3:19—Is human destiny the same as that of animals?

MISINTERPRETATION: Solomon seems to claim here that there is no difference between the death of humans and that of animals: "One thing befalls them: as one dies, so dies the other" (NKJV). The Jehovah's Witnesses cite this verse to prove that humans do not have an immaterial nature called the soul or spirit (*Reasoning from the Scriptures,* 1989, 378).

CORRECTING THE MISINTERPRETATION: There are both similarities and differences between the deaths of animals and humans. In both cases, their bodies die and return to dust. Likewise, their death is certain, and both are powerless to prevent it. In these respects, the *physical* phenomena are the same for both humans and animals.

On the other hand, humans have immortal souls (spirits), and animals do not (Eccles. 12:7; cf. 3:21). Of no beast does the Bible say, "to be absent from the body . . . [is] to be present with the Lord" (2 Cor. 5:8 NKJV). Likewise, nowhere does the Bible speak of the resurrection of animals, as it does of all human beings (cf. John 5:28–29; Rev. 20:4–6). So there is a big difference in the *spiritual* realm between humans and animals. Consider the following summary:

Human and Animal Deaths

Similarities	Differences
Physically	Spiritually
In the body	In the soul
Life before death	Life after death
Mortality of the body	Immortality of the person
How the body decays	That the body is raised
No control over death	Experience of a resurrection

ECCLESIASTES 3:20–21—If there is life after death, why does Solomon declare that man has no advantage over the beasts?

MISINTERPRETATION: Ecclesiastes 3:20–21 insists that "all go to one place: All are from the dust, and all return to dust." Hence, "man has no advantage over beasts, for all is vanity." The Jehovah's Witnesses cite this verse to prove that human beings do not consciously survive death. "Does each human have a spirit that goes on living as an intelligent personality after it ceases to function in the body? No" (*Reasoning from the Scriptures,* 1989, 383).

CORRECTING THE MISINTERPRETATION: The Bible very clearly teaches that the soul survives death (2 Cor. 5:8; Phil. 1:23; Rev. 6:9). The reference in Ecclesiastes 3:20–21 is to the human body, not to the soul. Both humans and beasts die and their bodies return to dust. However, humans are different in that their "soul goes upward" (v. 21). In fact, Solomon speaks of "eternity" in the human heart (Eccles. 3:11) and of its immortality when he declares that at death "man goes to his eternal home" (12:5). He also emphasized that we should fear God because there is a day when "God will bring you into judgment" after this life (11:9). So Ecclesiastes is not denying life after death; it is warning about the futility of living only for this life "under the sun" (cf. 1:3, 13; 2:18). See also comments under Ecclesiastes 3:19.

ECCLESIASTES 9:5—Does the fact that the dead do not remember anything prove there is no conscious existence after death?

MISINTERPRETATION: The Jehovah's Witnesses argue that "in deep sleep, we are conscious of nothing, which agrees with the Hebrew expression at Ecclesiastes 9:5." They interpret the Bible as saying that "man does not *have* a soul but *is* a soul." Hence "there is no conscious existence after death. There is no bliss, and there is no suffering. All the illogical complications of the 'hereafter' disappear" (*Mankind's Search for God,* 1990, 128, 249).

CORRECTING THE MISINTERPRETATION: As stated above, the Bible teaches that the soul survives death in a state of conscious awareness (see also comments on 2 Kings 14:29 and 2 Cor. 5:8). The passages that say there is no knowledge or remembrance after death are speaking of no memory *in this world,* not of no memory *of this world.* Solomon clearly qualified his comment by saying it was "in the grave" (Eccles. 9:10) that there was "no remembrance." He affirmed also that the dead do not know what is going on "under the sun" (9:6). The dead know nothing so far as their bodily senses and worldly affairs are concerned. But while they do not know what is happening *on earth*, they certainly do know what is going on *in heaven* (see Rev. 6:9). These texts refer to human beings in relation to life on earth. They say nothing about the life to come immediately after this one.

ISAIAH

ISAIAH 1:18—Must one bypass reason in order to be truly spiritual, as some Word-Faith teachers seem to imply?

MISINTERPRETATION: Some Word-Faith teachers minimize the role of reason in the Christian's life (Hagin, 1966, 27).

CORRECTING THE MISINTERPRETATION: In Isaiah 1:18 God invites us, "Come now, let us reason together." Obviously God himself thinks that reason is important for the Christian. The Hebrew word for "reason" (*yakah*) in this verse is a legal term that was used in contexts of arguing a case in court or providing convincing evidence for one's case. The word carries the meaning of "to decide," "to judge," and "to prove." The use of this word strongly argues against the idea that God's people should bypass reason.

Moreover, God created man in his own image (Gen. 1:26–27)—which certainly included the capacity to reason (Mark 12:30). God calls on man to use this endowed reason, as in the context of Isaiah 1.

See the discussion of Mark 12:30 for a fuller discussion on the importance of reason.

ISAIAH 9:6—Does this verse indicate that the Son of God is also God the Father, thereby showing that the doctrine of the Trinity is false, as Oneness Pentecostals believe?

MISINTERPRETATION: The orthodox Christian doctrine of the Trinity holds that God is one God in three persons—Father, Son, and Holy Spirit. However, Isaiah 9:6 calls the Messiah "everlasting Father." How can Jesus be both the Father and the Son? Oneness Pentecostals often cite this verse in attempting to prove that the Son of God is also God the Father, thereby attempting to disprove the doctrine of the Trinity (Sabin, see Boyd, 1992, 32).

CORRECTING THE MISINTERPRETATION: It is important to understand that, in view of the fact that Scripture interprets Scripture, the Father is considered by Jesus as someone *other* than himself more than 200 times in the New Testament. And more than 50 times in the New Testament the Father and Son are seen to be distinct *within the same verse* (see, for example, Rom. 15:6; 2 Cor. 1:3–4; Gal. 1:3; Phil. 2:10–11; 1 John 2:1; and 2 John 3). Since the Word of God does not contradict itself, these facts must be kept in mind when we interpret Isaiah 9:6.

Second, the phrase in question is better rendered into English, "Father of eternity." In reference to Jesus this phrase can mean several things:

Some believe the phrase is used here in accordance with the Hebrew mindset that says that he who possesses a thing is called the father of it. For example, *the father of knowledge* means "intelligent," and *the father of glory* means "glorious." According to this common usage, the meaning of *Father of eternity* in Isaiah 9:6 is "eternal." Christ as the "Father of eternity" is an eternal being.

A second view suggests that the first part of verse six makes reference to the incarnation of Jesus. The part that lists the names by which he is called expresses his *relationship* to his people. He is *to us* the Wonderful Counselor, the Mighty God, the Father of Eternity, the Prince of Peace.

In this sense of the word *Father*, Jesus is a provider of eternal life. By his death, burial, and resurrection, he has brought life and immortality to light (2 Tim. 1:10). Truly, he is the Father or provider of eternity for his people.

ISAIAH 9:6—Does the reference to Jesus as a "Mighty God" indicate that Jesus is a lesser God than God the Father?

MISINTERPRETATION: The Jehovah's Witnesses agree that Jesus is a "Mighty God," as Isaiah 9:6 indicates, but they say he is not God Almighty like Jehovah is. Does the fact that Jesus is referred to as a "Mighty God" indicate he is a lesser God than the Father (*Reasoning from the Scriptures*, 1989, 413–14)?

CORRECTING THE MISINTERPRETATION: The folly of the Watchtower position is at once evident in the fact that Jehovah himself is called a "Mighty God" in the very next chapter of Isaiah (10:21). That both Jehovah and Jesus are called "Mighty God" in the same book within the same section demonstrates their equality.

A good cross-reference is Isaiah 40:3, where Jesus is prophetically called both "Mighty God" *(Elohim)* and Jehovah *(Yahweh):* "A voice is calling, 'Clear the way for the LORD *[Yahweh]* in the wilderness; Make smooth in the desert a highway for our God *[Elohim]*'" (NASB; cf. John 1:23). Clearly Jesus is not a lesser God than the Father.

ISAIAH 21:7—Does this passage predict the coming of Muhammad?

MISINTERPRETATION: Some Muslim commentators take the rider on the "donkeys" to be Jesus and the rider on "camels" to be Muhammad, whom they believe superseded Jesus.

CORRECTING THE MISINTERPRETATION: This speculation has no basis in the text or the context. The passage is speaking of the fall of Babylon (v. 9) and the news of its fall that spread by various means, namely, those riding on horses, donkeys, and camels. There is absolutely nothing here about the prophet Muhammad.

ISAIAH 29:1–4—Does this prophecy speak about *The Book of Mormon?*

MISINTERPRETATION: Mormons believe this passage is speaking about *The Book of Mormon* being discovered on American soil. They argue that the passage refers to the so-called Nephites, who allegedly came to inhabit North America. The phrase, *from the ground,* is supposedly a reference to *The Book of Mormon,* which was translated from golden plates that came out of the ground (Talmage, 1982, 278).

CORRECTING THE MISINTERPRETATION: This passage deals not with the so-called "Nephites" but with God's judgment against the rebellious Israelites. Jerusalem is called "Ariel" (cf. Isa. 29:1; 2 Sam. 5:6–9), which literally means "hearth of God." God's judgment on Jerusalem would be so horrific that the bloodshed and flames would make the city seem like an altar on which sacrifices were consumed. This judgment found its fulfillment in Sennacherib's siege of the city in 701 B.C. Following this bloody siege, Jerusalem found itself brought down to the ground, buried under the tidal wave of Assyrian might. In place of the proud boasts the city's inhabitants had previously uttered, the inhabitants now whispered or mumbled from the ground, as it were. The great city had been humbled. In context, then, the verse has nothing to do with *The Book of Mormon* coming out of the ground on American soil.

ISAIAH 40:12—Does this verse indicate that God is a being of human proportions, as some Word-Faith teachers suggest?

MISINTERPRETATION: Isaiah 40:12 says, "Who has measured the waters in the hollow of his hand, And marked off the heavens by the span, And calculated the dust of the earth by the measure, And weighed the mountains in a balance, And the hills in a pair of scales?" Word-Faith teachers say that since God measured the waters "in the hollow of his hand," he must be a being of human proportions. God is someone "very much like you and me. . . . A being that stands somewhere around 6'2" [or] 6'3" that weighs somewhere in the neighborhood of a couple of hundred pounds, little better, [and] has a [hand] span nine inches across" (Copeland, "Spirit, Soul and Body I," 1985, audio tape).

CORRECTING THE MISINTERPRETATION: This verse does not indicate that God is a being of human proportions. Scripture is clear that God is a spirit (John 4:24), and a spirit does not have flesh and bones (Luke 24:39). Since God does not have flesh and bones, he has no literal hand or a hand-span. God is not a man (Hosea 11:9) and has no form that people can see (Deut. 4:12; John 1:18; Col. 1:15). God's "hand-span" is simply anthropomorphic language—that is, language that figuratively describes God in humanlike terms. Scripture often uses such metaphoric language to help us understand God better.

ISAIAH 53:4–5—Does this passage indicate that physical healing during mortal life is guaranteed in the atonement, as Word-Faith teachers often argue?

MISINTERPRETATION: Isaiah 53:4–5 states, "Surely our griefs He Himself bore, And our sorrows He carried; Yet we ourselves esteemed Him stricken, Smitten of God, and afflicted. But He was pierced through for our transgressions, He was crushed for our iniquities; The chastening for our well-being fell upon Him, And by His scourging we are healed" (NASB). Word-Faith teachers believe this passage means that physical healing during mortal life is guaranteed in the atonement. Hence, a true believer should never be sick. It is up to the believer to appropriate the guaranteed healing that has been made available in the atonement. If the believer has unbelief or sin, then this available healing is thereby prevented (Hagin, *Word of Faith*, August 1977, 9).

CORRECTING THE MISINTERPRETATION: While ultimate physical healing *is* in the atonement (a healing we will enjoy in our resurrection bodies), healing of our bodies while in the *mortal* state (prior to our death and resurrection) *is not* guaranteed in the atonement.

Moreover, it is important to note that the Hebrew word for "healing" *(napha)* can refer not just to physical healing but to spiritual healing. The context of Isaiah 53:4 indicates that spiritual healing is in view. In verse 5 we are clearly told, "He was pierced through for *our transgressions,* He was crushed for *our iniquities;* The chastening for our well-being fell upon Him, And by His scourging we are healed" (v. 5, emphasis added). Because "transgressions" and "iniquities" set the context, spiritual healing from the misery of sin is in view.

Numerous verses in Scripture substantiate the view that physical healing in mortal life is not guaranteed in the atonement and that it is not always God's will to heal. The apostle Paul couldn't heal Timothy's stomach problem (1 Tim. 5:23) nor could he heal Trophimus at Miletus (2 Tim. 4:20) or Epaphroditus (Phil. 2:25–27). Paul spoke of "a bodily illness" he had (Gal. 4:13–15). He also suffered a "thorn in the flesh" which God allowed him to retain (2 Cor. 12:7–9). God certainly allowed Job to go through a time of physical suffering (Job 1–2). In none of these cases is it stated that the sickness was caused by sin or unbelief. Nor did Paul or any of the others act as if they thought their healing was *guaranteed* in the atonement. They accepted their situations and trusted in God's grace for sustenance. It is noteworthy that on two occasions Jesus said that sickness could be for the glory of God (John 9:3; 11:4).

Other Scripture reveals that our physical bodies are continuously running down and suffering various ailments. Our present bodies are said to be perishable and weak (1 Cor. 15:42–44). Paul said "our outer man is decaying" (2 Cor. 4:16). Death and disease will be a part of the human condition until that time when we receive resurrection bodies that are immune to such frailties (1 Cor. 15:51–55). See comments on Philippians 2:25.

ISAIAH 53:9—Did Jesus die spiritually on the cross, as Word-Faith teachers argue?

MISINTERPRETATION: Word-Faith teachers largely base their view that Jesus died spiritually on the cross on Isaiah 53:9: "His grave was assigned to be with wicked men, Yet with a rich man in His death; Although He had done no violence, Nor was there any deceit in His mouth" (NASB). They typically argue that the Hebrew word for death in this verse is a plural word, thereby indicating that Jesus *died twice*— spiritually *and* physically. Is this interpretation correct?

CORRECTING THE MISINTERPRETATION: Word-Faith teachers have misunderstood the nature of the Hebrew language in regard to this verse. While a Hebrew plural often refers to numeric plurality, a plural can also be used to intensify the meaning of a single word. The Hebrew word for death in Isaiah 53:9 is what Hebrew grammarians call a *plural of intensity* (or *plur. exaggerativus,* as Keil and Delitzsch put it, 7:329). This kind of plural indicates not that there is more than one death in view but rather that the one death spoken of (a *physical* death) is particularly intense in terms of violence—like having to die *again and again.* Hence, Word-Faith teachers are reading a meaning into this verse that simply is not there. This verse cannot be cited to support the view that Jesus died twice—both physically *and* spiritually—on the cross.

ISAIAH 56:3—Did Isaiah predict there would be homosexuals in the kingdom?

MISINTERPRETATION: According to some prohomosexual interpreters, Isaiah 56:3 prophesied that homosexuals will be brought into the kingdom of God. The Lord said, "To them I will give within my temple and its walls a memorial and a name better than sons and daughters; I will give them an everlasting name that will not be cut off." Should this be taken to mean that Isaiah predicted the day of acceptance for homosexuals into God's kingdom?

CORRECTING THE MISINTERPRETATION: The Bible makes no predictions about homosexuals being accepted into the kingdom of God. Isaiah's prophecy is about "eunuchs," not homosexuals. And eunuchs are asexual, not homosexual. The "eunuchs" spoken of are probably spiritual, not physical. Jesus spoke of spiritual "eunuchs" who have given up the possibility of marriage for the sake of the kingdom of God (Matt. 19:11–12).

This interpretation is a classic example of reading one's beliefs into the text (eisogesis) rather than reading the meaning out of the text (exegesis). Eisogesis is the very thing homosexuals charge heterosexuals with doing with Scripture. However, the Bible says emphatically that "neither fornicators . . . nor homosexuals . . . will inherit the kingdom of God" (1 Cor. 6:9 NASB). The Scriptures repeatedly and consistently condemn homosexual practices (see comments on Lev. 18:22 and Rom. 1:26).

God loves all persons, including homosexuals. But he hates homosexuality, and those who practice it stand under God's wrathful judgment.

JEREMIAH

JEREMIAH 1:5—Is Jeremiah teaching reincarnation in this verse (New Age)? Is Jeremiah teaching that people preexist as spirit-children before taking on physical bodies (Mormon)?

MISINTERPRETATION: God informed Jeremiah, "Before I formed you in the womb I knew you; before you were born I sanctified you; And I ordained you a prophet to the nations" (NKJV). New Agers think this verse supports the doctrine of reincarnation since Jeremiah preexisted as a soul before he was incarnated into a body. Mormons think the verse proves their doctrine of "preexistence"—the idea that we all lived in the spirit world before we were born in the flesh (Talmage, 1977, 197).

CORRECTING THE MISINTERPRETATION: This verse does not speak of reincarnation or of the soul preexisting before birth. Rather it speaks of God calling and setting apart Jeremiah for the ministry long before he was born. "I knew you" does not refer to a *preexistent soul,* but to the *prenatal person.* Jeremiah was known by God "in the womb" (Jer. 1:5; cf. Ps. 51:5; 139:13–16).

The Hebrew word for "know" *(yada)* implies a special relationship of commitment (cf. Amos 3:2). It is supported by words like *sanctified* [set apart] and *ordained* which reveal that God had a special assignment for Jeremiah even before birth. *Know* in this context indicates God's act of making Jeremiah the special object of his sovereign choice. Therefore, this verse does not imply Jeremiah's *preexistence;* rather, it affirms Jeremiah's *preordination* to a special ministry.

EZEKIEL

EZEKIEL 1:5–28—Is this a manifestation of UFOs and extraterrestrial intelligences?

MISINTERPRETATION: Ezekiel speaks here of "living creatures" whose faces were in "the likeness of a man" which moved "like a flash of lightening" (v. 14). They were "lifted up from the earth" and their "wheels were lifted up together with them." Some—including many New Agers—have taken this to be a reference to UFOs and extraterrestrials.

CORRECTING THE MISINTERPRETATION: This is not a visit with UFOs but a vision of the glory of God. The text states clearly that "this was the appearance of the likeness of the glory of the LORD" (Ezek. 1:28 NIV).

The accounts are called "visions" in the very first verse. Visions are usually highly symbolic in form (cf. Rev. 1:9–20). Hence, the "likeness" (v. 28) given of things should not be taken literally but symbolically.

In this case the "living creatures" were angels, since they had "wings" (v. 6) and flew in the midst of heaven (cf. Ezekiel 10). They compare to the angels mentioned in Isaiah 6:2 and especially to the "living creatures" (angels) which were around God's throne in Revelation 4:6. The accompanying message was from the "Lord God" of Israel through the prophet Ezekiel (cf. 2:1–4) to his "rebellious nation" (2:3–4; cf. 3:4), not one from some alleged UFO beings.

There is no real evidence that any UFO humanlike creatures exist anywhere in the universe, but Scripture warns us of "lying spirits" (1 Kings 22:22) and "deceiving spirits" (1 Tim. 4:1). These demons or evil angels may deceive people into thinking they are extraterrestrials. But they can be known by their false teaching and the evil practices they encourage, such as idolatry, witchcraft, astrology, divination, fortune telling, and contacting departed spirits (cf. Deut. 13:1–9; 18:9–22; 1 Tim. 4:1–5).

EZEKIEL 16:49—Was the sin of Sodom selfishness rather than homosexuality?

MISINTERPRETATION: (See comments on Gen. 19:8.) Ezekiel described the sin of Sodom as selfishness: "Now this was the sin of your sister Sodom: She and her daughters were arrogant, overfed and unconcerned; they did not help the poor and needy" (16:49). No mention is made of homosexuality or related sexual sins. Contrary to the traditional view, they were apparently condemned simply because they were selfish, not because they were homosexuals.

CORRECTING THE MISINTERPRETATION: Beyond the comments on Genesis 19:8, the sin of selfishness related by Ezekiel does not exclude the sin of homosexuality. Sexual sins are a form of selfishness, a satisfaction of fleshly passions.

The very next verse (Ezek. 16:50) indicates that their sin was sexual by calling it an "abomination." This is the same word used to describe homosexual sins in Leviticus 18:22. Here, as throughout the Bible, the sin of Sodom is referred to as a sexual perversion. Jude 7 even calls their sin "sexual immorality."

EZEKIEL 18:4—Does this verse indicate that a human being does not have an immaterial part that survives death?

MISINTERPRETATION: Ezekiel 18:4 says, "For every living soul belongs to me, the father as well as the son—both alike belong to me. The soul who sins is the one who will die." The Jehovah's Witnesses argue that "the soul is not something with a separate existence. It can and does die" (*Mankind's Search for God*, 1990, 356). They say the word *soul* (Hebrew: *nephesh*) refers not to man's immaterial nature but to a living person.

CORRECTING THE MISINTERPRETATION: Words can have different meanings in different contexts. The word for soul *(nephesh)* is an example. In Ezekiel 18:4 "soul" indeed is used in the sense of "living person" or "person." However, just because the word is used in this one way in Ezekiel 18:4 does not mean the word must mean the same thing in *every other* verse. In Genesis 35:18, "soul" apparently refers to man's immaterial nature: "And it came about as her soul was departing (for she died), that she named him Ben-oni; but his father called him Benjamin." This verse recognizes the soul as distinct from the physical body which dies (see also 2 Cor. 5:8–10; Phil. 1:23; Rev. 6:9–11).

EZEKIEL 37:16–17—Is this passage a prophecy of *The Book of Mormon?*

MISINTERPRETATION: Mormons think this passage points to *The Book of Mormon*. They believe the sticks mentioned in Ezekiel 37:16–17 are pieces of wood around which a papyrus scroll was wrapped. "In ancient times it was the custom to write on parchment and roll it on a stick. Therefore, when this command was given, it was the equivalent of directing that two books or records should be kept" (Richards, 1969, 67). One of the sticks (Judah) is referring to the Bible; the other (Joseph) is allegedly referring to *The Book of Mormon*.

CORRECTING THE MISINTERPRETATION: The context clearly identifies the two "sticks." Ezekiel 37:22 says, "I will make them *one nation* in the land, on the mountains of Israel; and one king will be king for all of them; and *they will no longer be two nations,* and *they will no longer be divided into two kingdoms*" (emphasis added). The sticks are not two books but are rather two kingdoms.

The backdrop is that following Solomon's death, Israel became split into two smaller kingdoms (931 B.C.). The Southern Kingdom was called Judah; the Northern Kingdom was called Israel (or sometimes Ephraim). Israel was taken into captivity by Assyria (722 B.C.); Judah was taken into exile by Babylon (605, 597, and 586 B.C.). The division between the kingdoms, however, was not to last forever. The uniting of the "sticks" pictures God's restoring his people, the children of Israel, into a single nation again (Ezek. 37:18–28).

Amos

AMOS 3:7—Does this verse mean that there must *always* be a prophet—the Mormon president—on the earth?

MISINTERPRETATION: Amos 3:7 says, "Surely the LORD God does nothing unless He reveals His secret counsel to His servants the prophets" (NASB). Mormons say this verse proves that God in every age has a prophet on earth through whom he reveals his instructions. They believe the president of their church is God's prophet for today (McConkie, 1977, 606).

CORRECTING THE MISINTERPRETATION: This verse should not be interpreted to mean that God will always have a prophet on earth. In Amos 3:7 we find God about to bring judgment against the Israelites because of their disobedience. This passage affirms that God had previously warned the Israelites that judgment would follow disobedience, but they had ignored the prophets (cf. 2:12). In context, then, Amos 3:7 simply points to God's chosen pattern of not engaging in a major action with the Israelites (such as judgment) without first revealing it to the prophets.

Relevant to our discussion is the fact that in Old Testament times the biblical test for a prophet was 100-percent accuracy (cf. Deut. 18:20–22). Mormon prophets do not measure up. Mormon prophet (and founder) Joseph Smith, for example, once prophesied that the New Jerusalem would be built in Missouri in his generation (Smith, 1835, 84:3–5).

AMOS 8:14—Does this verse affirm that there is no literal resurrection?

See comments on Job 7:9.

JONAH

JONAH 3:4–10; 4:1–2—Do these verses indicate that biblical prophets sometimes made mistakes?

MISINTERPRETATION: Jonah's prediction about the destruction of Nineveh did not come to pass (Jonah 3:4–10; 4:1–2). Clearly, then, a biblical prophet made a mistake in this case. Some argue that if Jonah was not condemned, neither should modern "prophets" (such as the Watchtower Society) be condemned for making false prophecies.

CORRECTING THE MISINTERPRETATION: Jonah *did not* make a mistake, for he told the Ninevites *precisely* what God had told him to say (Jonah 3:1–4). Since God cannot err (Heb. 6:18; Titus 1:2), this is not a false statement. Rather, the message had an implied condition in Jonah's exhortation to Nineveh—"*Unless you repent,* God will destroy you." So the fulfillment of the threat of judgment was contingent on the intransigence of Nineveh—a fact proven by their repentence (cf. 3:5). Jonah selfishly admits that he was afraid from the beginning that they would repent and God would save them (Jonah 4:2).

God's allowance of repentance in the face of judgment is stated as a principle in Jeremiah 18:7–8: "If at any time I announce that a nation or kingdom is to be uprooted, torn down and destroyed, and if that nation I warned repents of its evil, then I will relent and not inflict on it the disaster I had planned." This principle is illustrated in the case of Nineveh.

Thus, Jonah's prophecy cannot be cited to lessen the guilt of the Watchtower Society in its numerous false predictions. Biblical prophets were 100-percent accurate (Deut. 18:22).

HABAKKUK

HABAKKUK 3:3—Is this a prediction of the prophet Muhammad?

MISINTERPRETATION: Many Muslim scholars believe this verse refers to the prophet Muhammad coming from Paran (Arabia), and use it in connection with a similar text in Deuteronomy 33:2. Is this a correct interpretation?

CORRECTING THE MISINTERPRETATION: As already noted (see comments on Deut. 33:2), Paran is nowhere near Mecca, where Muhammad came, but is hundreds of miles away. Furthermore, this verse is speaking of "God" coming, not Muhammad. Finally, the "praise" could not refer to Muhammad (whose name means "the praised one"), since the subject of both "praise" and "glory" is God, and Muhammad is not God.

MALACHI

MALACHI 3:6—Does this verse indicate that God will always communicate with new revelation and new scripture, as the Mormons argue?

MISINTERPRETATION: In Malachi 3:6 God affirmed, "For I, the LORD, do not change; therefore you, O sons of Jacob, are not consumed" (NASB). Mormons argue that because God does not change, he will always communicate with people through new revelation and new Scripture. Because God *once* gave Scripture, he must *always* give Scripture (Van Gorden, 1995, 25).

CORRECTING THE MISINTERPRETATION: All one need do is to consult the immediate context of Malachi 3 and the broader context of all of Scripture to see that this view is wrong.

Malachi 3:6 affirms that God is unchanging in his nature and in his sovereign purposes and promises to his people. Notice the second part of Malachi 3:6, which Mormons typically ignore: "therefore you, O sons of Jacob, are not consumed." In context, this verse is simply saying that the descendants of Jacob would not be destroyed because of God's covenant promises to Israel. God's *unchanging promises* to Israel are just as reliable and sure as his *unchanging person.* God's promises, *like himself,* are immutable. Clearly, then, the verse has nothing to do with the issue of continuing revelation.

Other verses in Scripture *do* address the issue of continuing revelation. For example, Jude 3 instructs us, "Contend earnestly for the faith which was once for all delivered to the saints." In the Greek text, the definite article ("the") preceding "faith" points to the *one and only* faith that was handed down to the church; there is no other true "faith."

The word translated "once for all" (Greek: *hapax*) refers to something that has been done for all time and never needs repeating. The revelatory process was completed after this faith had been delivered. Therefore there is no need of further revelation about the nature of God, the person of Christ, the way of salvation, or any other doctrine.

It is significant that the word *delivered* in this verse is an aorist passive participle, which indicates a once-for-all completed action. There would be no new "faith" or body of truth communicated through Joseph Smith or Mormon presidents or in books such as *The Pearl of Great Price.*

Even if one hypothetically granted that God might wish to reveal additional foundation truths today, any present-day revelation would have to be consistent with the previous revelation. The apostle Paul said that, "even if we or an angel from heaven should preach a gospel other than the one we preached to you, let him be eternally condemned!" (Gal. 1:8). Any teaching that contradicts previous authoritative teaching from God is anathema. Paul spoke of the importance of making sure that new claims to truth be measured against what we know to be true from Scripture (Acts 17:11; 2 Tim. 3:16). Using this criterion alone, Mormon "revelation" must be rejected because it sets forth a different Jesus, a different God, and a different gospel.

MALACHI 4:5, 6—Is this a prediction of baptism for the dead, as Mormon's claim?

MISINTERPRETATION: According to Mormon president James Talmage (*The Vitality of Mormonism,* 71), "For the dead who have lived and died in ignorance of the requirements of salvation, as, in another sense, for the disobedient who later come to repentance, the plan of God provides for the vicarious administration of the essential ordinances to the living posterity in behalf of their dead progenitors. Of this saving labor Malachi prophesied in solemn plainness (Mal. 4:5, 6); and the glorious fulfillment has been witnessed in this modern age."

CORRECTING THE MISINTERPRETATION: This text says nothing about baptism for the dead, as Mormons claim. Rather it is a prediction of the coming of "Elijah" (cf. Matt. 17:11) before "the great and terrible day of the Lord." This is evident from several things. First, the text makes no reference to any baptism for the dead. Second, this passage may be taken in part to be a reference to John the Baptist who "turned the hearts of the fathers to the children" (Luke 1:17), for Jesus called him "the Elijah who was to come" (Matt. 11:14). Of course, John was not literally Elijah reincarnated, as he himself said (John 1:21–23). But he did come "in the spirit and power of Elijah" (Luke 1:17), and

Jesus called John "the Elijah who was to come" (Matt. 11:14). But when John came he baptized only the *living* (cf. Matt. 3:1–6), not the dead, as Mormons claim should be done.

It is also important to note that there is no reference here or anywhere else in the Bible to any "ordinance," such as baptism for the dead. (See comments on 1 Cor. 15:29 for more on this.)

Further, salvation is not something that can be administered on behalf of another, whether by baptism or any other way. Each person bears his own responsibility before God (Ezek. 18:20; Rom. 14:12).

Finally, salvation is not a "labor," as Talmage claimed. It is totally by grace apart from any works on man's part (Rom. 4:5; 11:6; Eph. 2:8–9).

MATTHEW

MATTHEW 2:2—Why does the Bible commend the magi for following the star at the birth of Christ when it condemns astrology?

MISINTERPRETATION: The Bible condemns the use of astrology (see Lev. 19:26; Deut. 18:10; Isa. 8:19), yet God blessed the wise men (magi) for using a star to indicate the birth of Christ. Does not this verse support the claim of astrologers?

CORRECTING THE MISINTERPRETATION: Astrology is a belief that the study of the arrangement and movement of the stars can enable one to *foretell* events—whether they will be good or bad. The star used in the biblical account was to *announce* the birth of Christ, not to *foretell* this event. God gave the star to the magi to proclaim to them that the child had already been born. We know the child was already born because, in Matthew 2:16, Herod commanded the killing of all boys in Bethlehem and vicinity two years old or younger, in accordance with "the time which he had ascertained from the Magi."

Further, there are other cases in the Bible in which the stars and planets are used by God to reveal his desires. Psalm 19:1–6 affirms that the heavens declare God's glory, and Romans 1:18–20 teaches that creation reveals God's existence. Christ refers to what will happen to the sun, moon, and stars in connection with his second coming (Matt. 24:29–30), as did the prophet Joel (2:31–32).

Therefore, there is no contradiction between the Bible's use of the star to announce Christ's birth and the Bible's condemnation of the practice of astrology. The star guiding the Magi was not used to *predict*, but to *proclaim* the birth of Christ.

MATTHEW 3:16–17—Does this passage support polytheism?

MISINTERPRETATION: This passage—which describes Jesus' baptism, with the Holy Spirit descending on him as a dove and the Father verbally commending him—has been misinterpreted in a variety of ways. The Jehovah's Witnesses say that, just because the Father, Son, and Holy Spirit are mentioned together does not mean they are "one," as trinitarians argue. The Mormons argue that this passage gives support to their view that the Father, the Son, and the Holy Spirit are three separate personages or Gods (i.e., polytheism). These three cannot possibly be "one," as trinitarians teach (Talmage, 1977, 39–40).

CORRECTING THE MISINTERPRETATION: This passage does not support Mormon polytheism. Rather, it supports a crucial premise of trinitarianism—the truth that there are three distinct persons of the Godhead.

Matthew 3:16–17 supports the doctrine of the Trinity, though in itself it does not prove the doctrine. Trinitarians base their understanding of the nature of God on the accumulative evidence of the whole of Scripture. Taken by itself, all that the passage proves directly is that there are three different persons in the Godhead. It does not show that these three persons all share one and the same divine essence.

Other verses demonstrate the unity of God—that he is one in essence. Deuteronomy 6:4 declares: "Hear, O Israel: The LORD our God, the LORD is one." This truth of God's essential unity is repeated in the New Testament (Mark 12:29). Paul said explicitly: "We know that . . . there is no God but one" (1 Cor. 8:4).

Some passages show both the unity and plurality of God. For example, Matthew 28:19 declares: "Go therefore and make disciples of all the nations, baptizing them in the name of the Father and the Son and the Holy Spirit" (NASB). The word *name* is singular in the Greek, indicating that there is one God. But there are three distinct persons within the Godhead, each with a definite article in the Greek—*the* Father, *the* Son, and *the* Holy Spirit. This disproves the Jehovah's Witnesses' view since it proves the Father, Son, and Holy Spirit are subsumed under *one name* and therefore are indeed "one" (unlike Abraham, Isaac, and Jacob). This disproves the Mormon view, since it shows that the Father, Son, and Holy Spirit are not three separate individuals or gods but rather are three persons within *one* Godhead.

So, Scripture taken as a whole yields the doctrine of the Trinity that is based on three lines of biblical evidence: (1) evidence that there is only one true God; (2) evidence that there are three Persons who are recognized as God; and (3) evidence for three-in-oneness within the Godhead. Scripture uniformly teaches that *there is only one God* (Deut. 6:4;

32:39; 2 Sam. 7:22; Ps. 86:10; Isa. 44:6; John 5:44; 17:3; Rom. 3:29–30; 16:27; 1 Cor. 8:4; Gal. 3:20; Eph. 4:6; 1 Thess. 1:9; 1 Tim. 1:17; 2:5; James 2:19; 1 John 5:20–21; Jude 25). Yet Scripture also calls *three persons God*—the Father (1 Peter 1:2), the Son (John 20:28; Heb. 1:8), and the Holy Spirit (Acts 5:3–4). Scripture also indicates three-in-oneness in the Godhead (Matt. 28:19; 2 Cor. 13:14). The accumulative evidence of the whole of Scripture indicates that God is a Trinity.

MATTHEW 5:13—Does this verse refer to people who recognize their divinity and help others to recognize their divinity as well?

MISINTERPRETATION: In Matthew 5:13 Jesus instructs his followers, "You are the salt of the earth. But if the salt loses its saltiness, how can it be made salty again? It is no longer good for anything, except to be thrown out and trampled by men" (NASB). Some New Agers believe that in this verse Jesus has in mind enlightened individuals who not only recognize their own divinity, but who also help others recognize theirs. "What is seeking to emerge is a body of people who are nourishers and who are quite literally what Jesus called 'the salt of the Earth' . . . accepting their divinity without becoming inflated by it, and acting within the sphere of their influence to draw that same divinity out of others" (Spangler, 1981, 80).

CORRECTING THE MISINTERPRETATION: This New Age interpretation is contrary to the meaning of the text in its context. Salt is known for its preservative qualities. As the "salt of the earth" (Matt. 5:13), Christians serve as a preservative against the evils of society. Salt is also known for creating thirst. Christians can so influence others so as to cause them to thirst for more information about Christ and the gospel.

In order for Christians to function properly as "the salt of the earth," however, the salt must maintain its pure character. Christians must be careful lest, instead of being a preservative against evil, they themselves become tainted with evil, thereby compromising the influence they have on the world. They cannot influence the world for Christ without retaining their own virtue as Christians.

The idea that human beings are their own gods or can become gods is one example of the kinds of things Christians stand against as "the salt of the earth." One way we act as a preservative in the world is to preserve pure doctrine (Jude 3). And one way we cause people to thirst for the true God of Scripture is to argue against false gods—such as the New Age god of pantheism.

MATTHEW 5:14—Does this verse indicate that the "cosmic Christ" dwells in all of us?

MISINTERPRETATION: Jesus said, "You are the light of the world. A city on a hill cannot be hidden" (Matt. 5:14 NASB). New Agers interpret this passage in reference to what the "cosmic Christ" can accomplish in all humanity: "Jesus believed that Christ in him could save the world and we believe that Christ in him will save the world. But Jesus also believes that Christ in each one of us can and will save the world. He has told me so. He said it plain: 'Ye are the Light of the world. A city [citadel of Christ-consciousness] that is set on a hill [of attainment] cannot be hid'" (Prophet, 1988, 239).

CORRECTING THE MISINTERPRETATION: There is no indication in this text that the cosmic Christ of New Age pantheism is dwelling in us. Several considerations make this evident.

First, Jesus is a Jewish monotheist (cf. Mark 12:29) who believed that God *created* the world and humankind (Matt. 19:4), not that the world and mankind is God.

Second, Jesus is the ultimate Light of the world (Matt. 4:16; John 8:12; 1 John 1:7). Believers are lights only in a derivative sense, as we are reflective of his light.

Third, Christians by their good deeds "shine a light" so that people may "glorify your Father who is in heaven" (Matt. 5:16). In other words, the result of Christians shining as a light is that people turn to the *true God of Christianity,* not to the "Christ within us." Christians are to so radiate their commitment to the God of the Bible that others are pointed to the proper path.

Light by its very nature dispels darkness—including the darkness of false doctrine. The idea that we can become gods, or that we are Christ just as Jesus was the Christ, is such a false doctrine (Gen. 3:4–5) inspired of demons (1 Tim. 4:1). As we shine as lights in the world, we point people away from false gods (such as pantheism and self-godhood) to the one true God of the Bible.

MATTHEW 5:17–18—Are Christians still under the law of Moses?

MISINTERPRETATION: Jesus said very explicitly, "Do not think that I came to destroy the Law or the Prophets. I did not come to destroy, but to fulfill." This is an important issue, for certain cultic leaders—such as Herbert W. Armstrong—have emphasized the keeping of the law, including Sabbath observance, the annual feast days, and dietary regulations. Other aberrant groups like Seventh-Day Adventists also believe Christians are still under the Mosaic law.

CORRECTING THE MISINTERPRETATION: In the matter of whether the law of Moses was done away with by Christ, confusion results from failing to distinguish several things.

There is a confusion of time. During his lifetime, Jesus always kept the law of Moses himself, including offering sacrifices to the Jewish priests (Matt. 8:4), attending Jewish festivals (John 7:10), and eating the Passover lamb (Matt. 26:19). He did on occasion violate the pharisaical (and false) traditions that had grown up around the law (cf. Matt. 5:43–44), chiding them, "You have made the commandment of God of no effect by your tradition" (Matt. 15:6). The verses that indicate the law has been fulfilled refer to *after* the Cross when there is "neither Jew nor Greek . . . for you are all one in Christ Jesus" (Gal. 3:28).

There is a confusion of aspect. At least some of the references (if not all) to the law being done away with in the New Testament are speaking of Old Testament ceremonies and types. These ceremonial and typological *aspects* of the Old Testament law of Moses were clearly done away with when Jesus, our Passover lamb (1 Cor. 5:7), fulfilled the law's types and predictions about his first coming (cf. Heb. 7–10). Jesus himself apparently did away with the ceremonial law by declaring all meats clean (Mark 7:19). In this sense, believers are clearly not under the law of Moses.

There is a confusion about context. Even when the moral dimensions of the law are discussed, there is a confusion. For example, not only did Jesus fulfill the moral demands of the law for us (Rom. 8:2–4), but the *national* and *theocratic* context in which God's moral principles were expressed in the Old Testament no longer apply to Christians today. For example, we are not under the commands *as Moses expressed them for Israel,* since, when expressed for them in the Ten Commandments, it had as its reward that the Jews would live "long upon *the land* [of Palestine] which the Lord your God is giving *you* [Israelites]" (e.g., Exod. 20:12). When the moral principle expressed in this Old Testament commandment is stated in the New Testament, it is expressed in a *different context,* namely, one that is not national or theocratic, but is personal and universal. For all persons who honor their parents, Paul declares that they will "live long on the earth" (Eph. 6:3). Likewise, Christians are no longer under the commandment of Moses to worship on Saturday (Exod. 20:8–11). Since the resurrection, postresurrection appearances, and ascension were all on Sunday, Christians worship on Sunday instead (see Acts 20:7; 1 Cor. 16:2). Sabbath worship, declared Paul, was only an Old Testament "shadow" of the real substance that was inaugurated by Christ (Col. 2:16–17). Since even the Ten Commandments *as such* were expressed in a national Jewish, theocratic framework, the New Testament can speak correctly about that which was "engraved on stones" being "taken away in Christ" (2 Cor. 3:7, 13, 14).

However, this does not mean that the moral principles embodied in the Commandments, that reflect the very nature of an unchanging God, are not still binding on believers today. Indeed, every one of these principles contained in the Ten Commandments is restated *in another context* in the New Testament, except of course the command to rest and worship on Saturday. Christians today are no more under the Ten Commandments *as given by Moses to Israel* than we are under the Mosaic Law's requirement to be circumcised (see Acts 15; Gal. 3) or to bring a lamb to the temple in Jerusalem for sacrifice. Hebrews 7 declares that "when there is a change of the priesthood, there must also be a change of the law" (v. 12) and "the former regulation is set aside because it was weak and useless" (v. 18). The law was only a "shadow" and the "substance" is found in Christ (Col. 2:17).

Jesus' disciples clearly rejected much of the Old Testament law, including circumcision (Acts 15; Gal. 5:6; 6:15). Indeed, Paul declared that "You are not under law but under grace" (Rom. 6:14) and that the Ten Commandments engraved in stone have been "taken away in Christ" (2 Cor. 3:14). The fact that we are bound by similar moral laws against adultery, lying, stealing, and murder no more proves we are still under the Ten Commandments than the fact that there are similar traffic laws in North Carolina and Texas proves that a Texan is under the laws of North Carolina. The truth is that when one violates the speed laws in Texas he has not thereby violated a similar law in North Carolina, nor is he thereby bound by the penalties of such laws in North Carolina. In like manner, although both the Old and New Testaments speak against adultery, nevertheless, the penalty was different—capital punishment in the Old Testament (Lev. 20:10) and only excommunication from the church in the New Testament (1 Cor. 5), with the hope of restoration upon repentance (cf. 2 Cor. 2:6–8).

MATTHEW 5:26—Does this parable substantiate the doctrine of purgatory, as Roman Catholic scholars claim?

MISINTERPRETATION: In this parable the judge would not release his prisoner until he paid the last farthing. Roman Catholic authority

Ludwig Ott believes this lends support to the doctrine of purgatory, for "through further interpretation of the parable, a time-limited condition of punishment in the other world began to be seen expressed in the time-limited punishment of the prison" (Ott, 1960, 484).

CORRECTING THE MISINTERPRETATION: Purgatory is not envisioned in this text. Such an interpretation goes well beyond the context.

Jesus is not speaking about a spiritual prison *after* death but a physical prison *before* death. The previous verse makes the context clear: "Settle matters quickly with your adversary who is taking you to court. Do it while you are still with him on the way, or he may hand you over to the judge . . . and you may be thrown in prison" (v. 25 NIV). To be sure, Jesus was not speaking of mere external things here but of the spiritual matters of the heart (cf. vv. 21–22). However, nothing in the context warrants the conclusion that he intended the concept of a "prison" to refer to a place (or process) of purgation for sins in the next life, which is what one would have to conclude if this passage were made to speak of purgatory. Even orthodox Catholics, such as Cardinal Ratzinger, shy away from the prison image of purgatory, claiming that it is not "some kind of supra-worldly concentration camp" (Ratzinger, 1990, 230).

However, to make this an analogy or illustration of a spiritual prison after death (i.e., purgatory) is to beg the question, since one has to assume there *is* a purgatory where we "will not be released until we have paid" (v. 26) before it can be an illustration of it. Illustrations do not *prove* anything; they only *illustrate* something believed to be true. Hence, this passage cannot be used as a proof of purgatory.

If this text is taken as a reference to purgatory, it contradicts the clear teaching of Scripture that there is nothing left to pay for the consequences of our sins, temporal or eternal. While Catholic theology acknowledges that Christ's death paid the penalty for the guilt and eternal consequences of our sins, they deny that this means there is no purgatory in which we pay the temporal consequences for our sins. But Christ's death on the cross was both complete and sufficient for all our sins *and all their consequences*. To say there is some suffering for sins left for us is to insult the "once for all" finished work of Christ (cf. Heb. 10:14–15). Once Jesus suffered for our sins, there is nothing left for us to suffer, for there is "*now* no condemnation" for those in Christ (Rom. 8:1). The prophet Isaiah made it clear that Christ died for our griefs and sorrows as well as for our sins (Isa. 53:4–5).

MATTHEW 5:29—Is hell the grave or a place of conscious torment?

MISINTERPRETATION: Jesus refers here to the "body" being "cast into hell," and the psalmist speaks of "bones" being "scattered at the mouth of hell [*sheol*]" (Ps. 141:7). Jacob talked about his "gray hairs" being brought down to hell (Gen. 42:38; cf. 44:29, 31). However, Jesus referred to hell as a place where the soul goes after one dies and is in conscious torment (Luke 16:22–23). Is hell just the grave, as the Jehovah's Witnesses and some other cults claim (*Reasoning from the Scriptures*, 1989, 173)?

CORRECTING THE MISINTERPRETATION: The Hebrew word translated "hell" (*sheol*) is also translated "grave" or "pit." It simply means "unseen world," and can refer either to the grave, where the body is unseen after burial, or to the spirit world, which is invisible to mortal eyes.

Further, in the Old Testament, *sheol* often means grave, as indicated by the fact that it is a place where "bones" (Ps. 141:7), "gray hairs" (Gen. 42:38), and even weapons (Ps. 76:3–5) go at death. Even the resurrection of Jesus' body is said to be from "hell" (i.e., the grave), where it did not see corruption (Acts 2:30–31).

There may be allusions to "hell" as a spirit world in the Old Testament (cf. Prov. 9:18; Isa. 14:9); "hell" (Greek: *hades*) is clearly described as a place of departed spirits (souls) in the New Testament. Fallen angels are there and they have no bodies (2 Peter 2:4). Unrepentant human beings are in conscious torment there after they die and their bodies are buried (Luke 16:22–23). In the end those in hell will be cast into the lake of fire with the devil where they will be "tormented day and night forever" (Rev. 20:10, 14–15). Jesus spoke many times of hell as a place of conscious and eternal suffering (cf. Matt. 10:28; 18:9; Mark 9:43, 45, 47; Luke 12:5; 16:23).

MATTHEW 5:48—Does this verse indicate we must become more and more perfect in this life in order to attain exaltation in the next life?

MISINTERPRETATION: Matthew 5:48 says, "Therefore you are to be perfect, as your heavenly Father is perfect" (NASB). According to Mormons, people are required to perform every duty and keep every law and endeavor to be perfect just as the Father is perfect in his sphere. Everyone is on a road to perfection that ultimately leads to godhood (Smith, 1970, 7).

CORRECTING THE MISINTERPRETATION: This verse does not mean human beings can actually become perfect in this life. This is clear from the context.

The context of this verse is that the Jewish leaders had taught that we should love those near and dear to us (Lev. 19:18), but hate our enemies. Jesus, however, said we should love even our enemies. After all, Jesus said, God's love extends to all people (Matt. 5:45). And since God is our righteous standard, we should seek to be as he is in this regard. We are to be "perfect" (or "complete") in loving others as he is perfect.

Furthermore, the Bible certainly does not give support to the idea that we can actually attain sinless perfection in this life, for all of us are fallen and sin continually (1 John 1:8). The good news is that by trusting in Jesus, his perfection becomes ours: "For by one offering He has perfected for all time those who are sanctified" (Heb. 10:14 NASB).

MATTHEW 6:22—Does this verse refer to a mystical "third eye" that gives us spiritual perception?

MISINTERPRETATION: Jesus said, "The eye is the lamp of the body. If your eyes are good, your whole body will be full of light" (Matt. 6:22 NIV). New Agers often interpret this verse in reference to "the third eye," which devotees of Eastern religions believe to be a mystical instrument or organ of spiritual vision, allegedly located on the forehead directly between the two physical eyes (Prophet, 1988, 143).

CORRECTING THE MISINTERPRETATION: No such esoteric interpretation of this text is justified by the context. The backdrop to this verse is that the Pharisees were materialistic and coveted wealth. Their spiritual eyes were focused not on the God of the Bible but on the god of greed. They were blind to true spirituality. They were full of darkness. By contrast, Jesus calls his followers to focus on God and heavenly treasures (see Matt. 6:16–33). We are to maintain an eternal perspective with a focus on the next world, not a temporal perspective with a fixation on the fading things of this world (see esp. v. 20).

Also, it is by focusing our *two* God-given eyes on the Scriptures that we gain spiritual perception (Prov. 7:2; Ps. 119). Reading a "third eye" into the context of Matthew 6 is *eisogesis* ("reading a meaning into the text") instead of *exegesis* ("deriving a meaning out of the text").

MATTHEW 6:33—Does this verse mean we are to make our "inner divinity" a top priority?

MISINTERPRETATION: Jesus said, "Seek first His kingdom and His righteousness; and all these things shall be added to you" (Matt. 6:33).

New Agers often interpret this verse as referring to the alleged "inner divinity" of man. Jesus was supposedly teaching his disciples to seek "the state of identification with one's true individuality, the source within, the Divine center, that I AM THAT I AM" (Spangler, 1983, 23–24). Therefore, seeking the kingdom of heaven first in one's life amounts to making one's inner divinity a top priority. After a person does this one thing, "all else will be added."

CORRECTING THE MISINTERPRETATION: There is no indication that Jesus referred to any "inner divinity." As a Jewish monotheist (Mark 12:29), not a pantheist, Jesus believed God was as different from the world as a Creator (Matt. 19:4) is from his creation. New Agers believe that God is to the world what a pond is to drops of water in it. That is, we are part of God, not a distinct creation of God.

Unlike the pagans, whose focus is only on meeting external physical needs, followers of Christ are called to seek God and his kingdom first. "Seeking God's kingdom" certainly includes seeking the one true God (1 Tim. 4:10) of the Bible (as opposed to pantheism). It includes obeying the absolute truth contained in God's Word (Ps. 119) (as opposed to New Age mystical "revelations"). And it includes participating in spreading the good news of the gospel of Jesus Christ (1 Cor. 15:1–4), as opposed to the "Aquarian gospel" which says we are Christ. Hence, rather than supporting the idea of an "inner divinity" within, this verse opposes this and other ideas that have no legitimate part in God's kingdom.

Third, one must also wonder, if all of us are god and have an "inner divinity," why is it necessary for us to read New Age books and Bible verses to come into an awareness of this divinity? The fact that we "come to realize" we are God proves that we are not God. A God would never have passed from a state of unenlightenment to a state of enlightenment. To put it another way, God does not blossom; he is always in full bloom. That is, God is and *always has been* God.

Finally, numerous verses in Scripture show that God stands against human pretenders to the divine throne. For example, God instructed Moses to tell Pharaoh: "I will send all My plagues on you and your servants and your people, so that you may know that *there is no one like Me in all the earth*" (Exod. 9:14 NASB, emphasis added). These words were spoken to a man who was himself considered a god. The Pharaoh was thought to be the incarnation of the Egyptian sun god, Amon-Ra, and was therefore considered a god in his own right. But he was impotent in the face of the true God. Pharaoh discovered what all New Agers must come to discover: as a human being he has virtually no divine power.

MATTHEW 7:20—Does this verse show which cult or religious group is the true religion?

MISINTERPRETATION: Jesus said, "By your fruit you will recognize them." In other words, good fruit is a sign of true religion, and bad fruit a sign of the false. Some cults use this to prove that they are the true religion. Christian Scientists, for example, point to the "uplifting power" of their religion as a good fruit (Eddy, 10). From this they conclude that Christian Science is the true religion.

CORRECTING THE MISINTERPRETATION: This verse should not be used to prove that any religious organization (including one claiming to be Christian) is the one true religion. Jesus is not talking about a religious organization here. Rather, he is speaking *to his disciples* in the Sermon on the Mount—a sermon that begins in Matthew 5. Thus, the verse about good fruit applies to anyone who professes to be Jesus' disciple anywhere and in any organization.

Jesus is not speaking of inner peace or an inner state which cannot be tested by others, but rather of outward manifestations ("fruit") that can be seen by other persons. The context seems to indicate that Jesus is not even speaking of the "fruit" of someone's spiritual life as Paul did in Galatians 5:22–23. Rather, he refers to the fruit of their teaching. For he begins the section speaking of "false prophets" (v. 15) and their "fruit" (v. 16), one of which is false prophecy (cf. Deut. 18:22). He continues by noting that it is not those who give a false confession of him (v. 21) who enter heaven, nor those who show outward spiritual powers (v. 22). Instead, it is those who confess the truth about Christ from the heart (cf. Rom. 10:9) who are his true disciples. They do his will (v. 21). But the fruit of a false prophet's teaching is to produce disciples who do not do "the will of My Father in heaven" but who simply say "Lord, Lord" (v. 21).

MATTHEW 7:24–29—Does this verse teach that only those who recognize their "inner divinity" can stand against the storms of life?

MISINTERPRETATION: Some New Agers believe that when Jesus taught about those who build on sandy soil (Matt. 7:26–27), he was referring to those who do not have the ability to recognize the inner divinity within them. "When a person loses that ability to recognize the divinity that is within one then he loses his ability to withstand or to transmute or to deal creatively with the forces of adversity" (Spangler,

1981, 61). Thus, in the same way that a house built upon sand will not stand up well when a harsh wind comes along, so an individual who fails to recognize his own inner divinity will not stand up well when a force of adversity comes against him.

CORRECTING THE MISINTERPRETATION: That Jesus is not speaking about any ability to recognize his own divinity is clear from the context.

For one thing, those who build their lives on the *words of Christ* are likened to those who build a house on a rock (Matt. 7:24–25). Those who do not build their lives on the words of Christ are likened to those who build a house on sandy soil (vv. 26–27).

For another thing, the "words of Christ" include a commitment to wholehearted submission to the Scriptures (Matt. 5:17–18), a recognition of the one true God (6:9), and a warning against false prophets who teach things contrary to Scripture (7:15–23). This passage thus decisively stands against New Age scriptures which contradict the Bible (such as *The Aquarian Gospel of Jesus the Christ*), the false New Age god of pantheism, and New Age false prophets who preach another Jesus.

MATTHEW 8:12—Is hell a place of darkness, or is there light there?

MISINTERPRETATION: Jesus described hell as a place of "outer darkness" (Matt. 8:12; cf. 22:13; 25:30). By contrast, the Bible elsewhere says hell is a place of "fire" (Rev. 20:14) and "unquenchable flames" (Mark 9:48). But fire and flames give off light. How can hell be utterly dark when there is light there? Mormons often make reference to the "outer darkness" as the abode of Satan, demons, and sons of perdition (Talmage, 1977, 146–47). Is this correct?

CORRECTING THE MISINTERPRETATION: Both "fire" and "darkness" are powerful figures of speech that appropriately describe the unthinkable reality of hell. It is like fire because it is a place of destruction and torment. Yet, it is like outer darkness because people are lost there forever. While hell is a literal place, not every description of it should be taken literally. Some powerful figures of speech are used to portray this literal place. Its horrible reality, wherein body and soul will suffer forever, goes far beyond any mere figure of speech that may be used to describe it. But it is a serious mistake to take metaphorical language literally. By doing so, one can conclude that God has feathers, since he is described as having wings (Ps. 91:4). Other figures of speech used to describe the eternal destiny of the lost, if taken literally, contradict each other. For example, hell is depicted as an eternal garbage dump (Mark 9:43–48), which has a bottom. But, it is also portrayed as a bottomless pit (Rev. 20:3). Each is a vivid depiction of a place of everlasting punishment.

MATTHEW 8:20 (cf. Matt. 20:18; 24:30)—If Jesus was the Son of God, why did he call himself the "Son of Man"?

MISINTERPRETATION: Jesus referred to himself most often as the "Son of Man." This seems to point to his humanity more than his deity. If he was really the Messiah, the Son of God, why did he use the self-description, "Son of Man"? This issue has obvious relevance in regard to discussions with Jehovah's Witnesses.

CORRECTING THE MISINTERPRETATION: Even if the phrase *Son of Man* is a reference to Jesus' humanity, it is not a denial of his deity. By becoming man, Jesus did not cease being God. The incarnation of Christ did not involve the subtraction of deity, but the addition of humanity. Jesus clearly claimed to be God on many occasions (Matt. 16:16, 17; John 8:58; 10:30). But in addition to being divine, he was also human (Phil. 2:6–8). He had two natures conjoined in one person.

Jesus was not denying his deity by referring to himself as the Son of Man. Actually the term *Son of Man* is used to describe Christ's deity as well. The Bible says that only God can forgive sins (Isa. 43:25; Mark 2:7). But as the Son of Man, Jesus had the power to forgive sins (Mark 2:10). Likewise, Christ will return to earth as the Son of Man in clouds of glory to reign on earth (Matt. 26:63–64). In this passage, Jesus is citing Daniel 7:13 where the Messiah is described as the "Ancient of Days," a phrase used to indicate his deity (cf. Dan. 7:9).

What is more, when Jesus was asked by the high priest whether he was the "Son of God" (Matt. 26:63), he responded affirmatively, declaring that he was the "Son of Man," who would sit at the right hand of God and return on the clouds (v. 64). This indicated that Jesus himself used the phrase *Son of Man* to indicate his deity as the Son of God.

Finally, the phrase "Son of Man" emphasizes who Jesus is in relation to his incarnation and his work of salvation. In the Old Testament (see Lev. 25:25, 26, 48, 49; Ruth 2:20), the kinsman-redeemer was a close relative of someone who was in need of redemption. So Jesus, as our Kinsman-Redeemer, was identifying himself with humankind as the Savior and Redeemer of humankind. Those who knew the Old Testament truth about Messiah being the Son of Man understood Jesus' implicit claims to deity. Those who did not would not so recognize this. Jesus often said things in this way to test his audience and separate believers from unbelievers (cf. Matt. 13:10–17).

MATTHEW 11:14—Didn't Jesus say John the Baptist was Elijah reincarnated?

MISINTERPRETATION: Jesus refers here to John the Baptist as "Elijah who is to come" (cf. Matt. 17:12; Mark 9:11–13). But since Elijah had died many centuries before, some reincarnationists have argued that John must have been a reincarnation of Elijah.

CORRECTING THE MISINTERPRETATION: There are many reasons why this verse does not support the Eastern or New Age view of reincarnation.

Even if it could be shown to be a reference to Elijah being reincarnated in John the Baptist, it would still be vastly different from New Age reincarnation: (1) It would be a single reincarnation, not endless reincarnations such as are found in Eastern religions. (2) It is in a theistic context, not a pantheistic worldview. (3) There is no concept of karma by which one is punished for what happened in a previous existence. It could hardly be a punishment for Elijah to return as the greatest prophet before Jesus (cf. Matt. 11:11).

However, it is not necessary to take this passage as meaning a literal reincarnation of Elijah. There are several indications in the text that it simply means that John ministered in the spirit and power of Elijah.

First, John and Elijah did not have the same *being*—they had the same *function*. Jesus was not teaching that John the Baptist was literally Elijah, but simply that he came "in the spirit and power of Elijah" (Luke 1:17), to continue his prophetic ministry.

Second, Jesus' disciples understood that he was speaking about John the Baptist, since Elijah appeared on the Mount of Transfiguration (Matt. 17:10–13). Since John had already lived and died by then, and since Elijah still had the same name and self-consciousness, Elijah had obviously not been reincarnated as John the Baptist.

Third, Elijah does not fit the reincarnation model, for he did not die. He was taken to heaven like Enoch who did not "see death" (2 Kings 2:11; cf. Heb. 11:5). According to traditional reincarnation, one must first die before he can be reincarnated into another body.

Fourth, this passage should be understood in the light of the clear teaching of Scripture opposing reincarnation. Hebrews 9:27, for example, declares, "It is appointed for men to die once, and after this comes judgment" (NASB; cf. John 9:2).

MATTHEW 11:29—Does this verse support yoga?

MISINTERPRETATION: New Agers tell us that when Jesus said "Take my yoke upon you and learn from me" (Matt. 11:29 NIV), he was teaching his disciples to "take my yoke, *yoga*, upon you and learn of me [take my consciousness of my sacred labor, my Christhood bearing the burden of world karma . . . and learn of my Guru, the Ancient of Days]; for I am meek and lowly in heart, and ye shall find rest unto your souls. For my yoke, *yoga*, is easy and my burden in heaven and on earth is truly Light" (Prophet, 1988, 273–74).

CORRECTING THE MISINTERPRETATION: This verse has nothing to do with yoga or karma. All people are heavily burdened with sin and its destructive consequences. People can find rest for their souls only by coming to Jesus. By taking Jesus' "yoke" upon them, they become his disciples and trade their heavy burdens for his light "burden." Of course, to serve Jesus is not truly burdensome, for he is gentle and humble.

It is also important to recognize that when Jesus said "learn *from me*" (v. 29), he was essentially saying, "learn from the revelation that *I alone* impart." And what Jesus says takes precedence over what all others say— including false teachers like New Age gurus. Among the things that we "learn" from Jesus is that he is *uniquely* the divine Messiah. In fact, Jesus often made his identity as the Christ a primary issue of faith (see Matt. 16:13–20 and John 11:25–27). And when Jesus was acknowledged as the Christ, he did not say to people, "You, too, have the Christ within." Instead, he warned them that others would come *falsely* claiming to be the Christ (Matt. 24:4–5, 23–25).

MATTHEW 12:32—Does Jesus' statement about no forgiveness in this life for the sin mentioned in this verse support the Roman Catholic doctrine of purgatory?

MISINTERPRETATION: In this passage Jesus said there would never be forgiveness for blasphemy of the Holy Spirit. From this verse noted Roman Catholic scholar Ludwig Ott infers that this "leaves open the possibility that sins are forgiven not only in this world but in the world to come"

(Ott, 1960, 483). Does this verse really support the Catholic belief that believers will be punished for the temporal consequences of their sins in purgatory?

CORRECTING THE MISINTERPRETATION: The Catholic use of this passage to support the concept of forgiveness of the temporal consequences of our sins after death fails for several reasons. First, this text is not speaking about forgiveness in the next life after suffering for sins, but rather indicates that there will be no forgiveness for this sin in the world to come (Matt. 12:32). How can the denial that this sin will not ever be forgiven, even after death, be the basis for speculation that sins will be forgiven in the next life?

According to Catholic teaching, purgatory involves only venial sins, but this sin is not venial; it is *mortal,* being eternal and unforgivable. How can a statement about the unforgiveness of a mortal sin in the next life be the basis for an argument that nonmortal sins will be forgiven then?

What is more, the passage is not even speaking about punishment, which Catholics affirm will occur in purgatory. So how could this text be used to support the concept of purgatorial punishment?

Even *The New Catholic Encyclopedia* frankly acknowledges that "the doctrine of Purgatory is not explicitly stated in the Bible" (11:1034). Indeed, it is not implicitly taught in Scripture either, since the Roman Catholic use of Scripture to support purgatory does violence to the contexts of the texts employed.

If this passage did imply punishment, it is not for those who will eventually be saved (as Catholics believe is the case with those who go to purgatory) but of those who will never be saved. Again, how can a passage not speaking about punishment for the saved after death be used as a basis for belief in purgatory which affirms punishment for the saved? In view of these strong differences, the fact that Roman Catholic scholars cite this verse in support of the doctrine of purgatory indicates the lack of real biblical support for this doctrine.

MATTHEW 13:10–11—Did Jesus teach that we need to seek a hidden, secondary (esoteric) meaning in Scripture, as New Agers say?

MISINTERPRETATION: Some New Agers appeal to Matthew 13:10–11 in an attempt to show that we should seek secret and hidden (esoteric) meanings in Scripture (Spangler, in *Earth's Answer,* 1977, 203). Jesus is portrayed as being in front of a multitude composed of both believers and unbelievers. He did not attempt to separate the believers from the unbelievers and then instruct only the believers. Rather, he constructed his teaching in such a way that believers would understand what he said but unbelievers would not—by using parables. Then, after teaching one such parable, a disciple asked Jesus: "Why do you speak to the people in parables?" (Matt. 13:10). Jesus answered: "The knowledge of the secrets of the kingdom of heaven has been given to you [believers], but not to them [unbelievers]" (v. 11, inserts added).

CORRECTING THE MISINTERPRETATION: When this passage is taken in its proper context all support for an esoteric interpretation evaporates. Consider the following: The Greek word for *secret* simply means "mystery," and is even translated this way in the New American Standard Bible. A mystery in the biblical sense is a truth that cannot be discerned simply by human investigation, but requires special revelation from God. Generally speaking, this word refers to a truth that was unknown to people living in Old Testament times, but is now revealed to humankind by God (see Matt. 13:17; Eph. 3:3–5; Col. 1:26). In Matthew 13, Jesus provides information to believers about the kingdom of heaven that has never been revealed before.

Second, some have wondered why Jesus engineered his parabolic teaching so that believers could understand his teaching but unbelievers could not. The disciples, having responded favorably to Jesus' teaching and placed their faith in him, already knew much truth about the Messiah. Careful reflection on Jesus' parables would enlighten them even further. However, hardened unbelievers who had willfully and persistently refused Jesus' previous teachings—such as those set forth in the Sermon on the Mount—were prevented from understanding the parables. Jesus was apparently following an injunction he provided earlier in the Sermon on the Mount: "Do not give dogs what is sacred; do not throw your pearls to pigs" (Matt. 7:6). Yet there is grace even here. For it is possible that Jesus may have prevented unbelievers from understanding the parables because he did not want to add more responsibility to them by imparting new truth for which they would be held responsible.

Third, that Jesus wanted his parables to be clear to those who were receptive is evident in the fact that he carefully interpreted two of them for the disciples—the parables of the Sower (Matt. 13:3–9) and the Tares (13:24–30). He did this, not only so there would be no uncertainty as to their meaning, but to guide believers as to the proper method to use in interpreting the other parables. The fact that Christ did not interpret his subsequent parables indicates that he fully expected believers to understand what he taught by following the methodology he illustrated for them. Clearly, then, Matthew 13 does not support but rather argues against esotericism.

Finally, that Jesus held to a *literal* (not *esoteric*) method of interpreting Scripture is clear in that he literally interpreted the creation account of Adam and Eve (Matt. 13:35; 25:34; Mark 10:6), the account of Noah's Ark and the Flood (Matt. 24:38–39; Luke 17:26–27), the account of Jonah and the whale (Matt. 12:39–41), the account of Sodom and Gomorrah (Matt. 10:15), and the account of Lot and his wife (Luke 17:28–29).

MATTHEW 14:6–10—Does this passage prove that birthdays are evil?

MISINTERPRETATION: In this passage Herod on his birthday put John the Baptist to death. The Jehovah's Witnesses take this to mean that birthdays are evil and should not be celebrated by God's people (*Reasoning from the Scriptures,* 1989, 68–69).

CORRECTING THE MISINTERPRETATION: This is "guilt by association." All this verse proves is that Herod was evil, not that birthdays are evil. See the discussion of Genesis 40:20–22.

MATTHEW 15:24—Did the "lost sheep of the house of Israel" mentioned in this verse migrate to America?

MISINTERPRETATION: Mormons believe the "lost sheep of the house of Israel" mentioned in this verse refers not to Israelites in the Palestine area but to Israelites who migrated to America (Smith, 1975, 3:214).

CORRECTING THE MISINTERPRETATION: The Mormon understanding is not supported either by the text or its context. Jesus was referring to Israelites that were *spiritually* lost, not *geographically* lost, more specifically, Israelites in the Palestine area who were in a lost condition in God's eyes.

Further, recall that Jesus had instructed the disciples: "Go to the lost sheep of the house of Israel. And as you go, preach, saying, 'The kingdom of heaven is at hand'" (Matt. 10:6–7 NASB). Jesus' disciples fulfilled these instructions not by going to America to preach, but by preaching to Israelites in and around Palestine.

MATTHEW 16:16–18—Does this passage support papal infallibility, as Roman Catholics claim?

MISINTERPRETATION: Roman Catholics use the statement of Jesus to Peter that "upon this rock I will build my church" to support their doctrine of papal infallibility. Is Jesus giving unique authority to Peter as the head of the church?

CORRECTING THE MISINTERPRETATION: Properly understood, this text falls far short of supporting the dogma of papal infallibility.

Many Protestants insist that Christ was not referring to Peter when he spoke of "this rock" being the foundation of the church. They note that:

1. Peter is referred to in this passage in the second person ("you"), but "this rock" is in the third person.
2. "Peter" *(petros)* is a masculine singular term and "rock" *(petra)* is feminine singular. Hence, they do not have the same referent. Even if Jesus did speak these words in Aramaic (which does not distinguish genders), the inspired Greek original does make such distinctions.
3. The same authority Jesus gave to Peter in Matthew 16:18 is given to all the apostles in Matthew 18:18.
4. No Catholic commentator gives primacy in evil to Peter simply because he was singled out by Jesus' rebuke a few verses later: "Get behind me, Satan! You are a stumbling block to me; you do not have in mind the things of God, but the things of man" (Matt. 16:23). Why then should they give primacy in authority to Peter since Jesus singled him out in his response to Peter's affirmation? It only makes sense for Jesus to reply to Peter since only Peter spoke, even though he represented the group.
5. Authorities, some Catholic, can be cited that Peter is not the referent, including John Chrysostom and St. Augustine. The later wrote: "On this rock, therefore, He said, which thou hast confessed. I will build my Church. For the Rock *(petra)* is Christ; and on this foundation was Peter himself built" (Augustine, "On the Gospel of John," Tractate 12435, *The Nicene and Post-Nicene Fathers Series* I, 7:450).

Even if Peter is the rock referred to by Christ, as even some non-Catholic scholars believe, he was not the *only* rock in the foundation of the church. As noted above, Jesus gave all the apostles the same power ("keys") to "bind" and "loose" that he gave to Peter (cf. Matt. 18:18). These were common rabbinic phrases used of "forbidding" and "allowing." These "keys" were not some mysterious power given to Peter alone but the power granted by Christ to his church by which, when they proclaim the Gospel, they can proclaim God's forgiveness of sin to all who believe. As John Calvin noted, "Since heaven is opened to us by the doctrine of the gospel, the word 'keys' affords an appropriate metaphor. Now men are bound and loosed in no other way than when faith reconciles some to God, while their own unbelief constrains others the more" (Calvin, *Institutes of the Christian Religion* 4:6.4).

Further, the Scriptures affirm that the church is "built on the foundation of the apostles and prophets, with Christ Jesus himself as the capstone" (Eph. 2:20). Two things are clear from this: First, all the apostles, not just Peter, are the foundation of the church; second, the only one who was given a place of unique prominence was Christ, the capstone. Indeed, Peter himself referred to Christ as "the cornerstone" of the church (1 Peter 2:7) and the rest of believers as "living stones" (v. 5) in the superstructure of the church. There is no indication that Peter was given a special place of prominence in the foundation of the church above the rest of the apostles and below Christ. He is just one "stone" along with the other eleven apostles (Eph. 2:20).

Peter's role in the New Testament falls far short of the Catholic claim that he was given unique authority among the apostles. While Peter did preach the initial sermon on Pentecost, his role in the rest of Acts is scarcely that of the chief apostle but as *one of* the "most eminent apostles" (plural, 2 Cor. 21:11 NKJV). By inspiration of God the apostle Paul revealed that no apostle was superior to him when he affirmed, "I was in no way inferior to these [so-called] 'superapostles'" (2 Cor. 12:11).

No one reading Galatians carefully can come away with the impression that any apostle is superior to the apostle Paul. For Paul claimed to get his revelation independently of the other apostles (Gal. 1:12; 2:2), to be on the same level as Peter (Gal. 2:8), and he even used his revelation to rebuke Peter (Gal. 2:11–14).

Likewise, the fact that both Peter and John were sent by the apostles on a mission to Samaria reveals that Peter was not *the* superior apostle (Acts 8:4–13). Indeed, if Peter was the God-ordained superior apostle, it is strange that more attention is given to the ministry of the apostle Paul than to that of Peter in the Book of Acts. Peter is the focus through parts of chapters 1–12, but Paul is the dominant figure in chapters 13–28.

Though Peter addressed the first council (in Acts 15), he exercised no primacy over the others. The decision came from "the apostles and the elders [in agreement] with the whole church" (Acts 15:22; see v. 23).

Many scholars feel that James, not Peter, presided over the council, since he was the one who gave the final words to the council (cf. vv. 13–21; see, for example, Bruce, 86f.).

In any event, by Peter's own admission he was not *the* pastor of the church but only a "fellow presbyter [elder]" (1 Peter 5:1–2). And while he did claim to be "*an* apostle" (1 Peter 1:1) he nowhere claimed to be "*the* apostle" or the chief of apostles. He certainly was a leading apostle, but even then he was only one of the "pillars" (plural) of the church, along with James and John, not *the* pillar (see Gal. 2:9).

However Peter's role is understood in the early church, *there is absolutely no reference to any alleged infallibility he possessed*. Indeed, the word "infallible" never occurs in the New Testament. When parallel words or phrases do occur they are used in reference to Scripture alone, not to anyone's ability to interpret it. Jesus said, for example, that "Scripture cannot be set aside" (John 10:35). And "until heaven and earth pass away, not the smallest *letter* or stroke shall pass away from the law" (Matt. 5:18 NASB).

This is not to say that Peter did not have a significant role in the early church. He seems to have been the initial leader of the apostolic band. As already noted, along with James and John, he was one of the "pillars" of the early church (Gal. 2:9). It was Peter who preached the great sermon at Pentecost when the gift of the Holy Spirit was given, welcoming many Jews into the Christian fold. It was Peter also who spoke when the Spirit of God fell on the Gentiles in Acts 10. However, from this point on Peter fades into the background and Paul is the dominant apostle, carrying the gospel to the ends of the earth (Acts 13–28), writing some one-half of the New Testament (as compared to Peter's two Epistles) and even rebuking Peter for his hypocrisy (Gal. 2:11–14). In short, there is no evidence in Matthew 16 or any other text for the Roman Catholic dogma of the superiority, to say nothing of the infallibility, of Peter.

Most important, whatever apostolic powers Peter and the other apostles possessed, it is clear that they were not passed on to anyone after their deaths. For to be an apostle one had to be a first-century eyewitness of the resurrected Christ. This is the criterion repeatedly mentioned by the New Testament (cf. Acts 1:22; 1 Cor. 9:1; 15:5–8). Therefore, there could be no true apostolic succession in the bishop of Rome or in anyone else.

These select individuals were given certain unmistakable "signs of a true apostle" (2 Cor. 12:12). These sign-gifts included the ability to raise the dead on command (Matt. 10:8), heal diseases immediately that were naturally incurable (Matt. 10:8; John 9:1–7), perform immediately successful exorcisms (Matt. 10:8; Acts 16:16–18), speak messages in languages they had never studied (Acts 2:1–8; cf. 10:44–46), and pass on supernatural gifts to others so that they could assist them in their apostolic mission of founding the church (Acts 6:6; cf. 8:5–6; 2 Tim. 1:6). On one occasion the apostles pronounced a supernatural death sentence on two people who had "lied to the Holy Spirit," and they immediately dropped over dead (Acts 5:1–11).

It is noteworthy that these special miraculous powers ceased during the life of the apostles. The writer of Hebrews (c. A.D. 69) referred to these special sign-gifts of an apostle as already past when he spoke of the message "announced originally through our Lord" which "was confirmed [in the past] to us by those who heard him [namely, apostles]. God also testified to it by signs, wonders, and various miracles, and gifts of the Holy Spirit distributed according to his will" (Heb. 2:3–4 NIV). Jude, writing late in the first century (after A.D. 70), speaks of "the faith that was once for all entrusted [in the past] to the saints" (Jude 3), exhorting his hearers to "remember what the apostles of our Lord Jesus Christ foretold" (Jude 17 NIV). Here, too, the miraculously confirmed apostolic message was spoken of *as past* by A.D. 70. Despite the profusion of apostolic miracles (cf. Acts 28:1–10) up to the end of the Book of Acts (c. A.D. 60–61), there is no record of any apostolic miracle in Paul's later Epistles after this time. Indeed, when some of his trusted helpers were sick and Paul was apparently not able to heal them (Phil. 2:26–24; 2 Tim. 4:20), he asked for prayer for them or recommended that they take medicine instead (1 Tim. 5:23). The special apostle-confirming miracles had apparently ceased even before the death of the apostles.

Moreover, these special miraculous signs were given to the apostles to establish their authority as the representatives of Christ in founding his church. Jesus had promised them special "power" to be his witnesses (Acts 1:8). The apostle Paul spoke of "the signs of an apostle" in confirming his authority to the Corinthians, some of whom had challenged it (2 Cor. 12:12). Hebrews 2:3–4 speaks of the special apostolic miracles as being given to confirm their witnesses to Christ. Indeed, it was the pattern of God from the time of Moses on to give special miracles to his servants to confirm that their revelations were from God (Exod. 4; 1 Kings 18; John 3:2; Acts 2:22).

In summation, since to be an apostle one had to be a first-century eyewitness of the resurrected Christ, since these apostolic witnesses were given certain unmistakable "signs of an apostle" to establish their authority, and since these special miraculous powers ceased during the life of the apostles, it follows that no one since the first century has possessed apostolic authority. In brief, the absence of these special apostolic gifts proves the absence of the special apostolic authority. What remains today is the *teachings* of the apostles (in the New Testament), not the *office* of an apostle nor its authority. The authority of apostolic *writings* has replaced the authority of the first-century apostolic *writers*.

MATTHEW 16:19—Does this text prove that Peter, as the first Pope, was given special authority by Christ to forgive sins?

MISINTERPRETATION: After Peter's confession that Jesus was the Son of God, Jesus said, "I will give you the keys to the kingdom of heaven, whatever you bind on earth will be bound in heaven, and whatever you loose on earth will be loosed in heaven" (Matt. 16:19 NIV). According to Catholic teaching, "the keys of the kingdom of heaven" mean "supreme authority on earth over the earthly empire of God. The person who possesses the power of the keys has the full power of allowing a person to enter the empire of God or to exclude him from it [and] . . . the power to forgive sins must also be included in the power of the keys" (Ott, 1960, 418).

CORRECTING THE MISINTERPRETATION: That Jesus' disciples were given the power to pronounce the forgiveness of or retaining of sins by Christ is not disputed by Protestants. What *is* disputed is whether this is a unique power now possessed by those with proper ordination, such as Roman Catholic priests. There is absolutely nothing in this text to indicate that it is.

It is important to observe that Jesus gave this same power to *all* the apostles (Matt. 18:18), not just to Peter. So, whatever this power was it was not unique to Peter.

In fact, everyone who proclaims the gospel has the same power, for the gospel "is the power of God for the salvation of everyone who believes" (Rom. 1:16 NIV). Indeed, Paul defined the gospel in terms of Christ dying and rising "for our sins" (1 Cor. 15:1–4). So *every* preacher of the gospel—clergy *or* laity—has the power to say, on the basis of a person accepting Christ's death and resurrection for them, that their sins are forgiven. Likewise, all who evangelize can say to those who reject the gospel that their sins are retained. For, as the apostle Paul said, messengers of Christ are "the aroma of Christ among those who are being saved and those who are perishing. To the one we are the smell of death" (2 Cor. 2:15–16).

The Catholic claim that the Old Testament priesthood is somehow "translated" into a New Testament priesthood on the basis of Hebrews 7:12 misses the whole point of this passage. The writer of Hebrews is arguing that both the law and the Old Testament priesthood are done away with by Christ, our great High Priest, for he writes: "When there is a change of the priesthood, there must also be a change of the law" (Heb. 7:12 NIV). He then goes on to say "a former commandment is annulled . . ." (v. 18). Christ did not translate Aaron's Old Testament priesthood into a new one for priests in the New Testament. The whole point of this section of Hebrews is to show that Christ, by perfectly fulfilling what the Old Testament priesthood prefigured (cf. 7:11, 18–19), did away with it and replaced it with his own high priestly office, after the order of Melchizedek, not after Aaron (7:17–28).

Indeed, a vivid contrast is made here between the repeated offerings of the Aaronic priests and the once-for-all sacrifice of Christ our High Priest that should cause serious pause for Roman Catholics who believe that Catholic priests offer up continually the unbloody sacrifice of the Mass. The Book of Hebrews declares: "Every priest stands daily ministering and offering time after time the same sacrifices, which can never take away sins; but he [Christ], having offered one sacrifice for sins for all time, sat down at the right hand of God." For "by one offering he has perfected for all time those who are being sanctified" (Heb. 10:11–12, 14 NASB). Contrary to the Catholic claim that Hebrews is only speaking of a once-for-all *unbloody* sacrifice, no such qualifying word is found in the text. Hebrews says emphatically the opposite of what Catholics affirm, namely, that the Mass is a sacrifice that is repeated over and over. Holy Writ says explicitly that Christ offered one sacrifice for sins for all time. Then he sat (his work finished forever) at the right hand of God (Heb. 10:12). This sacrifice is called a "once for all" offering in the preceding verse, which is directly opposed to the Catholic view.

While Roman Catholicism acknowledges that "the entire Christian family" is "a kingdom of priests," nevertheless in practice it denies what the New Testament clearly affirms, namely, that all believers are priests. By making such a strong distinction between the common or universal priesthood and the ministerial or hierarchical priesthood they render ineffective the apostle Peter's teaching that all God's elect (1 Peter 1:1) are "a royal priesthood, a holy nation, a people belonging to God" (2:9). In fact, there is only one priest necessary in the New Covenant, our great High Priest Jesus Christ (cf. Heb. 7–8). The task left for all other priests (namely, all believers) is to minister the gospel (2 Cor. 3–4).

The appeal to the Old Testament to show that all Israelites were called priests (Exod. 19:21–21) even when God had established the Aaronic priesthood as a special ministerial class misses the whole point of Hebrews ("Quick Questions," *This Rock* [September 1993], 30). The Aaronic priesthood has been done away with—and every believer has direct access to only one High Priest, Jesus Christ, who ever lives to make intercession for us!

The fact is that nowhere in the New Testament are church leaders called "priests." They are called "elders" or "bishops" (overseers) who were exhorted by the apostle Peter (1 Peter 5:2) to "shepherd the flock of God among you, [overseeing] not under compulsion, but voluntarily, according to the will of God." Peter continues, exhorting overseers to be examples to the flock. "And when the Chief Shepherd appears you will receive the unfading crown of glory" (1 Peter 5:4 NASB). The whole hierarchical institution of the Roman Catholic priesthood as a special class of men endowed with special priestly powers to forgive sins and to transform the communion elements into the actual body and blood of Christ is contrary to the teaching of these verses. For in these verses: (1) no one is described as a priest nor has priestly powers except the Chief Shepherd Christ himself; (2) Peter describes himself as "a fellow elder" (v. 1); (3) the leaders of the flock are called elders, not priests; (4) they are depicted as undershepherds, not overlords (cf. v. 3) of the church; (5) they have no special binding power but are to lead by example, not by constraint (vv. 2–3). The whole spirit of this is contrary to the priestly powers claimed by the Roman Catholic church.

MATTHEW 17:4—Does the disciples' encounter with Moses and Elijah on the Mount of Transfiguration indicate that we should pray to the dead?

MISINTERPRETATION: Roman Catholic scholars appeal to the fact that Moses and Elijah appeared with Christ on the Mount of Transfiguration to support their belief that we should pray to the dead.

CORRECTING THE MISINTERPRETATION: The disciples never even spoke to Moses and Elijah, let alone prayed to them. Moses and Elijah were speaking *with Jesus* (Matt. 17:3) and with *each other*, not with the disciples.

The text explicitly says, "Peter said to Jesus" (Matt. 17:4), not to Moses or Elijah. This was a miraculous contact, not representing any normal way we can be in contact with the departed.

In addition, it does not follow that, simply because we should serve each other, we must do it by praying for the dead. There are other ways to serve fellow believers than talking to them. We can do many things in honor of the dead and their memory without attempting to communicate with them. The dead may be praying for us (cf. Rev. 6:9–10), but there is nothing in Holy Writ that says we should be praying to them.

Finally, there are good reasons why we should not pray to the dead. The most basic is that *only God* is the proper object of prayer. Nowhere in all of Scripture is a prayer actually addressed to anyone but God. Prayer is an act of religious devotion, and only God is the proper object of such devotion (Rev. 4:11). We witness prayers from Genesis (4:26) to Revelation (22:20), but not one of them is ever addressed to a saint, angel, or any other creature. Jesus taught us to pray, "Our Father who art in heaven." The God of Isaiah the prophet emphatically declared, "Turn to me and be safe, all you ends of the earth, for I am God; there is no other!" Indeed, there is no other person but God to whom anyone anywhere in the Holy Scriptures ever turned in prayer.

MATTHEW 18:15–18—Does this passage prohibit public criticism of a pastor's (or teacher's) doctrine, as Word-Faith teachers argue?

MISINTERPRETATION: Some Word-Faith teachers believe this passage prohibits Christians from publicly criticizing the doctrine of a pastor or a teacher. Even if the doctrine is clearly false, and the pastor is teaching it publicly from the pulpit or on television, the pastor should not be criticized publicly but rather should be contacted privately about the matter. Addressing the issue of speaking out against "God's anointed," Kenneth Copeland said, "There are people attempting to sit in judgment right today over the ministry that I'm responsible for, and the ministry that Kenneth E. Hagin is responsible for. . . . Several people that I know had criticized and called that faith bunch out of Tulsa a cult. And some of 'em are dead right today in an early grave because of it, and there's more than one of them got cancer" (Copeland, "Why All Are Not Healed," audio tape).

CORRECTING THE MISINTERPRETATION: This passage deals with personal ethics and morals, not with biblical doctrine. If a Christian does something *unethical* or he *sins*, he should first be contacted privately about the matter. If the individual fails to respond, increasingly confrontational steps are to be taken (Matt. 18:15–18).

False doctrine that is publicly proclaimed from a platform—such as from a pulpit, a television show, or a radio show—is to be confronted publicly according to the New Testament pattern. The apostle Paul publicly confronted Peter when his actions compromised the liberty of the gospel (Gal. 2:11–14). He publicly dealt with Hymenaeus and Alexander regarding their blasphemy (1 Tim. 1:20). He publicly dealt with Alexander the coppersmith for his harmful activities (2 Tim. 4:14). The apostle John publicly dealt with Diotrephes, who propagated false doctrine and refused to listen to what John and other Christian leaders had to say (3 John 9).

Though Word-Faith teachers often cite Matthew 18 in an effort to maintain church unity in an atmosphere of love, it is important to understand that true church unity is rooted not only in love but in truth. As Paul affirmed, the church is the "pillar and support of the truth" (1 Tim. 3:15). Members of the church are called to "contend earnestly for the faith which was once for all delivered to the saints" (Jude 3 NASB). We are to "examine everything carefully" and "hold fast to that which is good" (1 Thess. 5:21). We are to follow the example of the Bereans in testing all doctrinal teachings against the Scriptures (Acts 17:11). Without a commitment to the truth, there can be no true church unity.

MATTHEW 18:17—Does this verse refer to the visible authority of the Roman Catholic church on earth?

MISINTERPRETATION: Roman Catholics claim that the authority Jesus granted to his disciples here is invested in the Catholic church today as the visible representative of Christ on earth.

CORRECTING THE MISINTERPRETATION: Jesus said in Matthew 18:17: "If he [the offender] refuses to listen to them [the offended and his witnesses, vv. 15–16], tell it to the church" (NIV). But this is far short of the Roman Catholic claim that this proves the divine authority of the Roman See. "The church" referred to was a local assembly of believers, such as they were no doubt accustomed to having in their local synagogue. There is no reference here to a universal (catholic) church.

The New Testament church as a united, gifted, and empowered body of believers did not come into existence until the Day of Pentecost (Acts 1:8; 2:1–5, 42–47). So, whatever "church" means in the context of Matthew 18, it does not refer to what Roman Catholics mean by a visible church which administers the sacraments and infallibly teaches and disciplines the faithful.

Matthew 18 does not speak of any universal apostolic authority to settle all disputes of faith and practice. It refers only to cases involving "sins" and "faults" by which one "brother" has offended another (18:15). This falls short of what Catholics claim for the divine authority of the visible Roman church.

Even if this text spoke about the need for submission to God-ordained authority in all matters of doctrine and conduct (which it does not), it would not support the Catholic argument for a visible church. For clearly this passage does not show that this authority is to be found in the visible *Roman Catholic church*, as opposed to other visible churches, some of which, Eastern Orthodoxy, are even older.

MATTHEW 18:23–35—Can one's forgiveness be canceled once it is given, as Seventh-Day Adventists claim?

MISINTERPRETATION: Based on the Parable of the Unmerciful Servant (Matt. 18:23–35), Seventh-day Adventists teach that one's forgiveness can be canceled after it has been bestowed. They claim that "the actual blotting out of sin, therefore, could not take place the moment when a sin is forgiven, because subsequent deeds and attitudes may affect the final decision. Instead, the sin remains on the record until the life is complete—in fact, the Scriptures indicate it remains until the judgment" (*Seventh-day Adventists Answer Questions on Doctrine*, 1957, 441).

CORRECTING THE MISINTERPRETATION: This is a parable, and parables should not be taken literally. They have a point to make, and that point is illustrated in the parable of which not every aspect is to be taken literally. For example, God is illustrated as an "unjust judge" in one parable (Luke 18:1–18), but the point is not to teach about the attribute of God's justice but that he is merciful in answering persistent prayer.

The Bible makes it unmistakable that God does not renege on his promises. Paul declared that "God's gifts and his call are irrevocable" (Rom. 11:29 NIV). God does not take back what he gives in grace. Many other passages of Scripture teach that salvation is an unconditional gift (John 10:26–29; Rom. 8:36–39). And God's Word does not contradict itself.

MATTHEW 19:16–30 (cf. Mark 10:17–31; Luke 18:18–30)—If Jesus was God, why did he seem to rebuke the rich young ruler for calling him good?

MISINTERPRETATION: The rich young ruler called Jesus "Good Teacher," and Jesus rebuked him, saying, "Why do you call Me good? No one is good but One, that is, God." Was Jesus denying that he was God to the young ruler? Jehovah's Witnesses think so. "Jesus was saying that no one is as good as God is, not even Jesus himself. God is good in a way that separates him from Jesus" (*Should You Believe in the Trinity?* 1989, 17).

CORRECTING THE MISINTERPRETATION: Jesus did not deny he was God to the young ruler. He simply asked him to examine the implications of what he was saying. In effect, Jesus was saying to him, "Do you realize what you are saying when you call me good? Do you realize that this is something you should attribute only to God? Are you saying I am God?"

The young man did not realize the implications of what he was saying. Thus Jesus was forcing him to a very uncomfortable dilemma. Either Jesus was good and God, or else he was bad and man. A good God or a bad man, but not merely a good man. Those are the real alternatives with regard to Christ. For no good man would claim to be God when he was not.

MATTHEW 20:1–16—Are rewards the same for all, or do they differ in degree?

MISINTERPRETATION: Jesus told a parable of his kingdom in which each servant got the same pay even though each had worked a different number of hours. Yet in other places, the Bible speaks of different degrees of reward for working in God's kingdom (cf. 1 Cor. 3:11–15; 2 Cor. 5:10; Rev. 22:12). Mormons sometimes set up a straw man to knock down, alleging that Christians wrongly believe that "all who go to heaven share and share alike" (Richards, 1978, 253). Does Christianity teach that in the afterlife there will be different degrees of reward?

CORRECTING THE MISINTERPRETATION: There are different degrees of reward in heaven, depending on our faithfulness to Christ on earth. Jesus said, "I am coming quickly, and My reward is with Me, to render to every man according to what he has done" (Rev. 22:12 NASB). Paul said each believer's work will be tried by fire and "if anyone's work which he has built on it endures, he will receive a reward" (1 Cor. 3:14). In 2 Corinthians 5:10, he says we must all appear before the judgment seat of Christ "that each one may be recompensed for his deeds in the body, according to what he has done, whether good or bad" (NASB).

The point of the parable in Matthew 20 is not that all rewards will be the same, but that all rewards are *by grace*. It is to show that God rewards on the basis of *opportunity*, not simply on *accomplishment*. Not all the servants had the opportunity to work for the master the same amount of time, but all, nevertheless, were given the same pay. God looks at our *disposition* as well as our *actions* and judges accordingly.

MATTHEW 22:30—Does this verse support the "open sex" views of the Children of God?

MISINTERPRETATION: In Matthew 22:30 we are told, "At the resurrection people will neither marry, nor be given in marriage; they will be like the angels in heaven" (NIV). Are the Children of God (now called "the Family") correct in interpreting this verse to mean that we today are to be like the angels in heaven by not being "given in marriage"—so that we engage in open sex with one another outside the marriage relationship?

CORRECTING THE MISINTERPRETATION: This is a preposterous twisting of Scripture. Understood in its proper context, this verse strongly argues against the sexually perverted views of the Children of God.

The context indicates that once believers receive their glorified resurrection bodies, the need for procreation (one of the fundamental purposes for marriage) will no longer exist. We will be "like" the angels in the sense that we will not be married and will not procreate any longer. Angels do not procreate and reproduce. Rather all the angels in the universe were created at one time (see Ps. 148:2–5; cf. Col. 1:16). Hence, if the Children of God really want to "be like the angels," they would have to avoid sexual intimacy altogether, since angels do not procreate at all.

The Bible everywhere affirms that sexual intercourse is to be used only within the bonds of marriage (Exod. 20:14; 1 Cor. 7:2). See the discussion of John 15:12; Acts 2:44.

MATTHEW 22:37–39—Does obedience to the "greatest commandments" bring about a unity of religions?

MISINTERPRETATION: In Matthew 22:37–39 Jesus described the first and second greatest commandments as loving God and loving one's neighbor. According to New Agers, these commandments "describe the process by means of which the barrier of separation is broken down, by which microcosm (man) and macrocosm (God) can be one and synthesis and unity be expressed within the relative universe of I and thou, me and you." By being obedient to these commandments people "will build the most enduring bridges between creeds, paths, teachings, and philosophies" (Spangler, 1981, 30).

CORRECTING THE MISINTERPRETATION: First, the commandment about loving God takes priority over loving people. God is to be loved with all of one's heart; the neighbor is to be loved only as one loves oneself. The clear implication here is that God should be loved *supremely* but humankind only *finitely*. In light of this distinction, it is clear that the first priority is expression of love to the one true God— not to Buddha, or Krishna, or any idols set up by New Agers.

A serious flaw in New Age thinking is the assumption that loving God and loving one's neighbor automatically does away with all discrimination and separation (between religions, for example). However, such is clearly not the case. Jesus recognized the importance of love, exhorting his followers to "love your enemies and pray for those who persecute you" (Matt. 5:43–44). Yet, this same Jesus (at the Judgment) will say to unbelievers: "I never knew you; depart from me, you who practice lawlessness" (Matt. 7:23 NASB). God loves the world (John 3:16), but eternal torment nevertheless awaits those who reject his provision for salvation in Jesus Christ (Rev. 20:14).

MATTHEW 22:42—Does this verse support the doctrine of reincarnation, as the Unity School of Christianity argues?

MISINTERPRETATION: In Matthew 22:42 Jesus asked the Pharisees, "What do you think about the Christ, whose son is He?" The Pharisees responded, "The son of David." The Unity School of Christianity says this verse indicates that Jesus was a reincarnation of David.

CORRECTING THE MISINTERPRETATION: "Son of" in Hebrew thinking meant "descendent of" (see Matt. 1:1–17), not "reincarnation of." This verse indicates that Jesus came from the lineage of David, not that Jesus was a reincarnation of David. Jesus' birth in the line of David was important, for the Old Testament Scriptures taught that the Messiah *had* to come from the line of David (2 Sam. 7:12–16; Isa. 9:6–7; 11:1).

Reincarnation goes against the whole of Scripture. For example, while the doctrine of reincarnation teaches that people die over and over again until they reach perfection (Nirvana), the Bible teaches that "it is appointed for men to die once, and after this comes judgment" (Heb. 9:27 NASB). Each human being *lives once* as a mortal on earth, *dies once*, and then faces judgment. Jesus taught that people decide their eternal destiny in a single lifetime (Matt. 25:46). This is precisely why the apostle Paul emphasized that "now is the day of salvation" (2 Cor. 6:2). Scripture indicates that at the moment of death believers go into the presence of the Lord (2 Cor. 5:8) and unbelievers go to a place of suffering (Luke 16:19–31), not into another body.

From a practical perspective, if the purpose of karma is to rid humanity of its selfish desires, then why has there not been a noticeable improvement in human nature after all the millennia of reincarnations? And how do reincarnationists explain the immense and ever-worsening social and economic problems in India (including widespread poverty, starvation, disease, and horrible suffering), where reincarnation has been systematically taught throughout its history?

MATTHEW 23:2–3—Does Jesus' statement justify the Children of God cult's claim that today's churches are hypocritical?

MISINTERPRETATION: According to the late Moses David, leader of the Children of God, "That's the difference between the churches and us! Jesus said to the common people, 'The scribes and Pharisees (the church leaders) sit in Moses' seat. All therefore they bid you observe, that observe and do; but do not ye after their works: for they say and do not.' And that goes for today's churches too!" (David, 1974, 1–3).

CORRECTING THE MISINTERPRETATION: Jesus is speaking about the leaders of Judaism in *his* day—"those who sit in Moses's seat." He is not speaking about the Christian churches of our day. It is a total misapplication to claim this reveals that all church leaders are hypocritical. Even if all church leaders were hypocritical, it would not prove that the teachings and practices of the Children of God cult are right.

The life of Moses David is anything but exemplary, especially in sexual matters. He said, "Salvation set us free from the curse of clothing and shame of nakedness! We're as free as Adam and Eve in the Garden before they ever sinned! If you're not, you're not the fully saved!" (David, 1973, 2; see also comments on Acts 2:44).

MATTHEW 24:3—Does this verse support the idea that Jesus returned invisibly in 1914?

MISINTERPRETATION: Matthew 24:3 speaks of "the sign of Your coming" (NASB) in reference to the second coming of Christ. By contrast, the New World Translation speaks of "the sign of your presence." The Jehovah's Witnesses use this distorted translation to support their view that Jesus returned invisibly in 1914 and has been spiritually present on earth ever since (*The Greatest Man Who Ever Lived*, 1991, section 111).

CORRECTING THE MISINTERPRETATION: The Greek word *parousia* can mean "presence," but often means "*physically* present," "coming to a place," and "*physically* arriving." For example, in 2 Corinthians 7:6–7 we read, "But God, who comforts the depressed, comforted us by *the coming* of Titus" (NASB). Paul tells the Philippians: "So then, my beloved, just as you have always obeyed, not as in my *presence* only, but now much more in my absence, work out your salvation with fear and trembling" (2:12 NASB). The word is used in this same sense of "physical coming" in Matthew 24:3. Jesus will *physically* and *bodily* and *visibly* come again (cf. Acts 1:11).

This is in keeping with the other Greek words used to describe the second coming. *Apokalupsis* means "revelation," "visible disclosure," and "unveiling." This word is used of Christ's second coming in 1 Peter 4:13. *Epiphaneia* means "to appear." In Titus 2:13 Paul speaks of "looking for the blessed hope and *the appearing* of the glory of our great God and Savior, Christ Jesus" (NASB). It is interesting that Christ's first coming—which was both bodily and visible—was called an *epiphaneia* (2 Tim. 1:10).

MATTHEW 24:23–24—Does this verse support the idea that each of us has the "cosmic Christ" within?

MISINTERPRETATION: In Matthew 24:23–24, Jesus said, "If anyone says to you, 'Behold, here is the Christ,' or 'There He is,' do not believe him. For false Christs and false prophets will arise and will show great signs and wonders, so as to mislead, if possible, even the elect" (NASB).

New Agers believe Jesus is here refuting the idea that God or Christ is separate from humanity. Those who suggest such a separation are false prophets: "Jesus warned there would arise false Christs and false prophets proclaiming a flesh-and-blood messiah that could be located in time and space, saying: 'Look, here is Christ!' or 'Look, he is there!' But the Master said, 'Believe not, go not, for the kingdom of God is within you'" (Prophet, 1988, 56).

CORRECTING THE MISINTERPRETATION: Jesus is *uniquely* the Christ (Luke 2:11, 26). The Greek word for Christ *(Christos)* means "anointed one," and is a direct parallel to the Hebrew word for Messiah; "Messiah" and "Christ" refer to the same person. John 1:41 says that Andrew went to his brother Simon and said to him: "We have found *the Messiah* (that is, *the Christ*)." All the messianic prophecies in the Old Testament point to the coming of a single person, who is the Messiah/Christ (for example, Gen. 3:15; Isa. 7:14; Micah 5:2).

Jesus made his identity as *the* Christ the primary issue of faith (Matt. 16:13–20; John 11:25–27). When Jesus was acknowledged as the Christ, he did not say to people, "You, too, have the Christ within." Instead, he warned them that others would come *falsely* claiming to be the Christ (Matt. 24:4–5, 23–25). Likewise, when the Jewish leaders sought to stone Jesus to death for identifying himself as the promised Messiah and as God, he did not say to them, "Oh, no, you misunderstand. *You too* are Christ and *you too* have God within." Jesus continually affirmed that he was uniquely the Messiah/Christ.

MATTHEW 24:34—Does this verse indicate that the 1914 generation would not pass away before all other prophecies come to pass?

MISINTERPRETATION: In Matthew 24:34 Jesus says, "Truly I say to you, this generation will not pass away until all these things take place" (NASB). The Jehovah's Witnesses believe "this generation" is the 1914 generation. They say the 1914 generation "will by no means pass away until all these things (including the apocalypse) occur" (*Watchtower*, 15 February 1986, 5).

CORRECTING THE MISINTERPRETATION: There is no statement anywhere in Scripture that 1914 is a pivotal prophetic year that is foundational to the unfolding of all other prophecies. And there is certainly nothing in the context of Matthew 24:34 that the "generation" referred to is the 1914 generation.

Evangelical Christians have generally held to one of two interpretations of Matthew 24:34. One is that Christ is simply saying that the generation that witness the signs stated earlier in Matthew 24 dealing with the future Tribulation period will see the coming of Jesus Christ. The generation alive when these things (the abomination of desolation [v. 15], the great tribulation such as has never been seen before [v. 21], the sign of the Son of Man in heaven [v. 30], and similar events) begin to come to pass will still be alive when these judgments are completed. Since it is commonly believed that the Tribulation is a period of seven years (Dan. 9:27; cf. Rev. 11:2) at the end of the age, then Jesus would be saying that "this generation" alive at the beginning of the Tribulation will still be alive at the end of it.

Other evangelicals say the word *generation* is to be taken in its basic usage of "race, kindred, family, stock, or breed." Jesus' statement could mean that the Jewish race would not pass away until all things are fulfilled. Since there were many promises to Israel, including the eternal inheritance of the land of Palestine (Gen. 12; 14–15; 17) and the Davidic kingdom (2 Sam. 7), then Jesus could be referring to God's preservation of the nation Israel in order to fulfil his promises to them. Indeed, Paul speaks of a future of the nation of Israel when they will be reinstated in God's covenantal promises (Rom. 11:11–26). In either case, the year 1914 does not relate to this verse or any other verse of prophetic Scripture.

MATTHEW 24:45–47—Does the "faithful and discreet slave" mentioned in these verses refer to the Watchtower organization?

MISINTERPRETATION: The Jehovah's Witnesses believe Christ's words about the "faithful and discreet slave" refer to Christ's anointed followers headed by the Governing Body of the Watchtower Society. "Jesus said that he would have on earth a 'faithful and discreet slave' (his anointed followers viewed as a group), through which agency he would provide spiritual food to those making up the household of faith" (*Reasoning from the Scriptures*, 1989, 205). The "evil slave" mentioned in these verses refers to apostate Christians.

CORRECTING THE MISINTERPRETATION: This verse obviously does not refer to the Watchtower Society. Jehovah's Witnesses are practicing *eisogesis* (reading a meaning into the text) instead of practicing *exegesis* (deriving the meaning out of the text).

In this parable, Jesus likens a follower (*any* follower) to a servant who has been put in charge of his master's household. Jesus contrasts two possible ways that each professed disciple could carry out the task— *faithfully* or *unfaithfully*. The servant who chooses to be faithful makes every effort and focuses all his energies on fulfilling his commitments and obligations while his master is away. By contrast, the unfaithful servant calculates that his master will be away for a prolonged time and hence decides to mistreat his fellow servants and "live it up." He is careless and callous, utterly failing to live up to his obligations. Jesus' parable is a call to every Christian to be faithful. Those who are faithful will be rewarded at the Lord's return.

MATTHEW 25:46—Does this verse indicate that there is no eternal conscious punishment for the wicked?

MISINTERPRETATION: Jehovah's Witnesses believe the Greek words for "eternal punishment" in this phrase are better translated "everlasting cutting-off" (*The Greatest Man Who Ever Lived*, 1991, section 111). They believe this indicates that there is no eternal conscious punishment for the wicked.

CORRECTING THE MISINTERPRETATION: While the stem of *kolasis (kolazō)* originally meant "pruning," there is no justification for translating it "cutting-off" in Matthew 25:46. Greek authorities agree that the meaning here is "punishment." And the punishment is conscious and eternal in nature.

Several lines of evidence support the everlasting consciousness of those who are punished: First, the rich man who died and went to hell was in conscious torment (Luke 16:22–28), and there is absolutely no indication in the text that it was ever going to cease.

Second, Jesus spoke repeatedly of the people in hell as "weeping and gnashing their teeth" (Matt. 8:12; 22:13; 24:51; 25:30), which indicates they were conscious.

Third, hell is said to be of the same duration as heaven, "everlasting" (Matt. 25:41).

Fourth, the fact that their punishment is everlasting indicates that the damned too must be everlasting. One cannot suffer punishment, unless he exists to be punished (2 Thess. 1:9). It makes virtually no sense to say that the wicked will suffer "endless annihilation." Rather, the wicked will suffer a ruin which is everlasting—and this punishment will never end.

Fifth, the Beast and the False Prophet were thrown "alive" into the lake of fire at the beginning of the thousand years (Rev. 19:20), and they were still there, conscious and alive, after the thousand years passed (Rev. 20:10).

Sixth, the Scriptures affirm that the devil, the Beast, and the False Prophet "will be tormented day and night for ever and ever" (Rev.

20:10). But there is no way to experience torment forever and ever without being conscious forever and ever.

Seventh, Jesus repeatedly called hell a place of "unquenchable flames" (Mark 9:43–48) where the very bodies of the wicked will never die (cf. Luke 12:4–5). But it would make no sense to have everlasting flames and bodies without any souls in them to experience the torment.

Eighth, there are no degrees of annihilation, but Scripture reveals there will be degrees of suffering among the lost (see Matt. 10:15; 11:21–24; 16:27; Luke 12:47–48; Heb. 10:29; Rev. 20:11–15; 22:12).

MATTHEW 27:52–53—Is the opening of the graves in this verse evidence of the bodily assumption of Mary, as some Catholic scholars claim?

MISINTERPRETATION: Roman Catholic scholar Ludwig Ott argues that the fact that the graves were opened after Jesus' resurrection and many saints emerged shows the "probability" of the bodily assumption of Mary. For if "the justified of the Old Covenant were called to perfection of salvation immediately after the conclusion of the redemptive work of Christ, then it is possible and probable that the Mother of the Lord was called to it also" (Ott, 1960, 209).

CORRECTING THE MISINTERPRETATION: The fact that some saints arose immediately after Jesus' resurrection in no way indicates that Mary (who was still alive at the time) was bodily assumed into heaven. The text speaks *only* of being raised from the graves, not of ascension into heaven. Many scholars believe these saints, such as Lazarus, were only resuscitated in *mortal* bodies, not permanently resurrected in immortal bodies.

Mary is not mentioned in the group that was raised, nor is there any mention anywhere in Scripture of her being raised any time later. So the belief that Mary was bodily assumed into heaven has no real basis in this text or any text of Scripture.

It is significant that Catholic authorities admit that "the idea of the bodily assumption of Mary is first expressed in certain transitus-narratives of the fifth and sixth centuries." They acknowledge that these are apocryphal (Ibid., 209–10).

MATTHEW 28:18–20—How can three persons be God when there is only one God?

MISINTERPRETATION: Matthew speaks of the "Father, Son, and Holy Spirit" as all being part of one "name." The Jehovah's Witnesses argue that this verse does not say "that Father, Son, and Holy Spirit are coequal or coeternal or that all are God" (*Reasoning from the Scriptures,* 1989, 415). Therefore this verse does not support the doctrine of the Trinity.

CORRECTING THE MISINTERPRETATION: God is one in *Essence,* but three in *Persons.* God has one *Nature,* but three *Centers of Consciousness.* That is, there is only one *What* in God, but there are three *Whos;* there is one *It,* but three *Is.* This is a mystery, but not a contradiction. It would be contradictory to say God was only one person, but also was three persons, or that God is only one nature but has three natures. But to declare, as orthodox Christians do, that God is one essence, eternally revealed in three distinct persons, is not a contradiction.

A grammatical analysis of Matthew 28:19 is highly revealing. The verse says: "Go therefore and make disciples of all the nations, baptizing them in the *name* of *the* Father and *the* Son and *the* Holy Spirit" (NASB, emphasis added). The word *name* in Matthew 28:19 is singular in the Greek, indicating that there is one God. But there are three persons within the Godhead, each with a definite article (in the Greek language, firmly indicating distinctness)—*the* Father, *the* Son, and *the* Holy Spirit. The verse does not say "in the *names* [plural] of the Father, Son, and Holy Spirit," nor does it say "in the name of the Father, the name of the Son, and the name of the Holy Spirit." Nor does it say "in the name of Father, Son, and Holy Spirit" (omitting the definite articles). It says "in the *name* [singular, asserting the oneness of God] of *the* Father, *the* Son, and *the* Holy Spirit" (each distinct from the others as persons). This verse very clearly demonstrates the doctrine of the Trinity.

MATTHEW 28:19—Does this verse indicate that the Father, Son, and Holy Spirit are one person—*Jesus Christ*—as Oneness Pentecostals believe?

MISINTERPRETATION: In Matthew 28:19 Jesus instructs his followers to baptize "in the name of the Father and the Son and the Holy Spirit." But in Acts 2:38 we find reference to baptizing "in the name of Jesus." Putting these verses together, Oneness Pentecostals believe this means that "Jesus" is the "name" of the Father, Son, and Holy Spirit. Because the word "name" is singular in Matthew 28:19, this must mean that the Father, Son, and Holy Spirit are one person—the person of Jesus Christ.

CORRECTING THE MISINTERPRETATION: There is absolutely no indication in this text that Jesus was esoterically and cryptically referring to himself with the words "the Father, the Son, and the Holy Spirit." Oneness Pentecostals are reading something into the text that simply is not there. As noted above, Greek scholars universally recognize that the use of the definite articles before each noun (*the* Father, *the* Son, and *the* Holy Spirit) in Matthew 28:19 points to *distinct persons.* A study of the singular form of the word *name* in Scripture proves that the word does not have to refer to a single *person* (see, e.g., Gen. 5:2; 11:4; 48:16). *Name* in Matthew 28:19 (singular in the Greek) refers not to three designations or titles of *one person* but rather to three persons within the unity of the *one God.*

Scripture is abundantly clear that the Father, Son, and Holy Spirit are *distinct* persons. For example, it is clear that Jesus is not the Father, for the Father *sent* the Son (John 3:16–17). The Father and Son *love* each other (John 3:35). The Father and Son *speak* to each other (John 11:41–42). The Father *knows* the Son and the Son *knows* the Father (Matt. 11:27). Jesus is our *advocate* with the Father (1 John 2:1). Moreover, it is clear that Jesus is not the Holy Spirit, for the Holy Spirit is said to be *another* comforter (John 14:16). Jesus *sent* the Holy Spirit (John 15:26). The Holy Spirit seeks to *glorify* Jesus (John 16:13–14). The Holy Spirit *descended upon* Jesus (Luke 3:22). Nor is the Father the Holy Spirit, for the Father *sent* the Holy Spirit (John 14:16). And the Holy Spirit *intercedes* with the Father on our behalf (Rom. 8:26–27). It is impossible to argue that Jesus is the Father and the Holy Spirit.

Theologians throughout church history have consistently interpreted this verse as referring to the three persons of the Trinity, not to three designations or titles of the one person of Jesus Christ. It would be the height of human arrogance to suggest that all the theologians throughout church history have been wrong on this verse and only the Oneness Pentecostals understand it correctly.

MATTHEW 28:19—Does this text support the doctrine of the Trinity, as opposed to the conclusion of The Way International?

MISINTERPRETATION: According to Victor Paul Wierwille, founder of The Way International, this verse has been corrupted from its original form and cannot be used to support the orthodox doctrine of the

Trinity. He points to the fact that Eusebius, a prominent father of the early church, quoted this verse eighteen times without mention of the trinitarian formula prior to the Council of Nicea (A.D. 325)—which formally codified the doctrine of the Trinity. Only *after* the Council of Nicea did Eusebius include the trinitarian formula when quoting this verse. Thus, Wierwille concludes, "It would not have been difficult for scribes to insert 'in the name of the Father, and of the Son, and of the Holy Ghost,' in place of the original 'in my name.' This must have been what happened" (Wierwille, 1981, 19–20).

CORRECTING THE MISINTERPRETATION: The evidence supports the authenticity of this verse and its use in support of the doctrine of the Trinity. The divine authority rests in the biblical text itself, not in what any Father may or may not have said about it. Only the Bible is inspired, not the Church Fathers. But even Wierwille admits that Eusebius *did* use the verse to support the doctrine of the Trinity. It is understandable that he would use it for this purpose *after* the doctrine had been officially recognized by a general council of the Christian church as being biblical.

At best Wierwille's argument is the logical fallacy of arguing from silence. From the fact that this verse was not cited in support of the Trinity before Nicea, *nothing follows,* except that Eusebius had no occasion to cite it. Certainly, there is no manuscript support for Wierwille's speculation that a scribe added the verse. The verse is not only in our earliest and best manuscripts, but it is supported by thousands of Greek manuscripts.

As noted above, the text itself teaches the doctrine of the Trinity, since it refers to "the name" (singular) of "the Father, the Son, and the Holy Spirit" (plural). There are three in one "name" (or essence), which is what the Trinity is.

MATTHEW 28:19—Does "making" disciples justify the proselyting tactics of the International ("Boston") Church of Christ?

MISINTERPRETATION: Jesus told his followers to "make" disciples. According to Al Baird, an elder at Boston, "We tried to make a disciple do something rather than motivate him to do it out of his love for God and our love for him" (Baird, "A New Look at Authority," 18).

CORRECTING THE MISINTERPRETATION: According to the Scriptures, the true motivation for serving Christ is love, not fear. Paul said, "the love of Christ constrains me" (2 Cor. 5:14 NKJV). John adds that "perfect love casts out all fear" (1 John 4:18).

In the context of Jesus' command in Matthew, "make disciples" does not imply force. A disciple is one who learns from another, who attaches himself or herself to a discipler and becomes a follower in doctrine and conduct of life. The one who disciples helps to shape the whole life of his or her disciple and produce Christlikeness. But nowhere does Jesus imply or the Bible approve of using force or fear as a means of producing change in the life of the disciple. Changes should be made by nurture and development (Heb. 5:13–14; 1 Peter 2:2), not by control of the disciple's life. It is incorrect to attempt to directly orchestrate change in the disciple's life; the correct approach seeks to facilitate a relationship with Jesus, so that Jesus himself can produce the change in accordance with the desire of his disciple.

MARK

MARK 1:10—Does this verse indicate that the Holy Spirit is not a person, which the Jehovah's Witnesses argue?

MISINTERPRETATION: In Mark 1:10 we read regarding Jesus' baptism: "And immediately coming up out of the water, He saw the heavens opening, and the Spirit like a dove descending upon Him" (NASB). The Jehovah's Witnesses argue that the Holy Spirit is not a person since the Spirit came upon Jesus *in the form of a dove.*

CORRECTING THE MISINTERPRETATION: If we used this same kind of logic, we could disprove the personality of the Father and of Jesus. After all, we read in Exodus 3:2–4 that Jehovah appeared to Moses *in a burning bush.* And we are told that Jesus is the *bread of life* (John 6:48) and is *a door* (John 10:9). On the other hand, numerous evidences throughout Scripture mark the personality of the Holy Spirit—including the fact that the Holy Spirit has the personal attributes of *mind* (Rom. 8:27), *emotions* (Eph. 4:30), and a *will* (1 Cor. 12:11). See the discussion of Genesis 1:2 for detailed biblical argumentation on the personality of the Holy Spirit.

MARK 6:5—If Jesus is Almighty God, why couldn't he do mighty works in Nazareth?

MISINTERPRETATION: According to this verse Jesus while in Nazareth "could do no mighty work there." Why couldn't he, if he is all-powerful? The Jehovah's Witnesses argue that Jesus is not God Almighty but was rather a lesser God than God the Father (*Reasoning from the Scriptures,* 1989, 150).

CORRECTING THE MISINTERPRETATION: Jesus is almighty *as God*, but not almighty *as man*. As the God-man, Jesus has both a divine nature and a human nature. What he can do in one nature he cannot necessarily do in the other. For example, as God, Jesus never got tired (Ps. 121:4), but as man he did (John 4:6).

Just because Jesus *possessed* all power does not mean that he always chose to *exercise* it. The "could not" in Mark 6:5 is *moral*, not *actual*. That is, he chose not to perform miracles "because of their unbelief" (v. 6). Jesus was not an entertainer, nor did he cast pearls before swine. So the necessity here is moral, not metaphysical. He had the ability to do miracles there and in fact did some (v. 5), only he refused to do more because he deemed it a wasted effort.

MARK 10:17–31—Did Jesus deny he was God to the rich young ruler?

See comments on Matthew 19:16–30.

MARK 10:30—Did Jesus promise a "hundredfold return" for our financial and material gifts?

MISINTERPRETATION: Word-Faith teachers say that Jesus promised a hundredfold return for all our financial and material gifts.

> You give $1 for the Gospel's sake and $100 belongs to you; give $10 and receive $1,000; give $1,000 and receive $100,000. . . . Give one house and receive one hundred houses or one house worth one hundred times as much. Give one airplane and receive one hundred times the value of the airplane. Give one car and the return would furnish you a lifetime of cars. In short, Mark 10:30 is a very good deal. [Copeland, 1978, 54]

CORRECTING THE MISINTERPRETATION: This verse has nothing to do with money or riches. It is speaking specifically of those who forsake home and loved ones for the sake of Jesus and the gospel. These individuals will receive a "hundredfold return" in the sense that they become a part of a community of believers. It is in this new community that they find a multiplication of relationships—many of which are ultimately closer and more spiritually meaningful than blood relationships (cf. Mark 3:31–35; Acts 2:41–47; 1 Tim. 5:1–2).

God wants us to have a balanced perspective on money. The Bible does not condemn possessions or riches per se. It is not a sin to be wealthy; some very godly people in the Bible—Abraham and Job, for example—were quite wealthy. Rather, God condemns a love of possessions or riches (Luke 16:13; 1 Tim. 6:10; Heb. 13:5). A love of material things is a sign that a person is living according to a temporal perspective, not an eternal perspective.

Scripture tells us that a love of money and riches can lead to destruction. The apostle Paul flatly stated that "people who want to get rich fall into temptation and a trap and into many foolish and harmful desires that plunge men into ruin and destruction" (1 Tim. 6:9). Paul also warned that "there will be terrible times in the last days. People will be lovers of themselves, lovers of money . . . lovers of pleasure rather than lovers of God—having a form of godliness but denying its power" (2 Tim. 3:1–5 NIV).

Also, Jesus understandably warned his followers: "Watch out! Be on your guard against all kinds of greed; a man's life does not consist in the abundance of his possessions" (Luke 12:15). He then urged his followers to have an eternal perspective, exhorting: "Do not store up for yourselves treasures on earth, where moth and rust destroy, and where thieves break in and steal. But store up for yourselves treasures in heaven" (Matt. 6:19–20a NIV; see also John 6:27).

In view of the above, Jesus urges: "Seek first his kingdom and his righteousness, and all these things will be given to you as well" (Matt. 6:33 NIV). Living for God in a righteous way should be our top priority. When we do this, we can rest assured that God will provide us with the necessities of life. Our attitude should be that whether we are rich or poor (or somewhere in between), we are simply stewards of what God has provided us. Our attitude should mirror that of the apostle Paul, who said: "I know what it is to be in need, and I know what it is to have plenty. I have learned the secret of being content in any and every situation, whether well fed or hungry, whether living in plenty or in want. I can do everything through him who gives me strength" (Phil. 4:12–13 NIV).

MARK 11:23–24—Did Jesus promise to give literally anything we ask in faith?

MISINTERPRETATION: On the face of it, this verse seems to be saying that God will grant literally any request we make of him as long as we believe. Word-Faith teachers often cite this verse in support of their views (Hagin, 1972, 27–28).

CORRECTING THE MISINTERPRETATION: Limitations on what God will give are indicated both by the context and by other texts, as well as by the laws of God's own nature and the universe.

God cannot literally give us anything. Some things are actually impossible. For example, God cannot grant a request of a creature to be God. Neither can he answer a request to approve of our sin. God will not give us a stone if we ask for bread, nor will he give us a serpent if we ask for fish (Matt. 7:9–10).

The context of Jesus' promise in Mark 11 indicates that it was not unconditional, for the very next verse (v. 25) says "*If* you . . . forgive" your brother then God will forgive your trespasses. Thus, there is no reason to believe that Jesus intended us to take his promise to give us "whatever things" we ask without any conditions.

All difficult passages should be interpreted in harmony with other clear statements of Scripture. And it is clear that God does not promise, for example, to heal everyone for whom we pray in faith. Paul wasn't healed, though he prayed earnestly and faithfully (2 Cor. 12:8–9). Jesus taught that it was not the blind man's lack of faith that hindered his being healed. Rather, he was born blind "that the works of God should be revealed in him" (John 9:3). Despite the apostle Paul's divine ability to heal others (Acts 28:9), later he apparently could not heal either Epáphroditus (Phil. 2:25) or Trophimus (2 Tim. 4:20). It clearly was not unbelief that brought Job's sickness on him (Job 1:1). What is more, if the faith of the recipient were the condition for receiving a miracle, then none of the dead Jesus raised would have come back to life, since the dead cannot believe! See comments on Isaiah 53:4–5; Philippians 2:25.

The rest of Scripture places many conditions on God's promise to answer prayer in addition to faith. We must "abide in him" and let his Word "abide in us" (John 15:7). We cannot "ask amiss" out of our own selfishness (James 4:3). Furthermore, we must ask "according to His will" (1 John 5:14). Even Jesus prayed, "Father, *if it is possible*, let this cup [his death] pass from Me" (Matt. 26:39 NASB). Indeed, on all except God's unconditional promises, this "if it be your will" must always be stated or implied. For prayer is not a means by which God serves us. Rather, it is a means by which we serve God. Prayer is not a means by which we get our will done in heaven, but a means by which God gets his will done on earth.

MARK 12:30—Must one bypass reason in order to be truly spiritual, as some Word-Faith teachers seem to imply?

MISINTERPRETATION: Some Word-Faith teachers seem to minimize the role of reason in regard to true spirituality. Kenneth Hagin, for example, said: "One almost has to by-pass the brain and operate from the inner man (the heart or spirit) to really get into the things of God" (Hagin, 1966, 27).

CORRECTING THE MISINTERPRETATION: Mark 12:30 instructs believers to "love the Lord your God with all your heart and with all your soul and with *all* [literally 'the whole of'] *your mind* ['understanding,' 'intellect,' 'intellectual faculty'] and with all your strength" (emphasis added). One cannot love God with all one's mind without using one's God-given rational capacity.

We often see the importance of reason illustrated in Scripture. God himself invites us: "Come now, and let us reason together" (Isa. 1:18). God's wisdom is said to be "reasonable" (James 3:17). The apostle Paul often "reasoned with them [the Jews] from the Scriptures" (Acts 17:2). Scripture admonishes us, "Set your mind on the things above, not on the things that are on earth" (Col. 3:2). Moreover, Christians are to "prepare your minds for action" (1 Peter 1:13).

Though Word-Faith teachers place a heavy emphasis on the Holy Spirit, it is important to understand that the role of the Holy Spirit in illuminating our minds (1 Cor. 2:12) does not mean that Bible interpreters can ignore reason and logic. Since the Holy Spirit is "the Spirit of truth" (John 14:17; 15:26; 16:13), he would not teach truths that fail to meet the tests of truth—tests which involve the use of reason. The Holy Spirit does not guide people into beliefs that contradict each other or fail to have logical, internal consistency.

One further observation: If reason can be bypassed, as Word-Faith teachers often seem to imply, then why do they continually write and sell books that require the use of reason to understand? Moreover, Word-Faith teachers do not seem to realize that they must utilize reason in the very process of arguing against the need for reason.

MARK 13:32—Was Jesus ignorant of the time of his second coming, and does this mean he was not God Almighty?

MISINTERPRETATION: In this verse Jesus denied knowing the time of his own second coming, saying, "but of that day and hour no one knows, neither the angels in heaven, nor the Son, but only the Father." Jehovah's Witnesses argue, "That would not be the case if Father, Son, and Holy Spirit were coequal, comprising one Godhead" (*Reasoning from the Scriptures,* 1989, 409). Jesus' ignorance here proves that he is not God Almighty.

CORRECTING THE MISINTERPRETATION: We must distinguish between what Jesus knew *as God* (everything) and what he knew *as man*. As God, Jesus was omniscient (all-knowing), but as man he was limited in his knowledge. The situation can be schematized as follows:

Jesus as God	Jesus as Man
Unlimited in knowledge	Limited in knowledge
No growth in knowledge	Growth in knowledge
Knew time of his coming	Did not know time of his coming

Hence, in Mark 13:32 Jesus was speaking from the vantage point of his humanity. In his humanity, Jesus was not omniscient, but was limited in understanding, just as are all human beings. If Jesus had been speaking from the perspective of his divinity, he wouldn't have said the same thing.

That Jesus *as God* knew all things is illustrated in numerous verses of Scripture. For example, Jesus knew precisely where the fish were in the water (Luke 5:4, 6; John 21:6–11), and he knew just which fish contained the coin (Matt. 17:27). He knew that his friend Lazarus had died, even though he was nowhere in the vicinity of Lazarus (John 11:11). He knew beforehand those who would reject him (John 6:64) and those who would follow him (John 10:14). He knows the Father as the Father knows him, something that requires that Jesus have the same omniscience as the Father (Matt. 11:27; John 7:29; 8:55; 10:15; 17:25).

MARK 14:21—Does Jesus' statement about how it would have been better if Judas had never been born support the annihilationist's view?

MISINTERPRETATION: Jesus said of Judas, who was sent to perdition, that "it would be better for him if he had not been born" (Mark 14:21 NIV). But before one is conceived one does not exist. Thus, annihilationists argue that if hell will be like the *prebirth* condition, it must be a state of nonexistence. Annihilationism must therefore be true. Is this a proper conclusion?

CORRECTING THE MISINTERPRETATION: Jesus is not comparing Judas's perdition to his nonexistence before birth. This hyperbolic figure of speech indicates the severity of his punishment, not the superiority of nonbeing over being.

Further, *nothing* cannot be better than *something,* since they have nothing in common to compare them. So nonbeing cannot be actually better than being. It is a category mistake to assume they can.

In a parallel condemnation on the Pharisees, Jesus said Sodom and Gomorrah would have repented had they seen his miracles (Matt. 11:20–24). This does not mean that they actually would have repented (or God would surely have shown them these miracles—2 Peter 3:9). It is simply a powerful figure of speech indicating that their sin was so great that "it would be *more tolerable*" (Matt. 11:24) in the day of judgment for Sodom than for them. So even in this phrase about Judas there is no proof of annihilation of the wicked.

The Bible makes clear references to the lost being in conscious torment and punishment after their death. Jesus said it is a place "where there will be weeping and gnashing of teeth" (Matt. 8:12; cf. 22:13; 24:51; 25:30). But those who are not conscious do not weep. See comments on Matthew 25:46.

MARK 16:12—Did Jesus appear in different bodies after his resurrection?

MISINTERPRETATION: According to Mark, Jesus appeared here in "another form." From this, some argue that after the resurrection Jesus assumed different bodies on different occasions, but did not have the same continuously physical body he had before the resurrection. More specifically, the Jehovah's Witnesses argue that Jesus was not raised from the dead physically but was raised in a spirit body and that he appeared or "materialized" to his followers in different "bodies" than the one that was laid in the tomb. Indeed, "the bodies in which Jesus manifested himself to his disciples after his return to life were not the body in which he was nailed to the tree" (*The Kingdom Is At Hand,* 1944, 259).

CORRECTING THE MISINTERPRETATION: There are serious questions about the authenticity of the text involved. Mark 16:9–20 is not found in some of the oldest and best manuscripts. And in reconstructing the original texts from the existing manuscripts, many scholars believe that the older texts are more reliable, since they are closer to the original manuscripts. But even granting its authenticity, the event of which it is a summary (see Luke 24:13–32) simply says "their eyes were prevented from recognizing Him" (v. 16). This makes it clear that the miraculous element was not in Jesus' body, but in the eyes of the disciples (vv. 16, 31). Recognition of Jesus was kept from them until their eyes were opened.

At best this is an obscure and isolated reference. And it is never wise to base any significant doctrinal pronouncement on such a text. Whatever "another form" means, it certainly does not mean a form other than his real physical, material body. Later in this very chapter he ate, giving this as a proof that he was "flesh and bones" and not an immaterial "spirit" (vv. 38–43). "Another form" probably means other than that of a *gardener* for which Mary mistook him earlier (John 20:15). Here Jesus appeared in the form of a *traveler* (Luke 24:13–14).

MARK 16:16—Does this verse mean that baptism is necessary in order to be saved?

MISINTERPRETATION: Mark 16:16 says, "He who has believed and has been baptized shall be saved; but he who has disbelieved shall be condemned" (NASB). Cults and aberrant groups cite this in support of their belief that baptism is necessary for salvation. Mormons use this verse as a proof that mere belief is not enough; one must be baptized to be saved (Talmage, 1982, 129).

CORRECTING THE MISINTERPRETATION: A basic principle of Bible interpretation is that difficult passages should be interpreted in light of the easy, clear verses. One should never build a theology on difficult passages. The clear verses indicate that one is saved by faith in Christ (e.g., John 3:16–17; Acts 16:31).

In Mark 16:16 it is clear that it is *unbelief* that brings damnation, not a lack of being baptized: "he who has disbelieved shall be condemned." When a person rejects the gospel, refusing to believe it, that person is damned.

Other verses in Scripture support the view that baptism is not necessary for salvation.

1. Jesus told the repentent thief, "I tell you the truth, today you will be with me in paradise" (Luke 23:43). The thief was saved without a baptism.
2. In Acts 10 Cornelius exercised faith in Christ and was clearly saved *prior* to being baptized in water. The moment Cornelius believed in Christ, the gift of the Holy Spirit was poured out on him (Acts 10:45).
3. In 1 Corinthians 1:17 the apostle Paul said, "For Christ did not send me to baptize, but to preach the gospel"(NIV). Here a distinction is made between the gospel and being baptized. We are told elsewhere that it is the gospel that brings salvation (1 Cor. 15:2). And baptism is not a part of that gospel (see also comments on Acts 2:38).

LUKE

LUKE 1:28—Does Mary being "full of grace" prove that she was immaculately conceived, as Roman Catholics say?

MISINTERPRETATION: On December 8, 1854, Pope Pius IX, in the Bull "Ineffabilis," pronounced infallibly the following doctrine to be believed firmly and constantly by all the faithful: "The Most Holy Virgin Mary was in the first moment of her conception, by a unique gift of grace and privilege of Almighty God, in view of the merits of Jesus Christ, the Redeemer of mankind, preserved free from all stain of original sin" (Ott, 1960, 199). Ott argues that "the expression 'full of grace' [Luke 1:28] . . . in the angel's salutation, represents the proper name, and must on this account express a characteristic quality of Mary. . . . However, it is perfect only if it be perfect not only intensively but also extensively, that is, if it extends over her whole life, beginning with her entry into the world" (Ibid., 200).

CORRECTING THE MISINTERPRETATION: Nothing in this verse justifies a belief in the immaculate conception of Mary.

It is by no means necessary to take the phrase "full of grace" as a proper name. Even contemporary Catholic versions of the Bible do not translate it as a proper name (for example, the New American Bible). It could refer simply to Mary's state of being as a recipient of God's favor.

Even if it were a proper name and referred to Mary's essential character, it is not necessary to take it extensively all the way back to her birth. The only way one could conclude this is by factors beyond the biblical text itself (which does not teach the Immaculate Conception). Of course, Catholics believe that tradition fills in what the Scriptures do not declare. But if this is so, then why appeal to Scripture for support. Why not just admit what many contemporary Catholics are reluctant to acknowledge, that this teaching is not found in Scripture but was only added centuries later by tradition.

Even if it were taken extensively to Mary's beginning, it does not of necessity mean an immaculate conception. It could simply refer to God's grace being upon her life from conception. But that was true of others, including Jeremiah (Jeremiah 1) and John the Baptist (Luke 1), who were not immaculately conceived. Elliott Miller and Kenneth Samples note in *The Cult of the Virgin,* the Greek term for "full of grace" is *charitō.* But "*charitō* is used of believers in Ephesians 1:6 without implying sinless perfection. So again there is hence nothing about Luke 1:28 that establishes the doctrine of the immaculate conception. That Mary was uniquely favored to be the mother of her Lord is the only necessary inference" (Miller and Samples, 34). One must appeal to traditions outside the Bible, and late ones at that, to find support for this Catholic dogma.

LUKE 1:28b—Does the fact that Mary was "full of grace" prove that she lived a sinless life, as Roman Catholics claim?

MISINTERPRETATION: According to Roman Catholic teaching, "Mary's sinlessness may be deduced from the text: Luke 1, 28: 'Hail, full of grace!' since personal moral defects are irreconcilable with fullness of grace" (Ott, 1960).

CORRECTING THE MISINTERPRETATION: The Catholic argument that because Mary was "full of grace" at the annunciation she was sinless during her entire life cannot be sustained. The phrase "full of grace" is an inaccurate rendering based on the Latin Vulgate that has been corrected by the modern Catholic Bible, the New American Bible translation. The NAB translates it simply as "favored one." The Vulgate's misleading rendering became the basis for the idea that grace extended throughout Mary's life. But even if accurate, taken in context, the salutation of the angel is only a reference to Mary's state *at that moment,* not to her entire life. It does not affirm that she was *always* full of grace but only that she was full of grace in her selection by God at that time for this singular honor.

The grace given to Mary was not only limited in time but limited in function. The grace she received was for the task of being the mother of the Messiah. Nothing indicates that the purpose of this grace was to prevent her from any sin.

The stress on fullness of grace is misleading, since even Catholic scholars admit that Mary was in need of redemption. But why is this so if she was not a sinner? Ott says clearly of Mary that "she herself required redemption and was redeemed by Christ" (Ibid., 212). It is biblically unfounded to suggest that she was merely prevented from inheriting all this rather than being actually delivered from it. Nor does the Bible support the sinlessness of Mary. To the contrary, it affirms her sinfulness. Speaking as a sinner, Mary said, "My spirit rejoices in God my savior" (Luke 1:46 NIV). Contrary to Duns Scotus's solution that Mary was prevented from needing to be saved from sin, she confessed her *present need* (after her conception) of a Savior. Indeed, she even presented an offering to the Jewish priest arising out of her sinful condition (Luke 2:22) which was required in the Old Testament (Lev. 12:2). This would not have been necessary if she were sinless.

LUKE 1:42—Does the fact that Mary was called "Blessed" show that she was immaculately conceived?

MISINTERPRETATION: Luke 1:42 is offered by Catholics in defense of the doctrine of the immaculate conception of Mary. They claim that when Elizabeth said, "Blessed are you among women," the "blessing of God which rests upon Mary is made parallel to the blessing of God which rests upon Christ in His humanity. This parallelism suggests that Mary, just like Christ, was from the beginning of her existence, free from all sin" (Ott, 1960, 201).

CORRECTING THE MISINTERPRETATION: Ott's reasoning that this blessing is parallel to the one on Christ is farfetched. It grasps for straws in the lack of biblical evidence for a Catholic dogma proclaimed so many years after the events themselves. The passage nowhere sets a parallel between Mary and Christ. It simply says that Mary, the bearer of our Lord, was given grace for her task.

Even if the parallel could somehow be made, an immaculate conception would not necessarily follow from it. Jesus was conceived of a virgin. Mary was not so conceived; she had two natural parents. By Ott's illogic, one could make Mary a redeemer for our sins, something that some Catholics have sought to do and others approach in their extreme veneration of Mary. The church, however, has not officially proclaimed such a heresy.

Thomas Aquinas, one of the greatest Catholic theologians of all time, declared that the doctrine of the immaculate conception of Mary is impossible (Aquinas, *Summa Theologica* 3, 27, 2), since Mary, like all other humans except Christ, inherited a sin nature from Adam (cf. Rom. 5:12).

LUKE 1:42, 48—Do these verses show that Mary should be venerated above all creatures, as Roman Catholics claim?

MISINTERPRETATION: According to the teaching of the Catholic church, "Mary, the Mother of God, is entitled to the Cult of Hyperdulia" (Ott, 1960, 215). This means that Mary may be venerated and honored on a level higher than that of other creatures, whether angels or saints. However, "this [veneration due to Mary] is substantially less than the *cultus latriae* (or adoration) which is due to God alone, but is higher than the *cultus duliae* (or veneration) due to angels and to the other saints.

The Scriptural source of the special veneration due to the Mother of God is to be found in Luke 1. Verse 28 says: "Hail, full of grace, the Lord is with thee," in the praise of Elizabeth, filled with the Holy Ghost. Verse 42 adds: "Blessed are thou amongst women, and blessed is the fruit of thy womb." The prophetic words of the Mother of God are found in verse 48: "For behold, from henceforth all generations shall call me blessed" (Ibid., 215).

CORRECTING THE MISINTERPRETATION: Nothing in these verses supports the conclusion that Mary should be venerated above all creatures and below God.

The texts say nothing about veneration or prayers to Mary. They simply call Mary "blessed" of God, which she truly was. However, contrary to Catholic practice, Mary was not blessed *above* all women but simply was the most blessed *among* all women. Even in the Catholic Bible it reads, "Most blessed are you *among* [not above] women" (Luke 1:42). This is not a distinction without a difference. It is a strange logic to argue that being the most blessed among women makes her worthy of more honor than any other women. Eve was the mother of all humanity (Gen. 3:20), a distinctive honor held by no other person including Mary, and yet she is not venerated by Catholics in accord with her blessed status.

Further, even great sinners that are forgiven are highly blessed but need not be most highly esteemed because of that fact (see, for example, 1 Cor. 15:9; 1 Tim. 1:15). Abraham was called the Father of the faithful, yet he lied about his wife (Gen. 20:1–18). It was said of David that his heart was fully devoted to the LORD his God (1 Kings 11:4), yet he committed adultery and murder (2 Sam. 11).

There is not a single instance in the New Testament where any veneration was given to Mary. When the Magi came to the manger at the

Nativity to visit the Christ child, the Bible declares that they worshiped him, not her (Matt. 2:11).

In addition, bowing down in veneration before any creature, even angels (cf. Col. 2:18; Rev. 22:8–9), is *forbidden* in Scripture. The Bible makes it clear that we are not to make any "images" of any creature or even to "bow down" to them in an act of religious devotion (Exod. 20:4–5). To call Mary "Queen of Heaven," knowing that this phrase was borrowed directly from an old pagan idolatrous cult condemned in the Bible (cf. Jer. 7:18), only invites the charge of mariolatry. *And mariolatry is idolatry.*

In addition, despite theological distinctions to the contrary, in practice many Catholics do not distinguish between the veneration given to Mary and that given to Christ.

There is clearly a difference, both in theory and in practice, in the way Catholics honor other human beings and the way they venerate Mary. Consider the following book, *Novena Prayers in Honor of Our Mother of Perpetual Help,* with the Catholic imprimatur (and *nihil obstat* declaration) on it, which guarantees that there is nothing heretical in it (published by Sisters of St. Basil, 1968, 16, 19):

> Come to my aid, dearest Mother, for I recommend myself to thee. In thy hands I place my eternal salvation, and to thee I entrust my soul. Count me among thy most devoted servants; take me under thy protection, and it is enough for me. For, if thou protect me, dear Mother, I fear nothing: not from my sins, because thou wilt obtain for me the pardon of them; nor from the devils, because thou art more powerful than all hell together; not even from Jesus, my judge, because by one prayer from thee, He will be appeased.

LUKE 1:80; 2:52; 4:16—Did Jesus go to India as a child during the so-called "lost years" and learn to perform miracles from Hindu gurus?

MISINTERPRETATION: Russian writer Nicolas Notovitch, whose writings are popular among New Agers today, describes Luke as saying Jesus "was in the desert until the day of his showing unto Israel" (cf. Luke 1:80). This, Notovitch declared, proves that no one knew where the young Jesus was for about sixteen years. He said he had found documents substantiating that Jesus went to India and learned from Indian gurus to raise people from the dead and cast out demons (Prophet, 1987, 245f.; MacLaine, 1984, 233–34).

CORRECTING THE MISINTERPRETATION. Luke 1:80 refers to John the Baptist, not Jesus. At this point in Luke's narrative, Jesus has not even been introduced. The person in the prophecy is not the Lord but the prophet who "will go before the Lord" (v. 76), which was clearly John the Baptist (cf. Matt. 3:1–4).

Jesus' teaching was not pantheistic, as is that of the gurus of India. Jesus never cited the Hindu Vedas but always the Jewish Old Testament which proclaimed the monotheistic God of Judaism (see Mark 12:29) as part of the most important commandment. There is no evidence that Jesus studied in India, and Notovitch's alleged evidence has been thoroughly discredited.

Though the Gospels do not directly address Jesus' childhood, there are convincing indirect evidences that Jesus remained in Palestine. Luke 2:52 summarizes Jesus' life from age 12: "And Jesus kept increasing in wisdom and stature, and in favor with God and man" (NASB).

Jesus, of course, was God and human. As God, he was omniscient and all-wise; he could never "grow in wisdom" from the divine perspective. In his humanity, however, he probably gained wisdom as did other Jewish boys, by studying the Old Testament Scriptures (Ps. 1:2) and listening to the wisdom of the elders. He was known in his community as a carpenter (Mark 6:3) and a carpenter's son (Matt. 13:55). It was customary among the Jews for fathers to teach their sons a trade. Joseph would have taught Jesus the trade of carpentry. That carpentry played a role in his life is clear because some parables and teachings drew upon that experience. For example, he told of building a house on rock as opposed to sand (Matt. 7:24–27).

Luke 4:16 is a key text to refute the idea that Jesus went to India. At the beginning of his three-year ministry, Jesus "came to Nazareth, *where He had been brought up;* and *as was His custom,* He entered the synagogue on the Sabbath and stood up to read" (NASB, emphasis added). Clearly Jesus was brought up in Nazareth, not India, and his custom was to visit the synagogue, not Hindu temples.

After Jesus finished reading on this occasion, "all were speaking well of Him, and wondering at the gracious words which were falling from His lips; and they were saying, 'Is this not Joseph's son?'" (4:22). Those in the synagogue recognized Jesus as a local resident.

It also is noteworthy that Jesus read from the Old Testament Scriptures. The Old Testament, for which Jesus often displayed reverence (for example in Matt. 5:18), warns about staying away from false gods and religious systems such as Hinduism (see Exod. 20:2–3; 34:14; Deut. 6:14; 13:10; 2 Kings 17:35). The Old Testament clearly distinguishes creation from Creator, unlike Eastern pantheism, and teaches the need for redemption, not enlightenment. Not coincidentally does the New Testament show Jesus quoting from the Old Testament, not the Vedas.

LUKE 6:40—Does this text support the Boston Church of Christ's view of a perfect disciple?

MISINTERPRETATION: Jesus said, "A disciple is not above his teacher, but everyone who is perfectly trained will be like his teacher" (Luke 6:40). According to the Boston Church of Christ, one must be perfectly taught before he can be a true disciple of Christ.

CORRECTING THE MISINTERPRETATION: Common sense tells us that one need not be perfectly taught to be a "disciple" of Christ. Perfect learning is not something one can attain during a three-year crash course under some other disciple. It is a goal for a lifetime of learning from Christ.

The teacher in this text is Christ, not a member of the "Boston Church" or any other human being. This makes a world of difference.

The Boston Church changes the *goal* into the *prerequisite*. Many disciples have reached higher levels of growth than most Christians, but this does not mean that they are "fully taught."

LUKE 12:32—Does the reference to the "little flock" in this verse indicate there is an "anointed class" of believers who will dwell with God in heaven, as opposed to all other believers who will dwell eternally on earth?

MISINTERPRETATION: The Watchtower Society teaches that in Luke 12:32 Jesus "thus reveals that only a relatively small number (later identified as 144,000) will be in the heavenly Kingdom" (*The Greatest Man Who Ever Lived*, 1991, section 78). These individuals make up the "anointed class."

CORRECTING THE MISINTERPRETATION: This verse refers not to the so-called "anointed class" of Jehovah's Witnesses but to Jesus' disciples, as verse 22 makes patently clear ("Then Jesus said to his disciples . . ."). Jesus' point in using the metaphor of a "little flock" of his disciples is that they were a small group vulnerable to being "preyed upon" by dangerous "wolves" (cf. Matt. 10:16). Jesus "the Shepherd" admonished them not to worry, though, for he would take care of them and provide them food, clothing, and the other necessities of life (see vv. 22–34).

Jesus *never* restricted the kingdom of heaven to a mere 144,000 people. Indeed, Scripture indicates that *all* who believe in Jesus Christ can look forward to a heavenly destiny, not just some select group of 144,000 (see Eph. 2:19; Phil. 3:20; Col. 3:1; Heb. 3:1; 12:22; 2 Peter 1:10–11). See comments on Revelation 7:4.

LUKE 16:22–28—Does the human soul consciously exist following death?

MISINTERPRETATION: Because this passage so obviously supports the idea of conscious existence after death—as well as conscious suffering for the wicked following death—the Jehovah's Witnesses go to great lengths to reinterpret it. They argue that "the rich man represents the religious leaders who are favored with spiritual privileges and opportunities, and Lazarus pictures the common people who hunger for spiritual nourishment." They say that "since the rich man and Lazarus are not literal persons but symbolize classes of people, logically their deaths are also symbolic." Their "deaths" symbolize dying to their former circumstances. In God's program, the "repentant Lazarus class dies to their former spiritually deprived condition and come into a position of divine favor." By contrast, "those who make up the rich-man class come under divine disfavor because of persistently refusing to accept the kingdom message taught by Jesus." The "torment" referred to in this passage is the pain caused on evil people by the righteous message of Jesus and his disciples (*The Greatest Man Who Ever Lived*, 1991, section 88).

CORRECTING THE MISINTERPRETATION: If people at death simply lapse into a state of unconsciousness, then Jesus' comments in this passage lose their meaning. The elaborate reinterpretation offered by the Watchtower Society completely crosses the boundary of credulity.

Scholars have noted that whenever Jesus taught, he provided examples from real-life situations. For example, he spoke of a treasure buried in a field, a wedding feast, a man working in a vineyard, a woman sweeping her house, a shepherd watching his sheep, and a son returning home after squandering money. Jesus never illustrated a teaching with a falsehood. This being the case, we must conclude that in Luke 16 Jesus is giving a teaching based on a "real-life" situation—involving conscious existence after death. Certainly the verse is in perfect harmony with other verses that teach conscious existence in the afterlife (see Luke 23:46; Acts 7:59; 2 Cor. 5:6–8; Phil. 1:21–23; 1 Thess. 4:13–17; Rev. 6:9–10).

Jesus never calls this real story a "parable," and unlike parables, which never use real names, Jesus used a real name (Lazarus) of a person.

LUKE 17:21—Does Jesus' statement that "the kingdom of God is within you" mean that any human kingdom is unreal?

MISINTERPRETATION: Jesus in Matthew 4:17 said "the kingdom of heaven is near" and in Luke 17:21 that it is "in your midst" (NASB) or "within you" (NIV). According to Christian Science founder Mary Baker Eddy, this means that "God's kingdom is everywhere and supreme, and it follows that the human kingdom is nowhere, and must be unreal" (Eddy, 35). Eddy implies that *anything* that is not divine is unreal.

CORRECTING THE MISINTERPRETATION: There is no justification for the Christian Science claim that all that is not divine is unreal. Jesus in Luke 17:21 affirms the presence of God's kingdom; he is not negating the existence of anything opposed to it. In fact, Jesus elsewhere affirms the existence of Satan and his kingdom (Matt. 4:8), speaking of its everlasting separation from him (Matt. 25:41). This is an obvious example of something "real" but not divine. The reality of Satan is elsewhere attested by Jesus' personal encounter and discussion with Satan in his temptation (Matt. 4:1–11).

LUKE 17:21—Does this verse indicate that humankind is divine, as Christian Scientists argue?

MISINTERPRETATION: In Luke 17:21 Jesus said, "Behold, the kingdom of God is within you" (KJV). Christian Scientists sometimes argue that Jesus was here saying that man is divine and is therefore sinless and eternal (Eddy, 475–77).

CORRECTING THE MISINTERPRETATION: Jesus couldn't have meant that the kingdom of God was actually "*within you*," because Jesus was talking directly to the Pharisees—the religious hypocrites of the day. Certainly Jesus didn't believe that God's holy kingdom was "within" these men. Other interpretations of this verse are much more plausible. Many scholars believe the phrase translated "within you" in the King James Version (Greek: *entos hymon*) is better rendered, "in your midst."

In this understanding Jesus was simply saying that the kingdom of God is "in your midst" because Christ the King is "in your midst." The kingdom is present because the King is present.

Other interpreters believe the phrase is best translated, "within your possession" or "within your reach." In this understanding Jesus was saying that all his hearers had to do was acknowledge that he was the promised King/Messiah and he would issue in the kingdom. But the Pharisees to whom Jesus was talking rejected him as the King/Messiah.

Whichever interpretation is correct, Jesus was most certainly not saying that human beings can become divine. For biblical argumentation against the idea that human beings can become gods, see the discussion of Genesis 1:26.

LUKE 18:18–23—Was Jesus teaching salvation by works to the rich young ruler?

MISINTERPRETATION: Roman Catholics believe that meritorious works are a condition for salvation (see comments on Rom. 2:6–7). Luke 18:18–23 is sometimes cited as proof of this idea, since Jesus answered the question, "What must I do to inherit eternal life?" by telling the rich young ruler to keep the commandments (v. 20).

CORRECTING THE MISINTERPRETATION: There is no evidence here or elsewhere that Jesus taught that good works are a condition of salvation. Jesus' answer was not intended as a plan of salvation but as proof of the young man's condemnation. The law does not save (Rom. 3:28), but it does condemn (Rom. 3:19). The "law was put in charge to lead us to Christ that we might be justified by faith" (Gal. 3:24). Jesus was trying to demonstrate to the young man that he stood condemned before the law. His unwillingness to give his money to the poor revealed that he had not even kept the first great commandment to love God more than his money or anything else (cf. Matt. 22:36–37).

Further, Jesus was showing that even the rich young ruler's question was confused. For one does not "do" anything to get an inheritance of any kind, including eternal life. An "inheritance" is a gift. Indeed, eternal life is presented throughout the Bible as a gift (John 3:36; 5:24; 20:31; Rom. 6:23; 1 John 5:13). And one cannot work for a gift. As Paul said, "Now when a man works, his wages are not credited to him as a gift, but as an obligation. However, to the man who does not work but trusts God who justifies the wicked, his faith is credited as righteousness" (Rom. 4:4–5). The only "work" by which someone can be saved is "faith." For when Jesus was asked, "What can we do to accomplish the works of God?" Jesus replied, "This is the work of God, that you *believe* in Him who He sent" (John 6:29 NASB).

LUKE 23:43—Does this verse indicate there is no conscious existence after death?

MISINTERPRETATION: Luke 23:43 in the NASB reads, "And He said to him, 'Truly I say to you, today you shall be with Me in Paradise'" (NASB). By contrast, the New World Translation renders this verse, "And he said to him: 'Truly I tell you today, you will be with me in Paradise.'" The Jehovah's Witnesses place the comma after the word "today" in order to avoid the thief being with Jesus in paradise "today"—that is, to avoid the teaching that there is conscious existence after death. They say this promise will be fulfilled when Jesus "rules as King in heaven and resurrects this repentant evildoer to life on earth in the Paradise that Armageddon survivors and their companions will have the privilege of cultivating" (*The Greatest Man Who Ever Lived*, 1991, section 125).

CORRECTING THE MISINTERPRETATION: There is strong evidence to reject this interpretation. There is no warrant in the Greek text for inserting the comma where the New World Translation puts it. Out of seventy-four occurrences in the Gospels of the Greek for the phrase "Truly, I say to you," Luke 23:43 is the *only* place where the New World Translation places the comma in this way—an exception that would appear to be motivated by a desire to avoid teaching conscious existence after death.

In context here the thief apparently thought Jesus would come into power at the eschatological end of the world. He requested that Jesus remember him at that time. But Jesus promised the thief something much better: "*Today*—not just at the end of the world—you will be with me in Paradise."

This interpretation fits with the repeated teaching of the rest of Scripture that the soul is conscious between death and resurrection (Ps. 16:10–11; Matt. 17:3; 2 Cor. 5:8; Phil. 1:23; Heb. 12:23; Rev. 6:9).

LUKE 24:23—Were Jesus' resurrection appearances physical appearances or mere visions?

MISINTERPRETATION: Luke seems to say that Jesus' resurrection body was a "vision" in this passage. This implies that it was not a real physical appearance. The Jehovah's Witnesses deny that Jesus was raised physically from the dead but say he was raised as a spirit creature and then "materialized" on various occasions to prove that he had "resurrected" (*Aid to Bible Understanding,* 1971, 1395).

CORRECTING THE MISINTERPRETATION: The resurrection appearances were literal, physical appearances. The passage cited, Luke 24:23, does not refer to seeing Christ. It refers only to the women seeing angels at the tomb, not to any appearance of Christ. The Gospels never speak of a resurrection appearance of Christ as a vision, nor does Paul in 1 Corinthians 15.

The postresurrection encounters with Christ are described by Paul as literal "appearances" (1 Cor. 15:5–8), not as visions. The difference between a mere vision and a physical appearance is significant. Visions are of invisible, spiritual realities, such as God and angels. Appearances, on the other hand, are of physical objects that can be seen with the eye. Visions have no physical manifestations associated with them, but appearances do.

People sometimes "see" or "hear" things in their visions (Luke 1:11–20; Acts 10:9–16) but not with their physical senses. When someone saw angels with the naked eye, or had some physical contact with them (Gen. 18:8; 32:24; Dan. 8:18), it was not a vision but an actual appearance of the angel in the physical world. During these appearances the angels temporarily assumed a visible form after which they returned to their normal invisible state. However, the resurrection appearances of Christ were experiences of seeing Christ with physical eyes in his continued visible, physical form.

Vision	Appearance
Of a Spiritual Reality	Of a Physical Object
No Physical Manifestations	Physical Manifestations
Daniel 2, 7;	1 Corinthians 15:5–8;
2 Corinthians 12:1–5	Acts 9:1–8

Certainly the most common way to describe an encounter with the resurrected Christ is as an "appearance." These appearances were accompanied by physical manifestations, such as, the audible voice of Jesus, his physical body and crucifixion scars, physical sensations (such as touch), and eating on three occasions. These phenomena are not purely subjective or internal—they involve a physical, external reality.

The contention that Paul's experience must have been a vision because those with him did not see Christ is unfounded, since they both heard the physical sound and saw the physical light, just as Paul did. Only Paul looked into the light, so only he saw Jesus. See comments for Luke 24:31, 39.

LUKE 24:31—Did Jesus dematerialize when he suddenly disappeared from the disciples?

MISINTERPRETATION: Jesus could not only suddenly appear after his resurrection (see, for example, John 20:19), but he could also instantly disappear. Is this evidence, as some critics claim, that Jesus dematerialized on these occasions? This is an important question, for the Jehovah's Witnesses say Christ merely "materialized" on various occasions to prove his "resurrection" and then "dematerialized" (*Aid to Bible Understanding,* 1971, 1395).

CORRECTING THE MISINTERPRETATION: Jesus rose in the same physical, albeit glorified, body in which he died. Such a body is an important dimension of his continuing humanity both before (cf. John 1:14) and after (Luke 24:39; 1 John 4:2) his resurrection.

The fact that he could appear or disappear quickly does not diminish his humanity but enhances it. It reveals that, while the postresurrection body has *more* powers than a preresurrection body, it was not *less* than physical. That is, it did not cease to be a material body, even if by resurrection it gained powers beyond mere physical bodies.

It is the very nature of a miracle that it is immediate, as opposed to the natural gradual process. When Jesus touched the man's hand "*immediately* his leprosy was cleansed" (Matt. 8:3). Likewise, at Jesus' command the paralytic "rose and *immediately* took up the pallet, and went out in the sight of all" (Mark 2:12a NASB). When Peter proclaimed that the man born crippled be cured, "*immediately* his feet and ankles were strengthened. And with a leap he stood upright and began to walk" (Acts 3:7–8a NASB).

Philip was immediately transported from the presence of the Ethiopian eunuch in his physical preresurrection body. The text says that after Philip baptized the eunuch "the Spirit of the Lord snatched Philip away; and the eunuch saw him no more" (Acts 8:39). One moment Philip is with the eunuch; the next he suddenly and miraculously disappeared and later appeared in another city (Acts 8:40). Such a phenomenon does not necessitate an immaterial body. Hence, sudden appearances and disappearances are not proofs of the immaterial, but of the supernatural.

LUKE 24:31—If Jesus had the same physical body after his resurrection, why did his disciples not recognize him?

MISINTERPRETATION: Two disciples walked with Jesus, talked with him, and ate with him, and still did not recognize him. Other disciples had the same experience (see verses below). If he rose in the same physical body (cf. Luke 24:39; John 20:27), then why didn't they recognize him. The Jehovah's Witnesses explain this by saying Jesus "materialized" to his followers in different "bodies" than the one that was laid in the tomb (*Awake!* 22 July 1973, 4).

CORRECTING THE MISINTERPRETATION: Jesus did rise in the same body of flesh and bones in which he died (see comments on 1 Cor. 15:37). A number of reasons can account for why he was not immediately recognized by his disciples:

1. Dullness—Luke 24:25–26
2. Disbelief—John 20:24–25
3. Disappointment—John 20:11–15
4. Dread—Luke 24:36–37
5. Dimness of light at daybreak—John 20:1, 14–15
6. Distance—John 21:4
7. Different clothes—John 19:23–24; cf. 20:6–8

Notice, however, that the problem was only *temporary,* and before the appearance was over they were absolutely convinced that it was the same Jesus in the same physical body of flesh, bones, and scars he had before the resurrection. And they went out of his presence to turn the world upside down, fearlessly facing death, because they had not the slightest doubt that he had conquered death in the same physical body in which he had experienced it.

LUKE 24:34—Was Jesus invisible before and after he appeared?

MISINTERPRETATION: The phrase "he appeared" means "He made himself visible" to them (cf. 1 Cor. 15:5–8), say Jehovah's Witnesses as argument that the resurrected Jesus was not essentially material (see reasoning for Luke 24:23, 31).

CORRECTING THE MISINTERPRETATION: That Jesus' resurrection body was essentially material is clear.

Christ's resurrection body could be seen with the eye during his appearances. They are described by the word *horaō* ("to see"). Although this word is sometimes used of seeing invisible realities (cf. Luke 1:22; 24:23), it often means to see by the physical eye. John uses the same word *(horaō)* of seeing Jesus in his earthly body before the resurrection (6:36; 14:9; 19:35) and also of seeing him in his resurrection body (20:18, 25, 29). The same word for body *(soma)* is used of Jesus before and after the resurrection (cf. 1 Cor. 15:44; Phil. 3:21).

Even the phrase "he let himself be seen" (aorist passive, *ōphthē*) simply means that Jesus took the initiative to show himself to the disciples, not that he was essentially invisible. The same form ("He [they] appeared") is used in the Greek Old Testament (2 Chron. 25:21), in the Apocrypha (1 Mac. 4:6), and in the New Testament (Acts 7:26) of purely human beings appearing in normal physical bodies. In this passive form the word means to initiate an appearance for public view, to move from a place where one is not seen to a place where one is seen. It means more generally "to come into view." There is no reason to understand it as referring to something invisible by nature becoming visible, as some do. For in this case it would mean that these human beings in normal preresurrection bodies were essentially invisible before they were seen by others.

The same event that is described by "he appeared" or "let himself be seen" (aorist passive), such as the appearance to Paul (1 Cor. 15:8), is also described in the active mood elsewhere. Paul wrote of this same experience in the same book, "Have I not seen Jesus our Lord?" (1 Cor. 9:1). But if the resurrection body can be seen physically, then it is not invisible until it makes itself visible by some alleged "materialization."

Jesus also disappeared from the disciples on other occasions (see Luke 24:51; Acts 1:9). But if Jesus could disappear suddenly, as well as appear, then his ability to appear cannot be taken as evidence that his resurrection body was essentially invisible. For by the same reasoning his ability to disappear suddenly could be used as evidence that his body was essentially material and could suddenly become immaterial.

There are much more reasonable explanations for the stress on Christ's self-initiated "appearances." First of all, they were the proof that he had conquered death (Acts 13:30–31; 17:31; Rom. 1:4). Jesus said, "I am He who lives, and was dead, and behold I am alive forever more. Amen. And I have the keys of Hades and of Death" (Rev. 1:18 NKJV; cf. John 10:18). The translation "he let himself be seen" (1 Cor. 15:5–8) is a perfectly fitting way to express this self-initiated triumphalism. He was sovereign over death as well as over his resurrection appearances.

Further, no human being saw the actual moment of the resurrection. But the fact that Jesus appeared repeatedly in the same body for some forty days (Acts 1:3) to more than 500 different people (1 Cor. 15:6) on twelve different occasions is indisputable evidence that he really rose bodily from the dead. In brief, the reason for the stress on the many appearances of Christ is not because the resurrection body was essentially invisible and immaterial, but to show that it was actually material and immortal. Without an empty tomb and repeated appearances of the same body that was once buried in it, there would be no proof of the resurrection. So it is not surprising at all that the Bible strongly stresses the many appearances of Christ. They are the real proof of the physical resurrection.

LUKE 24:39—Did Jesus accommodate himself to the mistaken ideas of the disciples by speaking of his resurrection body as "flesh and bones," as Christian Scientists maintain?

MISINTERPRETATION: In Luke 24:39 Jesus told the disciples, "See My hands and My feet, that it is I Myself; touch Me and see, for a spirit does not have flesh and bones as you see that I have" (NASB). Christian Science interpreters say that because death is an illusion, Jesus did not really die on the cross. There could be no literal, physical resurrection because there is no such thing as death. The disciples were thus mistaken when they thought that Jesus had died. When Jesus spoke of his "resurrection body" as "flesh and bones," he was simply accommodating himself to the immature ideas of his disciples (Eddy, 593).

CORRECTING THE MISINTERPRETATION: There are numerous problems with the Christian Science view of this verse. First, if Jesus spoke about his resurrection body as a "flesh and bones" body merely to accommodate himself to the immature ideas of his disciples, then Jesus was *blatantly deceiving* his disciples, making them think he had a body when he really did not. Such a view makes a liar out of the Savior—thereby calling into question everything else he said.

On one occasion Jesus challenged Thomas to put his finger into the scar in Christ's hand and to put his hand into the wound in Christ's side and "stop doubting and believe" (John 20:27). Given the identity of the scars with his preresurrection body, the only impression these words could have left on the disciples' minds was that Jesus was claiming to have resurrected in the same literal, material body in which he died. However, if he did not rise in this physical body, he was intentionally misleading his disciples. Either Jesus rose in the same material body in which he died, or else he lied.

Second, there are numerous proofs in Scripture that Jesus rose from the dead in a physical, material body. In Luke 24:37–39 Jesus emphatically affirmed that spirits do not have material bodies *such as he had.* Numerous eyewitnesses—including more than 500 witnesses at one time—saw the resurrected Christ (1 Cor. 15:6). Speaking of the resurrection of Christ, Peter insisted that his "flesh did not see corruption" (Acts 2:31). Writing after the resurrection, John declared that Jesus "came in the flesh" (1 John 4:2; cf. 2 John 7). The use of the perfect participle ["has come"] in 1 John 4:2 implies that Jesus came in the flesh in the past and he remained in the flesh when John penned these words after the resurrection. The body that emerged from the tomb on Easter morning was *seen* (Matt. 28:17), *heard* (John 20:15–16), and even *touched* (Matt. 28:9). Jesus ate food at least four times after the resurrection (Luke 24:30; 24:42–43; John 21:12–13; Acts 1:4), thereby proving that he had a physical body.

Third, from a historical perspective, to embrace the Christian Science interpretation one must believe the claims of a woman who lived eighteen centuries after the time of Christ *over* the claims of numerous eyewitnesses who actually saw the physically resurrected Christ (1 Cor. 15:5–6). And many of these eyewitnesses gave up their lives defending the truth of what they knew to be true.

JOHN

JOHN 1:1—Is Jesus God or just *a* god?

MISINTERPRETATION: The Jehovah's Witnesses' New World Translation renders this verse, "The Word [Christ] was a god" (insert added). *The Watchtower* magazine states that "because there is no definite article 'the' *(ho)* it means Christ is only a god, not the God" (*The Watchtower*, 7 December 1995, 4). They in fact believe that Jesus is only a created being, Michael the Archangel (*The Watchtower*, 15 May 1969, 307). The Greek of John 1:1 "is not saying that the Word (Jesus) was the same as the God with whom he was but, rather, that the Word was godlike, divine, a god" (*Reasoning from the Scriptures*, 1989, 212).

CORRECTING THE MISINTERPRETATION: It is not proper to translate this verse "The Word was a god" so as to deny the deity of Christ. The full deity of Christ is supported by other references in John (e.g., 8:58; 10:30; 20:28) as well as the rest of the New Testament (e.g., Col. 1:15–16; 2:9; Titus 2:13; Heb. 1:8). Further, it is not necessary to translate Greek nouns that have no definite article with an indefinite article (there is no indefinite article in Greek). In other words, *theos* ("God") without the definite article *ho* ("the") does not need to be translated as "a God" as the Jehovah's Witnesses have done in reference to Christ. It is significant that *theos* without the definite article *ho* is used of Jehovah God in the New Testament. Because the lack of the definite article in Luke 20:38 in reference to Jehovah does not mean he is a lesser God, neither does the lack of the definite article in John 1:1 in reference to Jesus mean he is a lesser God. The fact is, the presence or absence of the definite article does not alter the fundamental meaning of *theos*. If John had intended an adjectival sense (the Word was *godlike* or *divine*—a god) he had an adjective *(theios)* ready at hand that he could have used. Instead, John says the Word is God *(theos)*.

Contrary to the claims of the Watchtower Society, some New Testament texts *do* use the definite article and speak of Christ as "the God" *(ho theos)*. One example of this is John 20:28 where Thomas says to Jesus, "My Lord and my God." The verse reads literally from the Greek: "The Lord of me and the God [*ho theos*] of me" (see also Matt. 1:23 and Heb. 1:8). So it does not matter whether John did or did not use the definite article in John 1:1—the Bible clearly teaches that Jesus is God, not just *a* god.

Greek scholars have thoroughly refuted the Watchtower translation. Dr. Julius Mantey says of the Jehovah's Witnesses' translation of John 1:1, "Ninety-nine percent of the scholars of the world who know Greek and who have helped translate the Bible are in disagreement with the Jehovah's Witnesses" (Mantey, 3:3, 5).

That Jesus is Jehovah *(Yahweh)* is clear from the fact that the New Testament consistently applies to Jesus passages and attributes which in the Old Testament apply only to Jehovah (compare Exod. 3:14 with John 8:58; Isa. 6:1–5 with John 12:41; Isa. 44:24 with Col. 1:16; Ezek. 43:2 with Rev. 1:15; Zech. 12:10 with Rev. 1:7).

JOHN 1:1—Does this verse teach that God is impersonal, as Mary Baker Eddy claimed?

MISINTERPRETATION: Christian Science leader Mary Baker Eddy concluded that the identification of the Word with God in this verse implies that God is an impersonal deity. Eddy said, "This great truth of God's impersonality and individuality . . . is the foundation of Christian Science" (Eddy, 117).

CORRECTING THE MISINTERPRETATION: Affirming that the "Word [*Logos*] is God" in no way implies that God is impersonal. "God" *(theos)* is the same Greek word used of God throughout the New Testament. And God is always presented as a personal being who has a mind (John 10:15), will (John 4:34; 7:17), and feeling (John 4:23). He is a personal being unto whom believers may cry, "Abba," an Aramaic term loosely meaning "daddy" (Mark 14:36; Rom. 8:15; Gal. 4:6).

Second, two of the three characteristics of personality can be found in this very passage. God is manifested as the Word *(Logos)* which means a rational discourse or reason. And God chose by his will to create (John 1:3).

Finally, there is nothing impersonal about the Logos (the Word), for he became flesh (human) and lived among us (John 1:14). He engaged in personal relations with other persons (humans).

JOHN 1:1—Did Jesus preexist only in God's foreknowledge, as some cults claim, or was he really eternal God?

MISINTERPRETATION: According to The Way International founder Paul Wierwille, Jesus was not God.

How was Jesus with God in the beginning? In the same way that the written Word was with Him, namely, in God's foreknowledge. . . . In the Old Testament, Jesus Christ was in God's foreknowledge and in the foreknowledge of God's people as God revealed this prophetic knowledge to them. When Jesus Christ was born, he came into existence. Foreknowledge became a reality. [cited in Martin, 87]

CORRECTING THE MISINTERPRETATION: All the evidence is contrary to Wierwille's conclusion. John asserts that the "Word" (*Logos*) was a *person* (John 1:14), not a mere *idea* in God's mind, as knowledge would be. The text does not say, as Wierwille claims, that "foreknowledge" was in God's mind eternally and that "foreknowledge" became flesh and dwelt among us. It says that the "Word [Christ] was God" (John 1:1) from all eternity—and that this same person (not God's *foreknowledge* of him) "became flesh and dwelt among us" (1:14).

John speaks of Christ "the Word [*Logos*]" being "with God" (1:1) eternally. Knowledge would not be "with" God. God would *have* wisdom, but it would not be *with* him. The word "with" implies *another along side* in an intimate relationship. Christ was another person in the Trinity, not the same person as the Father.

Numerous other verses in the New Testament declare the full deity of Christ (for example, John 20:28; Col. 2:9; Titus 2:13; Heb. 1:8).

JOHN 1:14—Does this verse mean that when Jesus became a human being he lost his deity, as Herbert Armstrong argued?

MISINTERPRETATION: In John 1:14 we read, "And the Word became flesh, and dwelt among us, and we beheld His glory, glory as of the only begotten from the Father, full of grace and truth." Herbert Armstrong, founder of the Worldwide Church of God, took the phrase "the Word *became* flesh" and concluded that it meant "*conversion into* flesh." Christ the Word did not merely assume an additional, human nature; rather, he experienced *metamorphosis* into human flesh. He became *exclusively* human.

CORRECTING THE MISINTERPRETATION: The Old Testament backdrop helps us to understand what John is saying in this important verse. John's choice of words in describing the incarnation is highly revealing. The phrase Jesus "dwelt among us," is more accurately translated "made his dwelling among us" or "pitched his tent [*tabernacle*] among us." In using this terminology, John was drawing heavily from the Old Testament. That Jesus "pitched his tabernacle" among us harkens back to the Old Testament tabernacle of Israel's wilderness wanderings. God's people had been instructed to erect the tabernacle as a reminder that God's dwelling-place was among them. Exodus 25:8 quotes God as saying, "Let them construct a sanctuary for Me, that I may dwell among them" (NASB). Hence, as God formerly dwelt among his people in Old Testament times in the tabernacle that was erected for him, so now in a fuller sense he has taken up residence on earth in a *tabernacle of human flesh.*

Furthermore, John's use of the Greek word *eskēnōsen* ("pitched his tabernacle") becomes even more significant when it is realized that the glory that resulted from the immediate presence of the Lord in the tabernacle came to be associated with the *shekinah,* a word that refers to the radiance, glory, or presence of God dwelling in the midst of his people. When Christ became flesh (John 1:14), the glorious presence of God was fully embodied in him, for he is the true shekinah. The same glory that Moses beheld in the tabernacle in Exodus 40:34–38 was revealed in the person of Jesus Christ on the Mount of Transfiguration (Matthew 17).

What is more, it is critical to recognize that Christ the Logos did not *cease to be* the Logos when he "became flesh." Christ still had the fullness of the shekinah glory in him, but that glory was *veiled* so he could function in the world of humanity. The Word did not cease to be what he was before; but he took on an *additional* nature—a human nature. This is the mystery of the Incarnation: Christ the Logos was *fully God* and *fully human.* The shekinah glory dwelt in the tabernacle of the flesh of Jesus. Of course, while Jesus' human body was, in one sense, a "temple" in which the shekinah glory dwelt, his body was not an *exact parallel* to the Old Testament tabernacle. For, in the Old Testament, God always remained *distinct from* the tabernacle, even though he dwelt *in* the tabernacle. In the New Testament, we learn that Jesus in the incarnation permanently took upon himself a human nature. Hence, Jesus' human body was not a *mere* temple that embodied the shekinah glory, but rather became a very real part of his person as the God-man.

JOHN 2:1–11—Does this passage indicate that Jesus married, as Mormons teach?

MISINTERPRETATION: Mormons believe that the description of the wedding at Cana in Galilee is actually a wedding in which Jesus took a Jewish bride (Van Gorden, 1995, 49).

CORRECTING THE MISINTERPRETATION: The Mormons are reading something into this passage that simply is not there. A simple look at the context indicates that Jesus and his disciples were "invited" to this wedding, so it could not possibly have been his own wedding (see v. 2). Jesus is portrayed, like his disciples, as a *guest* at this wedding, not as a *participant* in it.

Nowhere does the New Testament refer to Jesus having a wife, though it mentions his other relatives (Matt. 13:55–56). At least some of his disciples had wives (Matt. 8:14). The Gospels even record the time Jesus spent with his friends, Lazarus, Mary, and Martha. But there is not one word of any time he spent with a wife. Indeed, he had no home of his own (Luke 9:58).

JOHN 3:3—Does being "born again" indicate that Jesus taught reincarnation?

MISINTERPRETATION: Some cultic groups—including New Agers—cite this verse to support their view that Jesus taught that it was necessary to be reincarnated.

CORRECTING THE MISINTERPRETATION: What Jesus is teaching in this passage is not reincarnation, but regeneration.

The doctrine of reincarnation teaches that, after a person dies, he or she enters another mortal body to live on this earth again. This process repeats itself over and over in a virtually endless cycle of birth, death, and rebirth into yet another mortal body. If Jesus were advocating reincarnation, he should have said, "unless someone is born again and again and again and again. . . ."

The doctrine of reincarnation teaches that people die over and over until they reach perfection (Nirvana). However, the Bible clearly teaches that "it is appointed for men to die *once,* and after this comes judgment" (Heb. 9:27 NASB). Each human being *lives once* as a mortal on earth, *dies once,* and then faces judgment.

In the verses that follow, Jesus explains what he means by being born again. Jesus says, "unless one is born of water and the Spirit, he cannot enter the kingdom of God" (John 3:5). Although there are commentators who differ on exactly what this "water" means (see comments on John 3:5), they are all agreed that it cannot possibly refer to reincarnation. Being born again, then, is being cleansed from our sins, and being given the life of God by the Spirit of God (Rom. 3:21–26; Eph. 2:5; Col. 2:13).

Jesus taught that people decide their eternal destiny in a single lifetime (Matt. 25:46). This is precisely why the apostle Paul emphasized that "now is the day of salvation" (2 Cor. 6:2).

JOHN 3:3—Does the fact that Christians are "born again" mean that God imparts his divine nature into our human spirits, as some Word-Faith teachers suggest?

MISINTERPRETATION: Some Word-Faith teachers say that at the moment of the new birth God imparts his nature into us. When we are born again, God imparts "His very nature, substance, and being to our human spirits" (Hagin, *Word of Faith* January 1978, 3).

CORRECTING THE MISINTERPRETATION: The Word-Faith interpretation of this verse is an example of eisogesis (reading a meaning *into* the text) as opposed to exegesis (deriving the meaning *out of* the text). Scripture clearly views the new birth (Greek: *anōthen*) as a *spiritual* birth. It does not involve a change in essence or nature (i.e., becoming divine) but rather involves impartation of life to a uniquely human spirit by God (2 Cor. 5:17; Titus 3:5). Its spiritual *transformation* transfers a person from the kingdom of darkness to the kingdom of God (Col. 1:13). To belong to God's kingdom, one must be "born" into it. It is critical to realize that, while those who are "born again" become "new creatures" (2 Cor. 5:17), they most certainly *remain creatures*.

For scriptural argumentation against the idea that human beings can become God, see the discussion of Genesis 1:26.

JOHN 3:5—Does this verse indicate that only the "anointed class" are born again and live forever with God in heaven?

MISINTERPRETATION: The Jehovah's Witnesses teach that only the anointed class are born again, not the "other sheep." The new birth is necessary, they say, in order to enter heaven. "The 'other sheep' do not need any such rebirth, for their goal is life everlasting in the restored earthly paradise as subjects of the Kingdom" (*Watchtower,* 15 February 1986, 14).

CORRECTING THE MISINTERPRETATION: First John 5:1a affirms that "*whoever* believes that Jesus is the Christ is born of God" (NASB emphasis added). Hence, being born again cannot be limited to a mere 144,000 people. John 1:12 states, "But as many as received Him, to them He gave the right to become children of God" (NASB). Anyone who exercises faith in Christ is "born again" and is immediately placed into God's eternal family (1 Peter 1:23). The new birth also gives the believer a new capacity and desire to please the Father (2 Cor. 5:17). All who have this give evidence that they are born again (cf. 1 John 2:29; 3:9). See comments on Revelation 7:4.

JOHN 3:5—Does this verse teach that baptism is necessary for salvation?

MISINTERPRETATION: Jesus told Nicodemus that "unless one is born of water and the Spirit, he cannot enter the kingdom of God" (John 3:5 NASB). Certain groups, such as the Mormons, cite this verse as evidence that one must be baptized to be saved (Talmage, 1977, 129).

CORRECTING THE MISINTERPRETATION: Baptism is not necessary for salvation (see comments on Acts 2:38). Salvation is by grace through faith and not by works of righteousness (Eph. 2:8–9; Titus 3:5–6). But baptism is a work of righteousness (see Matt. 3:15). What then did Jesus mean when he referred to being "born of water"? There are three basic ways to understand this, none of which involve baptismal regeneration.

Some believe Jesus is speaking of the *water of the womb,* since he had just mentioned one's "mother's womb" in the preceding verse. If so, then he was saying "unless you are born once by water (at your physical birth) and then again by the 'Spirit' at your spiritual birth, you cannot be saved."

Others take "born of water" to refer to the "washing of *water by the word*" (Eph. 5:26). They note that Peter refers to being born again through the Word of God (1 Peter 1:23), the very thing John is speaking about in these verses (cf. John 3:3, 7).

Still others think that "born of water" refers to the *baptism of John* mentioned (John 1:26). John said he baptized by water for repentance, but Jesus would baptize by the Spirit (Matt. 3:11), saying, "Repent for the kingdom of heaven is at hand" (Matt. 3:2 NASB). If this is what is meant, then when Jesus said they must be "born of water and the Spirit" (John 3:5), he meant that the Jews of his day had to undergo the baptism of repentance by John and also later the baptism of the Holy Spirit before they could "enter the kingdom of God."

JOHN 3:16—Does "only begotten Son" indicate that Jesus Christ is a created being?

MISINTERPRETATION: This verse refers to Jesus as God's "only begotten Son." The Jehovah's Witnesses tell us that Jesus is God's only begotten son in the sense that he was directly created by the hand of God (*Aid to Bible Understanding*, 1971, 918). He is thus a lesser god than God the Father.

CORRECTING THE MISINTERPRETATION: The words *only begotten* do not mean that Christ was created but rather mean "unique" or "one of a kind" (Greek: *monogenēs*). Jesus was uniquely God's son *by nature*—meaning that he has the very nature of God. It is significant that when Jesus claimed to be the Son of God, his Jewish contemporaries understood him to be claiming deity in an unqualified sense and sought to stone him: "We have a law, and according to that law he [Jesus] ought to die, because he made himself out to be the Son of God" (John 19:7 NASB, insert added). They thought Jesus was committing blasphemy because he was claiming deity for himself.

Many evangelicals believe that Christ's sonship is an *eternal* sonship. Evidence for Christ's eternal sonship is found in the fact that he is represented as already the Son of God before his human birth in Bethlehem (John 3:16–17; cf. Prov. 30:4). Hebrews 1:2 says God created the universe *through* his "Son"—implying that Christ was the Son of God prior to the Creation. Moreover, Christ *as* the Son is explicitly said to have existed "before all things" (Col. 1:17; compare with vv. 13–14). As well, Jesus, speaking as the Son of God (John 8:54–56), asserts his eternal preexistence before Abraham (v. 58). Seen in this light, Christ's identity as the Son of God does not connote inferiority or subordination either of essence or position.

JOHN 4:23—Does this verse indicate that only God the Father—and not Jesus—is to be worshiped?

MISINTERPRETATION: John 4:23 says, "An hour is coming, and now is, when the true worshipers shall worship the Father in spirit and truth;

for such people the Father seeks to be His worshipers" (NASB). The Jehovah's Witnesses believe that only the Father is to be worshiped. Christ is to be shown "obeisance" (*Watchtower*, 15 February 1983, 18).

CORRECTING THE MISINTERPRETATION: The same Greek word used for worshiping the Father *(proskuneō)* is used of worshiping Christ in the New Testament. Jesus was worshiped by Thomas (John 20:28), angels (Heb. 1:6), wise men (Matt. 2:11), a leper (Matt. 8:2), a ruler (Matt. 9:18), a blind man (John 9:38), a woman (Matt. 15:25), the women at the tomb (Matt. 28:9), and the disciples (Matt. 28:17). In the Book of Revelation, the worship that the Father receives (4:10) is exactly the same as the worship received by Jesus Christ (5:11–14).

JOHN 5:28–29—Is Jesus advocating salvation by works?

MISINTERPRETATION: Jesus says in John's gospel that the time is coming when people in the graves will hear his voice "and come forth—those who have done good, to the resurrection of life, and those who have done evil, to the resurrection of condemnation" (vv. 28, 29 NKJV). This seems to indicate salvation by works—a common mark of cults, such as the Jehovah's Witnesses and the Mormons (e.g., Smith, 1975, 1:134).

CORRECTING THE MISINTERPRETATION: In the beginning of his gospel, John writes, "But as many as received Him, to them He gave the right to become children of God, even to those who *believe in His name*: who were born, not of blood, nor of the will of the flesh, nor of the will of man, but of God" (John 1:12, 13 NKJV, emphasis added). Jesus says in John 3:16–18 (NKJV),

> For God so loved the world that He gave His only begotten Son, that whoever *believes in Him* should not perish but have eternal life. For God did not send His Son into the world to condemn the world, but that the world through Him might be *saved*. He who *believes in Him* is not condemned; but he who does not believe is condemned already, because he has not *believed in the name* of the only begotten Son of God. [emphasis added]

Furthermore, in John 5:24, Jesus says, "Truly, truly, I say to you, he who hears My word, and *believes* Him who sent Me, has eternal life" (NASB). From these passages it is clear that Jesus did not believe in works salvation.

Jesus' reference to good works in John 5:28–29 is to that which occurs after saving faith. In order to be saved one needs the grace of God (Eph. 2:8–9), but authentic faith expresses itself in good works (v. 10). The apostle Paul in the Book of Romans says something very similar to what Jesus says in John 5:28–29. In Romans Paul says that God "will render to every man according to his deeds: to those who by perseverance in doing good seek for glory and honor and immortality, eternal life; but to those who are selfishly ambitious and do not obey the truth, but obey unrighteousness, wrath and indignation" (Rom. 2:6–8 NASB). But Paul also wrote, "For by grace you have been saved through faith, and that not of yourselves; it is the gift of God" (Eph. 2:8). In the passage in Romans, Paul is not talking about the one who obtains eternal life by faith, but the individual who shows this life in his good works. In Ephesians, Paul is saying that none can save himself by works *prior* to salvation. See also comments on James 2:17–18.

JOHN 5:43—Does this verse indicate that "Jesus" is the "Father's name" (or that Jesus is the Father), as Oneness Pentecostals believe?

MISINTERPRETATION: Jesus affirmed, "I have come in My Father's name, and you do not receive Me" (John 5:43 NASB). Oneness Pentecostals typically interpret "in My Father's name" to mean that Jesus' name *is* the Father's name (i.e., Jesus is the Father) (Campbell, 1975, 43).

CORRECTING THE MISINTERPRETATION: The use of the word *name* in this verse has to do with authority. Whereas many come in their *own* name or authority, Jesus comes not in his own authority but in the authority of the Father. Clearly, then, this verse, far from indicating that Jesus is the Father, in fact points to the *distinction* between the Father and Jesus. *One* comes in the authority of the *other.* See also the discussions of John 10:30 and 14:6–11.

JOHN 6:53a—When Jesus said to "eat his body," was he teaching what the Roman Catholics later called transubstantiation?

MISINTERPRETATION: Jesus said, "Unless you eat the flesh of the Son of Man and drink his blood, you do not have life within you." Roman Catholics use this verse to justify their belief in transubstantiation—the view that the communion elements actually become the physical body and blood of Christ at the moment of consecration. The Council of Trent made this doctrine an official part of Catholic faith that "by the consecration of the bread and wine a conversion takes place of the whole substance of the bread into the substance of the body of Christ our Lord, and of the whole substance of the wine into the substance of His blood. This conversion is appropriately called transubstantiation by the Catholic Church" (Denzinger, no. 877, 267–68).

Roman Catholic authority Ludwig Ott summarizes the argument as follows:

> The necessity of accepting a literal interpretation in this case [of John 6:53] is however evident: a) From the nature of the words used. One specially notes the realistic expressions *alathas brosis* = true, real food (v. 55); *alathas posis* = true, real drink (v. 55); *trogein* = to gnaw, to chew, to eat (v. 54 et seq.). b) From the difficulties created by a figurative interpretation. In the language of the Bible to eat a person's flesh and drink his blood in the metaphorical sense means to persecute him in a bloody fashion, to destroy him. Cf. Ps. 26, 2; Is. 9, 20; 49, 26; Mich. 3, 3. c) From the reactions of the listeners, which Jesus does not correct, as He had done previously in the case of misunderstandings (cf. John 3, 3 et seq.; 4, 32 et seq.; Mt. 16, 6 et seq.). In this case, on the contrary He confirms their literal acceptance of His words at the risk that His Disciples and His Apostles might desert Him (v. 60 et seq.). [Ott, 1960, 374]

CORRECTING THE MISINTERPRETATION: It is not *necessary* to take these phrases physically. Jesus' words need not be taken in the sense of ingesting his actual physical body and blood. Jesus often spoke in metaphors and figures of speech. He called the Pharisees "blind guides" (Matt. 23:16) and Herod a "fox" (Luke 13:32). Roman Catholic scholars do not take these terms literally. Neither do they understand Jesus to be speaking physically when he said, "I am the gate" (John 10:9). There is, therefore, no necessity to take Jesus in a literal, physical way when he said, "this is my body," or, "eat my flesh." Jesus often spoke in graphic parables and figures, as he himself said (Matt. 13:10–11). As we shall see, these can be understood from the context.

It is not even plausible to take Jesus' words physically. The vivid phrases are no proof of their literalness. Jesus used vivid phrases when speaking figuratively. For example, in John 15:1 Jesus said, "I am the true vine." Vividness is no necessary proof of identical meaning. The Psalms are filled with vivid figures of speech. God is depicted as a rock (Ps. 18:2), a bird (Ps. 63:7), a tower (Prov. 18:10), and many other ways. Further, the Bible often uses the language of ingesting in a figurative sense. "O taste and see that the Lord is good" is a case in point (Ps. 34:8 KJV). The apostle John himself was told to eat a scroll (God's Word) in the Apocalypse: "Take and eat it." John did as he was told and said, "When I had eaten it, my stomach turned sour" (Rev. 10:9b, 10

NIV). What could be more vivid? But it referred to his receiving God's Word (the scroll). Even the apostle Peter tells young believers, "Like newborn infants, crave pure spiritual milk" (1 Peter 2:2 NIV). And the writer of Hebrews speaks of "solid food" for mature Christians (5:14) and of others who fell away after they "tasted the heavenly gift" (6:4).

Neither is it necessary, as Catholic scholars suggest, to take "flesh and blood" literally because this phrase was used that way in many places in other contexts. As all biblical scholars know, identical words have different meanings in different contexts. The very word "flesh" *(sarks)*, for example, is used in the New Testament in a spiritual, nonphysical sense of the fallen nature of human beings, such as when Paul said, "I know that in me (that is, in my flesh) nothing good dwells" (Rom. 7:18 NKJV; cf. Gal. 5:17). Meaning is discovered by context, not by whether the same or similar words are used. The same words are used in very different ways in different contexts. Even the word "body" *(soma)*, which means a physical body when used of an individual human being, means the spiritual body of Christ, the church, in other contexts (cf. Eph. 1:22, 23), as both Catholics and Protestants acknowledge.

The fact that some of Jesus' listeners took his words in a physical sense without his explicit and immediate rebuke is not a good argument for several reasons. First of all, Jesus rebuked their understanding, at least implicitly, when he said later in the same discourse, "It is the spirit who gives life; the flesh profits nothing. The words that I speak to you are spirit, and they are life" (John 6:63 NKJV). To borrow a phrase from the apostle Paul, Jesus' words are to be "judged spiritually" (1 Cor. 2:14), not in a gross cannibalistic sense. Further, Jesus did not have to explicitly rebuke it in order for it to be wrong. A literalistic understanding in this context would have been so cannibalistic that no disciple should have expected the Lord to be making such an absurd statement.

Neither is the appeal to an alleged miraculous transformation called for in this context. The only miracle in this connection is the feeding of the 5,000 (John 6:11) which was the occasion for this discourse on the Bread of Life (John 6:35). An appeal to a miracle of transubstantiation here is *Deus ex machina*—that is, it is an unsuccessful attempt to evoke God to keep one's interpretation from collapse.

It is not *possible* to take a physical view. In at least one very important respect it is not physically or theologically possible for an orthodox Christian to hold to a literalistic interpretation of Jesus' words at the last supper, "This is my body." For when Jesus said "this is my body" in reference to the bread in his hand, no apostle present could possibly have understood him to mean that the bread was actually his physical body, *since he was still with them in his physical body, the hands of which were hold-*

ing that very bread. Otherwise, we must believe that Christ was holding his own body in his own hands. This reminds one of the medieval myth of the saint whose head was cut off, yet he put it in his mouth and swam across the river!

Jesus could not have been speaking physically when he said "This is My body" because ever since his incarnation he has always been a human being and also has always dwelt continuously in a human body (except for three days in a grave). Hence, if the bread and the wine he held in his hands at the Last Supper were actually his literal body and blood, then he would have been incarnated in two different places at the same time. But one physical body cannot be in two different locations at the same time. It takes two different bodies to do that. Hence, despite Catholic protest to the contrary, logically transubstantiation would involve two bodies and two incarnations of Christ, which is contrary to the orthodox doctrine of the Incarnation.

JOHN 6:53b—Are Roman Catholics correct in worshiping the "Consecrated Host" in the Mass, or is this a form of idolatry?

MISINTERPRETATION: Since Roman Catholics believe that the communion elements are transformed into the actual body and blood of Christ, it is appropriate to worship the consecrated hosts. The Council of Trent pronounced emphatically that "there is, therefore, no room left for doubt that all the faithful of Christ . . . offer in veneration . . . the worship of *latria* which is due to the true God, to this most Holy Sacrament" (Denzinger, no. 878, 268). The reasoning for this is that since Christ in his human form is God and, therefore, appropriately worshiped (e.g., John 20:28), and since in the Mass the bread and wine are transformed into the actual body and blood of Christ, then there is no reason that this sacrament should not be worshiped as God.

CORRECTING THE MISINTERPRETATION: Many Protestants believe this is a form of idolatry. It involves the worship of something which the God-given senses of every normal human being inform them is a finite creation of God, namely, *bread and wine.* It is to worship God under a physical image a form of worship that is clearly forbidden in the Ten Commandments (Exod. 20:4).

Furthermore, the appeal to some kind of ubiquitous presence of the body of Christ or omnipresence of Christ as God in the host does not resolve the charge of idolatry. That the eucharistic elements are only the "accidental clothing" under which Christ is somehow localized is the same kind of argument by which pagans have justified worshiping stones or statues. God is everywhere-present, including being present in their objects of worship. No animistic pagan really worships the stone but the spirit that animates it.

To claim that the consecrated host is anything but a finite creation undermines the very epistemological basis by which we know anything in the empirical world. It also undermines, indirectly, the historical basis of support for the truth about the incarnate Christ, his death, and resurrection. If the senses cannot be trusted when they experience the communion elements, then the apostles could not have verified Christ's claims to be resurrected. Jesus said, "*Look* at my hands and my feet. It is I myself. *Touch* me, and *see;* a ghost does not have flesh and bones, as you see I have" (Luke 24:39 NIV, emphasis added; cf. John 20:27). John said of Christ that he was "what was from the beginning, what we have *heard*, what we have *seen* with our eyes, what we *beheld* and our hands *handled*" (1 John 1:1 NASB, emphasis added).

A miracle is alleged to occur whenever the priest consecrates the host, but the Mass shows no evidence of the miraculous. To claim that the Mass involves the miraculous when there is *no evidence* for the miraculous makes the normal, natural way of observing things irrelevant. By the same kind of reasoning Roman Catholics use to justify an invisible material substance miraculously replacing the empirically obvious signs of bread and wine, one could justify the belief in Santa Claus at Christmas or that an invisible gremlin moves the hands on a watch. It is literally nonsense. It is not sensible, even though its object is a sensible (i.e., physical) body. Philosophically, it is an empirically unknowable event in the empirical world. And theologically, it is a matter of pure faith. One must simply believe in what the teaching Magisterium says, namely, that the host is really Jesus' body, even though human senses reveal otherwise.

If the Mass is a miracle, then virtually any natural empirical event could also be a miracle. But if this is true, then nothing is a miracle, since nothing is unique. Hence, claiming that the Mass is a miracle undermines the very nature of miracles, at least as special events that have apologetic value.

The appeal of Roman Catholic apologists to special divine appearances (theophanies) in an attempt to avoid these criticisms is futile. For there is a very important difference that they overlook: when God himself appears in a finite form it is an obvious miraculous appearance. One knows clearly that it is not a normal event. There are supernatural manifestations, voices, prophecies, or unusual events of nature connected with it (cf. Exod. 3:1–4:17). The Mass has no such events associated with it. Indeed, nowhere in the New Testament are the normal words for miracle (sign, wonder, or power) used of the communion. There is absolutely no evidence that it is anything but a natural event with natural elements on which Christ places special spiritual blessings as we "remember" his death (1 Cor. 11:25).

JOHN 8:58—Does this verse indicate that Jesus was merely preexistent (as opposed to being *eternally* preexistent)?

MISINTERPRETATION: In John 8:58 (NASB) we read, "Jesus said to them, 'Truly, truly, I say to you, before Abraham was born, I am.'" By contrast, the Jehovah's Witnesses' New World Translation reads, "Jesus said to them: 'Most truly I say to you, Before Abraham came into existence, I have been.'" This indicates that Jesus was preexistent but not *eternally* preexistent (certainly not as the great *I Am* of the Old Testament). "The question of the Jews (verse 57) to which Jesus was replying had to do with age, not identity. Jesus' reply logically dealt with his age, the length of his existence" (*Reasoning from the Scriptures*, 1989, 418).

CORRECTING THE MISINTERPRETATION: Greek scholars agree that the Watchtower Society has no justification for translating *ego eimi* in John 8:58 as "I have been" (a translation that masks its connection to Exodus 3:14 where God reveals his name to be *I Am*). The Watchtower Society once attempted to classify the Greek word *eimi* as a perfect indefinite tense to justify this translation—but Greek scholars have responded by pointing out that there is no such thing as a perfect indefinite tense in the Greek.

The words *ego eimi* occur many times in John's Gospel. Interestingly, the New World Translation elsewhere translates *ego eimi* correctly (as in John 4:26; 6:35, 48, 51; 8:12, 24, 28; 10:7, 11, 14; 11:25; 14:6; 15:1, 5; and 18:5, 6, 8). Only in John 8:58 does the mistranslation occur. The Watchtower Society is motivated to translate this verse differently in order to avoid it appearing that Jesus is the great *I Am* of the Old Testament. Consistency and scholarly integrity calls for John 8:58 to be translated the same way as all the other occurrences of *ego eimi*—that is, as "I am."

Finally, as noted above, *I Am* is the name God revealed to Moses in Exodus 3:14–15. The name conveys the idea of eternal self-existence. *Yahweh* never came into being at a point in time, for he has always existed. To know *Yahweh* is to know the eternal one. It is therefore understandable that when Jesus made the claim to be *I Am*, the Jews immediately picked up stones with the intention of killing Jesus, for they recognized he was implicitly identifying himself as *Yahweh*.

JOHN 8:58—Does this verse indicate that all human beings have the *I Am* presence of God within them?

MISINTERPRETATION: New Agers Mark and Elizabeth Clare Prophet interpret these words of Jesus with a New Age twist, exalting all human beings to the level of God. The Prophets tell us that "Jesus' I AM Presence looks just like yours. This is the common denominator. This is the coequality of the sons and daughters of God. He created you equal in the sense that he gave you an I AM Presence—he gave you a Divine Self" (Prophet, 1990, 83). Similarly, Christian Science founder Mary Baker Eddy said that "by these sayings Jesus meant, not that the human Jesus was or is eternal, but that the divine idea or Christ was and is so and therefore antedated Abraham; not that the corporeal Jesus was one with the Father, but that the spiritual idea, Christ, dwells forever in the bosom of the Father" (Eddy, *Science and Health,* 333–34). Is this a correct understanding of Jesus' claim here?

CORRECTING THE MISINTERPRETATION: John 8:58 cannot be interpreted to mean that all human beings have an "I AM Presence." In this verse, Jesus implicitly and uniquely ascribed the divine name *Yahweh* to himself. The backdrop of this is that *I Am* and *Yahweh* are equated in Exodus 3:14–15. Jesus was here equating himself with the God Almighty as God revealed himself in Exodus 3.

The Jews did not understand Jesus to be teaching that *they too* were identified as *I Am*. Nor did Jesus correct them, and say, "Oh, you misunderstand, for *you too* are *I Am*." Jesus uniquely and exclusively claimed to be the great *I Am* of the Old Testament.

The reaction of the Jewish audience demonstrates that they understood Jesus to be making a unique claim to be deity. For "they took up stones to throw at Him" (v. 59) which was the appropriate reaction for one who "being a man, make Yourself out to be God" (cf. John 10:32–33). See also comments on Matthew 6:33; 24:23–24.

JOHN 9:1—Does this verse support the doctrine of reincarnation, as the Unity School of Christianity teaches?

MISINTERPRETATION: In this passage we read that Jesus healed a man who had been born blind. The Unity School of Christianity teaches that this man was born blind because of the sins he committed in his previous incarnations (Ehrenborg, 77).

CORRECTING THE MISINTERPRETATION: Just the opposite is the case. Jesus' disciples asked him, "Rabbi, who sinned, this man or his parents, that he should be born blind?" (John 9:2 NASB). Jesus answered, "It was neither that this man sinned, nor his parents; but it was in order that the works of God might be displayed in him" (v. 3). If Jesus believed in the law of karma, he wouldn't have said this; rather he would have said that this man was born blind because of sin committed in a previous life.

The disciples who asked Jesus the question did not believe in reincarnation either. The Jewish theologians of that time gave two reasons for birth defects: *prenatal sin* (before birth, *but not* before conception) and *parental sin*. They claimed that when a pregnant woman worshiped in a heathen temple, the fetus committed idolatry as well. They also believed that the sins of the parents were visited upon the children (Exod. 20:5; Ps. 109:14; Isa. 65:6–7). Hence, when they saw this blind man, their assumption was either that his parents had committed some horrendous sin, or perhaps when he was in the womb his mother visited a pagan temple.

The New Testament speaks out clearly against reincarnation, affirming that "man is destined to die once, and after that to face judgment" (Heb. 9:27 NIV). For more arguments against reincarnation and karma, see the discussions of Matthew 22:42 and John 3:3.

JOHN 10:16—Does this verse refer to the "other sheep" who will live forever on a paradise earth?

MISINTERPRETATION: Jehovah's Witnesses say there are two flocks of God's people. "The 'little flock' in one fold will rule with Christ in heaven, and the 'other sheep' in the other fold will live on the Paradise earth" (*The Greatest Man Who Ever Lived,* 1991, section 80).

Mormons believe the "other sheep" mentioned in this verse are displaced Israelites who migrated to America (Smith, 1975, 3:214).

CORRECTING THE MISINTERPRETATION: The "other sheep" in John 10:16 are Gentile believers as opposed to Jewish believers. The lost Jews in the Gospels had been called "the lost sheep of Israel" (Matt. 10:6; 15:24). The Jews who followed Christ were called *his* "sheep" (John 10). When Jesus said "I have *other* sheep, which are not of this

[Jewish] fold" (insert added), he was clearly referring to non-Jewish, Gentile believers. The Gentile believers, along with the Jewish believers, "shall become one flock with one shepherd," not one flock on earth and one flock in heaven (see John 10:16).

JOHN 10:30—Was Christ one with the Father, or "one in purpose" with the Father?

MISINTERPRETATION: Jesus said, "I and the Father are one." The Jehovah's Witnesses do not believe this means that Jesus and the Father are one in essence, having the same divine nature. They point to John 17:21–22 where Jesus prayed to the Father that the disciples "may all be one, just as you, Father, are in union with me and I am in union with you" (New World Translation). "Obviously, Jesus' disciples do not all become part of the Trinity. But they do come to share a oneness of purpose with the Father and the Son, the same sort of oneness that unites God and Christ" (*Reasoning from the Scriptures*, 1989, 424).

CORRECTING THE MISINTERPRETATION: Jesus was one with the Father in *nature*, but distinct from him in *person*. The triune Godhead has one *essence*, but three distinct *persons* (see comments on John 14:28). So, Jesus was both the same in substance and yet was a different individual from the Father.

The context makes it very clear that Jesus is not just referring to being "one in purpose" with the Father. We know this is true because as soon as the Jews heard Jesus say he was "one" with the Father, they immediately picked up stones to put him to death for committing blasphemy. They didn't understand Jesus to be saying he was merely "one in purpose" with the Father (for, indeed, *they* considered *themselves* to be "one in purpose" with the Father). Rather they understood Jesus to be claiming to be God in an unqualified sense. The Jews understood precisely what Jesus intended to communicate.

JOHN 10:30—Does this verse prove that Jesus and the Father are the same Person, as Oneness Pentecostals believe?

MISINTERPRETATION: In John 10:30 Jesus affirmed, "I and the Father are one." Oneness Pentecostals, who deny the doctrine of the Trinity, believe this verse means that Jesus is God the Father (Bernard, 1983, 67).

CORRECTING THE MISINTERPRETATION: When Jesus said "I and the Father are one," he used the first person plural *esmen* ("we are"). If Jesus intended to say that he and the Father were one person, he certainly would not have used the first person plural, which implies *two* persons. Also, the Greek word for "one" (*hen*) in this verse refers *not* to personal unity (i.e., the idea that the Father and Son are one person) but to unity of essence or nature (i.e., that the Father and Son have the same divine nature). This is evident in the fact that the form of the word in the Greek is neuter, not masculine.

Contextually, the verses that immediately precede *and* follow John 10:30 distinguish Jesus from the Father (e.g., John 10:25, 29, 36, 38). It is also the uniform testimony of the rest of John's Gospel (not to mention the rest of the Bible) that the Father and Jesus are distinct persons (within the unity of the one God). For example, the Father *sent* the Son (John 3:16–17); the Father and Son *love* one another (3:35); the Father and Son *speak* to one another (11:41–42); and the Father *knows* the Son just as the Son *knows* the Father (7:29; 8:55; 10:15).

JOHN 10:34—Did Jesus advocate that people could become God?

MISINTERPRETATION: Jesus answered a group of Jews and said, "Is it not written in your law, 'I said, you are gods.'" Does this mean that humans can become God? New Agers tell us that "we can be the God that Jesus proclaimed us to be: 'Ye are Gods'" (Spangler, 1978, 47). Mormons also cite this verse to support their view on the plurality of gods (McConkie, 1977, 24).

CORRECTING THE MISINTERPRETATION: This text should not be used to support the view that we are (or can become) little gods, for such an interpretation is contrary to the overall context. Jesus is not speaking to pantheists (who believe that God is everything and everything is God) or polytheists (who believe in many gods). Rather, he is addressing strict Jewish monotheists who believe that only the Creator of the universe is God. So, his statement should not be wrenched out of this monotheistic context and given a pantheistic or polytheistic twist.

Jesus' statement must be understood as part of his overall reasoning here which is an *a fortiori* argument: "If God even called human judges 'gods,' then how much more can I call myself the Son of God." Christ had just pronounced himself one with the Father, saying, "I and My Father are one" (10:30). The Jews wanted to stone him because they thought Christ was blaspheming, making himself out to be equal with

God (vv. 31–33). Jesus responded by quoting Psalm 82:6 which says, "I said, you are gods." So, Jesus reasoned, if human judges could be called "gods," then why can't the Son of God be called "God"?

Note that not everyone is called "gods" but only a special class of persons, namely, judges about whom Jesus said, they are those to "whom the word of God came" (v. 35). Jesus was showing that if the Old Testament Scriptures could give some divine status to divinely appointed judges, why should they find it incredible that he should call himself the Son of God?

These judges were "gods" in the sense that they stood in God's place, judging even life and death matters. They were not called "gods" because they were divine beings. Indeed, the text Jesus cites (Ps. 82) goes on to say that they were "mere men" and would "die" (v. 7). It also affirms that they were "the sons of the Most High," but not because they were of the essence of God himself.

It is possible, as many scholars believe, that when the psalmist Asaph said to the unjust judges, "You are gods," he was speaking in irony. He was saying, "I have called you 'gods,' but in fact you will die like the men that you really are." If this is so, then when Jesus alluded to this psalm in John 10, he was saying that what the Israelite judges were called *in irony* and *in judgment*, he is *in reality*. Jesus was giving a defense for his own deity, not for the deification of man.

JOHN 11:1–33—Did Jesus have sexual relations with Mary and Martha, as the Children of God cult maintains?

MISINTERPRETATION: Some cults believe that Jesus was married, others that Jesus lived sexually with Mary and Martha. Moses David of the Children of God confessed: "I even believe that he [Jesus] lived with her and Mary and Martha later, which was no sin for Him, because He couldn't commit sin. Everything that he did He did in love, He probably did it for their sakes as much as His own—he had physical needs just like they did" (David, 1977, 4). He adds that Jesus

may have even contracted a disease from Mary Magdalene, who had been a known prostitute, and several other women that were prostitutes that followed him, or Mary and Martha. If so, then He was certainly tempted in all points like as we are, and He bore it for their sakes because they needed His love! Well, if He'd never suffered their sexual diseases, He could never really have full compassion on their sufferings, could He?—to be willing to even contract their disease!—That seemed to me too much. Isn't that something?" [David, 1976, 2–5, 7]

CORRECTING THE MISINTERPRETATION: Not only is such fanciful speculation without the slightest hint of support from this or any other passage of Scripture, it is blasphemous. It is contrary to the impeccable character of Christ. Jesus challenged people, "Can any of you prove me guilty of sin?" (John 8:46 NIV). He "knew no sin" (2 Cor. 5:21) and was "without sin" (Heb. 4:15). He was the "lamb without blemish and without spot" (1 Peter 1:19 KJV).

There is not even the slightest hint in this text that Jesus was romantically attracted to Mary or Martha. He was present in their home as a guest, not as a lover. Jesus was not even alone with these women in their home. Their brother Lazarus was present. When Lazarus died, Jesus met Mary and Martha outside the house (John 11:20, 29).

His "love" for them was one of friendship, not romance. This is evident from the fact that the passage says that "Jesus loved Martha and her sister and Lazarus"—the whole family (John 11:5 NIV).

JOHN 11:11–14—Does this passage prove there is no conscious existence following death, as the Jehovah's Witnesses teach?

MISINTERPRETATION: In John 11:11–14 Jesus said that Lazarus had "fallen asleep"—meaning that he had died. The Jehovah's Witnesses argue that, since death is described as "sleep," this proves there is no conscious existence of the soul following death (*Mankind's Search for God*, 1990, 128).

CORRECTING THE MISINTERPRETATION: Scripture consistently teaches that the souls of both believers and unbelievers are conscious between death and the resurrection. Unbelievers are in conscious woe (Mark 9:43–48; Luke 16:22–23; Rev. 19:20) and believers are in conscious bliss (2 Cor. 5:8; Phil. 1:23).

The term *sleep* when used in contexts of death in Scripture, always refers to the body, not the soul. Sleep is an appropriate figure of speech for the death of the body since the body takes on the appearance of sleep.

For strong evidence that the soul (or spirit) is conscious between death and resurrection, see the discussion of 1 Thessalonians 4:13.

JOHN 11:49–52—Does this text support the Catholic claim for papal infallibility?

MISINTERPRETATION: Some Catholic scholars claim that since the high priest in the Old Testament had an official revelatory function connected with his office, it is to be expected that there be an equivalent in the New Testament, the Pope. Catholics use this passage about the Jewish high priest exercising authority to substantiate their claim. Is this a correct interpretation?

CORRECTING THE MISINTERPRETATION: Roman Catholics are making an argument from analogy that is not based on any New Testament affirmation. The Catholic view cannot be derived from any proper exegesis of the text. The New Testament explicitly says that the Old Testament priesthood has been abolished. The writer to the Hebrews declared that "there is a change of priesthood" from that of Aaron (Heb. 7:12). The Aaronic priesthood has been fulfilled in Christ, who is a priest forever after the order of Melchizedek (vv. 15–17).

Even Catholics acknowledge that there is no new revelation after the time of the New Testament. So no one after the first century (Popes included) can have a revelatory function in the sense of giving new revelations. There is a New Testament revelatory function in the apostles and prophets (cf. Eph. 2:20; 3:5). But their revelation ceased when they died. To assume that a revelatory function was passed on after them and is resident in the Bishop of Rome is to beg the question.

JOHN 14:6–11—Does this passage prove that Jesus is God the Father, as Oneness Pentecostals believe?

MISINTERPRETATION: In this extended passage Jesus said, "If you had known Me, you would have known My Father also. . . . He who has seen Me has seen the Father. . . . Do you not believe that I am in the Father, and the Father is in Me?. . . . Believe Me that I am in the Father, and the Father in Me" (John 14:6–11 NASB). Oneness Pentecostals believe these verses prove beyond any doubt that Jesus is God the Father (Bernard, 1983, 68).

CORRECTING THE MISINTERPRETATION: These verses prove only that the Father and the Son are one in *being*, not that they are one *person* (see the discussion of John 10:30). In John 14:6 Jesus clearly distinguishes himself from the Father when he says, "No one comes *to* the Father, but *through* Me" (emphasis added). The words *to* and *through* would not make any sense if Jesus and the Father were one and the same person. They only make sense if the Father and Jesus are distinct persons, with Jesus being the Mediator between the Father and humankind.

When Jesus said, "He who has seen Me has seen the Father" (John 14:9), he wasn't saying he *was* the Father. Rather, Jesus is the perfect revelation of the Father (cf. John 1:18). And the reason Jesus is the perfect revelation of the Father is that Jesus and the Father, along with the Holy Spirit, are one, indivisible divine Being (John 10:30). This is in keeping with a proper definition of the Trinity: There is only one God, but within the unity of the Godhead there are three coequal and coeternal persons who are equal in substance but distinct in subsistence. Jesus, the second person of the Trinity, is the perfect revelation of the Father, the first person of the Trinity.

The Oneness Pentecostal belief that Jesus' statement "the Father is in Me" means that deity ("Father") dwells in the humanity ("Son") of Jesus is clearly faulty. According to this logic, Jesus' statement that "I am in the Father" would have to mean that the human nature of Jesus dwells in deity, which no Oneness Pentecostal believes.

JOHN 14:8–9—Does this passage support pantheism?

MISINTERPRETATION: New Agers believe that certain sayings of Jesus in the Bible teach pantheism. For example, in John 14:8–9 Jesus said to Philip, "Anyone who has seen me has seen the Father. . . . Don't you believe that I am in the Father, and that the Father is in me?" (NIV). Jesus was here teaching that God permeates all things (Besant, 1966, 30, 35, 36, 37).

CORRECTING THE MISINTERPRETATION: John 14:8–9 proves *only* that Jesus is the perfect revelation of the Father. Jesus—as eternal God—took on human flesh so he could be God's fullest revelation (Heb. 1:2–3). Jesus was a revelation of God not just in his person (as God) but in his life and teachings as well. By observing the things Jesus *did* and the things Jesus *said*, we learn a great deal about God.

Furthermore, God's awesome power was revealed in Jesus (John 3:2). God's incredible wisdom was revealed in Jesus (1 Cor. 1:24). God's boundless love was revealed and demonstrated by Jesus (1 John 3:16). God's unfathomable grace was revealed in Jesus (2 Thess. 1:12). Verses such as these serve as the backdrop as to why Jesus told a group of Pharisees, "When a man believes in me, he does not believe in me only, but in the one who sent me" (John 12:44 NIV). Jesus likewise told Philip that "anyone who has seen me has seen the Father" (John 14:9). Jesus was the ultimate revelation of God.

Jesus didn't teach the impersonal pantheistic God of the New Age, but rather taught a personal Creator-God with whom one can enter into a relationship (Matt. 17:5; Mark 1:11; Luke 2:49; John 16:32; 17:5). The biblical idea of God involves a loving personal Father unto whom believers may cry, "Abba" (which can loosely be translated "daddy") Mark 14:36; Rom. 8:15; Gal. 4:6). Moreover, the God of the Bible is distinct from the creation (Eccles. 5:2; cf. Gen. 1:1; Neh. 9:6; Ps. 33:8–9; 148:5).

If Jesus was an "enlightened teacher" who taught pantheism, as New Agers say, he was a lousy teacher, for all who followed him ended up being not pantheists but theists who believed in a personal Creator-God.

JOHN 14:16—Are Muslims right in referring this promise of the coming "Helper" to Muhammad?

MISINTERPRETATION: Muslim scholars see in this reference of the promised "Helper" (Greek, *paraclete*) a prediction of Muhammad, because the Qur'an (Sura 61:6) refers to Muhammad as *"Ahmad" (periclytos)*, which Muslims take to be the correct rendering of "paraclete."

CORRECTING THE MISINTERPRETATION: There are absolutely no grounds for concluding the "Helper" *(paraclete)* Jesus mentioned here is Muhammad.

Of the 5,366 Greek manuscripts of the New Testament, not a single manuscript contains the word *periclytos* ("praised one"), as the Muslims claim it should read.

Jesus clearly identifies the Helper as being the Holy Spirit, not Muhammad. Jesus refers to "the Helper, the Holy Spirit, whom the Father will send" (John 14:26).

The Helper was given to Christ's disciples ("you," v. 16), but Muhammad was not. And the Helper was to abide with them "forever" (v. 16), but Muhammad has been dead for thirteen centuries. Jesus said to the disciples, "You know him [the Helper]" (v. 17), but they did not know Muhammad. He wasn't even born for six more centuries.

Jesus told his apostles, the Helper will be "in you" (v. 17). In no sense was Muhammad "in" Jesus' apostles. The Helper would be sent "in my [Jesus'] name" (John 14:26). But no Muslim believes Muhammad was sent by Jesus in his name. The Helper Jesus would send would not "speak on his own authority" (John 16:13), whereas Muhammad constantly testifies to himself in the Qur'an (cf. Sura 33:40). The Helper would "glorify" Jesus (John 16:14), but Muhammad claims to supersede Jesus as later prophet.

Finally, Jesus asserted that the Helper would come in "not many days" (Acts 1:5), whereas Muhammad did not come for 600 years.

JOHN 14:16—Does this text support the claim of Christian Scientists that it refers to "Divine Science"?

MISINTERPRETATION: Mary Baker Eddy once boasted, "This Comforter I understand to be Divine Science [Christian Science]" which she founded. She also claimed that "when the Science of Christianity appears, it will lead you into all truth" (Eddy, 55, 271).

CORRECTING THE MISINTERPRETATION: It is clear from both the words of Jesus here and the context that he was not referring to Mary Baker Eddy or her "Divine Science." First of all, Jesus refers to the Comforter (or Helper) as "he"—not "she" (as Mary Baker Eddy was) or "it" as Divine Science is. Jesus identified the Helper as the "Spirit of truth" in the very next verse. A little later the Helper is called "the Holy Spirit" (v. 26) who is identified with the Father and the Son in the Holy Trinity (Matt. 28:19; 2 Cor. 13:14). There is absolutely no evidence that the Helper is anyone but God the Holy Spirit.

JOHN 14:18—Does this verse prove that Jesus is God the Father, as Oneness Pentecostals believe?

MISINTERPRETATION: In John 14:18 Jesus affirmed to his disciples, "I will not leave you as orphans; I will come to you" (NIV). Oneness Pentecostals argue that since Jesus himself said he would not leave his disciples as "orphans," Jesus must be their Father (see Haywood, n.d., 17). Does this verse prove that Jesus is the Father?

CORRECTING THE MISINTERPRETATION: The Oneness Pentecostal interpretation of this verse confuses *action* with *identity*. Christ *in action* functions as a divine parent-figure who guides, nurtures, protects, and leads his disciples. But this doesn't mean that Christ *in identity* is the Father. The apostle John speaks of the recipients of his first epistle as "my little children" (2:1), "little children" (v. 12), and "children" (v. 18) but this does not mean that John was claiming to be God the Father. Neither is Christ "the Father" simply because he watches after his disciples and doesn't leave them without his Spirit.

The uniform testimony of Scripture is that the Father and Son are distinct persons within the unity of the one God. See the discussion of Matthew 28:19.

JOHN 14:28—Did Jesus think of himself as less than God?

MISINTERPRETATION: Jesus said in John 14:28, "The Father is greater than I." The Jehovah's Witnesses say this verse proves that Jesus is a lesser god than the Father. Because Jehovah is "greater" than Jesus, Jesus cannot be God Almighty (*Let God Be True*, 1946, 110).

According to Christian Science, this verse proves that "Christ is not God, but an impartation of Him," just as "one ray of light is light, and it is one with light, but it is not the full-orbed sun" (Eddy, 1901, 8).

CORRECTING THE MISINTERPRETATION: The Father is greater than the Son *by office*, but not *by nature*, since both are God (see John 1:1; 8:58; 10:30; 20:28). Just as an earthly father is equally human with but holds a higher office than his son, even so the Father and the Son in the Trinity are equal in *essence*, but different in *function*. There is no contradiction in affirming ontological equality and functional hierarchy. In like manner, we speak of the President of our country as being greater, not by virtue of his *character or nature*, but by virtue of his *position*. Jesus cannot ever be said to say that he considered himself anything less than God by nature. The following summary helps to crystallize the differences:

Jesus Equal to the Father	Jesus Is Less Than the Father
In essence	In function
In nature	In office
In character	In position
As God	As man

JOHN 15:8—Is soul-winning a necessary sign of fruit-bearing, as the authoritarian discipleship movement claims?

MISINTERPRETATION: "By this My Father is glorified, that you bear much fruit, and so prove to be My disciples" (John 15:8 NASB). In the

Boston Church of Christ movement, people are accused of being unfruit-ful unless they personally bring others to Christ.

CORRECTING THE MISINTERPRETATION: This verse says noth-ing about winning souls. That may be included in fruit-bearing, but it is not stated as *the evidence* of fruit-bearing here or anywhere else in the Bible. There are many gifts in the body (Rom. 12; 1 Cor. 12; Eph. 4). Evangelism is only one of them, and only some people have it (Eph. 4:11). Likewise, "fruit" is far broader than evangelism. According to Galatians 5:22–23, "the fruit of the Spirit is love, joy, peace, patience, kindness, goodness, faithfulness, gentleness and self-control." In fact, spiritual fruit is anything that brings glory to God (cf. 1 Cor. 10:31).

JOHN 15:12—Does God's command to "Love one another" support the "open sex" views of the Children of God?

MISINTERPRETATION: In John 15:12 we are instructed, "This is My commandment, that you love one another, just as I have loved you." The Children of God, now known as "The Family," have said that the command to "love one another" supports engaging in open sex with one another outside the marriage relationship.

CORRECTING THE MISINTERPRETATION: This is a preposter-ous twisting of Scripture. This verse teaches us to love one another in the sense of *caring for* and *nurturing* one another. The standard of our love for one another is Jesus Christ himself. Certainly the love that Jesus expressed toward his followers was not sexual in nature but rather involved care and nurture. In the same way, our love for our Christian brothers and sisters is to be one of care and nurturing.

It is noteworthy that the Greek word for "love" in John 15:12 is *aga-paō*. This word is often used of God's love for man. This benevolent, self-sacrificing kind of love that seeks the highest good and optimal wel-fare of the one loved finds its highest expression in Jesus Christ. *Aga-paō* love has nothing to do with sexuality. If Jesus had intended to com-municate the idea of sexual love in this verse, a different Greek word, *eros,* was available. He purposefully chose *agapaō* to communicate the idea of caring and nurturing.

Scripture is consistent in its emphasis that sexual intercourse in a rela-tionship can only be engaged in within the confines of marriage (1 Cor. 7:2). The apostles urged all Christians to abstain from fornication (Acts 15:20). Paul said that the body is not for fornication and that a man should flee it (1 Cor. 6:13, 18). The Ephesians were told that fornication should not even be spoken of (5:3). Adultery is also condemned in Scripture: "You shall not commit adultery" (Exod. 20:14). In the Old Testament the adulterers were to be put to death (Lev. 20:10). The New Testament is also emphatically against adultery. Jesus pronounced it wrong even in its basic motives (Matt. 5:27–28). Paul called it an evil work of the flesh (Gal. 5:19), and John envisioned in the lake of fire some of those who practiced it (Rev. 21:8).

Sexual expression of intimacy within marriage, however, is good (see Gen. 2:24; Matt. 19:5; 1 Cor. 6:16; Eph. 5:31). Sexuality was a part of God's "good" creation. Indeed, God created maleness and femaleness in body and mind, and "everything created by God is good" (1 Tim. 4:4). But sexual intercourse is good only within the confines of the marriage covenant, which God himself ordained (see Heb. 13:4).

JOHN 16:12–13—Did Jesus predict the coming of Bahā'u'llāh, as the Baha'is say?

MISINTERPRETATION: Members of the Baha'i Faith believe each age needs updated revelation from God. Jesus was one among many prophets. He communicated revelation from God specifically for his age. However, the greatest of the prophets is Bahā'u'llāh (1817–1892). And John 16:12–13 is said to be a prophecy of him. Bahā'u'llāh is interpreted to be the "Spirit of truth" who has come to guide us into all truth (Effendi, 1955, 93–96).

CORRECTING THE MISINTERPRETATION: Jesus clearly identifies the Spirit of truth as being the Holy Spirit (John 14:16–17, 26), not Bahā'u'llāh. Furthermore, Jesus said almost 2000 years ago that his promise of the Holy Spirit would be fulfilled "in a few days" (Acts 1:5), not in the 1800s (when the Baha'i Faith was founded). Indeed, the fulfillment came in Acts 2 on the day of Pentecost.

Jesus also said the Holy Spirit would make known his teaching, not replace it with the teaching of another prophet (John 16:14). And the Holy Spirit would "be with you forever" (John 14:16). Bahā'u'llāh lived a mere 75 years. This hardly constitutes "forever."

JOHN 16:24—Does this verse mean we can obtain anything we want if we ask for it in the name of Jesus, as Word-Faith teachers suggest?

MISINTERPRETATION: In John 16:24 Jesus said, "Until now you have asked for nothing in My name; ask, and you will receive, that your joy may be made full" (NASB). Some Word-Faith teachers say this verse means that we can obtain virtually anything we want if we ask for it in the name of Jesus. In his book *The Name of Jesus*, Kenneth Hagin claimed, "I have not prayed one prayer in 45 years . . . without getting an answer. I always got an answer—and the answer was always yes" (1981, 16).

CORRECTING THE MISINTERPRETATION: Hagin and other Word-Faith teachers cite this verse in isolation from other verses that qualify Jesus' intended meaning. In John 15:7, for example, Jesus said, "If you abide in Me, and My words abide in you, ask whatever you wish, and it shall be done for you" (NASB). Here *abiding* is a clear condition for receiving answers to prayer. We are also told that "whatever we ask we receive from Him, because we keep His commandments and do the things that are pleasing in His sight" (1 John 3:22 NASB). "This is the confidence which we have before Him, that, if we ask anything *according to His will*, He hears us. And if we know that He hears us in whatever we ask, we know that we have the requests which we have asked from Him" (1 John 5:14–15 NASB, emphasis added). Finally, we are told that if we ask for something with *wrong motives* we won't receive what we asked for (James 4:3). These are important qualifications to keep in mind when seeking to understand what Jesus meant in John 16:24. The verse is certainly not a magic formula, as Word-Faith teachers portray it.

JOHN 17:20–21—Did Jesus' prayer "that they all may be one" intend the visible hierarchical unity expressed in the Roman Catholic Church?

MISINTERPRETATION: Catholic scholars believe that the unity of faith "consists in the fact that all members of the Church inwardly believe the truths of faith proposed by the teaching office of the [Roman Catholic] Church, at least implicitly and outwardly confess them." This unity "consists, on the one hand, in the subjection of the members of the Church to the authority of the bishops and of the Pope (unity of government or hierarchical unity); on the other hand, in the binding of the members among themselves to a social unity by participation in the same cult and in the same means of grace (unity of cult or liturgical unity)" (Ott, 1960, 303).

CORRECTING THE MISINTERPRETATION: When Jesus spoke of all believers being "one" in John 17, he was not speaking about *organizational* unity but *organic* unity. Jesus was not referring to an *external uniformity* but to the visible manifestation of our *spiritual unity*, for example, in our love for one another, which Jesus said unbelievers can detect (John 13:35). That the unity was truly spiritual is evident in what was said of early Christians: "Behold, how they love one another!" Christ's true followers are one in faith, hope, and love. But they are not one in denomination, synod, or jurisdiction.

Even though the immediate discussion in Jesus' prayer is a visible unity of the church, it is clear that Jesus did not envision this as organizational unity, such as that claimed by the Roman See. No such governmental unity is mentioned anywhere in the passage. Jesus is speaking of "all those who will believe" in him in the future too, including those who couldn't be seen (v. 20), which is a description of the whole spiritual body of believers, not simply the organized believers on earth. The unity for which he prayed is compared to that among the persons of the Godhead ("as you, Father, are in me and I in you"), a unity that is clearly spiritual and invisible, not visible and organizational. The primary sense in which the world was to observe the manifestation of this unity was by "love" (v. 23), a spiritual tie, not an organizational one. Indeed, Jesus said, "By this all men will know that you are my disciples, if you love one another" (John 13:35 NIV). So clearly the kind of unity envisioned here is not a visible organization, as Catholics claim, but a true spiritual unity.

JOHN 19:26–27—Did Jesus' statement about Mary from the cross confer on her the role of "Meatrix" in redemption, as Catholic scholars believe?

MISINTERPRETATION: Jesus said to his mother from the cross, "'Dear woman, here is your son,' and to the disciple, 'Here is your mother'" (John 19:26b–27a). Largely on the basis of this passage Mary has earned the role of "meatrix" and "coredemptrix" (or "coredemptress") (Ott, 1960, 212). Catholics insist that this "must not be conceived in the sense of an equation of the efficacy of Mary with the redemptive activity of Christ, the sole Redeemer of humanity" (1 Tim. 2:5). For "she herself required redemption and was redeemed by Christ" (Ibid.). Nonetheless, Catholic scholars point out, "In the power of the grace of Redemption merited by Christ, Mary, by her spiritual entering into the sacrifice of her Divine son for men, made atonement for the sins of men, and *(de congruo)* merited the application of the redemptive grace of

Christ. In this manner she co-operates in the subjective redemption of mankind" (Ibid., 213).

Mary's role as meatrix is described this way:

> Theologians seek a biblical foundation in the words of Christ, John 19:26 *et seq.*: 'Woman behold thy son, son behold thy mother'. . . . The mystical interpretation . . . sees in John the representative of the whole human race. In him Mary was given as the spiritual mother of the whole of redeemed humanity that she, by her powerful intercession, should procure for her children in need of help all graces by which they can attain eternal salvation. [Ott, 214]

CORRECTING THE MISINTERPRETATION: The scriptural evidence for calling Mary a mediator or coredemptrix is totally lacking. For one thing, the context itself provides the meaning of Jesus' statement. It adds, "From that time on, this disciple took her into his home" (John 19:27). Jesus as the oldest (Catholics say "only") son was dying and committed his mother to the care of John, the only apostle standing at the cross.

For another thing, even a classic Roman Catholic authority on Catholic dogma confesses: "Express scriptural proofs are lacking." He says merely that "theologians *seek* a biblical foundation" (Ibid., 214) in a "mystical" interpretation of John 19:26. But such an interpretation is far removed from the actual meaning of the text and by virtue of its implausible nature only weakens the case for the doctrine. Indeed, the clear meaning of many passages of Scripture declare that there is only "one mediator between God and man, the man Christ Jesus" (1 Tim. 2:5 NIV; cf. John 10:1, 9–11; 14:6; Heb. 1:2–3; 10:12).

The Catholic claim that the word "one" *(monos)* in 1 Timothy 2:5 does not mean *only* one *(eis)* is a false disjunction. Obviously, the apostle Paul intended to convey here that there is *only one God* and *only one mediator* between God and man. There are other human intercessors to God on earth (2:1–4), but only one Mediator between humans and God. For if *monos* does not mean only one, then the apostle leaves open the door for polytheism too, since the construction applies equally to God.

There is an inherent dilemma in Catholic Mariology. Catholic theology admits that everything we need as believers we can get from Christ. Yet many Catholic theologians have exalted the role of Mary as the dispenser of all grace. Either the role of Mary is superfluous or Christ's mediation is diminished. The only way out of the dilemma is to hold, as Protestants do, that Mary "dispenses" no grace at all. Mary, as the earthly mother of Jesus, was the *channel* through whom God's grace entered the world. But Mary is not now in heaven the *dispenser* of God's grace to us.

JOHN 20:17—Does this verse prove that Jesus is not God Almighty?

MISINTERPRETATION: John 20:17 quotes Jesus as saying to Mary, "Stop clinging to Me, for I have not yet ascended to the Father; but go to My brethren, and say to them, 'I ascend to My Father and your Father, and My God and your God'" (NIV). The Jehovah's Witnesses say that since Jesus had a God, his Father, he could not at the same time *be* that God (*Reasoning from the Scriptures,* 1989, 212, 411).

CORRECTING THE MISINTERPRETATION: Prior to the incarnation, Christ had only a divine nature (John 1:1). But in the incarnation (John 1:14) Christ took on a human nature. In his humanity (Phil. 2:6–8) it was proper that Christ acknowledge the Father as "my God." After all, Jesus was "made like His brethren in all things" (Heb. 2:17). As a human Jesus acknowledges God as do all other humans. However, Jesus in his divine nature could never refer to the Father as "my God," for Jesus was fully equal to the Father in every way regarding his divine nature (John 10:30).

JOHN 20:19—How could Jesus walk through a closed door with a physical body?

See comments on Luke 24:31, 34; 1 Corinthians 15:5–8.

JOHN 20:22–23—Does this text support the Roman Catholic claim that its priests have the power to forgive sins?

MISINTERPRETATION: On the basis of this text, Roman Catholics hold that "the Church has received from Christ the power of remitting sins committed after Baptism" (Ott, 1960, 417). And "with these words Jesus transferred to the Apostles the mission which He Himself had received from the Father. . . . As He Himself had forgiven sins on earth (Mt. 9, 2 et seq.; Mark 2, 5 . . .), He now invested the Apostles also with the power to forgive sins" (Ibid., 419). Catholics believe that this unique power to forgive sins has been passed on to Roman Catholic priests today.

CORRECTING THE MISINTERPRETATION: There is no dispute that the apostles were given the power to pronounce the forgiveness and/or retaining of sins. However, the Catholic claim that this is a spe-

cial power possessed only by those ordained under true apostolic authority—such as that allegedly held by the Roman Catholic church, and who
are true successors of the apostles—is not supported by this text.

No claim is made anywhere in the text that only validly ordained
priests in the line of apostolic authority, such as is claimed for Roman
Catholic priests (along with clergy in Eastern Orthodox, Old Catholic,
and some Anglican communions) were to alone possess this power.

All the early believers, including laypersons, proclaimed the gospel
by which sins are forgiven (Rom. 1:16; 1 Cor. 15:1–4). This ministry
of forgiveness and reconciliation was not limited to any special class
known as "priests" or "clergy" (2 Cor. 3–5). Philip, who was a deacon
(Acts 6:5), not an elder or priest in the Roman Catholic sense, preached
the gospel to the Samaritans. This resulted in the conversion of many
of them (8:1–12), which involved the forgiveness of their sins. The apostles later came, not to convert them, but to give them the special "gift
of the Holy Spirit" (2:38; 8:18) and an outward manifestation of speaking in tongues (cf. 2:1–4) that accompanied this special gift (cf. 1:5;
2:38; 10:44–46).

This passage in John is parallel to the Great Commission in which Jesus
instructed all his disciples to take the gospel into all the world and make
disciples of them (Matt. 28:18–20; Mark 16:15–16; Luke 24:46–49). In
this mandate to evangelize Jesus promised, as he did here in John, that they
would "preach the gospel" (Mark 16:15) which would result "in the forgiveness of sins" (Luke 24:47) for those who believe, and that by his Spirit
he would be with them to the end of the age (Matt. 28:20). All three of
these aspects find a parallel in John, where we find Jesus giving them the
Holy "Spirit" (John 20:22), charging them to proclaim the "forgiveness
of sins" (John 20:23), and commissioning them to go on their mission on
the authority of the Father: "As the Father has sent me, I am sending you"
(John 20:21 NIV). So, on more careful examination, there is no greater
power given here than that all the disciples possessed as a result of the Great
Commission which, even as Vatican II acknowledged, is the obligation of
all Christians to help fulfill (*The Documents of Vatican II*, section 120).

In short, contrary to Roman Catholic claims, there is nothing in John
20:21–23 to support either the primacy or infallibility of the bishop of
Rome, nor any special priestly power. It is simply an affirmation about
Jesus giving to his disciples the ability to pronounce the forgiveness of
sins for all who believe the message the apostles were commissioned to
proclaim.

JOHN 20:28—Does this verse support the deity of Christ?

MISINTERPRETATION: When doubting Thomas saw the risen Christ, he said, "My Lord and my God!" Jehovah's Witnesses reinterpret this verse in a way to avoid making it appear that Christ is God. They say Thomas may have been expressing surprise at seeing Jesus—something like, "My God!" (*Should You Believe in the Trinity?* 1989, 29).

CORRECTING THE MISINTERPRETATION: Thomas couldn't have been expressing mere surprise at seeing Jesus. If Thomas said "My Lord and My God" as a gesture of surprise, Jesus would have rebuked him for taking God's name in vain. Instead of rebuking Thomas, Jesus commended him for recognizing his true identity as "Lord" and "God" (v. 29). The acknowledgment of Jesus as God is consistent with what we're told elsewhere in John's Gospel about Jesus (see John 1:1; 8:58; 10:30). In fact, it is the culmination of the very theme of the Gospel of John (cf. 20:31).

JOHN 21:15–19—Does this passage support the Roman Catholic claim that Peter was the first Pope?

MISINTERPRETATION: In this text Jesus says to Peter, "Feed my lambs" and "tend my sheep" and "feed my sheep" (vv. 15, 16, 17). Roman Catholic scholars believe this shows that Peter *alone* was given infallible authority to be *the* pastor of the whole Christian church.

CORRECTING THE MISINTERPRETATION: A careful examination of the text reveals that Catholics make a serious overclaim for the passage. Whether this text is taken of Peter alone or of all the disciples, there is absolutely no reference here to any infallible authority. A matter of pastoral care concerns Jesus here. Feeding is a God-given pastoral function that even nonapostles had in the New Testament (cf. Acts 20:28; Eph. 4:11–12; 1 Peter 5:1–2). One does not have to be an infallible shepherd to feed his flock properly.

If Peter had infallibility (the ability not to mislead), then why did he mislead believers and have to be rebuked by the apostle Paul for so doing (Gal. 2:11–21)? The infallible Scriptures, accepted by Roman Catholics, declared of Peter on one occasion, "he clearly was wrong" and "stood condemned" (v. 11). Peter "acted hypocritically . . . with the result that even Barnabas was carried away by their hypocrisy" (v. 13). And hypocrisy here is defined by the Catholic New American Bible (NAB) as "pretense, play-acting; moral insincerity." It seems difficult to exonerate Peter from the charge that he led believers astray—something hard to reconcile with the Catholic claim that Peter was an infallible pastor of the church.

The Catholic response—that Peter was not infallible in his actions, but only his *ex cathedra* words, rings hollow when we remember that actions are the domain of morals, and the Pope is alleged to be infallible in Faith *and Morals*. In view of this, even the Roman Catholic admission of the despicable behavior of some of its popes is highly revealing. The fact is that Peter cannot be both an infallible guide for Faith and Morals *and* at the same time mislead other believers on an important matter of faith and morals, of which Galatians speaks.

Contrary to the Catholic claim, the overall import of this passage speaks more to Peter's weakness and need of restoration than to his unique powers. The reason Peter is singled out for restoration, being asked three times by Jesus "Do you love me more than these?" (other disciples), was that only Peter denied the Lord three times and so only Peter needed to be restored. Thus Jesus was not exalting Peter above the other apostles here but bringing him up to their level.

In view of the New Testament titles used of Peter, it is clear that he would never have accepted the terms used of the Roman Catholic Pope today: "Holy Father" (cf. Matt. 23:9) or "Supreme Pontiff" and "Vicar of Christ." The only Vicar of Christ on earth today is the blessed Holy Spirit (John 14:16, 26; 16:13–14). As noted earlier, Peter referred to himself in much more humble terms as "*an* apostle," not *the* apostle (1 Peter 1:1, emphasis added) and "*fellow*-presbyter [elder]" (1 Peter 5:1, emphasis added), not the Supreme Bishop, the Pope, or the Holy Father.

ACTS

ACTS 1:9–11—Does this verse prove that the Second Coming of Christ will be an invisible event?

MISINTERPRETATION: At the ascension, several disciples witnessed Christ vanishing into the clouds. Then some angels told the disciples that Christ at the second coming "will come in just the same way as you have watched him go into heaven" (Acts 1:9–11 NASB)—that is, he disappeared from view. The Jehovah's Witnesses say this passage indicates that the second coming will be an invisible event (*Reasoning from the Scriptures,* 1989, 243).

CORRECTING THE MISINTERPRETATION: Jesus ascended *bodily* and *visibly,* as witnessed by the disciples (v. 9). He disappeared from view only *after* he had bodily and visibly ascended ("a cloud received Him out of their sight"). In the same way, Christ will come again *bodily* and *visibly* (v. 11). A bodily and visible second coming is the consistent teaching of Scripture. For example, Revelation 1:7 says, "Behold, He is coming with the clouds, and every eye will see Him, even those who pierced Him; and all the tribes of the earth will mourn over Him. Even so. Amen" (NASB). Matthew 24:30 says, "And then the sign of the Son of Man will appear in the sky, and then all the tribes of the earth will mourn, and they will see the Son of Man coming on the clouds of the sky with power and great glory" (NASB).

ACTS 2:4—Does the fact that the Holy Spirit "filled" the disciples prove that he is not a person?

MISINTERPRETATION: This verse says the disciples were filled with the Holy Spirit. The Jehovah's Witnesses reason, "A comparison of Bible texts that refer to the holy spirit shows that it is spoken of as 'filling' people." This expression would not "be appropriate if the holy spirit were a person" (*Reasoning from the Scriptures,* 1989, 380).

CORRECTING THE MISINTERPRETATION: Ephesians 3:19 makes reference to being filled with God himself. Ephesians 4:10 speaks of Christ filling all things. Since these verses do not disprove the personhood of God and Christ, so Acts 2:4 does not disprove the personhood of the Holy Spirit.

The Holy Spirit's personhood is the testimony of Scripture. The Holy Spirit has the essential attributes of personality—mind (1 Cor. 2:11), emotions (Eph. 4:30), and will (1 Cor. 12:11). He does things only a person can do—such as teaching (John 14:26), testifying (John 15:26), guiding (Rom. 8:14), commissioning (Acts 13:4), issuing commands (Acts 8:29), praying (Rom. 8:26), and speaking to people (2 Peter 1:21). He is also treated as a person. For example, he can be lied to (Acts 5:3). One does not lie to a mere power or force.

ACTS 2:38—Did Peter declare that baptism was necessary for salvation?

MISINTERPRETATION: Mormons often cite this verse as a proof that one must be baptized to receive forgiveness of sins and be saved (Talmage, 1977, 122). Oneness Pentecostals also cite this verse in support of their view of baptismal regeneration (Bernard, 1984, 170–80).

CORRECTING THE MISINTERPRETATION: What Peter means here becomes clear when we consider the possible meaning of being baptized "for" the remission of sins in the light of its usage, the whole context, and the rest of Scripture.

First, the word "for" *(eis)* can mean either "with a view to" or "because of." In the latter case, water baptism would be *because* they had been saved, not *in order to be saved.*

Second, people are saved by receiving God's Word, and Peter's audience "gladly received his word" before they were baptized (Acts 2:41).

Third, verse 44 speaks of "all who believed" as constituting the early church, not all who were baptized.

Fourth, later, those who believed Peter's message clearly received the Holy Spirit *before* they were baptized. Peter said, "Can anyone forbid water, that these should not be baptized who have received the Holy Spirit just as we have?" (Acts 10:47).

Fifth, Paul separates baptism from the gospel, saying, "Christ did not send me to baptize, but to preach the gospel" (1 Cor. 1:17a NASB). But it is the gospel that saves us (Rom. 1:16). Therefore, baptism is not part of what saves us.

Sixth, Jesus referred to baptism as a work of righteousness (Matt. 3:15). But the Bible declares clearly it is "not because of righteous things we have done, but because of his mercy. He saved us through the washing of rebirth and renewal by the Holy Spirit" (Titus 3:5 NIV).

Seventh, not once in the entire Gospel of John, written explicitly so that people could believe and be saved (John 20:31), is baptism noted as a condition of salvation. Rather this Gospel instructs people to "believe" to be saved (cf. John 3:16, 18, 36).

It seems best to understand Peter's statement like this: "Repent and be baptized *as a result of* the forgiveness of sins." That this view looked backward to their sins being forgiven at the moment when they were saved is made clear by the context and the rest of Scripture. Believing or repenting and being baptized are placed together, since baptism should follow belief. But nowhere does it say, "He who is not *baptized* will be condemned" (cf. Mark 16:16). Yet Jesus said emphatically that "whoever does not *believe* stands condemned already" (John 3:18b NIV, emphasis added). Scripture does not make baptism a condition of salvation.

ACTS 2:38—Is the only legitimate baptism a baptism "in the name of Jesus," as Oneness Pentecostals believe?

MISINTERPRETATION: In Acts 2:38 Peter said, "Repent, and let each of you be baptized in the name of Jesus Christ for the forgiveness of your sins; and you shall receive the gift of the Holy Spirit" (NASB). Oneness Pentecostals believe this means that the only legitimate Christian baptism is a baptism in the name of Jesus (Bernard, 1984, 170–80). A "Trinitarian baptism" (in the name of the Father, Son, and Holy Spirit) is viewed as invalid. The phrase "in the name of Jesus" *must* be pronounced over the person being baptized. Is this view correct?

CORRECTING THE MISINTERPRETATION: The phrase "in the name of" in biblical times often carried the meaning "by the authority of." Seen in this light, the phrase in Acts 2:38 cannot be interpreted to be some kind of a magic baptismal formula. The verse simply indicates that people are to be baptized *according to the authority of* Jesus Christ. The verse does not mean that the words "in the name of Jesus" must be liturgically pronounced over each person being baptized. And, if Acts

2:38 was intended to be a baptismal formula, then why is this formula never repeated in exactly the same way throughout the rest of Acts or the New Testament (cf. Matt. 28:19)?

To consistently use Oneness Pentecostal logic, we would have to pronounce the words "in the name of Jesus" over everything we do, for Colossians 3:17 instructs us, "Whatever you do in word or deed, do all in the name of the Lord Jesus, giving thanks through Him to God the Father." Clearly the words "in the name of Jesus" are not intended as a formula.

Baptism "in the name *of Jesus*" makes good sense in the context of Acts 2, because the Jews ("men of Judea" [v. 14], "men of Israel" [v. 22]), to whom Peter was preaching, had rejected Christ as the Messiah. It is logical that Peter would call on them to repent of their rejection of Jesus the Messiah and become publicly identified with him via baptism.

From a historical perspective, the trinitarian baptism (Matt. 28:19) was certainly dominant from the second century. Are we to conclude that all those who were baptized from the second century to the present century in this manner are unsaved? The suggestion is preposterous. Moreover, it is highly revealing that no church leaders quibbled over the trinitarian baptism in the early centuries of Christianity. If salvation depended upon one being baptized in the name of Jesus, there certainly would have been major debate when trinitarian baptism was widely practiced. But church history reveals there wasn't even a *ripple* in the ocean of theological debate on this issue. Clearly the early believers did not consider "in the name of Jesus" *or* "in the name of the Father, Son, and Holy Spirit" to be rigid formulas.

ACTS 2:44—Does the reference to having "everything in common" in this verse support free sex?

MISINTERPRETATION: The Children of God, now known as "The Family," believe that the injunction in Acts 2:44 regarding having everything in common applied even to husbands and wives. They believe one could exercise sexual freedom in fulfillment of the law of God to "love one another" (John 15:12) and to begin at last to be "like the angels of God in heaven," who "neither marry, nor are given in marriage" (Matt. 22:30). They have finally reached the "glorious liberty of the children of God" (Rom. 8:21) and can now be truly considered Children of God (Lynch, 1990, 17).

CORRECTING THE MISINTERPRETATION: This verse describes how the early Christians shared *material* provisions among themselves to further the gospel in those early and crucial days of the Christian church.

From the very beginning, God set the pattern by creating a monogamous marriage relationship of one man with one woman, Adam and Eve (Gen. 1:27; 2:21–25). Jesus reaffirmed God's original intention. In Matthew 19:4 he teaches that God created one "male and [one] female" and joined them in marriage. The New Testament stresses that "each man should have his own wife, and each woman her own husband" (1 Cor. 7:2 NIV). See discussion of the Children of God views on Matthew 22:30 and John 15:12 and of faithful monogamy in 1 Kings 11:1.

ACTS 2:44–45—Did early Christians practice communism?

MISINTERPRETATION: Some have inferred from the fact that these early Christians "sold their possessions" and had "all things in common" that they were practicing a form of communism. Some cultic groups have cited such verses in forcing members to surrender all material possessions to the group.

CORRECTING THE MISINTERPRETATION: These passages are not *prescriptive*, but are simply *descriptive*. Nowhere does it lay this down as normative. It simply describes what the believers were doing. So far as the text indicates, the system was a temporary arrangement. They apparently stayed together in Jerusalem, since that is where the Holy Spirit had descended and the first great turning to Christ had occurred. The necessities of living together away from home occasioned this sort of common arrangement.

The communal arrangement was voluntary. There is absolutely no indication in the text that this was a compulsory arrangement. And it was only partial. The text implies that they sold extra land and possessions, not that they sold their only place of residence. Most eventually left Jerusalem, to which they had come for the feast of Pentecost (Acts 2:1), and went back to their homes, which were scattered all over the world (cf. Acts 2:5–13).

ACTS 3:21—Will all things be restored to God or just some things?

MISINTERPRETATION: The reference to the "restoration of all things" in this verse has been misinterpreted in a variety of ways. Among cults, universalists think this means that all people will eventually be saved.

Mormons say this passage points to a restoration of the church (through Joseph Smith) following total apostasy (Richards, 1958, 35).

CORRECTING THE MISINTERPRETATION: This verse does not support universalism. God desires that all men be saved (1 Tim. 2:4; 2 Peter 3:9). However, some will not accept his grace (cf. Matt. 23:37). See comments on Ephesians 1:10.

Acts 3:20–21 does not even remotely hint that there will be an apostasy through the entire church. Other passages of Scripture totally refute such an idea. Jesus said the gates of hell would not prevail against the church (Matt. 16:18). He also promised his followers, "Lo, I am with you always, even to the end of the age" (Matt. 28:20b NASB). Jesus could not be with his followers to the end of the age if the entire church went into complete apostasy soon after its founding. In Ephesians 3:21, the apostle Paul says, "To Him be the glory in the church and in Christ Jesus to all generations forever and ever" (NASB). How could God be glorified in an apostate church throughout all ages? Ephesians 4:11–16 speaks of the church growing to spiritual maturity, not spiritual degeneracy.

What then does "the restoration of all things" mean? Peter is speaking to the Jews when he refers to the "restoration of all things, about which God spoke by the mouth of His holy prophets from ancient time" (Acts 3:21 NASB). Clarification comes in verse 25, when Peter speaks of the "covenant which God made with your [Jewish] fathers, saying to Abraham, 'And in your seed all the families of the earth shall be blessed'" (NASB). It is to the future fulfillment of this Abrahamic covenant that Peter refers. It is the restoration of all *things* to God's people. See comments on Rom. 11:26.

ACTS 4:12—Is Christ the only way of salvation?

MISINTERPRETATION: Peter declares that "there is no other name under heaven given to men by which we must be saved" (NIV). But isn't this a narrow exclusivism? What about the sincere pagan or Buddhist? Hindus, Baha'is, and New Agers tell us that there are many roads to God, like spokes on a wheel (see Spangler, 1978, 46–47).

CORRECTING THE MISINTERPRETATION: Sincerity is not a good test of truth. People can and have been sincerely wrong about many things (Prov. 14:12). Whether someone sincerely believes to the contrary, all truth is exclusive. "Two plus three equals five" does not allow for any other conclusion. The same is true of value statements, such as, "Racism is wrong" and "People should be tolerant." These views do not tolerate any alternatives.

All truth claims are exclusive. If humanism is true, then all nonhumanisms are false. If atheism is true, then all who believe in God are wrong. If Jesus is the only way to God, then there are no other ways. This is no more exclusive than any other truth claim. The question is whether it is true. Jesus and the New Testament clearly and repeatedly emphasize that Jesus is the *only* way of salvation. Jesus said, "I am the way, and the truth, and the life. No one comes to the Father except through me" (John 14:6 NIV). He claimed he was the door (John 10:9), insisting that "the man who does not enter the sheep pen by the gate . . . is a thief and a robber" (v. 1 NIV). The apostle Peter added, "Nor is there salvation in any other, for there is no other name under heaven given among men by which we must be saved" (Acts 4:12). And Paul contended that "there is one God and *one Mediator* between God and men, the Man Christ Jesus" (1 Tim. 2:5 NIV).

ACTS 4:34–35—Did early Christians practice communism?

See comments on Acts 2:44–45.

ACTS 15:6–29—Was Peter the head of the church who presided over the first church council?

MISINTERPRETATION: Roman Catholics believe Peter was the first Pope who, as such, presided over the first church council in Acts 15.

CORRECTING THE MISINTERPRETATION: There is no evidence that Peter exercised any special authority as the divinely appointed vicar of Christ on earth by presiding over this gathering of early church leaders. Indications are that this meeting only confirmed the revelation already given to an apostle (Gal. 1:11–12).

The inquiry into the issue was from the church in Antioch (Acts 15:1–3). There was no apostolic mandate calling the council. The event was more of a conference than a church council, since it was not only apostles and elders but the other "brethren" who made the decision (Acts 15:2–3).

Contrary to the Catholic claim, if anyone dominated the conference it was not Peter but James, who gave the last word in the discussion

(15:13–21). That conclusion was moderate, using phrases like, "we all agreed" (Acts 15:25a). Indeed, the result of the conference was only a "letter" (15:30), not a papal encyclical with the typical language of anathema.

The conference recognized the supernatural confirmation of God on the message of Paul (Acts 15:12), which was the divinely appointed sign that he spoke by revelation from God (2 Cor. 12:12; Heb. 2:3–4). Peter was never called the chief apostle, let alone the vicar of Christ. He was only one of the "chief apostles" (2 Cor. 12:11; Gal. 1:18–19). Indeed, he called himself only "an apostle" (1 Peter 1:1) and a "fellow elder" (5:1) and declared Christ to be "the Chief Shepherd" (5:4).

Finally, Paul, not Peter, played the dominant role in most of the New Testament. Paul wrote thirteen or fourteen books. Peter wrote only two. Peter is the central figure only in Acts 1–8. Paul is the chief personage in Acts 9–28. Peter waffled on the relation of Jews and Gentiles and Paul had to rebuke him for his error (Gal. 2:14–16).

ACTS 15:20—Does this passage indicate it is a sin to receive a blood transfusion?

MISINTERPRETATION: The Jehovah's Witnesses say this verse proves that blood transfusions are against God's will (*Aid to Bible Understanding*, 1971, 245).

CORRECTING THE MISINTERPRETATION: This passage is talking about the Old Testament restriction against eating or drinking blood (Gen. 9:3–4; cf. Acts 15:28–29). However, a blood transfusion is not "eating" or "drinking" blood. See comments on Genesis 9:4.

It is clear that this Old Testament passage is not primarily concerned with the eating of blood. Rather, it is primarily concerned with the fact that the life is in the blood. Leviticus 17:10–12 makes this plain:

And whatever man of the house of Israel, or of the strangers who sojourn among you, who eats any blood, I will set My face against that person who eats blood, and will cut him off from among his people. *For the life of the flesh is in the blood,* and I have given it to you upon the altar to make atonement for your souls; for it is the blood that makes atonement for the soul. Therefore I said to the children of Israel, 'No one among you shall eat blood, nor shall any stranger who sojourns among you eat blood' (emphasis added; see also comments on Leviticus 7:26–27; 17:11–12).

The prohibitions in Genesis 9:3–4 and Leviticus 17:10–12 were primarily directed at eating flesh that was still pulsating with life because the life-blood was still in it. But the transfusion of blood is not eating flesh with the life-blood still in it.

Finally, the prohibition in Acts was not given as a law by which Christians were to live, for the New Testament clearly teaches that we are not under law (Rom. 6:14; Gal. 4:8–31). Rather, the Jerusalem Counsel was advising Gentile Christians to respect their Jewish brethren by observing these practices thereby not giving offense "either to the Jews or to the Greeks or to the church of God" (1 Cor. 10:32).

ACTS 17:1–3—Does Paul's Sabbath preaching in the synagogue support the Adventist view that the Sabbath is still binding?

MISINTERPRETATION: Seventh-Day Adventists argue that Paul sanctioned the practice of the Sabbath for Christians by his custom of going into the Jewish synagogue on Saturday and preaching.

CORRECTING THE MISINTERPRETATION: Paul's practice of speaking to assembled Jews was merely part of his missionary strategy to reach the Jews where they were assembled and from their Scriptures, which they came to read. It no more sanctioned the Sabbath for Christian use than Paul's meeting with pagan philosophers sanctioned their meeting time (Acts 17:22–34). On the contrary, Paul told the Colossians that the Sabbath was only a "shadow" that had passed away when the "substance" came with Christ (Col. 2:16–17). Paul affirmed that the entire table of the Mosaic Law "written and engraved on stone" (which included the Sabbath law) "was passing away" (2 Cor. 3:7, 10) and found its "end" (v. 13) in Christ. The New Testament repeatedly mentions that the Old Testament Jewish Law has been fulfilled by Christ (Rom. 10:4). Because of this fulfillment, "there is a change in the law" (Heb. 7:12).

The Sabbath command is the only one of the Ten Commandments that is not restated in the context of grace in the New Testament. This is a significant omission if it is supposed to be practiced by Christians today. Rather, the New Testament sanctions the first day of the week for Christian worship—a day which Paul himself practiced. The reasons for this are obvious. It is the day Christ arose, thus initiating the first day of the week for Christian celebration. Jesus' first postresurrection appearances were on Sundays, thus establishing a pattern of expecting his presence on the first day of the week (cf. Mark 16:2; John 20:19,

26). Sunday is also the day the Holy Spirit baptized the disciples into the body of Christ (Acts 2:1–4; cf. 1 Cor. 12:13)—providing the birthday of the Christian church.

Thus, it became the practice of the apostolic church to meet on the first day of the week (Acts 20:7; 1 Cor. 16:2). In the last book of the New Testament, John the apostle was meditating on Sunday, the "Lord's Day," when he received a vision of Christ (Rev. 1:10), showing that the practice continued for many decades after the time of Christ. Indeed, the Christian church has continued this practice from the first century to the present. See comments on Exodus 20:8–11.

ACTS 17:28—Does Paul's quotation support the pantheistic belief that God is everything?

MISINTERPRETATION: The apostle Paul told the philosophers on Mars Hill, "In him we live, move, and have our being." Christian Scientists see in this verse support for their pantheistic belief that "as a drop of water is one with the ocean, a ray of light one with the sun, even so God and man, Father and son, are one in being" (Eddy, 361).

CORRECTING THE MISINTERPRETATION: There is no reason here or anywhere else in the New Testament to believe that the apostle Paul was teaching pantheism. First of all, he was by training and conviction an orthodox Jew—a Pharisee (Phil. 3:4–6)—and accordingly a strict monotheist (Deut. 6:4; 1 Cor. 8:4, 6). Second, Paul referred here to the "God who *made* the world and everything in it" (Acts 17:24 NIV), whereas pantheists believe that God *is* the world and everything in it. Third, Paul only asserted that we have our life and being "*in* him" (God), not that we *are* him, as pantheists claim. That is to say, God is the sustaining Cause of all, as well as the originating Cause (Heb. 1:3; Col. 1:17).

ACTS 17:28–29—Does this verse support the idea that the heavenly Father and a heavenly mother gave birth to spirit-children in the "preexistence"?

MISINTERPRETATION: This verse refers to believers as God's "offspring," which, according to Mormons, means we were born as spirit children prior to being born physically on earth. "Man, as a spirit, was begotten and born of heavenly parents, and reared to maturity in the eternal mansion of the Father, prior to coming upon the earth in a temporal [physical] body" (*Gospel Principles*, 1979, 9).

CORRECTING THE MISINTERPRETATION: In this context Paul was preaching to some men in Athens who didn't even believe in God. Drawing on glimpses of truth in their writings, Paul affirmed that we are all "offspring of God" in the sense that we were all created by him. Paul earlier affirmed that God "made from one, every nation of mankind to live on all the face of the earth, having determined their appointed times, and the boundaries of their habitation" (Acts 17:26 NASB). Paul may have been thinking of Malachi 2:10: "Do we not all have one father? Has not one God created us?" (Mal. 2:10 NASB).

It is important to understand that humankind did not preexist as a spirit being prior to physical birth on earth. Genesis 2:7 tells us, "Then the LORD God formed man of dust from the ground, and breathed into his nostrils the breath of life; and man became a living being" (NASB). Notice that no preexisting spirit entered a physical tabernacle of flesh. Rather, God created the physical being, and then "breathed into his nostrils the breath of life," and the man became a living being *at that point*. It appears that at that moment God created both man's material *and* immaterial aspects. Since then, human beings—in both their material and immaterial aspects—are born into the world through the natural union of their parents (cf. Gen. 5:3).

ACTS 19:12—Do the miracles via the clothes from the apostles support the Catholic dogma of venerating religious relics?

MISINTERPRETATION: According to Acts 19:12 "even handkerchiefs and aprons that had touched him [the apostle Paul] were taken to the sick, and their illnesses were cured and the evil spirits left them" (NIV). Does this historical occurrence in biblical times lend credence to the Roman Catholic veneration of relics?

CORRECTING THE MISINTERPRETATION: The supernatural cures achieved by clothes from the apostle Paul does not prove we should venerate anything.

The apostles were given the special "signs of an apostle" (2 Cor. 12:12) to confirm God's special revelation through them (the New Testament). The signs of an apostle are no longer needed for that purpose (Heb. 2:3–4).

Regarding their relics, nowhere does it say here or anywhere else in the New Testament to venerate articles through which miracles were performed. God forbade such idolatry in general in the Old Testament. When any object, such as the brazen serpent, was venerated, it was considered idolatry (cf. 2 Kings 18:4).

God clearly commanded his people not to make graven *images* or to *bow* down to them in an act of religious devotion. This is the same error of the pagans who worshiped the creature rather than the Creator (Rom. 1:25). The Bible forbids us ever to make or even to "bow" down before an "image" of any creature in an act of religious devotion: "You shall not make for yourselves any *carved image,* or *any likeness* of anything that is in heaven above, or that is in the earth beneath, or that is in the waters under the earth; you shall not bow down nor serve them" (Exod. 20:4–5 NKJV).

ROMANS

ROMANS 1:5—Does this verse support the Roman Catholic view that the true church of Christ is a visible church on earth today, *viz.* the Roman Catholic church?

MISINTERPRETATION: Catholic dogma teaches that "the biblical proof of the visibility of the Church springs from the Divine institution of the hierarchy." And "the teaching office [of the Roman Catholic church] demands from its incumbents the duty of obedience to the faith (Rom. 1, 5)" (Ott, 1960, 301–2). Is this text a proof that the true church is a *visible* church on earth today—namely, the Roman Catholic church? Some other sects use the same or similar reasoning

CORRECTING THE MISINTERPRETATION: The claim that the Roman Catholic church demands obedience as the true visible church is not supported by this text. The text states, "through him [Christ] we have received the grace of apostleship, to bring about obedience of faith." Paul is speaking here about his apostleship (v. 1), not Peter's, or Peter's alleged successors, the Roman Catholic popes.

Further, to be an apostle in this authoritative sense, one had to be an eyewitness of the resurrected Christ (Acts 1:22; 1 Cor. 9:1; 15:5–8), which clearly disqualifies anyone after the first century. This would negate the claim that the "teaching office" of the Roman Catholic church is somehow implied here. The Church's argument would have more force if they related their authority to Paul, rather than Peter. The added requirement of being a witness of Jesus' earthly ministry (Acts 1:22) was pertinent only in regard to being one of the twelve apostles who have a special place in the foundation of the church (Eph. 2:20), their very names being written on the foundation of the eternal city (Rev. 21:14) and their reigning with Christ on twelve thrones when he returns (Matt. 19:28). Paul was not one of the twelve and, hence, need not fulfil this requirement. However, he *was* an apostle (Gal. 1:1) who received direct revelation from God (Gal. 1:12). His apostolic authority compared with that of the twelve apostles (Gal. 1:17; 2:5–9) and he displayed the miraculous "signs of an apostle" (2 Cor. 12:12). But neither was Paul's apostleship transferable. Paul explicitly listed the appearance of the resurrected Christ to him as a prerequisite for being an apostle. He wrote, "Am I not an apostle? Have I not seen Jesus our Lord?" (1 Cor. 9:1). Likewise, he listed Jesus' resurrection appearance to him along with that of the other apostles, saying, "After that He was seen by James, then by all the apostles. Then last of all He was seen by me also" (1 Cor. 15:7–8).

There were no more appearances of Christ to anyone after Paul to confirm apostleship in this special sense. None are listed on the official list of 1 Corinthians 15, and Paul describes himself as "last of all" among those personally visited and commissioned. The miraculous signs which confirmed an apostle are referred to as past events by A.D. 69 when the Book of Hebrews was written (Heb. 2:3–4). The Book of Jude, which was written after Paul's death, refers to the apostles as having lived in the past (Jude 17). Jude said the faith he preached had been "once for all" handed down to us by them (v. 3).

The "signs of an apostle" (2 Cor. 12:12) included the ability to heal all diseases (Matt. 10:1), even incurable ones, immediately (cf. Acts 3:7), the power of exorcising demons immediately on command (Matt. 10:8; cf. Acts 16:18), authority to condemn with death those who lie to the Holy Spirit (Acts 5:1–11), and even the ability to perform resurrections from the dead (Matt. 10:8; cf. Acts 20:7–11). This excludes anyone alive today, including the Pope. No one possesses the power to perform these kinds of apostolic signs. But without these kinds of apostolic signs (cf. Heb. 2:3–4), there is no proof of apostolic authority. The authority of the New Testament apostles existed after their miracles had ceased, but only because these apostolic signs already had confirmed their apostolic authority, expressed in the abiding apostolic writings. But once these apostles so confirmed had died, there was no living apostolic authority. The only apostolic authority present today is the New Testament. Only New Testament writings were confirmed by apostolic signs, so only the New Testament contains this apostolic authority.

ROMANS 1:7—Does this verse prove that Jesus is God the Father, as Oneness Pentecostals believe?

MISINTERPRETATION: In Romans 1:7 we read the salutation, "Grace to you and peace from God our Father and the Lord Jesus Christ" (NASB).

Oneness Pentecostals argue that the word "and" (Greek *kai*) in the phrase "God our Father *and* the Lord Jesus Christ" should be translated "even." It should thus read, "God our Father, *even* the Lord Jesus Christ." Translated this way, Jesus and the Father are seen to be one and the same person (Graves, 1977, 50–51; cf. Bernard, 1983, 207–11). This means Jesus is the Father.

CORRECTING THE MISINTERPRETATION: While it is true that the Greek word *kai* can be translated "even" in certain verses, context determines the appropriate translation. Even Oneness Pentecostal scholar Brent Graves admits this (Graves, 52). The fact is, Greek scholars universally agree that in context, *kai* in Romans 1:7 should be translated "and." Most occurrences of *kai* in the New Testament are translated "and," not "even." This means that the burden of proof is on Oneness Pentecostals to demonstrate that the word must be translated with its secondary meaning ("even") and not its primary meaning ("and") in Romans 1:7.

However *kai* is translated, the verses immediately *prior to* and immediately *after* Romans 1:7 show personal distinction between the Father and Jesus Christ. For example, Jesus is called God's "Son" in verse 3, and in verse 8 Paul thanks "God *through* Jesus Christ" for the Roman Christians. It is the uniform testimony of Scripture that Jesus and the Father are distinct persons (within the unity of the one God). See the discussion of Matthew 28:19.

ROMANS 1:19–20—Are those who have never heard the gospel lost?

MISINTERPRETATION: Jesus said, "I am the way, the truth, and the life, No one comes to the Father, except through Me" (John 14:6 NIV). Also, Acts 4:12 says of Christ, "And there is salvation in no one else; for there is no other name under heaven that has been given among men, by which we must be saved" (NASB). Will someone who has never heard the gospel of Christ be eternally lost? Paul seems to answer this in the affirmative. But is it fair to condemn people who have never even heard about Christ? Some New Agers point to this problem in support of the idea that all the world religions are paths to God (see Fox, 1989, 288).

CORRECTING THE MISINTERPRETATION: Paul's answer is clear. He said the heathen are "without excuse" (Rom. 1:20) because "what may be known of God is manifest in them, for God has shown it to them. For since the creation of the world His invisible attributes are clearly seen, being understood by the things that are made" (1:19–20 NIV). So, the heathen are justly condemned.

Romans 2:12 states, "For as many as have sinned without law will also perish without law, and as many as have sinned in the law will be judged by the law" (NKJV). This passage teaches that the Jew is judged by the law (the Hebrew Scriptures), but the Gentile is condemned by "the law written in their hearts" (v. 15). "For when Gentiles who do not have the law by nature do the things contained in the law, these, although not having the Law, are a law to themselves, *who show the work of the law written in their hearts,* their conscience also bearing witness, and between themselves their thoughts accusing or else excusing them" (Rom. 2:14, 15 NKJV, emphasis added).

The question of God's fairness in judging the heathen assumes innocence on the part of the unsaved who haven't heard the gospel. But the Bible tells us that "all have sinned and fall short of the glory of God" (Rom. 3:23). In addition, Romans 1:18–20 says that God clearly reveals himself through natural revelation "so that they are without excuse." Human beings are not innocent regarding God's natural revelation.

If a person who has not heard the gospel and lives to the best of his or her ability, that person is simply doing works in an attempt to achieve salvation. But salvation is by grace, "For by grace you have been saved through faith, and that not of yourselves; it is the gift of God" (Eph. 2:8 NKJV). No one can do anything to gain access into heaven. If there was such a way, then the work of Christ on the Cross was a futile act.

The Bible says in essence, "seek and you will find." That is, those who seek the light they have through nature, which is not sufficient for salvation, will get the light they need for salvation. Hebrews 11:6 says, "But without faith it is impossible to please Him, for he who comes to God must believe that He is, and that He is a rewarder of those who diligently seek Him." Acts 10:35 adds, "But in every nation whoever fears God and works righteousness is accepted by Him" (NKJV). God has many ways to get the truth about salvation through Christ to those who seek him. He can send a missionary (Acts 10), a radio broadcast, or a Bible (Ps. 119:130). Theoretically God could send a vision (Dan. 2, 7) or an angel (Rev. 14) though he no longer gives new revelation. But those who turn their back on the light they have (through nature) and find themselves lost in darkness have no one to blame but themselves. For "men loved darkness rather than light, because their deeds were evil" (John 3:19 NKJV).

ROMANS 1:26—Does this verse mean that homosexuals should not be heterosexual because it is unnatural to them?

MISINTERPRETATION: According to some homosexuals, when Paul spoke against what is "unnatural" in Romans 1:26 he was not declaring that homosexuality was morally wrong but simply that it was unnatural for heterosexuals. "Unnatural" is used in a *sociological*, not a *biological* way. So rather than condemning homosexual practices, it is argued that this Romans passage actually approves of homosexual practices for homosexuals.

CORRECTING THE MISINTERPRETATION: When the Bible declares that homosexual practices are "contrary to nature" (Rom. 1:26 KJV) it is referring to biological, not sociological nature. This passage cannot be used to justify homosexuality.

Sexuality and sexual expression are defined biologically in Scripture from the beginning. In Genesis 1 God created "male and female" and then told them to "be fruitful and increase in number" (Gen. 1:27–28). This reproduction was only possible if he was referring to a biological male and female. Sexual orientation is understood biologically, not sociologically, when God said "for this reason a man will leave his father and mother and be united to his wife, and they will become one flesh" (Gen. 2:24 NIV). Only a biological father and mother can produce children, and the reference to "one flesh" simply cannot be understood in any relationship except heterosexual physical marriage.

The Romans passage says that "men committed indecent acts with other men." This clearly indicates that the class of sinful act condemned was homosexual in nature (Rom. 1:27). What they did was not natural to them but was "exchanged" for "natural relations" (v. 26). So the homosexual acts were pronounced unnatural for homosexuals too. Homosexual desires are also called "shameful lusts" (v. 26). So it is evident that God is condemning sexual sins between those of the same biological sex. Homosexual acts are contrary to human nature as such, not just to a heterosexual's sexual orientation.

ROMANS 2:6–7—Does this passage teach that good works are a condition of salvation, as Roman Catholic scholars claim?

MISINTERPRETATION: The Roman Catholic Council of Trent declared that for "those who work well 'unto the end' [Matt. 10:22], and who trust in God, life eternal is to be proposed, both as a grace mercifully promised to the sons of God through Christ Jesus, 'and as a recompense' which is . . . to be faithfully given to their good works and merit" (Denzinger, 1957, no. 809, 257). It adds that "if anyone shall say that the good works of the man justified are in such a way the gift of God that they are not also the good merits of him who is justified, or that the one justified by the good works . . . does not truly merit increase of grace, eternal life, and the attainment of eternal life (if he should die in grace), and also an increase of glory; let him be anathema" (Ibid., no. 842, 261). Further, "St. Paul, who stresses grace so much, also emphasized on the other hand, the meritorious nature of good works performed with grace, by teaching that the reward is in proportion to the works: 'He [God] will render to every man according to his own labor' (Rom. 2, 6)" (Ibid., 265).

CORRECTING THE MISINTERPRETATION: Neither this nor any other passage of Scripture teaches that works are a necessary condition for receiving salvation. Paul makes it very clear that salvation is by grace apart from any works both in Romans (cf. 3:28; 4:5) and elsewhere (cf. Eph. 2:8–9; Titus 3:5).

When Paul speaks here (and elsewhere) of works in connection with salvation, the works are always the *result* of, not the *condition* of, salvation. We are saved by grace through faith (Eph. 2:8–9) but "to do good works" (Eph. 2:10). We are told to "work out" our salvation (Phil. 2:12) because it is "God who works in" us (Phil. 2:13). Likewise, in Titus we are told that "he saved us, not because of righteous things we had done, but because of his mercy" (3:5 NIV). Then he says immediately that "those who have trusted in God may be careful to devote themselves to doing what is good" (v. 8). In every case in the Bible we are saved *by* grace but *for* works. We do not work *for* grace but *from* grace (cf. 2 Cor. 5:14; Titus 2:11–12).

Paul in the next chapter of Romans says: "For we maintain that a man is justified by faith apart from observing the law" (Rom. 3:28 NIV). And in the following chapter he adds, "To the man who does not work but trusts God who justifies the wicked, his faith is credited as righteousness" (4:5). Unless one assumes that the apostle contradicts himself, then good "deeds" or "works" in Romans 2:6–7 must be understood as the result or manifestation of salvation, not the condition for receiving it.

A careful look at the context in Romans 2:6–7 reveals that the good "works" in view are a result of faith. Paul speaks of the need for repentance (v. 4) and obeying the truth (v. 8) in order to obtain it. And, like James, he is stressing the need for good works as an *evidence* that one has saving faith. "For it is not those who hear the law who are righteous in God's sight, but it is those who obey the law who will be declared righteous" (v. 13 NIV).

Like elsewhere human deeds are mentioned in the Bible (cf. Rev. 20:11–15), the context in Romans 2 relates to the judgment of God (see v. 3). And when judgment is the subject, the stress is always on works as a *manifestation* of one's faith (or lack thereof), not simply on the faith from which these works follow. So it is understandable that in this context Paul would stress the works that are a manifestation of the faith by which one receives eternal life (2:6–7).

"Eternal life" in Romans and elsewhere in the New Testament is a result of faith alone (albeit the kind of faith that produces good works). Just a few chapters later Paul wrote, "For the wages of sin is death, but the gift of God is eternal life in Christ Jesus our Lord" (Rom. 6:23 NIV). If eternal life is a gift, then it is not something for which one works (Rom. 4:5). Likewise, in John (NIV) we read, "Whoever believes in the Son has eternal life" (John 3:36), and "whoever hears my word and believes him who sent me has eternal life and will not be condemned; he has crossed over from death to life" (John 5:24). From these verses it is clear that eternal life is a present possession of believers on the basis of their faith alone.

ROMANS 2:7—Is immortality acquired or possessed?

MISINTERPRETATION: Paul speaks of "seeking" immortality, and of being clothed with, or acquiring, immortality at the resurrection (1 Cor. 15:53). Does personal existence cease, then, as Jehovah's Witnesses insist it does, between death and the day of resurrection when the Christian is returned to consciousness and clothed with eternal life? (*Reasoning from the Scriptures*, 1989, 377).

CORRECTING THE MISINTERPRETATION: The Bible does reserve the term *immortality* for the day of final resurrection. Scripture insists, though, that the believer enjoys eternal life as a continuous existence from the moment of salvation and after the body dies. It is necessary then to carefully sort out what the believer has in Christ from what the believer will have. One way to summarize this difference might be that immortality is something Christians have *acquired* but will not fully *possess* until they have resurrection bodies. Before the final resurrection of the dead, only Christ has an immortal body.

Since only Christ has experienced his final bodily resurrection, 1 Corinthians 15:20–23 describes him as the "firstfruits" from the dead. Unlike him, in this sense we are not yet "fruits" from the dead and so are not immortal. Verses 24–26 explain that at the culmination of history, Christ will put an end to the Adamic curse, destroying only at the very last the curse of physical death of the body. Until Christ puts this enemy under his feet, physical death remains unavoidable, with its separation of soul from body and the decay of the physical body. At the final resurrection, when a glorified body is united with the soul, believers will finally be able to say they possess immortality. The perishable will clothe itself with the imperishable, and the mortal with immortality (1 Cor. 15:53).

Meanwhile that ultimate physical-spiritual union and everlasting life belong to the Christian as a certain promise. Now justified and made holy in the death and resurrection of Christ, believers' souls will go at death to a conscious existence in heaven (2 Cor. 5:8; Phil. 1:23). Bodies will "sleep," awaiting the moment of change (1 Cor. 15:51–52) when we will be able to say with Paul, "Death has been swallowed up in victory" (v. 54 NIV).

ROMANS 3:27–28—When Paul speaks of "works" (deeds) not being a condition of salvation, does he mean only works of the Mosaic Law or *any* good works?

MISINTERPRETATION: Paul declares that "a man is justified by faith apart from the deeds of the law" (Rom. 3:28 NKJV). Roman Catholics claim that Paul is not speaking against good "deeds" or "works" in general (which they believe are essential to salvation) but only of the "works of the law" of Moses (as in Rom. 3:27–28).

CORRECTING THE MISINTERPRETATION: This misrepresents the teachings of the apostle Paul.

Paul often speaks of "works of the law," since that was the particular kind of works that members of his audience were prone to perform, being Jewish (cf. Acts 15:5; Rom. 4; Gal. 3). However, when speaking to churches with a large Gentile constituency, Paul sometimes used the word *works* without limiting it to works of the law of Moses. In Ephesians he declares, "For by grace you have been saved through faith, and that not of yourselves; it is the gift of God, not of works, lest anyone should boast" (2:8–9 NKJV). Likewise, in Titus 3 (NKJV; see vv. 5–7) he affirmed that it is "not by works of righteousness which we have done, but according to His mercy He saved us. . . ." So, it is not just "works of the law" of Moses but *any* "works" or "works of righteousness" that are insufficient for salvation.

To limit all of Paul's condemnations of "works" to only works of the law of Moses is like limiting God's condemnation of homosexuality in the Old Testament (cf. Lev. 18, 20) to Jews since these passages occur only in the Mosaic law which was written to Jews. And, to grant that a moral law (e.g., natural law) exists outside the law of Moses is to grant the Protestant point that "works" here are not just limited to works of the Mosaic law. The truth is that the condemnations are more broadly applicable than the immediate context in which they arose. The same is true of Paul's condemnation of meritorious "works" as a means of salvation. To limit Paul's condemnation to works of self-righteousness as opposed to meritorious works is reading into the text a distinction that is not there.

What is more, if good works of any kind play even a small part in obtaining salvation, then we would have grounds to boast and, hence, would still come under Paul's condemnation (Eph. 2:9).

Finally, the basic moral character of God expressed in the Ten Commandments is the same as that expressed through the natural law to all humanity. The fact that someone is not consciously or deliberately doing works according to the law of Moses does not mean that the basic moral standard is not the same. Hence, in one sense all moral "works" are "works of the law" in that they are in accord with the moral principles expressed in the law of Moses. This is why the apostle Paul said that "when Gentiles who have not the law [of Moses], by nature do the things contained in the law [of Moses], these . . . show the works of the law written in their hearts" (Rom. 2:14–15a NKJV). In the final analysis, when it comes to the *moral* demands of the law, there is no substantial difference between "works of righteousness" and the "works of the law."

In brief, the Catholic argument that Paul meant the latter but not the former is a distinction without a difference. The simple truth is that no works *of any kind* merit salvation. Eternal life is a gift received only by faith (John 3:16, 36; 5:24; Rom. 6:23).

ROMANS 5:18–19—Does Paul teach universalism when he affirms that "many [all] will be made righteous"?

MISINTERPRETATION: In Romans 5:18–19 Paul wrote:

Consequently, just as the result of one trespass was condemnation for all men, so also the result of one act of righteousness was justification that brings life for all men. For just as through the disobedience of the one man the many were made sinners, so also through the obedience of the one man the many will be made righteous. [NIV]

Many liberal and some neo-orthodox scholars, such as Karl Barth, insist that this passage teaches that everyone will eventually be saved. Is this a proper understanding of the text?

CORRECTING THE MISINTERPRETATION: From these verses universalists infer that Christ's death "for all" guarantees salvation "for all." This conclusion, however, is contrary to the context here and in Romans as a whole as well as to the rest of Scripture.

Even in this context Paul speaks of being "justified *by faith*" (5:1), not automatically by what Christ did for us. He also refers to salvation as a "gift" (5:16) that has to be received; in 5:17 he declares that salvation comes only to those who receive the gift of righteousness.

The rest of the Book of Romans makes it unmistakably clear that not everyone will be saved. Romans 1–2 speaks of the heathen who are "without excuse" (Rom. 1:20) and upon whom the wrath of God falls (1:18). It declares that "as many as have sinned without law will also perish without law" (Rom. 2:12 NKJV).

In the very heart of his argument Paul concludes that apart from justification by faith, the world is accountable before God (Rom. 3:19). Later, speaking of the destiny of both saved and lost, Paul affirms that "the wages of sin is death, but the gift of God is eternal life in Christ Jesus our Lord" (Rom. 6:23 NIV). Likewise, Paul recognized that, despite his prayers, not all of his kinsmen would be saved (Rom. 11:1–10) but that many would be "accursed" (Rom. 9:3). Indeed, the whole point of Romans is to show that only those who believe will be justified (Rom. 1:17; cf. 3:21–26).

Romans 9 could not be clearer that *only the elect*, not everyone, will be saved (cf. 9:14–26). The rest God patiently endured, waiting for them to repent (2 Peter 3:9), so they would not be "vessels of wrath prepared for destruction" (Rom. 9:22 NKJV).

Numerous passages elsewhere in Scripture speak of the eternal destiny of lost people, including the vivid passage at the end of Revelation when John said:

And I saw the dead, great and small, standing before the throne, and books were opened. Another book was opened, which is the book of life. The dead were judged according to what they had done as recorded in the books . . . and each person was judged according to what he had done. Then death and Hades were thrown into the lake of fire. The lake of fire is the second death. If anyone's name was not found written in the book of life, he was thrown into the lake of fire. [Rev. 20:11–15 NIV]

There simply is no evidence for universalism in Romans 5, and it is contrary to the clear teaching of other Scriptures. Since the Bible does not contradict itself, the verses that can be interpreted in more than one way must be understood in the light of those that cannot.

ROMANS 8:7—Does this verse support the idea that one should seek a spiritual meaning of Bible verses as opposed to reading the text literally?

MISINTERPRETATION: Romans 8:7 (RSV) says, "The mind set on the flesh is hostile toward God; for it does not subject itself to the law of God, for it is not even able to do so." Some advocates of Christian Science believe that a literal reading of the biblical text is the reading of the fleshly or carnal mind, which is enmity against God (Eddy, *Miscellaneous Writings*, 319–20). One should therefore seek the spiritual or esoteric interpretation of the biblical text.

CORRECTING THE MISINTERPRETATION: This verse and all of Romans 8 is contrasting the unregenerate life dominated by the flesh or sin nature with the life controlled by the Holy Spirit. The verse thus deals with the issue of *sanctification,* not biblical *interpretation.* Christian Scientists are reading something into the text that is not there.

An esoteric or "spiritual" approach to interpreting Scripture is untestable and therefore useless. Unlike objective methodology, in which interpretations can be rationally evaluated and tested by comparing Scripture with Scripture and by objectively weighing historical and grammatical considerations, there is no objective way to test esoteric interpretations of Scripture. Interpretations are subjective and nonverifiable; there is no way to *prove* that a given interpretation is right or wrong, since "proof" presupposes rationality and objectivity. This produces irreconcilable contradictions. In the subjective approach of esotericism, the basic authority ceases to be Scripture and becomes the mind of the interpreter. Hence, two people approaching the same verse can subjectively come up with radically contradictory interpretations and there is no objective way to determine which (if either) is correct.

If the primary purpose of God's originating of language was to make it possible for him to communicate with human beings, as well as to enable human beings to communicate with each other, then it must follow that he would generally use language and expect man to use it in its literal, normal, and plain sense. This view of language is a prerequisite to understanding not only God's spoken word but his written Word (Scripture) as well. The Bible as a body of literature exists because human beings need to know certain spiritual truths to which they cannot attain by themselves. Thus these truths must come to them from without—via objective, special revelation from God (Deut. 29:29). And this revelation can only be understood if one interprets the words of Scripture according to God's original design for language—that is, according to the ordinary, plain sense of each word. This is not to suggest a "wooden literalism" that interprets figures of speech or metaphors literally. But what is understood to be a figure of speech and what is taken literally should be based on the biblical text itself—such as when Jesus used obviously figurative parables to communicate spiritual truth.

Jesus never sought an esoteric meaning when interpreting the Old Testament Scriptures. On the contrary, he consistently interpreted quite literally the accounts of creation and Adam and Eve (Matt. 13:35; 25:34; Mark 10:6), Noah's Ark and the Flood (Matt. 24:38–39; Luke 17:26–27), Jonah and the whale (Matt. 12:39–41), Sodom and Gomorrah (Matt. 10:15), and the account of Lot and his wife (Luke 17:28–33). Jesus' interpretation of the Old Testament was always in accord with the grammatical and historical meaning.

If Jesus had intended to teach his followers to use an esoteric method of interpreting Scripture, he was a failure as a teacher, for his words led those who followed him in the precise opposite direction than he would have intended. Indeed, his followers interpreted his words literally—believing in the reality of sin, death, and the need for salvation, unlike Christian Science, which teaches that sin and death are illusions. Contrary to the Christian Science spiritual meaning of biblical texts, Jesus taught openly and with clarity. Following his arrest, Jesus was questioned by the High Priest about his disciples and his teaching. Jesus responded: "I have spoken openly to the world; I always taught in synagogues, and in the temple, where all the Jews come together; and I said nothing in secret" (John 18:20 NIV). There were no hidden meanings beneath his words.

Following the example of Jesus and the apostles, the objective interpreter of Scripture must seek the author's *intended* meaning of the biblical text. Meaning is *determined* by the author; it is *discovered* by readers. Our goal must be *exegesis* (drawing the meaning out of the text) and not *eisogesis* (superimposing a meaning onto the text).

ROMANS 8:16—Does this verse mean that prior to being born physically on earth, we were born as spirit children of our heavenly Father and heavenly mother?

MISINTERPRETATION: In Romans 8:16 the apostle Paul says, "The Spirit Himself bears witness with our spirit that we are children of God" (NKJV). Mormons believe we are "children of God" in the sense that we were born as "spirit children" prior to our earthly existence (McConkie, 1966, 589).

CORRECTING THE MISINTERPRETATION: The context of Romans 8 tells us in what sense believers become "children of God." Verse 15 affirms that we become children of God *by adoption*: "For you have not received a spirit of slavery leading to fear again, but you have received a spirit of adoption as sons by which we cry out, 'Abba! Father!'" This adoptive status takes place the moment we believe in Jesus for salvation (John 1:12; see also Gal. 4:5–6; Eph. 1:5).

ROMANS 8:17—Does this verse indicate we can become exalted as gods?

MISINTERPRETATION: Romans 8:17 says, "And if children, heirs also, heirs of God and fellow-heirs with Christ, if indeed we suffer with Him in order that we may also be glorified with Him" (NASB). Mormons believe this verse teaches that we can eventually become exalted as gods (McConkie, 1966, 237).

CORRECTING THE MISINTERPRETATION: As noted in the discussion of Romans 8:16, believers become children of God, not *by nature* but *by adoption* into God's family. Being a "fellow-heir" with Christ involves, not exaltation as a God, but an inheritance of all spiritual blessings in this life (Eph. 1:3), and all the riches of God's glorious kingdom in the next life (1 Cor. 3:21–23).

God throughout Scripture takes a strong stand against human pretenders to the divine throne (Acts 12:22–23; cf. Exod. 9:14; Acts 14:11–15). The only true God emphatically declared, "Before Me there was no God formed, and there will be none after Me" (Isa. 43:10). This verse completely obliterates the possibility of a human being becoming a god.

ROMANS 8:21—Does this verse support the "open sex" views of the Children of God?

MISINTERPRETATION: In Romans 8:21 we find reference to "the freedom of the glory of the children of God" (NASB). Does the "freedom" referred to in this verse include the liberty to have open sex outside the marriage relationship, as the Children of God argue?

CORRECTING THE MISINTERPRETATION: A look at the context of Romans 8 helps us to understand what is really going on in verse 21.

Paul affirmed that our sufferings are far outweighed by the glory that will be revealed in us (v. 18). The glory lasts forever (2 Cor. 4:17); suffering will come to an end. Paul said this to strengthen his readers so they could endure their present sufferings. The anticipation of a coming glory helps us to have an eternal perspective during tough times.

Paul then discussed the relationship between believers and the creation—both in their present state of travail and in their future glory (Rom. 8:19–21). He said the whole creation waits in eager expectation for the sons of God to be revealed. The verb for "eagerly waits" (v. 19) is used seven times in the New Testament. In each case it is used in reference to the second coming of Christ (Rom. 8:19, 23, 25; 1 Cor. 1:7; Gal. 5:5; Phil. 3:20; Heb. 9:28). The "revealing" of the sons of God will take place when Christ comes again.

As to the reason for this present state of waiting, Paul said the creation was subjected to frustration (Rom. 8:20). The word *frustration* carries the idea of "futility," "frailty," and "purposelessness." As a part of his judgment against man's sin, God subjected the creation to frustration (v. 20). Humankind had been assigned to a position of authority *over* the creation as God's representative (Gen. 1:26–30; 2:8, 15). Hence, God's judgment for rebellion included a judgment against the human domain.

All this was done "in hope" that the creation will one day be *liberated* (v. 21). There is a time coming when the creation will be free from sin, Satan, and physical decay. Our destiny as believers is to dwell in "a new heaven and a new earth" (2 Peter 3:7–13; Rev. 21:1). *This* is the glorious freedom and liberty to which we look forward. The verse obviously has nothing to do with *sexual* freedom and liberty.

The Bible everywhere condemns such promiscuous behavior (Exod. 20:14; 1 Cor. 5:1; 6:18; 7:2). See the discussion of John 15:12 for biblical argumentation regarding God's instruction that sex is to be engaged in *only* within the confines of marriage.

ROMANS 10:13—Does this verse indicate that we must call upon the actual name of "Jehovah" in order to be saved?

MISINTERPRETATION: The New World Translation renders Romans 10:13, "Everyone who calls on the name of Jehovah will be saved." Jehovah's Witnesses cite this verse in arguing for the necessity of using God's proper name, Jehovah, in attaining salvation (*Reasoning from the Scriptures,* 1989, 149).

CORRECTING THE MISINTERPRETATION: The New World Translation mistranslates this verse. It is correctly rendered, "Whoever will call upon the name 'of the Lord' (Gk: *kuriou*) will be saved" (NASB). In context, "Lord" refers to Jesus Christ, as is made clear in verse 9: "If you confess with your mouth Jesus as Lord, and believe in your heart that God raised Him from the dead, you shall be saved." So, by their own argument, if *Lord* means "Jehovah"—and *Lord* refers to Jesus here—then Jesus must be Jehovah, a doctrine they emphatically reject.

Likewise, if "Lord" *(kurios)* means Jehovah, then Jehovah's Witnesses should accept Jesus as Jehovah, since Philippians 2:10–11 (NIV) declares that "at the name of Jesus every knee should bow . . . and every tongue should confess that Jesus Christ is Lord *(kurios)."* Hence, if *kurios* is Jehovah, then Jesus is Jehovah.

1 CORINTHIANS

1 CORINTHIANS 1:3—Does this verse prove that Jesus is God the Father, as Oneness Pentecostals believe?

MISINTERPRETATION: In 1 Corinthians 1:3 we read the salutation, "Grace to you and peace from God our Father and the Lord Jesus Christ" (NASB). Oneness Pentecostals argue that the word *and* (Greek: *kai*) in the phrase "God our Father *and* the Lord Jesus Christ" should be translated "even." It should thus read, "God our Father, *even* the Lord Jesus Christ." Translated this way, Jesus and the Father are seen to be one and the same person (Graves, 1977, 50–51; cf. Bernard, 1983, 207–11).

CORRECTING THE MISINTERPRETATION: See comments on Romans 1:7. Note that the verse immediately *after* 1 Corinthians 1:3 points to the distinction between the Father and Jesus Christ (see v. 4).

1 CORINTHIANS 1:17—Is water baptism a condition for salvation?

MISINTERPRETATION: Paul declares that Christ did not send him to baptize. Yet Christ commissioned his disciples to "make disciples of all the nations, baptizing them in the name of the Father, and of the Son, and of the Holy Spirit" (Matt. 28:19 NIV). Is baptism necessary for salvation? Some groups, such as the Mormons, think so (Pratt, 1854, 255).

CORRECTING THE MISINTERPRETATION: Paul was not opposed to baptism, but neither did he believe it was a condition of salvation (see comments on Acts 2:38). Paul himself was baptized by water (Acts 9:18; 22:16), and he taught the significance and importance of water baptism in his Epistles (cf. Rom. 6:3–4; Col. 2:12). Indeed, in this very passage (1 Cor. 1), Paul admits that he baptized several people (vv. 14, 16) as he did the Philippian jailor after he was saved (Acts 16:31–33). While Paul believed water baptism was a symbol of salvation, he did not believe it was part of the gospel or essential to salvation.

1 CORINTHIANS 3:15—Does the reference to being saved by fire refer to purgatory, as Roman Catholic scholars claim?

MISINTERPRETATION: In 1 Corinthians 3:15 Paul declares that "if someone's work is burned up, that one will suffer loss; the person will be saved, but only as through fire." Roman Catholic scholars argue that "the Latin Fathers take the passage to mean a transient purification punishment in the other world" (Ott, 1960, 483).

CORRECTING THE MISINTERPRETATION: Here Paul, speaking of believers who will one day be given a "reward" for their service for Christ (v. 14), says: "But if someone's work is burned up, that one will suffer loss; the person will be saved, but only as through fire." The verse says *nothing* about a believer suffering the temporal consequences for his sins in purgatory.

First of all, the believer is not burned in the fire, only his *works* are burned. The believer sees his works burn but he himself escapes the fire. Even Roman Catholic authority Ludwig Ott seems to admit that this text "is speaking of a transient punishment *of the Day of General Judgment,* probably consisting of severe tribulations after which the final salvation will take place" (Ibid., 483, emphasis added). If so, then it is not speaking of what has traditionally been called purgatory at all. Further, the Book of Corinthians is written to those "who have been sanctified in Christ Jesus" (1 Cor. 1:2). Since they were already positionally sanctified in Christ, they needed no further purification to give them a right standing before God. They are already "in Christ." After listing a litany of sins, including fornication, idolatry, and coveting, Paul adds, "that is what some of you were; But you were washed, you were sanctified, you were justified in the name of the Lord Jesus Christ" (1 Cor. 6:11). From this and other Scriptures (cf. 2 Cor. 5:21), it is evident that their sins were already taken care of by Christ's suffering (cf. 1 Peter 2:22–24; 3:18) and that they stood, clothed in his righteousness, perfect before God. They needed no further suffering for sins to attain such a standing, nor to get them into heaven. And the fact that God desired them to improve their practical state on earth does not diminish for one moment their absolutely perfect standing in heaven. No sudden rush of practical sanctification (in purgatory) is needed to get into heaven.

What is more, the context reveals that the passage is not speaking about the *consequence* of sin but of *reward* for service for those who are already saved. Paul states clearly: "If what he has built [on the foundation of Christ] survives, he will receive his reward" (1 Cor. 3:14). The Greek word *(misthos)* used here refers to a "payment for work done" or a "reward" or "recompense given (mostly by God) for the moral quality of an action" (cf. 1 Cor. 9:17) (Arndt, *Greek-English Lexicon,* *"Mithos"*). So, the issue here is not *sin* and its punishment but *service* and its reward. Likewise, as even Catholic theologians acknowledge, the loss is clearly not of salvation, since "the person will be saved" (v. 15). Thus, the loss must be a loss of reward for not serving Christ faithfully. There is absolutely nothing here about suffering for our sins after death. Christ suffered for all our sins by his death (1 Cor. 15:3; Heb. 2:9).

In addition, the "fire" here does not purge our soul from sins; rather, it will "disclose" and "test" our "work." Verse 13 says clearly, "the work will come to light, for the Day will *disclose* it. It will be revealed with fire, and the fire [itself] will test the quality of each one's work" (emphasis added). There is virtually nothing here related to purging from sin. Contrary to the Catholic claim, the aim of the cleansing here is not ontological (actual) but functional. The focus is on what "crowns" believers will receive for service (2 Tim. 4:8), not with how their character is cleansed from sin. It is simply a matter of revealing and rewarding our work for Christ (2 Cor. 5:10). This does not mean that this experience will have no impact on the believer's character. It is only to point out that the purpose is not to cleanse the soul from sins in order to make it fit for heaven. This is what Christ did on the cross for us objectively and was subjectively applied to the believer at the moment of initial justification when he was dressed in the alien righteousness of Christ (John 19:30; Heb. 1:3; 2 Cor. 5:21).

Finally, when Christ died on the cross, he cried, "It is *finished*" (John 19:30). Speaking of his work of salvation on earth, Jesus said to the Father, "I have brought you glory on earth by completing the work you gave me to do" (John 17:4 NIV). The writer of Hebrews declared emphatically that salvation by Christ's suffering on the cross was a once-for-all, accomplished fact. For "by one sacrifice he has made perfect forever those who are being made holy" (Heb. 10:14 NIV). To affirm that we must suffer for our own sins, as the doctrine of purgatory does, is the ultimate insult to the all-sufficiency of Christ's atoning sacrifice! There is a purgatory, but it is not *after* our death; it was *in* Christ's death. For "when he had made *purification* of sins, He sat down at the right hand of the Majesty on high" (Heb. 1:3 NASB, emphasis added). Purification or purging from our sins was accomplished (in the past) on the cross. Thank God that this is the only purgatory we will ever have to suffer for our sins. Of course, there is a destiny of *hell* for those who reject this marvelous provision of God's grace (2 Thess. 1:8–9; Rev. 20:11–15). And there are temporal cause-effect relations in this life to the effect that what we sow, we reap (Gal. 6:8–9). But there is no evidence that we will have to pay for the results of our sins in the next life, either eternally or temporally. As Paul put it, "There is therefore *now* no condemnation for those who are in Christ Jesus" (Rom. 8:1 NASB).

1 CORINTHIANS 5:9—If Paul wrote an inspired Epistle, how could God allow it to be lost?

MISINTERPRETATION: Paul refers to a previous epistle he wrote to the Corinthians which is not in existence. But since it was written by an apostle to a church and contained spiritual and authoritative instruction, it must be considered inspired. This raises the question as to how an epistle inspired of God could be allowed by him to be lost. Mormons believe that because there are lost books of the Bible, this proves that the Bible has become corrupt and that the Book of Mormon is required.

CORRECTING THE MISINTERPRETATION: There are three possibilities regarding Paul's lost letter. First, it may be that not all apostolic letters were intended to be in the canon of Scripture. Luke refers to "many" other Gospels (1:1). John writes that there was much more Jesus did that was not recorded (20:30; 21:25). Perhaps this so-called "lost" letter to the Corinthians was not intended by God to be collected in the canon and preserved for the faith and practice of future generations, as were the twenty-seven books of the New Testament and thirty-nine of the Old Testament.

Second, others believe that the letter referred to in 1 Corinthians 5:9 may not be lost at all, but is incorporated into an existing book in the Bible. For example, it could be chapters 10 through 13 of what we know as 2 Corinthians, which some believe was later joined to chapters 1–9. Chapters 1–9 have a decidedly different tone from the rest of 2 Corinthians. This may indicate that it was written on a different occasion. The word *now* in 5:11 may contrast with an implied "then" when the former book was written. Paul refers to "letters" (plural) he had written in 2 Corinthians 10:10.

Third, Paul could be referring to 1 Corinthians itself in 1 Corinthians 5:9, that is, to the very Epistle which he was writing at the time. Evidence for this possibility is that he uses the Greek aorist tense.

Even though the aorist tense "I wrote" may refer to a past letter, it could also refer to the book at hand. This is called an "epistolary aorist," because it refers to the very book in which it is being used. The aorist tense is not a past tense as such. It identifies a completed action that may have even taken a long time to be accomplished (as in John 2:20).

The aorist tense often implies a decisive action, in which case Paul would be saying something like this: "I am now decisively writing to you. . . ." This certainly fits the context of this passage in which he is urging the church to take immediate action to excommunicate a wayward member. An "epistolary aorist" is used by Paul in 9:15 in this very letter: "I am not writing these things that it may be done so in my case."

There is absolutely no record from early church history of a third Corinthian letter of Paul. The reference in 2 Corinthians 10:10 that, "his letters are weighty" may mean no more than that "what he writes is weighty." And the "now" of 1 Corinthians 5:11 need not indicate a later letter. It can be translated "rather" (RSV) or "actually" (NASB).

1 CORINTHIANS 6:9b—Was Paul's condemnation of homosexuality merely his own idea? Was he against all homosexual acts, or only offensive ones?

MISINTERPRETATION: Paul told the Corinthians that homosexuals would not inherit the kingdom of God. But only a chapter later he makes a distinction between what is not his own but the Lord's command (7:10) and what is his own "opinion" (7:25). He doesn't give the source of his comments on homosexuality, so they may be his own nonbinding opinion on the issue. Also, the New International Version translation of 1 Corinthians 6:9 speaks only against "homosexual offenders," not against all homosexuality. Several New Age and other groups have used the reasoning that Paul was not against loving, faithful homosexual relationships.

CORRECTING THE MISINTERPRETATION: Paul's words on homosexuality in this text must be clarified by what he says elsewhere. His clearest condemnation of all homosexuality is in Romans 1:26–27. The divine authority of that text is not challenged by anyone who accepts the inspiration of Scripture anywhere.

We cannot make too much of the distinction between declarations that came out of Paul's divinely established apostolic office and direct revelations he received and passed on. He stated in Galatians 1:12 that none of his words were humanly conceived but received by revelation.

He had demonstrated his apostleship among the Corinthians (2 Cor. 12:12) and exercised apostolic authority in his ministry. He meets challenges to his authority forcefully in 1 Corinthians. He claims that his words were "taught by the Spirit" (2:13). At the end of his book he states that "what I am writing to you is the Lord's command" (14:37). Even in the disputed chapter 7 he declares his authority from the Holy Spirit (v. 40).

So when he speaks of words coming from himself and not the Lord, Paul is talking about Jesus Christ in his earthly ministry. At some points he can directly anchor his arguments in the words said on earth by the Lord. Elsewhere, he draws on divine revelation handed down since the ascension to him through the Holy Spirit. Jesus did not speak of these matters directly while on earth. But Jesus did promise that the Holy Spirit would "guide you into all truth" (John 16:13). Paul here fulfils that promise.

Again from Romans 1, it is obvious that Paul does condemn all homosexual behavior, not just an "offensive" class of behaviors. In Greek the word *homosexual* qualifies *offenders*. There are other kinds of offenders, which are not in view here. Paul establishes a category of offender—homosexuals. These are not "offending homosexuals" but "homosexual offenders." If only offensive acts were evil, what about adulterers and idolaters, condemned in the same passage. Are only offensive kinds of adultery and idolatry evil? There are simply too many places and ways in which Scripture condemns homosexuality for there to be waffling room on the subject. See comments on Leviticus 18:22; Romans 1:26–27 (see also 1 Tim. 1:10; Jude 7).

1 CORINTHIANS 6:13—If God is going to destroy the body, then how can it be resurrected?

MISINTERPRETATION: Paul said, "Food for the stomach and the stomach for food; but God will destroy both it and them" (1 Cor. 6:13). On this basis, some cults—including New Agers and Jehovah's Witnesses—argue that the resurrection body will not have the anatomy or physiology of the preresurrection body (*Things in Which It Is Impossible for God to Lie*, 1965, 354).

CORRECTING THE MISINTERPRETATION: The body that goes into the grave is the same body, now immortal, that comes out of it. This is proven by the fact that Jesus' tomb was empty. He had the crucifixion scars on his body (John 20:27). His body was "flesh and bones"

(Luke 24:39). People could and did touch Jesus (Matt. 28:9), and he could and did eat physical food (Luke 24:40–42).

As for 1 Corinthians 6:13, a careful study of the context reveals that, when Paul says God will destroy both food and the stomach, he is referring to the *process* of death, not to the *nature* of the body thereafter. Further, while the resurrection body may not have the need to eat, it does, however, have the ability to eat. Eating in heaven will be a joy without being a need. So, the body that death "destroys" (decays), is the same one that resurrection restores. To argue that there will be no resurrection body because the stomach will be "destroyed" is tantamount to claiming that the rest of the body—head, arms, legs, and torso—will not be resurrected because decay will turn them into dust.

1 CORINTHIANS 8:4—If idols are nothing, why does God condemn idolatry?

MISINTERPRETATION: Many cultic and aberrant groups justify the use of images. Indeed, the Roman Catholic church has done so since medieval times. Some appeal to Paul's affirmation here that an idol is nothing as in 1 Corinthians 10:19–20. Yet the Bible repeatedly condemns idolatry (Exod. 20:4), and even Paul said there are demons behind idols (1 Cor. 10:20). Is he here claiming that demons are nothing?

CORRECTING THE MISINTERPRETATION: Paul does not deny the *existence* of idols, simply their *ability* to affect mature believers who eat meat butchered in the context of idol worship, as most meat then was (cf. 8:1). It is not the *reality* of idols, but their *divinity* which Paul denies. The devil does deceive idolaters, but he cannot contaminate the meat God has created and pronounced good (Gen. 1:31; 1 Tim. 4:4), even if someone else has offered it to an idol.

Elsewhere, the Bible clearly condemns the use of images in worship, saying, "Thou shalt not make unto thee any graven image, or any likeness [of any thing] that [is] in heaven above, or that [is] in the earth beneath, or that [is] in the water under the earth" (Exod. 20:4 KJV).

1 CORINTHIANS 8:5—Does this verse support the idea that there are many gods in the universe?

MISINTERPRETATION: First Corinthians 8:5 says, "For even if there are so-called gods whether in heaven or on earth (as indeed there are many gods and many lords). . . ." Mormons believe this verse supports their view that there are many gods in the universe (McConkie, 1977, 579). They claim this is not polytheism, however, since Mormons do not worship *pagan* deities.

CORRECTING THE MISINTERPRETATION: The context of 1 Corinthians 8:5 is monotheistic. The preceding verse (v. 4) says, "We know that there is no such thing as an idol in the world, and that there is no God but one." The verse that follows (v. 6) says, "For us there is but one God, the Father, from whom are all things, and we exist for Him; and one Lord, Jesus Christ, by whom are all things, and we exist through Him." Obviously, then, Paul in verse 5 was referring to false pagan entities who are *called* gods (such as the Baals in the Old Testament). These are "gods" *by name* but not *by nature.*

1 CORINTHIANS 8:6—Does this verse prove that Jesus is not God Almighty like the Father is?

MISINTERPRETATION: 1 Corinthians 8:6 says, "For us there is but one God, the Father, from whom are all things, and we exist for Him; and one Lord, Jesus Christ, by whom are all things, and we exist through Him." Some cults claim that, since this verse clearly presents God the Father "as being in a class distinct from Jesus Christ" (*Reasoning from the Scriptures,* 1989, 411), it follows that Jesus is not God in the same sense that the Father is.

CORRECTING THE MISINTERPRETATION: If the reference to the Father being the "one God" proves Jesus is not God, then the reference to Jesus as the "one Lord" likewise proves the Father is not Lord. This is obviously faulty logic. Scripture calls the Father God (1 Peter 1:2) *and* Lord (Matt. 11:25), and calls Jesus God (John 20:28; Heb. 1:8) and Lord (Rom. 10:9). Clearly, the Father's designation as God in this verse is not intended to exclude Jesus and the Holy Spirit (Matt. 28:19; 2 Cor. 13:14). In the same way, Jesus' identification as "God and Savior" in Titus 2:13 does not exclude the Father and the Holy Spirit. When the Holy Spirit is called God in Acts 5:4, it is not to the exclusion of the Father and Jesus.

1 CORINTHIANS 10:14—Does this verse indicate that Christians should not wear a cross?

MISINTERPRETATION: The Jehovah's Witnesses argue that the command against idolatry in this verse encompasses a command not to wear a cross. To wear a cross, they say, is a form of idolatry (*Reasoning from the Scriptures,* 1989, 89).

CORRECTING THE MISINTERPRETATION: The command to avoid idolatry was relevant to the Corinthian believers because Corinth was an idolatrous city. Idolatry in Corinth led to such things as sexual immorality, drunkenness, and reveling. Because idolatry and its accompanying vices were rampant, Paul instructs the Corinthian believers to "flee" (run away from) idolatry.

Wearing a cross *is not* idolatry because the cross is not worshiped or venerated. Christians wear a cross because they worship and venerate Christ. It is an *outward* expression of an *inner* worshipful attitude toward Christ. Only if a Christian bowed down before a cross in worship or veneration would it become a forbidden object of worship (cf. Exod. 20:4).

1 CORINTHIANS 11:1—Does Paul's statement "Imitate me" justify authoritarianism, as some cultic groups claim?

MISINTERPRETATION: Paul sometimes calls on his followers to imitate him (see also 1 Cor. 4:16). Some authoritarian cults, such as the Boston Church of Christ, use this to justify their authoritarianism. Is this a legitimate inference from these verses?

CORRECTING THE MISINTERPRETATION: The New Testament often exhorts believers to submit to their leaders (1 Cor. 16:16; Heb. 13:17; 1 Peter 5:5). It also says wives are to submit to their husbands, children to their parents (Col. 3:18–20), and citizens to their governments (Titus 3:1). But this should not be twisted into ecclesiastical authoritarianism.

This submission is qualified. Children are to obey their parents only "in the Lord" (Eph. 6:1), not in literally anything their elders may command. The same is true of citizens submitting to their respective governments. There are many instances of justified disobedience to government, such as when the Pharaoh commanded the midwives to kill every male baby that was born (Exod. 1:15–21) or when the three Hebrew children were commanded to bow before an idol (Dan. 3). We should submit to a proper authority only when it takes its place under God but not when it takes the place of God.

There is an important difference between legitimate submission and illegitimate authoritarianism. Proper submission to a church leader is voluntary, not compulsory. It involves a free choice to join or leave that organization without intimidation or reprisal. It is done out of love and respect (cf. Heb. 13:7), not out of fear. While the Bible speaks of voluntary submission from the bottom up, it nowhere enjoins compulsory obedience from the top down. That is, it never says that leaders should command (or demand) obedience; only that followers should freely give it. Church leaders themselves are reminded not to "lord it over the flock" but rather to be "examples" to it (1 Peter 5:2–3). They are to lead by their life, not their lips; by their character, not their commands.

1 CORINTHIANS 11:2—Does this reference to tradition support the Roman Catholic view that the Bible alone is not sufficient for faith and practice?

See comments on 2 Thessalonians 2:15.

1 CORINTHIANS 11:3—Since God is called the "head" of Christ in this verse, is this an indication that Jesus is not God?

MISINTERPRETATION: The Jehovah's Witnesses argue that because the Father is said to be the head of Christ, then Christ cannot be God in the same sense the Father is. If Christ were God, then he would be the head (*Should You Believe in the Trinity?* 1989, 20).

CORRECTING THE MISINTERPRETATION: Paul in the same verse said the man is the head of the woman, even though men and women are equal in terms of their human nature (Gen. 1:26–28; cf. Gal. 3:28). Obviously, equality of nature and functional hierarchy are not mutually exclusive. Likewise, Christ and the Father are equal in their divine nature (John 10:30), but Jesus is functionally under the Father's headship.

1 CORINTHIANS 12:28—Does this verse indicate that the true church on earth today must have a living apostle and/or prophet?

MISINTERPRETATION: First Corinthians 12:28 says, "And God has appointed in the church, first apostles, second prophets, third teachers, then miracles, then gifts of healings, helps, administrations, various kinds of tongues" (NASB). Mormons believe that the true church must have living prophets and apostles (McConkie, 1977, 606). Since Mormons have "prophets" and "apostles," they claim to be the only true church.

CORRECTING THE MISINTERPRETATION: According to Ephesians 2:20, the church is "built upon the foundation of the apostles and prophets." Once the foundation is built, it is never built *again*. It is built *upon*. Scripture describes the work of the apostles and prophets as foundational in nature.

The first-century apostles understood that God was providing unique revelation through them (1 Cor. 2:13). They were handpicked by the Lord (Matt. 10:1–2; Acts 1:26) and had divine authority (Acts 20:35; 1 Cor. 7:10). Biblical apostles had to be eyewitnesses to the resurrected Christ (1 Cor. 9:1; cf. 1 Cor. 15:7–8).

The Book of Acts clearly attests to the uniqueness and authority of the apostles. In Acts 2:42 the first church "devoted themselves to the apostles' teaching and fellowship." The pronouncements of the apostles were final (cf. 15:2). By their voice the church was born (Acts 2); miracles were performed (Acts 3); rulers were restricted (Acts 4); the disobedient were judged (Acts 5); the Holy Spirit was given to the Samaritans (Acts 8) and the Gentiles (Acts 10).

The biblical apostles were authenticated by incredible miracles (2 Cor. 12:12)—miracles like raising people from the dead (Acts 9:36–42). Anyone claiming to be an apostle must be *authenticated* by the signs of an apostle. Mormon "apostles" and "prophets" have no such miraculous attestation.

Moreover, the revelation given by Mormon prophets and apostles clearly contradicts the revelation decisively ("once for all") handed down by the first-century apostles (Jude 3). Mormon apostles teach that Jesus is a created being and is the spirit-brother of Lucifer. The biblical apostles taught that Jesus is God and Creator (Col. 2:9; 1:16 [cf. Isa. 44:24]). Mormon apostles teach that God is an exalted man of flesh and bones. The biblical apostles taught that God is spirit (2 Cor. 3:17–18). The Mormon apostles teach that there are many gods in the universe. The biblical apostles taught that there is only one God (1 Tim. 2:5). Mormon apostles teach that human beings may become gods. The biblical apostles taught that human beings never become God (see Acts 14:14–15).

1 CORINTHIANS 14:33—Does the fact that God is not a God of disorder or confusion prove that the doctrine of the Trinity is not true?

MISINTERPRETATION: The Jehovah's Witnesses think that the doctrine of the Trinity cannot possibly be true because God is not a God of confusion, and the doctrine of the Trinity is definitely confusing (*Should You Believe in the Trinity?* 1989, 4).

CORRECTING THE MISINTERPRETATION: Such an interpretation takes this verse out of its context. It is not speaking about confusing *doctrine* but disorderly church *practices.* This verse is in an extended section of Scripture in which Paul deals with the proper exercise of the spiritual gifts. In 1 Corinthians 14:33 Paul's point is that because God is not a God of confusion, the Corinthians should make every effort to end the confusion in their church services resulting from too many people speaking in tongues and giving prophecies at the same time (see vv. 27–30). God does not move his people to handle themselves in a disorderly and tumultuous manner. Rather, God is a God *of peace* (harmony and order), and hence his people should be harmonious and ordered in their services.

Further, the doctrine of the Trinity is not *confusing;* it is a *mystery.* The doctrine of the Trinity is clear: There is one God manifest in three persons. This is just as clear as affirming there is one triangle with three sides (an analogy which cannot be pressed too far in describing the Trinity). Or, that love is one, and yet to have love there must be a lover, a loved one, and a spirit of love between them. We can apprehend the truth of the Trinity, even if we cannot completely comprehend it. The Trinity is not *contrary* to reason; it simply goes *beyond* our reason.

Just because a doctrine is difficult to comprehend does not mean it must be a false doctrine. Even a strict monotheistic concept of God, such as the Jehovah's Witnesses hold, cannot be completely comprehended. For us to fully understand God's nature, we would have to have the mind of God. But Scripture indicates that we cannot understand everything about God. Romans 11:33 (NASB) affirms, "How unsearchable are His judgments and unfathomable His ways!" In Isaiah 55:8–9 (NASB) God says, "'As the heavens are higher than the earth, so are My ways higher than your ways, and My thoughts than your thoughts.'" Just as an infant cannot possibly understand everything his father does or says, so we as God's finite children cannot understand everything about our infinite heavenly Father.

1 CORINTHIANS 15:5–8—Did Jesus only appear to believers?

MISINTERPRETATION: Some cults and critics have cast doubt on the validity of Christ's resurrection by insisting that he appeared only to believers, but never to unbelievers.

CORRECTING THE MISINTERPRETATION: It is incorrect to claim that Jesus did not appear to unbelievers. For one case, he appeared to the most hostile unbeliever of all, Saul of Tarsus (Acts 9, 22, 26).

Even Jesus' disciples did not accept the resurrection when Jesus first appeared to them. When Mary Magdalene and others reported that Jesus was resurrected "their words seemed to them like idle tales, and they did not believe them" (Luke 24:11 NASB). Later, Jesus had to chide the two disciples on the road to Emmaus about disbelief in his resurrection, "O foolish ones, and slow of heart to believe in all that the prophets have spoken!" (Luke 24:25 NASB). Even after Jesus had appeared to the women, to Peter, to the two disciples, and to the ten apostles, Thomas said, "Unless I see the nail marks in his hands and put my finger where the nails were, and put my hand into his side, I will not believe it" (John 20:25 NIV). He was hardly a believer in the resurrection.

In addition to appearing to his unbelieving disciples, Jesus also appeared to some who were not his disciples at all. He appeared to his brother James (1 Cor. 15:7), who, with his other brothers, was not a believer before the resurrection (John 7:5). Also, Scripture does not claim to be making an exhaustive list of those who saw the resurrected Christ, only some significant encounters.

1 CORINTHIANS 15:5–8—Why did Jesus appear to only a select few?

MISINTERPRETATION: Some critics have suggested that the fact that only a few saw Jesus after his resurrection indicates that he was essentially invisible to the physical human eye, and only materialized to a few people on select occasions. The Jehovah's Witnesses believe Jesus "materialized" on occasions in different bodily forms to prove his "resurrection" (*Aid to Bible Understanding*, 1971, 1395).

CORRECTING THE MISINTERPRETATION: Jesus did not appear to only a few people. He appeared to more than 500 people (1 Cor. 15:6), including many women, his own apostles, his brother James, and to Saul of Tarsus, the chief anti-Christian of the day. Jesus did not simply appear on a few occasions. He appeared on at least twelve different occasions. These were spread over a forty-day period (Acts 1:3) in different geographical locations.

Jesus did not allow just anyone to lay hands on him even before his resurrection. On one occasion, an unbelieving crowd tried to take Jesus and "throw Him down over the cliff. But passing through their midst, He went his way" (Luke 4:29b–30; cf. John 8:59; 10:39) Even before his resurrection, Jesus was selective about those for whom he performed miracles. He refused to perform miracles in his own home area because of their unbelief (Matt. 13:58). Jesus even disappointed Herod who had hoped to see him perform a miracle (Luke 23:8). The truth is that Jesus refused to cast pearls before swine (Matt. 7:6). In submission to the Father's will (John 5:30), he was sovereign over his activity both before and after his resurrection. But this in no way proves that he was essentially invisible and immaterial either before or after his resurrection. See also comments on Luke 24:23, 31; 1 John 4:2.

1 CORINTHIANS 15:23—Does the verse support the Roman Catholic dogma of the bodily assumption of Mary?

MISINTERPRETATION: According to Catholic dogma, "Mary was assumed body and soul into heaven" (Ott, 1960, 208). On November 1, 1950, the Roman Pontiff spoke *ex cathedra* to proclaim infallibly that "just as the glorious resurrection of Christ was an essential part, and final evidence of the victory, so the Blessed Virgin's common struggle with her son was to be concluded with the 'glorification' of her virginal body" (Denzinger, 1957, no. 2331, 647). Some Catholic theologians appeal to 1 Corinthians 15:23 to support this dogma, arguing that Christ is the "firstfruits" of the resurrection and "then, at his coming, those who belong to Christ" (Ott, 208).

CORRECTING THE MISINTERPRETATION: It is a far-fetched use of 1 Corinthians 15:23 to support the Bodily Assumption dogma. Even noted defenders of Catholic dogma admit that "direct and express scriptural proofs are not to be had" (Ibid.). They speak rather of the "possibility" of it in this text. But one is hard-pressed to find even that.

The text speaks about Christ being the "firstfruits" of the resurrection. Mary is not in view in the text at all.

1 CORINTHIANS 15:25–28—Does Paul teach universalism when he affirms that "all things" will be put under Christ?

MISINTERPRETATION: Speaking of the eschaton or end times, Paul affirmed in 1 Corinthians 15:24–28 (NIV) that "then the end will come, when he hands over the kingdom to God the Father after he has destroyed all dominion, authority and power. For he must reign, until he has put all his enemies under his feet. . . . When he has done this, then the Son Himself will be made subject to him who put everything under him, so that God may be all in all." The early church father Origen based his universalism on this text (Origen [2], 1.6.1), as do other universalists.

CORRECTING THE MISINTERPRETATION: In order to make this text support their view, universalists ignore both the content and context of this passage. Paul is not speaking of the salvation of the lost but of their condemnation. This is evident in words and phrases such as "destroy," "put under his feet," and "put an end to all rule." The text is speaking about the subjugation of the lost (vv. 24, 27, 28). It says nothing about salvation. These individuals are spoken of as God's enemies, not his friends or children. They are subjugated *as enemies*, not saved *as friends*.

That God will be "all in all" (v. 28) does not mean that all will be *in God*. It means he will reign supreme in all the universe. The phrase *all things* must be understood in its context. It does not say that all things will be saved. Rather, it merely asserts that "all things are made subject to Him" (v. 28), but, as "enemies" (v. 25). In fact, *all things* is used in parallel with *enemies* in successive verses (vv. 26–27).

Heaven is not a place where God overpowers the will of his enemies and forces them into his fold. This is precisely what a God of love cannot do—force people against their will to love him. Jesus said so (Matt. 23:37). So, there is not a hint here of salvation for all unbelievers.

1 CORINTHIANS 15:29—Does this verse support the Mormon doctrine of baptism for the dead?

MISINTERPRETATION: Paul said, "What will they do who are baptized for the dead?" Mormons believe this means that living believers should be baptized on behalf of the dead (Talmage, 1982, 149–50).

CORRECTING THE MISINTERPRETATION: This is an obscure and isolated passage. It is unwise to base any doctrine on such a passage. Rather, one should always use the clear passages of Scripture to interpret the unclear ones. The clear texts are emphatic that baptism does not save. We are saved by grace through faith, not by works (Rom. 4:5; Eph. 2:8–9; Titus 3:5–7). We cannot do anything that would obtain salvation for another person. Each person must believe for himself (John 1:12). Everyone must make his own free choice (Matt. 23:37; 2 Peter 3:9).

As to this text, scholars differ as to what Paul means. There are several possibilities.

Paul may refer sarcastically to a cultic practice existing among the Corinthians, who had many false beliefs (see 1 Cor. 5). In effect, Paul would be saying, "If you don't believe in the resurrection, then why engage in the practice of baptizing people for the dead. You are inconsistent in your own (false) beliefs." Paul finds the practice so obviously wrong that he does *not* need to explicitly condemn it. Paul says "they" (others) not "we" baptize the dead (15:29). Elsewhere in 1 Corinthians, Paul emphasizes intimacy with the Corinthian believers by using first-person pronouns. At verse 29 he switches to the third-person "they."

Paul may also refer to the fact that baptism of new converts is replenishing the depleted ranks of believers who have died. If so, his sense here would be, "Why do you continue to fill the church with baptized converts, who replace those who have died, if you do not really believe there is any hope for them beyond the grave?" Or Paul may be reminding his readers that baptism symbolizes the believer's death with Christ (Rom. 6:3–5). The Greek word *for (eis)* can mean "with a view to." In this sense, he would be saying, "Why are you baptized with a view to your death and resurrection with Christ, if you do not believe in the resurrection?"

Some scholars point out that the preposition *for* in Greek *(eis)* can mean "for the sake of." In this case, baptism would be for the sake of those who are dead. Paul says "If the dead do not rise at all; Why then are new converts who one day will die baptized?" (v. 29). Since it was common in the New Testament period to be baptized as one accepted the gospel, this was a sign of one's faith in Christ. But why be baptized if there is no resurrection? Paul later says that if there is no resurrection, "let us eat and drink, for tomorrow we die" (v. 32).

Whatever the correct interpretation, there is no reason to believe Paul is here contradicting his own clear teaching elsewhere, or the rest of Scripture, which insists that every person must freely choose or reject God's gift of salvation for himself. Paul certainly did not urge his hearers to practice the principle, nor did he command it. He merely used the case *as an illustration.* There is no mention of baptism for the dead in the Bible up until Paul—and no mention afterward. Christ does not mention it, nor do any of the other apostles.

1 CORINTHIANS 15:33—By quoting a pagan poet as part of Scripture, doesn't Paul thereby pronounce this pagan writing a part of Scripture?

MISINTERPRETATION: Some have argued that Paul's use of non-Christian sources here shows that there are other inspired writings not found in the Bible.

CORRECTING THE MISINTERPRETATION: Paul is not quoting this non-Christian source *as inspired*, but simply *as true*. All truth is God's truth, no matter who said it. Caiaphas the Jewish high priest uttered a truth about Christ (John 11:49). The Bible often uses non-inspired sources (cf. Num. 21:14; Josh. 10:13; 1 Kings 15:31). Three times Paul cites non-Christian thinkers (Acts 17:28; 1 Cor. 15:33; Titus 1:12). Jude alludes to truths found in two non-canonical books (Jude 9, 14). But never does the Bible cite them as divinely authoritative, but simply as containing the truth quoted. The usual phrases, such as, "thus saith the Lord" (cf. Isa. 7:7; Jer. 2:5 KJV) or "it is written" (cf. Matt. 4:4, 7, 10) are never found when these non-inspired sources are cited. Nonetheless, truth is truth wherever it is found. And there is no reason, therefore, that a biblical author, by direction of the Holy Spirit, cannot utilize truth from whatever source he may find it. See comments on Titus 2:2.

1 CORINTHIANS 15:37—Is Paul teaching that the resurrection body is a different one from the one that is sown—a kind of reincarnation?

MISINTERPRETATION: Just as seeds change when they are sown, so this verse says that the body will change when it is resurrected. Some take this to mean the resurrection body is a different one, a "spiritual" (v. 44) body that is not essentially material. Does this prove that we are not raised in the same physical body of flesh and blood in which we die? This verse is relevant to discussions with the Jehovah's Witnesses (*Aid to Bible Understanding*, 1971, 1395).

CORRECTING THE MISINTERPRETATION: There are real changes in the resurrection body, but it is not changed into a nonphysical body—one substantially different from the one we possess now. The seed that goes into the ground brings forth more seeds that are the same kind, not immaterial seeds. It is in this sense that Paul can say "you do not sow [cause to die] the body that shall be," since it is immortal and cannot die. The body that is raised is different in that it is immortal (1 Cor. 15:53), not in that it is immaterial. Of his resurrection body Jesus said,

"It is I Myself. Handle Me and see, for a spirit does not have flesh and bones as you see I have" (Luke 24:39).

Jesus' resurrection body, though transformed and glorified, is the *numerically same body* of flesh and bones Jesus possessed before his resurrection. And since our resurrection bodies will be like his (Phil. 3:21), the same is true of the believer's resurrection body. Notice these characteristics of Jesus' resurrection body: (1) It was the same body, with the crucifixion scars, it had from before the resurrection (Luke 24:39; John 20:27). (2) It was the same body that left the empty tomb behind (Matt. 28:6; John 20:5–7; cf. John 5:28–29). (3) The physical body of Jesus did not corrupt in the tomb (Acts 2:31). (4) Jesus said his body would be destroyed and built up again (John 2:19–22). (5) It was a body of "flesh and bones" (Luke 24:39) that could be touched (Matt. 28:9; John 20:27) and could eat physical food (Luke 24:41–42).

Further, Scripture teaches that the immortal body is "put on" over, but does not replace, the mortal body (1 Cor. 15:53). The plant that springs forth from the seed is both genetically and physically connected with the seed. What is sown is what is reaped (1 Cor. 15:37–38).

The "change" (1 Cor. 15:51) Paul referred to at the resurrection is a change *in* the body, not a change *of* body. The changes in the resurrection are *accidental,* not *substantial.* They are changes in *secondary qualities,* not changes in *primary qualities.* It is changed from a corruptible physical body to an incorruptible physical body. It is not changed from a physical body into a nonphysical body. It is changed from a mortal to an immortal physical body. But it not changed from a material to an immaterial body.

1 CORINTHIANS 15:40–42—Does this support the idea that there are three kingdoms of glory one may inhabit in the next life?

MISINTERPRETATION: Mormons believe the reference to "celestial bodies" and "terrestrial bodies" in this passage (KJV) gives support to their view that all people will inhabit one of three kingdoms of glory in the next life—the Celestial Kingdom, the Terrestrial Kingdom, or the Telestial Kingdom (McConkie, 1966, 420). One's faithfulness in this life determines which kingdom one will end up in.

CORRECTING THE MISINTERPRETATION: This passage does not refer to three kingdoms of glory. First Corinthians 15:40–42 does not even make reference to the word *telestial.* This in itself disqualifies the passage as a support for the idea that there are three kingdoms.

The context of the passage very clearly has to do with resurrection bodies (see v. 35). Paul in this verse is talking about the heavenly (celestial) body as opposed to the earthly (terrestrial) body. He says the earthly body is fallen, temporal, imperfect, and weak (vv. 42–44), while the heavenly body will be eternal, perfect, and powerful (cf. 2 Cor. 5:1–4).

1 CORINTHIANS 15:44—Is the resurrection body material or immaterial?

MISINTERPRETATION: Paul declares that the resurrection body is a spiritual body (1 Cor. 15:44). Jehovah's Witnesses believe such verses indicate that Jesus was raised from the dead in a spirit body. They say, "It is true that Jesus appeared in physical form to his disciples after his resurrection. . . . Jesus evidently materialized bodies on these occasions" (*Reasoning from the Scriptures*, 1989, 215). But his resurrection body was a spirit body.

CORRECTING THE MISINTERPRETATION: A "spiritual" body denotes an immortal body, not an immaterial body. A "spiritual" body is one dominated by the spirit, not one devoid of matter. The Greek word *pneumatikos* (translated "spiritual" here) means a body directed by the spirit, as opposed to one under the dominion of the flesh. It is not ruled by flesh that perishes, but by the spirit that endures (1 Cor. 15:50–58). So "spiritual body" does not mean immaterial and invisible, but immortal and imperishable. Notice the parallels drawn by Paul:

Preresurrection body	Postresurrection body
Earthly (v. 40)	Heavenly
Perishable (v. 42)	Imperishable
Weak (v. 43)	Powerful
Natural (v. 44)	[Supernatural]
Mortal (v. 53)	Immortal

The complete context shows that *spiritual (pneumatikos)* could be translated "supernatural" in contrast to "natural" from the parallels of perishable and imperishable, corruptible and incorruptible. *Pneumatikos* is translated "supernatural" in 1 Corinthians 10:4 when it speaks of the "supernatural rock that followed them in the wilderness" (RSV). In its translation of "spiritual" *pneumatikos* refers to physical objects. Again turning to 1 Corinthians 10:45, Paul spoke of the "spiritual rock" that followed Israel in the wilderness from which they got "spiritual drink" (1 Cor. 10:4). But the Old Testament story (Exod. 17; Num. 20) reveals that it was a physical rock from which they got literal water to drink. But the actual water they drank from that material rock was produced supernaturally. When Jesus supernaturally made bread for the five thousand (John 6), he made literal bread. However, this literal, material bread could have been called "spiritual" bread because of its supernatural source in the same way that the literal manna given to Israel is called "spiritual food" (1 Cor. 10:3).

Further, when Paul spoke about a "spiritual man" (1 Cor. 2:15) he obviously did not mean an invisible, immaterial man with no corporeal body. He was, as a matter of fact, speaking of a flesh and blood human being whose life is lived by the supernatural power of God, a literal person whose life is Spirit directed. A spiritual man is one who is taught by the Spirit and who receives the things that come from the Spirit of God (1 Cor. 2:13–14). The resurrection body can be called a "spiritual body" in much the same way we speak of the Bible as a "spiritual book." Regardless of their spiritual source and power, both the resurrection body and the Bible are material objects.

1 CORINTHIANS 15:45—Was Christ a life-giving spirit after his resurrection, or did he have a physical body?

MISINTERPRETATION: Paul asserts here that Christ was made a "life-giving spirit" after his resurrection. Some—including the Jehovah's Witnesses—have cited this passage to prove that Jesus had no physical resurrection body (*Aid to Bible Understanding*, 1971, 1395).

CORRECTING THE MISINTERPRETATION: "Life-giving spirit" does not speak of the *nature* of Christ's resurrection body, but of the divine *origin* of the resurrection. Jesus' physical body came back to life only by the power of God (cf. Rom. 1:4). So Paul is speaking about its spiritual *source*, not its physical *substance* as a material body. See also comments on 1 Corinthians 15:44.

If "spirit" describes the nature of Christ's resurrection body, then Adam, with whom he is contrasted, must not have had a soul, since he is described as "of the earth, made of dust" (v. 47). But the Bible clearly says that Adam was "a living being [soul]" (Gen. 2:7).

Christ's resurrection body is called "spiritual body" (v. 44) which, as discussed under 1 Corinthians 15:44, is the same word used by Paul to describe material food and a literal rock (1 Cor. 10:4). It is called a "body" *(soma),* which always means a physical body when referring to an individual human being.

In summation, the resurrection body is called "spiritual" and "life-giving spirit" because its source is the spiritual realm, not because its substance is immaterial. Christ's supernatural resurrection body is "from heaven," as Adam's natural body was "of the earth" (v. 47). But just as the one from "earth" also has an immaterial soul, even so the One from "heaven" also has a material body.

1 CORINTHIANS 15:50—If flesh and blood cannot enter heaven, then how can there be a physical resurrection?

MISINTERPRETATION: According to this verse, "flesh and blood cannot inherit the kingdom of God." Hence, Jesus must have had a spiritual resurrection, since flesh and blood bodies cannot exist in heaven (*Aid to Bible Understanding*, 1971, 1395). Mortality and corruption belong to the fleshly body. The resurrection body is immortal and incorruptible because it is by nature a spiritual body.

CORRECTING THE MISINTERPRETATION: To conclude from this phrase that the resurrection body will not be a body of physical flesh is without biblical justification. The very next phrase omitted from the above quotation clearly indicates that Paul is speaking not of flesh as such, but of *corruptible* flesh. For he adds, "*nor does corruption inherit the incorruption*" (v. 50 NKJV). So, Paul is not affirming that the resurrection body will not have flesh; he is saying that it will not have *perishable* flesh.

In order to convince the frightened disciples that he was not an immaterial spirit (Luke 24:37), Jesus emphatically told them, "Look at my hands and my feet. It is I myself! Touch me and see; a ghost does not have flesh and bones, as you see I have" (Luke 24:39 NIV). Peter declared that the resurrection body would be the same body of flesh that went into the tomb and never saw corruption (Acts 2:31). Paul also reaffirmed this truth in a parallel passage (Acts 13:35). And John implies that it is against Christ to deny that he remains "in the flesh" even after his resurrection (1 John 4:2; 2 John 7).

This conclusion cannot be avoided by claiming that Jesus' resurrection body had flesh and bones, but not flesh and blood. For if it had flesh and bones, then it was a literal, material body, whether or not it had blood. Flesh and bones stresses the solidity of Jesus' physical postresurrection body. They are more obvious signs of tangibility than blood, which cannot be as easily seen or touched. The phrase *flesh and blood* in this context apparently means "*mortal* flesh and blood," that is, a mere human being. This is supported by parallel uses in the New Testament. When Jesus said to Peter, "Flesh and blood has not revealed this to you" (Matt. 16:17 KJV), he could not have been referring to the mere substance of the body as such, which obviously could not reveal that he was the Son of God. Rather, the most natural interpretation of 1 Corinthians 15:50 seems to be that a human being, as an earth-bound and perishable creature, cannot have a place in God's glorious, heavenly kingdom.

2 Corinthians

2 CORINTHIANS 3:17—Does this verse prove that Jesus *is* the Holy Spirit, supporting the modalistic views of Oneness Pentecostals?

MISINTERPRETATION: In 2 Corinthians 3:17 we read, "Now the Lord is the Spirit; and where the Spirit of the Lord is, there is liberty" (NIV). Oneness Pentecostals say Jesus is the Lord in this verse, and he is explicitly identified as the Holy Spirit who opens up the heart of believers (Bernard, 1983, 132). Hence, Jesus is the Holy Spirit.

CORRECTING THE MISINTERPRETATION: Many expositors view this verse as saying that the Holy Spirit is Lord, not in the sense of being Jesus but in the sense of being *Yahweh*, the Lord God (see v. 16, which cites Exod. 34:34–35).

Another problem with the Oneness Pentecostal interpretation is that just earlier in 2 Corinthians 3:3–6, the apostle Paul clearly distinguishes between Jesus and the Holy Spirit. More broadly, the whole of Scripture makes that distinction. Indeed, the Holy Spirit is said to be *another* comforter (John 14:16). Jesus *sent* the Holy Spirit (John 15:26; 16:7). The Spirit *seeks* to *glorify* Jesus (John 16:13–14). The Holy Spirit *descended upon* Jesus at his baptism (Luke 3:22). Jesus distinguishes the Holy Spirit from himself in the Great Commission (Matt. 28:19).

The question above refers to the Oneness position as "modalism." This ancient error has occasionally turned up to trouble the church with the idea that God has revealed himself in three successive modes as Father, Son, and Spirit, but he cannot be all three at one time. The Oneness theology is a contemporary version of this heresy.

2 CORINTHIANS 5:19—Does Paul mean all will be saved when he says the world will be reconciled to God?

MISINTERPRETATION: Paul told the Corinthians "that God was reconciling the world to himself in Christ, not counting men's sins against them. And he has committed to us the message of reconciliation." On this basis universalists argue that the entire "world" of humanity was reconciled to God by Christ's work. Thus, *all* are saved on the basis of Jesus' work on the cross.

CORRECTING THE MISINTERPRETATION: Reconciliation is regarded in this passage as a process according to God's purpose, not an accomplished fact for the whole world. It is God's desire to save all (2 Peter 3:9), but not all will be saved (Matt. 7:13–14; Rev. 20:11–15). The context indicates that actual reconciliation is only for those who are "in Christ," not for all persons (v. 17).

If all were already saved, then Paul's exhortation to be "ambassadors for Christ" and to "plead" with the world to "be reconciled to God" would be meaningless. It is senseless to beg people to be reconciled to God if in fact they already are reconciled. Certainly Scripture denies this reconciliation, so to interpret this passage in favor of universalism is to say that Scripture contradicts itself (see, for example, Matt. 25:31–46).

2 CORINTHIANS 5:21—How could Jesus be made sin when he was sinless?

MISINTERPRETATION: Paul asserts here that Jesus was "made to be sin." However, many other Scriptures insist that Jesus was "without sin" (Heb. 4:15; cf. 1 Peter 3:18). How could Jesus be without sin if he was made sin for us? This is an especially important question in view of the fact that Word-Faith teachers say that when Jesus was "made sin," he took on the nature of Satan (Copeland, "What Happened from the Cross to the Throne," 1990, audio tape).

CORRECTING THE MISINTERPRETATION: Christ did not take on the nature of Satan, for Christ as God is immutable (Heb. 13:8; cf. Mal. 3:6). His divine nature cannot change. In Hebrews 1:12b the Father says of Jesus, "You remain the same, and your years will never end" (NIV).

Regarding as Jesus being "made to be sin," Jesus was always without sin *actually*, but he was made to be sin for us *judicially*. That is, by his death on the cross, he paid the penalty for our sins and thereby canceled the debt of sin against us. So, while Jesus never committed a sin *personally*, he was made to be sin for us *substitutionally*. The issue can be summarized:

Christ was not sinful	Christ was made to be sin
In himself	For us
Personally	Substitutionally
Actually	Judicially

One must also keep in mind the Old Testament backdrop of the concept of substitution. The sacrificial victim had to be "without defect" (see Lev. 4:3, 23, 28, 32). A hand would be laid on the unblemished sacrificial animal as a way of symbolizing a transfer of guilt (Lev. 4:4, 24, 33). The sacrificial animal did not thereby actually become sinful by nature; rather, sin was *imputed* to the animal and the animal acted as a sacrificial substitute. In like manner, Christ the Lamb of God was utterly unblemished (1 Peter 1:19), but our sin was *imputed* to him and he was our sacrificial substitute on the cross of Calvary. Simply because our sin was imputed to him does not mean he changed in nature. Christ was not sinful *personally;* he was made to be sin *substitutionally.*

2 CORINTHIANS 8:9—Does this verse indicate that financial prosperity is in the atonement, as Word-Faith teachers argue?

MISINTERPRETATION: Second Corinthians 8:9 says, "For you know the grace of our Lord Jesus Christ, that though he was rich, yet for your sake he became poor, that you through his poverty might become rich" (NIV). Word-Faith teachers cite this verse in support of their view that financial prosperity is provided for in the atonement.

CORRECTING THE MISINTERPRETATION: If Paul intended to say that prosperity is provided for in the atonement, he was offering the Corinthians something that he himself did not possess at the time. Indeed, in 1 Corinthians 4:11 Paul informed these same individuals that he was "hungry and thirsty," "poorly clothed," and "homeless." He also exhorted the Corinthians to be imitators of his life and teaching (1 Cor. 4:16).

In 2 Corinthians 8:9 it seems clear that Paul was speaking about spiritual prosperity, not financial prosperity. This fits both the immediate context in 2 Corinthians and the broader context of Paul's other writings. For example, if financial prosperity was provided for in the atonement, one must wonder why Paul informed the Philippian Christians that he had learned to be content even when going hungry (Phil. 4:11–12). One would think he would have instead claimed the prosperity promised in the atonement to meet his every need.

For more on the biblical perspective on money, see the discussion of Mark 10:30.

2 CORINTHIANS 12:2—Does this verse indicate that there are three degrees of glory in the afterlife, as Mormons believe?

MISINTERPRETATION: In 2 Corinthians 12:2 we read, "I know a man in Christ who fourteen years ago—whether in the body I do not know, or out of the body I do not know, God knows—such a man was caught up to the third heaven" (NASB). Mormons say this verse proves there are three heavens or three degrees of glory in the next life—the Celestial Kingdom for faithful Mormons, the Terrestrial Kingdom for less-than-valiant Mormons and moral non-Mormons, and the Telestial Kingdom for worldly people (Richards, 1978, 255).

CORRECTING THE MISINTERPRETATION: It is true that there are three "heavens" mentioned in the Bible, but these are not the Celestial Kingdom, Terrestrial Kingdom, and Telestial Kingdom. Scripture reveals that the three heavens are the atmospheric heaven (Deut. 11:11), the starry heaven (Gen. 1:14), and the highest heaven where God dwells (Isa. 63:15). It is to this last heaven—the "third heaven"—that Paul refers in 2 Corinthians 12:2. This third heaven is the seat of the divine Majesty, the residence of the holy angels, and the abode where the souls of departed saints go immediately upon death.

2 CORINTHIANS 12:15—Does Paul's desire to be "spent" for the Corinthians support the Roman Catholic doctrine of indulgences?

MISINTERPRETATION: In this verse Paul says to the Corinthians, "I will very gladly spend and be spent for your sakes" (KJV). Catholic scholars have cited this in support of the doctrine of indulgences by which the merits of one person are transferred to another.

CORRECTING THE MISINTERPRETATION: This admirable desire to serve others does not support the doctrine of indulgences. There are several significant leaps one must take from this and the Roman Catholic teaching that the living can offer prayers and indulgences on behalf of the suffering of those in purgatory.

First, this passage says absolutely nothing about purgatory or indulgences. Second, the action on behalf of others in this text is for the living, not for the dead. Third, the suffering is not for their *sins* or their temporal consequences but in order to bear their *burden* or help minister the grace of Christ to them. So there is no support here for the doctrines of purgatory and indulgences.

2 CORINTHIANS 13:14—Does this verse support the doctrine of the Trinity?

MISINTERPRETATION: Second Corinthians 13:14 records a benediction of the apostle Paul: "The grace of the Lord Jesus Christ, and the love of God, and the fellowship of the Holy Spirit, be with you all" (NIV). Though Trinitarians often cite this verse in support of the Trinity, the Jehovah's Witnesses believe it is "'insufficient' to prove the Trinity." It does not prove "that Father, Son, and Holy Spirit are coequal or coeternal or that all are God" (*Reasoning from the Scriptures,* 1989, 415).

CORRECTING THE MISINTERPRETATION: This verse provides *supportive* evidence—not *conclusive* evidence—for the doctrine of the Trinity. Trinitarians base their understanding of God on the accumulative evidence of the whole of Scripture, not on any isolated verse. While it is true that 2 Corinthians 13:14 by itself does not prove the truth of the doctrine of the Trinity, when taken with other Scriptures there is no doubt that the doctrine is true.

Scripture declares that there is only one true God (Deut. 6:4). In the unity of the Godhead, however, there are three distinct persons. Each of the three persons is called God in Scripture: the Father (1 Peter 1:2), the Son (John 20:28), and the Holy Spirit (Acts 5:3–4). Moreover, each possess the attributes of deity. For example, each of the three are *everywhere-present* (Ps. 139:7; Matt. 19:26; 28:18), *all-knowing* (Rom. 11:33; Matt. 9:4; 1 Cor. 2:10), and *all-powerful* (Matt. 28:18; Rom. 15:19; 1 Peter 1:5). Finally, there is three-in-oneness within the Godhead. Just prior to his ascension, Jesus told the disciples, "Therefore go and make disciples of all nations, baptizing them in the *name* of the Father and of the Son and of the Holy Spirit" (Matt. 28:19 NIV). The word *name* is singular in the Greek, indicating that there is one God. But there are three distinct persons within the Godhead—the Father, the Son, and the Holy Spirit. This three-in-oneness is reflected in 2 Corinthians 13:14.

GALATIANS

GALATIANS 1:8—Does this verse mean the early church became apostate, bringing about the need for a restoration in the Mormon Church?

MISINTERPRETATION: Galatians 1:6–8 records the apostle Paul's warning against believing a different gospel. According to Mormons, the early church believed a false gospel and ended up in total apostasy (McConkie, 1977, 334). This made a restoration of the church through Joseph Smith necessary.

CORRECTING THE MISINTERPRETATION: Galatians 1:8 does not indicate there would be a total apostasy of the entire church throughout the world. Rather, the local church in Galatia was the focus of Paul's statements.

The Galatians had apparently succumbed to a gospel that added works to faith. Some false teachers of a Jewish bent had thrown the Galatians into confusion (Acts 15:24; 20:29–30). These Jewish teachers sought to "Judaize" the Gentile believers by telling them they must take the additional step of getting circumcised. This added law to grace in Paul's mind (see Gal. 3:1–2).

Paul emphasized that any gospel that contradicted the gospel already authoritatively handed down to them is to be rejected. Even Paul held himself accountable to the authoritative gospel already handed down (Gal. 1:8; cf. 1 Cor. 15:3). The gospel of Mormonism is itself a gospel of works that clearly contradicts the gospel of grace that Paul taught. The Mormon gospel thus falls into the category of "a different gospel" and accordingly falls under Paul's condemnation.

GALATIANS 1:15–16—Is the apostle Paul teaching the doctrine of reincarnation in this passage?

See comments on Jeremiah 1:5.

GALATIANS 6:2—Does the idea of bearing one another's burdens support the Roman Catholic view of a "Treasury of Merit" where one saint's merit can be given to another by indulgences?

MISINTERPRETATION: In Galatians 6:2 the apostle exhorts us to "bear one another's burdens." Roman Catholic scholars cite this verse to support their belief in indulgences based on the merit of other saints that are stored in a so-called Treasury of Merit (Ott, 1960, 317).

CORRECTING THE MISINTERPRETATION: A study of this text in its context shows there is no justification for the Catholic dogma about one saint's merits atoning for another.

It does not say we can bear the *punishment* for someone else's sin. There is solidarity here but no substitution for sins. We are to bear our "own load" (v. 5) and then help bear our brother's load. But that we cannot bear his sins is made clear only two verses later when Paul reminds us that "a person will reap only what *he* sows" (v. 7).

Christ's sacrifice *alone* atoned for all our sins and their consequences. This is made clear in many passages of Scripture (cf. Isa. 53:1–12; John 19:30; Heb. 1:3; 10:14–15).

GALATIANS 6:7–8—Does this verse support the doctrine of reincarnation, as the Unity School of Christianity teaches?

MISINTERPRETATION: In Galatians 6:7–8 we read, "Do not be deceived, God is not mocked; for whatever a man sows, this he will also reap. For the one who sows to his own flesh shall from the flesh reap corruption, but the one who sows to the Spirit shall from the Spirit reap eternal life" (NASB). The Unity School of Christianity teaches that this passage refers to the unrelenting law of karma, which says that if a person does good things in this life, he or she will build up good karma, leading to a better condition in the next life. If the person does bad things in this life, bad karma will cause him or her to be born in a worse condition in the next life.

CORRECTING THE MISINTERPRETATION: The concepts of reincarnation and karma are nowhere to be found in the context of Galatians 6, not to mention the rest of the Bible.

In context, these verses are dealing with the impartial judgment of God on Christians in specific regard to their financial support of Christian workers (cf. v. 6).

Further, what is reaped is not another life of punishment but "everlasting life" (v. 7). But this is contrary to the doctrine of karma.

The Bible condemns the doctrine of reincarnation, insisting that "man is destined to die once, and after that to face judgment" (Heb. 9:27). For other arguments against reincarnation and karma, see the discussions of John 3:3 and Matthew 22:42.

EPHESIANS

EPHESIANS 1:10—Does Paul teach universalism when he says God will gather "all things in Christ"?

MISINTERPRETATION: Paul wrote in Ephesians 1:10 that in "the fullness of the times He might gather together in one all things in Christ, both which are in heaven and which are under the earth—in Him." Unitarian-universalists, liberals, some neo-orthodox, and other groups use this verse to support their belief that everyone will eventually be saved.

CORRECTING THE MISINTERPRETATION: A careful examination of this verse reveals that Paul is speaking here *only* of believers, so, there is no support for universalism. The whole context is about those chosen in Christ "before the foundation of the world" (Eph. 1:4). The phrase "in Christ" is never used in Scripture of anyone but believers.

That unbelievers are excluded is clear from the fact that Paul does not refer to those "under the earth" as he does elsewhere when speaking of the lost (Phil. 2:10). There is abundant evidence elsewhere in Paul (cf. 2 Thess. 1:7–9) and in the rest of Scripture that some will go to their eternal destiny without Christ (e.g., Matt. 25:31–46).

EPHESIANS 4:3–6—Is the apostle Paul speaking of an organizational unity in the Roman Catholic Church in this passage?

MISINTERPRETATION: The apostle Paul urges the Ephesians to strive "to preserve the unity of the spirit" in "one body." Roman Catholic authorities (see Ott, 1960, 303) believe that Paul is speaking about a unity manifest in the divinely appointed Roman Catholic church.

CORRECTING THE MISINTERPRETATION: Ephesians 4:3–6 does speak about "striving to preserve the unity of the spirit" in "one body." However, it is evident that he does not have in mind an organizational unity of the Christian church and certainly not the kind claimed by the Roman Catholic church.

For one thing, according to the Roman Catholic (NAB) translation, it is not an organizational unity, since he spoke of "unity of the spirit" (v. 3). Even if it is rendered "the unity of the [Holy] Spirit" (NIV, RSV), there is no indication that it is more than a spiritual unity wrought by the source of all true spiritual unity, the Holy Spirit.

Further, the spiritual unity is made by God, not people. Christians are merely urged to strive to *maintain* this unity that God has *made* in the body. What is more, the "one body" is the body (cf. 1 Cor. 12:13) into which believers are baptized by "one Spirit" (v. 4). But the spiritual body of Christ is the only body to which all believers belong, since many believers, those who are dead, are not part of the visible church.

Furthermore, this spiritual unity connects us with the invisible (spiritual) body of Christ. Water baptism, which is different (Acts 1:5; 10:47) joins us to part of the visible body of Christ on earth. So the unity here is a unity of faith, not of communion, since the apostle Paul refers to "one Lord, one faith, [and] one baptism," all of which are a matter of confession. There is nothing in this text about unity of government or organization, certainly not on a universal scale, as Roman Catholics believe.

EPHESIANS 4:9—Did Jesus descend into hell, as some Word-Faith teachers argue?

MISINTERPRETATION: The apostle Paul claims here that Jesus "descended into the lower parts of the earth." And the Apostles' Creed declares that after Jesus died he "descended into hell." Word-Faith teachers cite this verse in attempting to prove that upon his death Jesus went to hell for three days (Copeland, 1991, 3).

CORRECTING THE MISINTERPRETATION: There are two views as to where Jesus went the three days his body was in the grave before his resurrection.

The Hades View. One position claims that Christ's spirit went to the spirit world, while his body was in the grave. Here, they believe, he spoke to the "spirits in prison" (1 Peter 3:19) who were in a temporary holding place until he would come and "lead captivity captive," that is, take them to heaven. According to this view, there were two compartments in Hades (or *sheol*)—one for the saved and another for the unsaved. They were separated by a "great gulf" (Luke 16:26) which no man could pass.

The section for the saved was called "Abraham's bosom" (Luke 16:22). When Christ, as the "firstfruits" of the resurrection (1 Cor. 15:20), ascended, he led these Old Testament saints into heaven for the first time with him.

The Heaven View. This teaching holds that the souls of Old Testament believers went directly to heaven the moment they died. Jesus affirmed that his spirit was going directly to heaven, declaring, "Father, into your hands I commit my spirit" (Luke 23:46b NIV). Jesus promised the thief on the cross, "Today, you will be with me in Paradise" (Luke 23:43). "Paradise" is defined as "the third heaven" in 2 Corinthians 12:2–4.

When Old Testament saints departed this life, they went directly to heaven. God took Enoch to be with himself (Gen. 5:24; cf. Heb. 11:5), and Elijah was caught up into "heaven" when he departed (2 Kings 2:1).

"Abraham's bosom" (Luke 16:23) is a description of heaven. At no time is it ever described as hell. It is the place to which Abraham went, which is the kingdom of heaven in Matthew 8:11. When Old Testament saints appear before the cross, they appear from heaven, as Moses and Elijah did on the Mount of Transfiguration (Matt. 17:3).

Old Testament saints had to await Christ's resurrection before their *bodies* could be resurrected (1 Cor. 15:20; cf. Matt. 27:53), but their *souls* went directly to heaven. Christ was the Lamb slain "from the foundation of the world" (Rev. 13:8), and they were there on the merits of what God knew Christ would accomplish.

"Descending into the lower parts of the earth" is not a reference to hell, but to the grave. Even a woman's womb is described as "lowest parts of the earth" (Ps. 139:15). The phrase simply means caves, graves, or enclosures on the earth, as opposed to higher parts, like mountains. Besides, hell itself is not in the lower parts of the earth—it is "under the earth" (Phil. 2:10).

The phrase *descended into hell* was not in the earliest Apostles' Creed. It was not added until the fourth century. Whenever this phrase was added, the Apostle's Creed is not inspired—it is only a human confession of faith.

The "spirits in prison" were unsaved beings. Indeed, they may be angels, rather than human beings. See comments on 1 Peter 3:19.

When Christ "led captivity captive," he was not leading friends into heaven, but bringing foes into bondage. It is a reference to his conquest of the forces of evil. Christians are not "captives" in heaven. We get there by our own free choice (see Matt. 23:37; 2 Peter 3:9).

Even if it could be shown that Jesus visited the spirit world during this time, the Bible is clear that he was not "born again" while there, nor did he gain victory over the devil at that time. Jesus was not a sinner and, therefore, did not need to be born again (cf. John 2:25; 3:3, 6–7; see comments on 2 Cor. 5:21). His work for our salvation was completed on the cross (John 19:30; Heb. 1:3; 10:14–15 before he entered the grave.

EPHESIANS 4:11—Are Mormons correct in saying that their church structure—with living prophets and apostles—is the same as that of the early church?

MISINTERPRETATION: In Ephesians 4:11 the apostle Paul says, "And he gave some, apostles; and some, prophets; and some, evangelists; and some, pastors and teachers" (KJV). Mormons believe their present structure (with apostles and prophets) is the same as that of the early church (McConkie, 1977, 607). Therefore, Mormons form the one true church. Proponents of the Kingdom Now movement and other groups that claim new revelation from God also use this text to argue that there still are apostles and prophets.

CORRECTING THE MISINTERPRETATION: According to Ephesians 2:20, the church is "built upon the foundation of the apostles and prophets." Once the foundation is built, it is never built *again*. It is built *upon*. Scripture indicates that apostles and prophets were foundational gifts.

The first-century apostles understood that God was providing unique revelation through them (1 Cor. 2:13). They were handpicked by the Lord (Matt. 10:1–2; Acts 1:26) and had divine authority (Acts 20:35; 1 Cor. 7:10). Biblical apostles had to be eyewitnesses to the resurrected Christ (Acts 1:22; 1 Cor. 9:1; cf. 1 Cor. 15:7–8).

The Book of Acts clearly attests to the uniqueness and authority of the apostles. In 2:42 the first church "devoted themselves to the apostles' teaching and the fellowship." Throughout Acts the pronouncements of the apostles were final (Acts 15). By their voice the church was born (ch. 2); miracles were performed (ch. 3); rulers were restricted (ch. 4); the disobedient were judged (ch. 5); the Holy Spirit was given to the Samaritans (Acts 8) and the Gentiles (ch. 10).

The biblical apostles were authenticated by incredible miracles (2 Cor. 12:12)—miracles like raising people from the dead (Acts 9:36–42). Anyone claiming to be an apostle must be *authenticated* by the signs of an apostle. Mormon apostles and prophets have no such miraculous attestation.

Moreover, the revelation given by Mormon prophets and apostles clearly contradicts the revelation decisively ("once for all") handed down by the first-century apostles (Jude 3). Mormon apostles teach that Jesus is a created being and is the spirit-brother of Lucifer. The biblical apostles taught that Jesus is God and Creator (Col. 1:16; 2:9; cf. Isa. 44:24). Mormon apostles teach that God is an exalted man of flesh and bones. The biblical apostles taught that God is spirit (2 Cor. 3:17–18). The Mormon apostles teach that there are many gods in the universe. The biblical apostles taught that there is only one God (1 Tim. 2:5). Mormon apostles teach that human beings may become gods. The biblical apostles taught that human beings never become God (see Acts 14:14–15).

PHILIPPIANS

PHILIPPIANS 2:7—If Christ emptied himself of deity while on earth, then how could he be God?

MISINTERPRETATION: Paul seems to say that Jesus "emptied" himself of his deity or "equality with God" (vv. 6–7) in order to become human (v. 8). How could Jesus be God while on earth if he left his deity aside to become man? Jehovah's Witnesses say he could not. (See *Reasoning from the Scriptures,* 1989, 198, 419.)

CORRECTING THE MISINTERPRETATION: Jesus did not cease being God while on earth. Rather, in addition to being God, he also became man. His incarnation was not the subtraction of deity, but the addition of humanity.

This text does not say Christ gave up or emptied himself of his deity, but merely that he gave up his *rights* as deity, assuming the "form of a servant" (v. 7) so as to be an example for us (v. 5). The text declares that Jesus was in the "form of God" or "being in very nature God" (v. 6 NIV). Just as the "form of a servant" (v. 7) is a servant by nature, so the "form of God" (v. 6) is God by nature. Notice also that the word *being* (in the phrase "being in very nature God") is a present tense participle. This carries the idea of *continued existence* as God. The thought is that Christ always has been and still is in the form of God.

This very passage also proclaims that every knee will one day confess that Jesus is "Lord." This cites Isaiah 45:23, which refers to Yahweh, a name used exclusively of God.

PHILIPPIANS 2:10—Does Paul teach here that everyone will be saved by confessing Christ is Lord?

MISINTERPRETATION: Paul predicts that one day "that at the name of Jesus every knee should bow, of those who are in heaven, and on earth, and under the earth, and that every tongue should confess that Jesus Christ is Lord to the glory of God the Father" (NASB). Here, the universalists insist, unbelievers are clearly in view in the phrase "under the earth." Does this mean that everyone will eventually be saved?

CORRECTING THE MISINTERPRETATION: While it is admitted by all that unbelievers will eventually confess Jesus is Lord, nevertheless there is no evidence here or elsewhere that they will be saved.

Unbelievers only confess "that" Jesus is Lord. There is no reference to their believing "in" him, something that is necessary for salvation. Even demons believe *that* but do not believe *in* God (cf. James 2:19). But believing *that* Jesus is Lord will not save anyone. Only belief *in* Christ will save (James 2:21–26). As for "those under the earth" (the lost) in this text, they are said to utter a mere confession from the mouth. For salvation, Paul insisted, one must both "confess with your mouth and believe in your heart" (Rom. 10:9). Unbelievers do not believe in the heart.

Numerous other passages of Scripture teach that many will be lost forever. This includes the devil and his angels (Matt. 25:41), the Beast and the False Prophet (Rev. 19:20), Judas (John 17:12), a multitude of unsaved people from all nations (Matt. 25:32, 41), and all who are not written in the Book of Life (Rev. 20:15).

PHILIPPIANS 2:12—Does this verse mean we must earn our salvation?

MISINTERPRETATION: Philippians 2:12 says, "Work out your salvation with fear and trembling." A number of cults cite this verse to support a works-oriented view of salvation. The Jehovah's Witnesses conclude from this verse that salvation is not assured for anyone (*Reasoning from the Scriptures,* 1989, 358). The Mormons say people must "work out" their salvation by self-effort in order to attain godhood (McConkie, 1977, 329).

CORRECTING THE MISINTERPRETATION: The whole of Scripture emphasizes that works have nothing to do with salvation (e.g., Rom. 3:20, 28; Eph. 2:8–9). Hence this verse cannot be interpreted to mean that we must add works in order to attain our final salvation.

Many scholars believe this verse deals, not with the assurance of *final* personal salvation for individual believers, but rather with the *corporate* salvation of the church in Philippi in regard to some temporal problems the church was facing. This church was suffering under intense rivalries (Phil. 2:3–4), disturbances caused by Judaizers (3:1–3), and libertinism

(3:18–19). Because of these internal problems, which severely hindered spiritual growth, the Philippian church as a whole was in need of "salvation" in the sense that it needed to deal with and overcome these problems. If this scenario is correct, the Philippians were called to "work out" their salvation on these issues. The Greek word for "work out" *(katergazomai)* indicates bringing something to a conclusion. Paul was calling the Philippians to end their internal problems.

PHILIPPIANS 2:25—If Paul had the gift of healing, why couldn't he heal his coworker, Epaphroditus?

MISINTERPRETATION: Word-Faith teachers say that full physical healing *in this life* is guaranteed in the atonement and that it is God's will for every single person to be healed of all physical afflictions (cf. Hagin, *Word of Faith,* August 1977, 9). In the Book of Acts, Paul healed the sick and raised the dead (20:9–10). On one occasion he even healed everyone in an entire city (28:9). But here, he apparently could not even heal a needed coworker.

CORRECTING THE MISINTERPRETATION: Some believe that possessing the gift of healing did not guarantee that one could always heal everyone. On one occasion the disciples could not heal a demon-possessed young man (Matt. 17:16). They insist that the gift of healing did not make a person 100-percent successful, any more than the gift of teaching makes one infallible.

Others insist that the gift of healing was always successful, noting that Jesus healed the young man (Matt. 17:14–20) and rebuked the disciples for not exercising their God-given power to do it (vv. 17–18). They claim that the gift of healing was 100-percent successful, in the same way that no one with the gift of prophecy ever uttered a false prophecy. For a false prophecy was a proof that someone did not possess the true gift of prophecy (cf. Deut. 18:22).

The reason Epaphroditus was not healed is not stated in the text. But neither does it say Paul attempted to heal him and failed. Since no exercise of the gift of healing is recorded past about A.D. 60 (Acts 28:8), it may be that the special apostolic gift of healing (cf. 2 Cor. 12:12; Heb. 2:4) had passed away by this time (c. A.D. 61). It is not listed in the much briefer list of gifts in Ephesians 4, as it was earlier in 1 Corinthians 12:28.

From any perspective the Word-Faith claim that full physical healing (*in this life*) is guaranteed in the atonement is incorrect. We *will* be *ultimately* healed when we receive our resurrection bodies—and that *is* guaranteed in the atonement.

COLOSSIANS

COLOSSIANS 1:15–17—If Jesus is the "firstborn," then wasn't he created first, and then he created all other things?

MISINTERPRETATION: Colossians 1:15 says, "and He is the image of the invisible God, the firstborn of all creation" (NASB). The Jehovah's Witnesses say this passage proves that Jesus is a creature, the "first-created." They argue that Jesus is the eldest in Jehovah's family of sons (*Reasoning from the Scriptures,* 1989, 408). The Jehovah's Witnesses New World Translation subtly changes Colossians 1:16–17 so that it seems the first-created Christ was used by the Father to create all other things in the universe: "By means of him all [other] things were created in the heavens and upon the earth, the things visible and the things invisible, no matter whether they are thrones or lordships or governments or authorities. All [other] things have been created through him and for him. Also, he is before all [other] things and by means of him all [other] things were made to exist" (bracketed words from the translation).

"Thus he is shown to be a created being, part of the creation produced by God" (*Reasoning from the Scriptures,* 1989, 409).

CORRECTING THE MISINTERPRETATION: *Firstborn* does not carry the meaning "first-created." In biblical times the word meant "first in rank" or "preeminent." King David was actually the last-born son of Jesse, yet he was called "firstborn" because he was the preeminent son (Ps. 89:27). Christ is preeminent because he is Creator (John 1:3). Moreover, Jesus could not be Michael, the first angel created, since he created all the angels (Col. 1:16) and they all worship him (Heb. 1:6).

Nor is there justification for inserting the word *other* into Colossians 1:16–17. The fact is, Colossians 1:16 teaches that Christ created "all things"—and this being so, Christ himself cannot be a created being. A good cross-reference is Isaiah 44:24, where God himself asserts: "I, the

LORD [Yahweh], am maker of *all things*, stretching out the heavens *by Myself*, and spreading out the earth *all alone*" (emphasis added). If Yahweh made all things by himself and all alone, obviously he didn't create Jesus first and then create everything else through Jesus. If Yahweh is called the creator of the universe, and if Jesus is called the creator of the universe, then Scripture equates Jesus with God.

COLOSSIANS 1:18—Was Christ "born again" in hell?

MISINTERPRETATION: Word-Faith teachers argue that this verse means that Jesus was "born again" in hell after suffering there for three days. "Jesus was born again—the firstborn from the dead the Word calls Him—and He whipped the devil in his own backyard" (Copeland, "The Price of It All," 1991).

CORRECTING THE MISINTERPRETATION: Christ is "firstborn" in the sense that he is the preeminent one over all creation. He wasn't born again in hell. Indeed, he didn't need to be born again in any way (John 3:3, 6–7). Besides, Christ never went to hell. See the discussion of Ephesians 4:9 for discussion of the idea that Christ went to hell.

COLOSSIANS 1:20—Does this verse teach that all will be saved?

MISINTERPRETATION: The apostle Paul wrote to the Colossians, "For it was the Father's good pleasure . . . through Him [Christ] to reconcile all things to Himself, having made peace through the blood of His cross; through Him, I say, whether things on earth or things in heaven" (Col. 1:19–20 NASB). If Paul says that all things are reconciled to Christ by his death and resurrection, this seems to imply that all people are saved. Is this universalist interpretation true?

CORRECTING THE MISINTERPRETATION: Paul is not speaking about *universal salvation*, but the *universal sovereignty* of Jesus Christ. All authority has been given to Jesus Christ in heaven and on earth (Matt. 28:18). By virtue of his death and resurrection, Christ as the Last Adam is Lord over all that was lost by the First Adam (cf. 1 Cor. 15:45–49). Note the contrast between two crucial passages by Paul:

All "in" Christ	All bow "before" Christ
Texts: Eph. 1:3–10; Col. 1:19–20	Text: Phil. 2:9–11
Who: All the saved . . .	Who: All who are in subjection . . .

—in heaven	—in heaven
—on earth	—on earth
	—under the earth
Purpose: Sinners' reconciliation	Purpose: Christ's exaltation

When Paul speaks of being "in Christ" (i.e., being saved), he does not include "those under the earth" (i.e., the lost). However, all persons, saved and unsaved, will one day bow *before* Christ and acknowledge his universal lordship. But nowhere do the Scriptures teach that all people will be saved. Jesus will say to many, "Depart from Me, you cursed, into the everlasting fire prepared for the devil and his angels" (Matt. 25:41). John spoke of the devil, the beast, and the false prophet, and all whose names are not written in the Book of Life being cast into the Lake of Fire forever (Rev. 20:10–15). Luke speaks of a great impassable gulf between heaven and hell in which those who have rejected God are living in torment (Luke 16:19–31). Paul speaks of punishment on the wicked as "everlasting destruction from the presence of the Lord" (2 Thess. 1:9). Jesus declared Judas was lost and called him "the son of perdition" (John 17:12). It is evident from all these passages that not everyone will be saved.

COLOSSIANS 1:24—Does this verse teach that Christ's suffering on the cross was not sufficient for our sins?

MISINTERPRETATION: According to Roman Catholic teaching, believers will have to suffer in purgatory for the temporal consequences of their venial sins unpaid for in this life.

CORRECTING THE MISINTERPRETATION: Colossians 1:24b (NASB), Paul says, "I do my share on behalf of His body (which is the church) in filling up that which is lacking in Christ's afflictions." In no way does this support the Roman Catholic dogma of purgatory. This verse does not mean that Christ's atoning sacrifice does not satisfy both the eternal and temporal consequences for all our sins. And if it is sufficient, as even Catholics say they believe, then we cannot add to the atonement's sufficiency. If we could, then God's work would necessarily be insufficient to save, a blasphemous notion that contradicts many other passages (for example, John 17:4; 19:30; Heb. 1:2; 10:14).

In one sense, Christ still suffers after his death. Jesus said to Paul, "Why are you persecuting Me?" (Acts 9:4). Since Christ was not then literally on earth to be persecuted, this must be a reference to his Body (the church) which Paul, as the Pharisee Saul of Tarsus, had been persecuting (cf. 8:1; 9:1–2). In a similar sense, we too can suffer for Christ, since "it has been granted on behalf of Christ, not only to believe in Him, but also to suffer for His sake" (Phil. 1:29 NKJV). But in no sense is our suffering for Christ a means of atoning for sin. Only Jesus suffered *for* sin. We suffer because of our sins but never to satisfy God's judgment on our sins or anyone else's. Each person must bear the guilt of his own sin (Ezek. 18:20) or else accept the fact that Christ suffered for his sin (2 Cor. 5:21; 1 Peter 2:21; 3:18). When we suffer for Christ, we are undergoing pain as part of his spiritual body, the church (cf. 1 Cor. 12:26), but only what Christ suffered in his physical body on the cross is efficacious for our sins. Our suffering, then, is in service to Christ, an act of love, obedience, and gratitude, but not merit.

Even in the nonsalvific sense in which this verse declares we can suffer for others, there is no intimation here or elsewhere in the accepted canon of Holy Scripture that we can do this on behalf of *those who are dead*. Our sacrificial lives can only be exercised on behalf of the living.

COLOSSIANS 2:8—Does this verse mean Christians should not study philosophy?

MISINTERPRETATION: Paul warned in Colossians 2:8 (NKJV), "Beware lest anyone cheat you through philosophy and empty deceit." The Jehovah's Witnesses cite this verse in warning against the study of philosophy (*Reasoning from the Scriptures*, 1989, 291).

CORRECTING THE MISINTERPRETATION: The Bible is no more against philosophy as a body of knowledge than it is against religion. It is not philosophy, but *vain* philosophy, that Paul calls "empty deceit" (v. 8). Likewise, the Bible is not opposed to religion, but against *vain* religion (cf. James 1:26–27).

In this context, Paul is not speaking about philosophy *in general*, but about a *particular* philosophy, usually understood as an early form of Gnosticism. This is indicated by his use of the definite article (Greek *tēs*). *Tēs philosophias* should be translated "*the* philosophy" or "*this* philosophy." Paul was referring to this particular philosophy that had invaded the church in Colossae and involved legalism, mysticism, and asceticism (cf. Col. 2) and not to all philosophy.

Paul himself was well trained in the philosophies of his day, even quoting them from time to time (cf. Acts 17:28; Titus 1:12). Paul successfully "reasoned" with the philosophers on Mars Hill, even winning some to Christ (Acts 17:17, 34). Elsewhere he said that a bishop should be able "to exhort and convict those who contradict" (Titus 1:9). Peter exhorted believers to "always be ready to give a defense to everyone who asks you a reason for the hope that is in you" (1 Peter 3:15b). Indeed, Jesus said the great command is to love the Lord "with all your *mind*" (Matt. 22:37). In its pure form as the study of life and wisdom, philosophy stimulates deeper affection for God.

God places no premium on ignorance. In fact, he knows we cannot "beware of philosophy" unless we are aware of it. No one would go to a doctor who did not study sickness. But, herein lies the danger: The Christian should approach the false philosophies of the world the way a medical researcher approaches the HIV virus. He should study them objectively and carefully to find out what is wrong with them, but not subjectively and personally so that he catches the "disease" himself.

COLOSSIANS 2:9—Does this verse indicate that Jesus merely has divine qualities, or does it indicate that Jesus is really God?

MISINTERPRETATION: The Jehovah's Witnesses translate Colossians 2:9 this way: "Because it is in him that all the fullness of the divine quality dwells bodily." They say this verse does not mean Jesus is intrinsically God Almighty like the Father is, but merely has divine qualities (*Reasoning from the Scriptures,* 1989, 421).

CORRECTING THE MISINTERPRETATION: This verse does not say Jesus just has divine qualities but rather that the absolute "fullness [literally, 'full measure,' 'completeness,' 'totality,' 'sum-total'] of Deity" dwells in Christ in bodily form (see the NASB translation). The verse means Christ has the very nature of God and is the very essence of deity. All that God is has its permanent home in the Lord Jesus Christ in bodily form. This is supported by numerous other verses, both here in Colossians (cf. 1:15–18) and elsewhere (John 1:1; 8:58; 20:28; Phil. 2:6–8; Titus 2:13).

COLOSSIANS 2:9—Does this verse prove that Jesus is God the Father and the Holy Spirit, as Oneness Pentecostals believe?

MISINTERPRETATION: In Colossians 2:9 the apostle Paul said of Christ, "For in Him all the fullness of Deity dwells in bodily form" (NASB). Oneness Pentecostals believe this verse is impossible to square with trinitarianism. Indeed, they say, "Trinitarianism denies that the fullness of the Godhead is in Jesus because it denies that Jesus is the Father and the Holy Spirit" (Bernard, 1983, 289). Because the *fullness* of the Godhead is said to dwell in Jesus, this must mean that Jesus is the Father and the Holy Spirit.

CORRECTING THE MISINTERPRETATION: In this verse the term *Godhead* simply means deity. The word indicates that the fullness of deity—the very divine essence itself, including all the divine attributes—dwells fully in Jesus. The verse indicates, then, that Jesus is fully God, *but it does not say that Jesus is the only person who is fully God.*

Scripture interprets Scripture. And Scripture indicates that in the unity of the one God (Deut. 6:4), there are *three distinct persons.* Each of the three persons is called God in Scripture: the Father (1 Peter 1:2), the Son (John 20:28), and the Holy Spirit (Acts 5:3–4). Moreover, each possess the attributes of deity. For example, each of the three are *everywhere-present* (Ps. 139:7; Matt. 28:18), *all-knowing* (Matt. 9:4; Rom. 11:33; 1 Cor. 2:10), and *all-powerful* (Matt. 28:18; Rom. 15:19; 1 Peter 1:5). Finally, there is three-in-oneness within the Godhead. In one good example, just prior to his ascension, Jesus told the disciples, "Therefore go and make disciples of all nations, baptizing them in the *name* of the Father and of the Son and of the Holy Spirit" (Matt. 28:19 NIV). The word *name* is singular in the Greek, indicating that there is one God. But there are three distinct persons within the Godhead—the Father, the Son, and the Holy Spirit. This three-in-oneness is also reflected in 2 Corinthians 13:14. Colossians 2:9 simply cannot mean that Jesus is the Father and the Holy Spirit.

For more on the distinction between the Father, Son, and Holy Spirit *as persons,* see the discussion of Matthew 28:19.

COLOSSIANS 2:16—Are Christians obligated to keep the Sabbath?

See comments on Exodus 20:8–11 and Matthew 5:17–18.

COLOSSIANS 4:16—What happened to the lost epistle of the Laodiceans?

MISINTERPRETATION: Paul refers to the "epistle from Laodicea" as a book he wrote that should be read by the church at Colossae, just as the inspired Book of Colossians was to be read by the Laodiceans. However, no such first-century epistle to the Laodiceans exists (though there is a fourth-century fraudulent one). But, it is very strange that an inspired book would perish. Why would God inspire it for the faith and practice of the church (2 Tim. 3:16–17) and then allow it to be destroyed?

Some Mormons try to make much of the fact that the Bible mentions specific books that are not contained in the Bible as Scripture (see *A Sure Foundation: Answers to Difficult Gospel Questions,* 1988). They thereby argue that the Bible is incomplete, and so people also need the Book of Mormon.

CORRECTING THE MISINTERPRETATION: First, it is possible that not all divinely authoritative or inspired books were intended by God to be in the Bible. Luke refers to other Gospels (Luke 1:1), and John affirmed that there were many other things Jesus did that are not recorded in his Gospel (John 20:31; 21:25). Simply because a book is *cited* in the Bible does not mean that the book *belongs in* the Bible.

Second, there are some good reasons to believe that the epistle from Laodicea is not really lost, but only renamed. It may be the Book of Ephesians. Colossians 4:16 does not call it the epistle *of* the Laodiceans, but the "epistle [coming] from Laodicea," whatever name it may have had. Moreover, it is known that Paul wrote Ephesians at the same time he wrote Colossians and sent it to another church in the same general area.

Third, there is evidence that the Book of Ephesians did not originally bear that title, but was a kind of cyclical letter sent to the churches of Asia Minor. As a matter of fact, some early manuscripts do not have the phrase "in Ephesus" in Ephesians 1:1. It is certainly strange that Paul, who spent three years ministering to the Ephesians (Acts 20:31), sent no personal greetings to them, if the book known as "Ephesians" were intended for them alone. By contrast, Paul had never visited Rome, but he greeted numerous people in his letter to them (Rom. 16:1–16).

Fourth, no epistle of the Laodiceans is cited by any early church father, though they make over 36,000 New Testament citations to every book and almost every verse of the New Testament. A fraudulent Epistle of the Laodiceans appeared in the fourth century, but no scholars believe it is the one referred to by Paul. Indeed, it is largely a collection of quotations from Ephesians and Colossians which the Second Council of Nicea (A.D. 787) rejected as a "forged epistle."

1 THESSALONIANS

1 THESSALONIANS 4:13—Did Paul teach the doctrine of soul-sleep?

MISINTERPRETATION: Several times the Bible refers to the dead as being asleep. Many aberrant groups, such as the Seventh Day Adventists, believe this means that the soul is not conscious between death and resurrection (*Seventh-day Adventists Answer Questions on Doctrine*, 1957, 515, 520).

CORRECTING THE MISINTERPRETATION: The souls of both believers and unbelievers are conscious between death and the resurrection. Unbelievers are in conscious woe (see Mark 9:43–48; Luke 16:22–23; Rev. 19:20) and believers are in conscious bliss (Phil. 1:23). "Sleep" is a reference to the body, not the soul. Sleep is an appropriate figure of speech for death of the body, since death is temporary until the resurrection when the body will "awake" from it. See comments on Romans 2:7.

Biblical evidence that the soul (spirit) is conscious between death and resurrection is very strong:

1. Enoch was taken to be with God (Gen. 5:24; Heb. 11:5).
2. David spoke of bliss in God's presence after death (Ps. 16:10–11).
3. Elijah was taken up into heaven (2 Kings 2:1, 11–12).
4. Moses and Elijah were conscious on the Mount of Transfiguration (Matt. 17:3).
5. Jesus said he went to the Father the day he died (Luke 23:46).
6. Jesus promised that the repentant thief would be with him in paradise the very day he died (Luke 23:43).
7. Paul said it was far better to die and be with Christ (Phil. 1:23).

8. Paul affirmed that when we are "absent from the body" then "we are present with the Lord" (2 Cor. 5:8).
9. The writer of Hebrews refers to heaven as a place where "the spirits of just men [are] made perfect" (Heb. 12:23).
10. The "souls" of those martyred during the tribulation were conscious in heaven, singing and praying to God (Rev. 6:9).
11. Stephen, as he was being stoned to death, said, "Lord Jesus, receive my spirit!" (Acts 7:59).
12. Jesus, in speaking about Old Testament saints Abraham, Isaac, and Jacob, said that God "is not the God of the dead, but *of the living*" (Luke 20:38). Jesus was saying, "Abraham, Isaac, and Jacob, though they died many years ago, are actually living today. For God, who calls himself the God of Abraham, Isaac, and Jacob, is not the God of the dead but of the living."

1 THESSALONIANS 4:16—Does this verse teach that Jesus is the archangel Michael?

MISINTERPRETATION: The Jehovah's Witnesses think this verse proves that Jesus is the archangel Michael. "The command of Jesus Christ for the resurrection to begin is described as 'the archangel's call,' and Jude 9 says that the archangel is Michael" (*Reasoning from the Scriptures,* 1989, 218). Hence, Jesus and Michael are one and the same.

CORRECTING THE MISINTERPRETATION: This verse does not relate that Jesus speaks but that he descends from heaven when the voice of the archangel speaks. Jesus' coming at the rapture will be *accompanied* by the archangel Michael since it is the archangel's voice (not that of Jesus) that issues the shout. This is not unlike what will happen at the second coming of Christ, for "the Lord Jesus shall be revealed from heaven with His mighty angels in flaming fire" (2 Thess. 1:7 NASB).

Among numerous reasons that Jesus is not Michael the archangel is that Jesus is God (John 1:1; 8:58; 20:28; Col. 2:9) and Creator of all angels (John 1:3; Col. 1:15–16). The angel Michael was created by Jesus and, like all other angels, he worships Jesus (Heb. 1:6).

2 THESSALONIANS

2 THESSALONIANS 1:9—Will the wicked be annihilated or will they suffer conscious punishment forever?

MISINTERPRETATION: This verse says the wicked will suffer "eternal destruction." The Jehovah's Witnesses believe such verses indicate that the destruction of the wicked is everlasting in the sense that they are forever annihilated, so cease to exist (*Reasoning from the Scriptures,* 1989, 171–72).

CORRECTING THE MISINTERPRETATION: "Destruction" does not mean annihilation here, otherwise it would not be "everlasting" destruction. Annihilation only takes an instant, and it is over. If someone undergoes everlasting destruction, then they have to have everlasting existence. Just as endless life belongs to Christians, so endless destruction belongs to those opposed to Christ. The "destruction" suffered by the wicked does not involve a cessation of existence. Rather, it involves a continual and perpetual state of ruin.

Further, Scripture's definition of *death* never means annihilation, but separation. Adam and Eve died spiritually the moment they sinned, yet they still existed and could hear God's voice (Gen. 2:16–17; cf. 3:10). Likewise, before one is saved, he is "dead in trespasses and sins" (Eph. 2:1), and yet he is still in God's image (Gen. 1:27; cf. Gen. 9:6; James 3:9) and is called on to believe (Acts 16:31) and to repent (Acts 17:30) and be saved.

When the wicked are said to go into "perdition" (2 Peter 3:7), and Judas is called the "son of perdition" (John 17:12), it does not mean they will be annihilated. The word "perdition" *(apoleia)* simply means to perish or to come to ruin. Junk cars have perished in the sense of having been ruined. But they are still cars, ruined as they may be, and they are still in the junkyard. In this connection, Jesus spoke of hell as a junkyard or dump where the fire would not cease and where a person's resurrected body would not be consumed. See comments on Mark 9:48.

Other evidence supports the everlasting consciousness of the lost. The rich man who died and went to hell was in conscious torment (Luke 16:22–28). There is absolutely no indication in the text that it was ever going to cease. Jesus spoke repeatedly of the people in hell as "weeping and gnashing their teeth" (Matt. 8:12; 22:13; 24:51; 25:30), which indicates they were conscious.

Hell is said to be of the same duration as heaven, namely, "everlasting" (Matt. 25:41). The fact that their punishment is everlasting indicates that they too must be everlasting. One cannot suffer punishment, unless he exists to be punished (2 Thess. 1:9). It makes virtually no sense to say that the wicked will suffer "endless annihilation." Rather, the wicked will suffer a ruin which is everlasting—and this punishment will never end.

The beast and the false prophet were thrown "alive" into the lake of fire at the beginning of the thousand years (Rev. 19:20), and they were still there, conscious and alive, after the thousand years passed (Rev. 20:10). The Scriptures affirm that the devil, the beast, and the false prophet "will be tormented day and night forever and ever" (Rev. 20:10). But there is no way to experience torment forever and ever without being conscious for ever and ever.

Jesus repeatedly called hell a place of "unquenchable flames" (Mark 9:43–48) where the bodies of the wicked will never die (cf. Luke 12:4–5). But it would make no sense to have everlasting flames and bodies without any souls in them to experience the torment. The same word used to describe the wicked perishing in the Old Testament *(abad)* is used to describe the righteous perishing (see Isa. 57:1; Micah 7:2). The term also describes things that are merely lost, but then later found (Deut. 22:3), which proves that *lost* does not here mean nonexistent. So, if perish means to annihilate, then the saved would be annihilated too, but we know they are not.

It would be contrary to the created nature of human beings to annihilate them, since they are made in God's image and likeness, which is everlasting (Gen. 1:27). For God to annihilate his image in man would be to destroy the reflection of himself. Annihilation would be demeaning both to the love of God and to the nature of human beings as free moral creatures. It would be as if God said to them, "I will allow you to be free only if you do what I say! If you don't, then I will snuff out your very freedom and existence." This would be like a father telling his son he wanted him to be a doctor, and, when he chose instead to be a park ranger, the father shot him. Eternal suffering is an eternal testimony to the freedom and dignity of humans, even unrepentant humans.

There are no degrees of annihilation, but Scripture reveals there will be degrees of suffering among the lost (see Matt. 10:15; 11:21–24; 16:27; Luke 12:47–48; John 15:22; Heb. 10:29; Rev. 20:11–15; 22:12).

2 THESSALONIANS 2:15—Does the apostle Paul deny the Protestant doctrine of *sola Scriptura* ("the Bible alone") by affirming the need for oral traditions?

MISINTERPRETATION: Paul told the Thessalonian Christians to "stand firm and hold to the teachings we passed on to you, whether by word of mouth or by letter." Roman Catholics argue that this supports their view of the authority of oral apostolic traditions as well as the Bible. See also 2 Thessalonians 3:6.

CORRECTING THE MISINTERPRETATION: The Bible does teach that the apostles affirmed that their oral teaching was authoritative, being on the same level as the written Word of God. However, this was because there were living apostles who spoke with the authority of Christ through the *Holy Spirit* (John 14:26; 16:13). Several things are important to note here.

Their oral teachings are the content that would become Scripture. Since they had not yet committed all their teaching to writing and since they had not yet died, it was necessary to depend on their oral teaching. However, once the apostles committed their teachings to writing and died, so that they could no longer exercise their living authority, then the Bible alone became our authority for faith and practice (2 Tim. 3:16–17).

The revelatory traditions (teachings) of the apostles were written down and are inspired and infallible. They comprise the New Testament. Since God deemed it essential for the faith and morals of the faithful to inspire the writing of twenty-seven books of apostolic teaching, it is not reasonable to suppose that he left out some important revelation in this book. So, however authoritative the apostles were by virtue of their office, only their words in Scripture are inspired and infallible (2 Tim. 3:16–17; cf. John 10:35).

There are good reasons to believe that the Bible alone is the full and final authority for faith and practice for all believers. First, the Bible makes it clear that God, from the very beginning, desired that his normative revelations be written down and preserved for succeeding generations. "Moses wrote down all the words of the LORD" (Exod. 24:4

NASB). Indeed, Moses said in Deuteronomy, "these are the words of the covenant which the Lord commanded Moses to make with the sons of Israel" (Deut. 29:1 NASB). And Moses's book was preserved in the Ark (Deut. 31:26). "So Joshua made a covenant with the people that day and made for them a statute and an ordinance in Shechem. And Joshua wrote these words in the book of the law of God" (Josh. 24:25–26 NASB) along with Moses's (cf. Josh. 1:7).

Likewise, "Samuel told the people the ordinances of the kingdom, and wrote them in the book, and placed it before the LORD" (1 Sam. 10:25 NASB). Isaiah was commanded by the Lord, "Take for yourself a large tablet and write on it in ordinary letters" (Isa. 8:1) and to "inscribe it on a scroll, That it may serve in the time to come as a witness forever" (Isa. 30:8). Daniel had a collection of "the books" of Moses and the prophets right down to his contemporary Jeremiah (Dan. 9:2).

Jesus and New Testament writers used the phrase "Scripture has it" or "It is written" (cf. Matt. 4:4, 7, 10) more than ninety times, stressing the importance of the written Word of God. When Jesus rebuked the Jewish leaders it was not because they did not follow the traditions but because they did not "understand the Scriptures" (Matt. 22:29). The apostles were told by Jesus that the Holy Spirit would guide them to all truth (John 16:13). But Jesus said in the very next chapter, "Your word is truth" (John 17:17) and the apostles claimed that their writings to the churches were Scripture inspired of God (2 Peter 3:15–16; cf. 2 Tim. 3:16–17). Clearly, God intended from the very beginning that his revelation be preserved in Scripture. No similar intent is demonstrated to preserve religious traditions.

Second, the Bible states that inspired Scripture is competent to equip a believer for every good work (2 Tim. 3:16–17). If the Bible is sufficient to do this, then nothing else is needed. The fact that Scripture, without mention of tradition, is said to be "God-breathed" *(theopnuestos)* and thus by it believers are "competent, equipped for every good work" (2 Tim. 3:16–17), supports the Protestant doctrine of *sola Scriptura.*

Third, Jesus and the apostles constantly appealed to the Old Testament (which was all the Bible written to their time) as the final court of appeal. Jesus appealed to Scripture as the final authority in his dispute with Satan (Matt. 4:4, 7, 10). Of course, since God was still giving new revelation, Jesus (Matt. 5:22, 28, 31; 28:18) and the apostles (1 Cor. 5:3; 7:12) sometimes referred to their own God-given authority. But since even Catholics agree that new revelation ceased with the death of the last apostles, there is no reason to believe there is any revelation outside the Bible. No oral revelation in New Testament times can be cited as evidence that nonbiblical infallible authority exists today.

Fourth, Jesus made it clear that the existing Bible was in a class of its own, exalted above all tradition. He rebuked the Pharisees for not accepting *sola Scriptura* and negating the final authority of the Word of God by their religious traditions, saying, "And why do you break the command of God for the sake of your tradition? . . . You have nullified the word of God, for the sake of your tradition" (Matt. 15:3, 6b NIV). Jesus applied his statement specifically to the traditions of the religious authorities who used their traditions to misinterpret the Scriptures.

Fifth, Solomon affirmed that "every word of God is tested. . . . Do not add to his words, lest he reprove you, and you will be proved a liar" (Prov. 30:5–6 NASB). And John closed the last chapter of the Apocalypse with the same exhortation: "I testify to everyone who hears the words of the prophecy of this book: if anyone adds to them, God will add to him the plagues which are written in this book, and if anyone takes away from the words of the book of this prophecy, God shall take away his part from the tree of life and from the holy city, which are written in this book" (Rev. 22:18–19 NASB). While John referred specifically to his revelation, the principle and its warning logically fit the situation of the other books of the Bible. It is clear that God does not wish anything that claims divine authority to be added to his inspired words, whether oral or written.

Sixth, the Bible teaches *sola Scriptura* by stressing its own status as revelation from God (Gal. 1:12; cf. 1 Cor. 2:11–13), as over the mere words of human beings. A revelation from God is a divine unveiling or disclosure. The apostle Paul put the contrast vividly when he wrote, "I want you to know, brothers, that the gospel I preached is not something that man made up. I did not receive it from any man, nor was I taught it; rather I received it by revelation from Jesus Christ" (Gal. 1:11–12 NIV). Note that "man" includes the other apostles, of whom Paul adds, "nor did I go up to Jerusalem to those who were apostles before I was" (Gal. 1:17 NIV). So even the preaching of an apostle was not on the same level as direct revelation from God. Neither the words of an apostle nor of an angel (Gal. 1:8). This vividly expresses *sola Scriptura*.

Seventh, although written revelation was progressive, Catholics and Protestants agree that normative revelation ended by the time of the completion of the New Testament. Indeed, Jesus told the apostles that he would lead them into "all truth" (John 14:26; 16:13). And to be an apostle one must have lived in the first century in order to be an eyewitness of the resurrected Christ (cf. Acts 1:22; 1 Cor. 9:1; 15:4–8). But the only infallible record we have of apostolic teaching is in the New Testament. Therefore, it follows that Jesus predicted the Bible alone would be the summation of "all truth." This being the case, then, since canonical revelation ceased at the end of the first century, *sola Scriptura* means nothing more, nothing less, and nothing else has infallible authority.

Eighth, apostolic "traditions" or oral teachings were authoritative in their days, but the apostles are dead and all of their essential teaching is the Bible. The New Testament speaks of following the traditions or teachings of the apostles, whether oral or written because they were living authorities set up by Christ (Matt. 18:18; Acts 2:42; Eph. 2:20). However, when they died there was no longer a living apostolic authority since, as already noted, only those who were eyewitnesses of the resurrected Christ could have apostolic authority (Acts 1:22; 1 Cor. 9:1). For to have apostolic authority one must be able to perform apostolic signs (2 Cor. 12:12). Since these special apostolic signs have admittedly ceased (Heb. 2:3–4), there is no longer apostolic authority, except in the inspired writings the apostles left us. And since the New Testament is the only inspired (infallible) record of what the apostles taught, it follows that, since the death of the apostles, the only apostolic authority we have today is the inspired record of their teaching in the New Testament. This does not necessarily mean that everything the apostles ever taught is *in* the New Testament, anymore than everything Jesus said is there (cf. John 20:30; 21:25). Jesus did promise that "all the truth" (John 14:26; 16:13) he had taught them would be brought to their remembrance, but he no doubt said the same truth in different ways at different times. The context of Jesus' statement refers to all truth necessary for faith and morals (cf. 2 Tim. 3:15–17).

Ninth, oral traditions are notoriously unreliable. They are the stuff of which legends and myths are made. What is written is more easily preserved in its original form. Dutch theologian Abraham Kuyper notes four advantages of a written revelation: (1) It has durability whereby errors of memory or accidental corruptions, deliberate or not, are minimized; (2) It can be universally disseminated through translation and reproduction; (3) It is fixed and can be kept pure; (4) It is given a finality and normativeness which other forms of communication cannot attain (Milne, 28). By contrast, what is not written is more easily polluted. There is an example of that in the New Testament. There was an unwritten "apostolic tradition" (i.e., one coming from the apostles) based on a misunderstanding of what Jesus said. They wrongly assumed that Jesus said that the apostle John would not die. John, however, debunked this false tradition in his authoritative written record (John 21:22–23).

1 TIMOTHY

1 TIMOTHY 2:1–2—Does Paul's exhortation to pray for kings and others include those who are dead?

MISINTERPRETATION: Some Catholic scholars appeal to 1 Timothy 2:1 to support their dogma of praying for the dead. Paul said, "I urge, then, first of all, that requests, prayers, intercession and thanksgiving be made for everyone" (NIV). Does this include those who are dead?

CORRECTING THE MISINTERPRETATION: This passage does not envision prayers for the dead. Paul urged believers to pray for the living, namely, "for Kings and for all those [who *are*] in authority" (v. 2, insert added) at the present. There is absolutely nothing here to imply that he includes the dead. The Bible elsewhere condemns praying for the dead. See comments on 2 Timothy 1:18.

1 TIMOTHY 2:5–6—Does the fact that Christ is the mediator between humanity and God mean that Christ himself is not God?

MISINTERPRETATION: The Jehovah's Witnesses say that, since Christ is the Mediator, he must not be God, for the Mediator must be separate and distinct from those who need mediation (*Should You Believe in the Trinity?* 1989, 16).

CORRECTING THE MISINTERPRETATION: If Jesus as mediator cannot be God, then, by the same logic, he cannot be human. Such reasoning is clearly faulty. From a scriptural perspective, Jesus can mediate between God and man *precisely because* he is both God and man. It was only as a man that Christ could represent all humankind and die *as* a man. However, since Christ was also God, his death had infinite value sufficient to provide redemption for the sins of all humankind (see Heb. 2:14–16; 9:11–28). Thus, only the death of the perfect God-man can truly mediate for sinful humanity to God.

1 TIMOTHY 4:1–2—Does this verse indicate that the early church would fall into total apostasy, thereby pointing to the need for a restoration?

MISINTERPRETATION: This passage says that in the latter days "some will depart from the faith, giving heed to deceiving spirits, and doctrines of demons" (NKJV). Mormons say this is a prophecy of a *total* apostasy of the entire church (McConkie, 1977, 205).

CORRECTING THE MISINTERPRETATION: Though this verse speaks of apostasy, it does not speak of a *total* apostasy of the *entire* church. Notice that the text does not say, "in the latter times *all* shall depart from the faith." Rather it says, "*some* shall depart from the faith."

The apostasy of 1 Timothy 4:1–3 is a particular kind of apostasy related to Gnostic dualism. This school of thought said spirit is good and matter is evil. Apparently, there were some false teachers who believed that all appetites relating to the (material) body—including sex and food— were evil and should be avoided. Hence these false teachers forbade people to get married and ordered them to abstain from certain foods. The apostasy to which Paul referred occurred specifically in Timothy's day (see use of present tense in vv. 2–3). The phrase *last days* often means the period beginning with Christ's first coming (cf. Acts 2:16–17; Heb. 1:1) and extending to his second coming (2 Peter 3:3–4), or any era of it.

Even if this were a reference to the later apostasy of the whole church, it would not thereby justify the Mormon claims that the text of the Bible was corrupted and/or that Mormonism is the true restoration of the New Testament church.

1 TIMOTHY 6:17–18—Should wealth be avoided or retained?

MISINTERPRETATION: Jesus urged the rich young ruler to "sell what you have and give to the poor" (Matt. 19:21). The early disciples sold their possessions and laid the money at the apostles' feet (Acts 4:34, 35). And Paul warned that "the love of money is a root of all kinds of evil" (1 Tim. 6:10). Some cultic communal groups refer to these texts to justify the demand that members surrender all wealth and material possessions to the group.

CORRECTING THE MISINTERPRETATION: Jesus' instruction to "sell what you have and give to the poor" (Matt. 19:21) was to a rich young man who had made money his god. There is nothing wrong with *possessing riches*—there is something wrong with *being possessed by riches*. God blessed Abraham and Job with great riches, and the apostle Paul does not instruct the rich to give away all they have, but to use and enjoy their blessings (1 Tim. 6:17–18).

Further, there is no indication that the early disciples in Acts were either urged to sell all, or that they actually did. The land that was sold (Acts 4:34–35) may have been extra property. It is noteworthy that the narrative does not say they sold their homes. See the discussion of Acts 2:44–45.

Paul does not say that money is evil, but only that the *love* of money is the root of all kinds of evil. Seeking riches for their own sake is wrong, but seeking to have something to share with others in need is not. Thus, while God "gives us richly all things to enjoy" (1 Tim. 6:17), in the same breath he warns us not "to trust in uncertain riches."

2 TIMOTHY

2 TIMOTHY 1:18—Does Paul's prayer for Onesiphorus support the Roman Catholic doctrine of praying for the dead?

MISINTERPRETATION: The apostle Paul prayed for Onesiphorus, "May the Lord grant that he will find mercy from the Lord on that day! You know very well in how many ways he helped me in Ephesus" (NIV). Some Catholic scholars cite this verse to support the doctrine of praying for the dead. Is this what Paul referred to here?

CORRECTING THE MISINTERPRETATION: That Paul prayed that God would have mercy on Onesiphorus on the day of his reward does not at all support praying for the dead for one very fundamental reason—Onesiphorus was still alive when Paul prayed for him! Praying that someone alive will receive mercy on the day of judgment is a far cry from praying for them *after* they have already died.

There is no indication in the Bible that anyone should ever pray for another after they die. Luke 16 speaks of a "great chasm" between the living and the dead (v. 26). Paul speaks of death separating loved ones until they are reunited at the resurrection (1 Thess. 4:13–18). Any attempted contacts with the dead are not only futile but forbidden (Deut. 18:11) because of the possibility of demonic deception (cf. 1 Tim. 4:1).

When David's baby was alive but seriously ill he prayed for him fervently. However, when the baby died he ceased praying for him immediately (2 Sam. 12:22–23). When Jesus lost his close friend Lazarus by death he never prayed to God for him. He simply resurrected him with the command, "Lazarus, come forth!" Rather than pray for the dead, *Jesus prayed for the living.*

Praying for the dead is contrary to the all-sufficiency of the sacrifice of Christ. His mediation and intercession for them (1 John 2:1–2) is more than sufficient to address the needs of those who die in him. When

Jesus died and rose again the work of salvation was finished (John 19:30; cf. 17:4; Heb. 10:14). When he purged our sins he "sat down" at the right hand of God (Heb. 1:3) since there was absolutely nothing more to do for our salvation. So the whole concept of praying for the dead, that they might be freed from sin, is an insult to the finished work of Christ, who freed us from our sins by his blood (Rev. 1:5). Jesus not only obtained salvation from all our sins at one time but, as our great High Priest (Heb. 7), he alone implements it for all time.

Praying for the dead can be an idolatrous practice. Praying the rosary focuses on the intercession of Mary, or the saints are invoked. It is a form of worship and only God should be worshiped (Exod. 20:3). One of the Ten Commandments declares clearly, "You shall have no other gods before me. You shall not make for yourself a carved image, or any likeness of anything that is in the sky above or on the earth beneath or that is in the water under the earth; you shall not bow down to them nor serve them" (Exod. 20:3–5a NKJV). Praying to saints, making images of them, and/or bowing down to them violate this command.

The practice also insults the intercession of the Holy Spirit. Much of the Catholic justification for praying to the saints is based on the seemingly plausible argument that, because of their position in heaven, they may be better able to intercede on our behalf. This is a practical denial of the ministry of the Holy Spirit, whose task it is to do this very thing on our behalf. And who is better able to make intercessions for us than another person of the blessed Trinity? The Bible says, "we do not know how to pray as we should, but the Spirit Himself intercedes for us with groanings too deep for words" (Rom. 8:26b NASB). Paul adds in Ephesians, "For through him [Christ] we both have access in one Spirit to the Father" (Eph. 2:18 NASB). Since beyond our explicit prayers to God the Holy Spirit intercedes for us perfectly "according to God's will" (Rom. 8:27) there is no need to call on anyone else in heaven to do so. To expect any human being to be more efficacious with God the Father than God the Son and God the Holy Spirit (1 John 2:1–2) is to insult his divinely-appointed role.

2 TIMOTHY 2:2—Does this text support hierarchial discipleship, as some groups claim?

MISINTERPRETATION: Paul said to Timothy, "The things that you have heard from me among many witnesses, commit these to faithful men who will be able to teach others also" (2 Tim. 2:2 NKJV). This is often quoted by advocates of hierarchical discipleship, such as the Boston Church of Christ.

CORRECTING THE MISINTERPRETATION: This verse certainly teaches that the gospel is to spread from person to person and from teacher to disciple. But it does not justify a hierarchical or authoritarian relationship. The reference here is to personal discipleship, not to ecclesiastical authority. It speaks of how to teach, not how to exercise authority.

Even where the Bible does speak of submission to leaders it does not justify authoritarianism (see comments on 1 Cor. 11:1). It is submission out of love, not fear. It is voluntary, not compulsory subservience out of fear.

2 TIMOTHY 4:6—When Paul speaks of being made an offering, is he speaking about indulgences to save people from purgatory?

MISINTERPRETATION: Does this verse lend support to the Roman Catholic doctrine of purgatory or the idea that one can atone for another's sins?

CORRECTING THE MISINTERPRETATION: When Paul speaks of being "poured out as a libation [offering]" he is referring to his death as a martyr. There is nothing here about purgatory, indulgences, prayers for the dead, or anything supporting the Catholic doctrine of a Treasury of Merit contributed to by good deeds from which those in need in purgatory can draw.

This Catholic dogma is biblically unfounded and contrary to the biblical doctrine of salvation by grace through faith (Rom. 3:28; 4:5; Eph. 2:8–9; Titus 3:5–6). The concept of human beings helping to atone for the sins of other humans contradicts the all-sufficiency of the death of Christ. Regarding his redemptive work for our salvation, Jesus on the cross said, "It is finished" (John 19:39; cf. 17:4). For "because by one sacrifice he has made perfect for ever those who are being made holy" (Heb. 10:14).

TITUS

TITUS 2:13—Does this verse refer to two persons (God almighty *and* Jesus Christ) or one person (God almighty *who is* Jesus Christ)?

MISINTERPRETATION: The Jehovah's Witnesses translate this verse in such a way as to make it appear that two persons are in view—the "great God" (the Father) and the "Savior" (Jesus Christ). They argue that this verse "clearly differentiates between [God] and Jesus Christ, the one through whom God provides salvation" (*Reasoning from the Scriptures*, 1989, 421).

CORRECTING THE MISINTERPRETATION*:* Greek grammarians tell us that when two nouns in the same case are connected with the word *and* (Greek: *kai*)—and the first noun is preceded by the definite article ("the") while the second noun *is not* preceded by the definite article— then the second noun refers to the identical person or thing that the first noun refers to. This is the case in Titus 2:13. Two nouns—*God* and *Savior*—are joined by *and,* and the definite article precedes the first noun *(God)* but not the second noun *(Savior).* The sentence literally reads: "the great God and Savior of us." Hence, the two nouns in question— *God* and *Savior*—are referring to the same person, Jesus Christ.

The teaching in Titus 2:13 that God (Jesus) is Savior is consistent with what we read elsewhere in Scripture. In Isaiah 43:11, God asserts: "I, even I, am the LORD [*Yahweh*], and apart from me there is no savior" (NIV). This verse indicates that a claim to be Savior is a claim to deity, and there is only one Savior—God. It is against this backdrop that the New Testament refers to Jesus as Savior (Luke 2:11). The parallel truths that only God is the Savior (Isa. 43:11) and that Jesus is himself the Savior constitute a powerful evidence for Christ's deity.

PHILEMON

PHILEMON 16—Does the apostle Paul approve of the institution of slavery?

MISINTERPRETATION: The Apostle Paul seems to favor the institution of human slavery by sending a runaway slave, Onesimus, back to his owner. But slavery is an unethical violation of the principles of human freedom and dignity. This is relevant to cult studies because Identity movements (cultlike groups who hold to white supremacy) cite such verses in support of their racist views.

CORRECTING THE MISINTERPRETATION: Slavery is unethical and unbiblical and neither Paul's actions nor his writings approve of this debasing form of treatment. In fact, it was the application of biblical principles that ultimately led to the overthrow of slavery.

From the very beginning, God declared that all humans have the image of God (Gen. 1:27). The apostle reaffirmed this, declaring, "We are the offspring of God" (Acts 17:29), and he "has made from one blood every nation of men to dwell on all the face of the earth" (Acts 17:26 NKJV).

Despite the fact that slavery was countenanced in the Semitic cultures of the day, the Mosaic law demanded that slaves eventually be set free (Exod. 21:2; Levit. 25:40). Meanwhile, servants had to be treated with respect (Exod. 21:20, 26). Israel, a nation of slaves in Egypt, was constantly reminded by God of this (Deut. 5:15), and their emancipation became the model for the liberation of all slaves (cf. Levit. 25:40).

In the New Testament, Paul declared that in Christianity "there is neither Jew nor Greek, there is neither slave nor free, there is neither male nor female; for you are all one in Christ Jesus" (Gal. 3:28 NKJV). All social classes are broken down in Christ; we are all equal before God. The New Testament explicitly forbids the evil system of this world that traded in the "bodies and souls of men" (Rev. 18:13). Slave trade is so repugnant to God that he pronounces his final judgment on the evil system that perpetrated it (Rev. 17–18).

When Paul urges, "Servants, be obedient to those who are your masters" (Eph. 6:5 NKJV; cf. Col. 3:22), he is not thereby approving of the institution of slavery, but simply alluding to the de facto situation in his day. He is instructing slaves to be good employees, just as believers should be today, but he was not thereby commending slavery. Paul also instructed all believers to be obedient to existing oppressive governments for the Lord's sake (Rom. 13:1; cf. Titus 3:1; 1 Peter 2:13). But this in no way condones oppression and tyranny which the Bible repeatedly condemns (Exod. 2:23–25; Isa. 10:1). Law and order are necessary for peace and security (Rom. 13:2–5; 1 Tim. 2:2; 1 Peter 2:13–14).

A closer look at Philemon reveals that Paul did not perpetuate slavery, but actually undermined it. He urged Philemon, Onesimus's owner, to treat the runway as "a beloved brother" (v. 16). So, by emphasizing the inherent equality of all human beings, both by creation and redemption, the Bible laid down the very moral principles that overthrew slavery and helped restore the dignity and freedom of all persons, whatever their color or ethnic group.

HEBREWS

HEBREWS 1:3—Does this verse indicate that the Father has a physical body of flesh and bones?

MISINTERPRETATION: Hebrews 1:3 (NASB) says of Jesus, "He is the radiance of His glory and the exact representation of His nature. . . . When He had made purification of sins, He sat down at the right hand of the Majesty on high." Mormons think this verse indicates the Father has a physical body. After all, Jesus (who has a physical body) is an "exact representation" of the Father. Moreover, Jesus sat down at the Father's (literal) "right hand" (Talmage, 1982, 42).

CORRECTING THE MISINTERPRETATION: It is the uniform teaching of Scripture that God is a spirit (John 4:24). And a spirit does not have flesh and bones (Luke 24:39). Hence, it is incorrect to think of God as a physical being.

But if God is a Spirit, how are we to interpret the references in Scripture to God's "right hand"? This doesn't mean the Father has physical parts. Rather in Jewish thinking the "right hand" metaphorically referred to a place of honor. Christ was accorded supreme honor as the triumphant Lord who rose from the dead.

That Christ is the "exact representation" of God does not mean the Father has a physical body. Rather it means that Christ is fully God— just as much God as the Father is. The glory of God radiates from Jesus because Jesus is the God of glory. Because Jesus is the exact representation of God, Jesus could say, "He who has seen Me has seen the Father" (John 14:9).

Finally, Mormons fail to recognize that the incarnate Jesus is one person with two natures—a *divine* nature and a *human* nature. The incarnate Jesus is fully God (John 1:1; 8:58; 20:28) and is fully man (John 1:14; Rom. 8:3; 1 Tim. 3:16; 1 John 4:2; 2 John 7). In his divine nature, Jesus was (is) spirit (cf. John 4:24). In his human nature he has a physical body (John 1:14). The Father—who in his divine nature is spirit (as is Jesus in his divine nature)—never became incarnate (as Jesus became incarnate), and hence does not have a human body as does Jesus. It is therefore correct to say that in regard to Jesus' *divine* nature, he is the "exact representation" of God, because he is just as much God as is the Father.

HEBREWS 1:6—Does this verse indicate that Christ is just to be honored or is he to be worshiped?

MISINTERPRETATION: Though legitimate translations show Christ being worshiped by the angels in this verse, the New World Translation shows Christ being shown *obeisance* by the angels. The Jehovah's Witnesses say worship is to be "directed only toward God," not toward Jesus Christ (*Reasoning from the Scriptures,* 1989, 215).

CORRECTING THE MISINTERPRETATION: First of all, Jesus is often seen being worshiped (not just being shown obeisance) in Scripture. In Matthew 14:33, for example, Jesus accepts worship from his disciples on the Sea of Galilee. Again, in Mark 14:3–9, Jesus accepts worship from a woman who anoints him with costly perfume. It is noteworthy that Jesus always accepted such worship as *perfectly appropriate* (Matt. 28:9; John 9:38). Knowing that *only God* is to be worshiped (Exod. 20:5), Jesus never once corrected anyone who bowed down before him in worship.

Second, the exact same Greek word used of worshiping the Father (*proskuneō*) (John 4:24) is used of worshiping Jesus (Mark 14:3–9). There is no justification for translating *proskuneō* as "worship" in contexts dealing with the Father and as "obeisance" in contexts dealing with Jesus. In both contexts worship is the clear meaning of the word.

Third, in the Book of Revelation Jesus is seen to be receiving exactly the *same kind* of worship the Father receives (compare Rev. 4:10 with 5:11–14).

Clearly, then, the reference in Hebrews 1:6 points to Christ being worshiped—not being shown "obeisance"—by the angels. This is as it should be, since Christ is not only God but is the Creator of the angels (Col. 1:16).

HEBREWS 7:3—Does this verse support reincarnation?

MISINTERPRETATION: Hebrews 7:3b tells us that Melchizedek, "having neither beginning of days nor end of life, but made like the Son of God, abides a priest perpetually." Since Jesus assumed this priesthood (v. 21), some reincarnationists use this verse to prove that Jesus is a reincarnation of Melchizedek.

CORRECTING THE MISINTERPRETATION: This passage says Melchizedek was *made like* Jesus, not that Jesus *was* Melchizedek (Heb. 7:3). Christ is a priest "according to the order of" Melchizedek (v. 21). What one person, Melchizedek, symbolized, Jesus—another person— is the reality of.

That Melchizedek had a mysterious and unrecorded birth and death (Heb. 7:3) does not prove reincarnation. The mystery behind the man was used merely as an analogy for the kind of office filled by the eternal Messiah, Jesus Christ.

HEBREWS 11:1—Does this verse indicate that faith is an actual substance that God used to create the universe, as Word-Faith teachers argue?

MISINTERPRETATION: Hebrews 11:1 says, "Now faith is the substance of things hoped for, the evidence of things not seen" (KJV). Word-Faith teachers think this means that faith is an actual substance. Kenneth Copeland says that faith is a substance and "has the ability to effect natural substance" ("Forces of the Recreated Human Spirit," 1982, 8). Moreover, "faith was the raw material substance that the Spirit of God used to form the universe" ("Authority of the Believer II," 1987, audio tape).

CORRECTING THE MISINTERPRETATION: This verse does not indicate that faith is an actual substance. The Greek word translated "substance" in the King James Version is *hypostasis*, and literally means "assurance," "confidence," "confident expectation," or "being sure." Hence, Hebrews 11:1 teaches that faith is the certainty or assurance that God will do as he promises. Our hope for those things is a certainty in the person with faith (2 Peter 1:4).

HEBREWS 11:3—Did God create the universe according to his own faith, as Word-Faith teachers say?

MISINTERPRETATION: Hebrews 11:3 says, "Through faith we understand that the worlds were framed by the word of God, so that things which are seen were not made of things which do appear" (KJV). Faith teachers say this means that God, by means of his own faith, created the world. Hence, God is a faith being (Copeland, "Spirit, Soul, and Body," 1985, audio tape). And Christians can allegedly have this same God-kind of faith to accomplish miracles today.

CORRECTING THE MISINTERPRETATION: As the context clearly reveals, all Hebrews 11:3 says is that human beings, by faith, *understand* that God created the world. In other words, it isn't God who exercised faith in order to create the world. Rather, God created the world by his sovereign power (Gen. 1–2; John 1:3; Col. 1:16)—and our *understanding* of this fact rests upon faith. Our understanding must rely on faith, because none of us was there to witness this miracle.

Hebrews 11:35—Is this a citation from the Apocrypha which confirms these books to be a part of the Canon, as Roman Catholics claim?

MISINTERPRETATION: Roman Catholics accept as lesser authorities eleven extra books in the Old Testament canon in addition to the thirty-nine accepted by Protestants and Jews. These books include 1 and 2 Maccabees. One of the evidences they offer for accepting these books as authoritative is that the New Testament reflects the thought of the Apocrypha, and even refers to events recorded in it. One such reference is that "women received back their dead, raised to life again" (Heb. 11:35 KJV). Some Catholic scholars believe this is a reference to 2 Maccabees 7:12. Roman Catholics also say that because the Septuagint (the Greek translation of the Old Testament) contained the Apocrypha, the Apocrypha must therefore belong in the canon.

CORRECTING THE MISINTERPRETATION: Even if this verse alluded to the Apocrypha, it is not a quotation of it. There are no clear New Testament quotations from *any* book in the Apocrypha. Citations of an apocryphal book in the New Testament would not prove that the book was inspired. There are allusions in the New Testament to pseudepigraphal books (false writings) that are rejected even by Roman Catholics, as well as Protestants, such as the Book of Enoch (Jude 14–15) and the Bodily Assumption of Moses (Jude 9). There are also citations of pagan poets and philosophers (Acts 17:28; Titus 1:12; 1 Cor. 15:33). But neither Catholics nor Protestants accept these as inspired. Why? Because none of these are cited as Scripture. The New Testament simply refers to a truth contained in these books, which otherwise may (and do) have many errors. Nowhere is any apocryphal book cited as divine authority. For example, no allusion begins with the introductory phrases "Thus says the Lord" or "As it is written" or "The Scriptures say." Such phrases are found when canonical books are quoted.

The fact that the New Testament often quotes from the Greek Old Testament (the Septuagint) in no way proves that the Apocryphal books contained in Greek manuscripts of the Old Testament are inspired. It is not certain that the Greek Old Testament, the Septuagint (LXX), of the first century contained the Apocrypha. The earliest Greek manuscripts so far found that include these books date from the fourth century after Christ. If they were in the LXX of apostolic times, Jesus and the apostles are never once said to have quoted them, although they are supposed to have been included in the very Greek text that the apostles usually cited. Even the notes in the current Roman Catholic Bible (NAB) make the revealing admission that the Apocrypha contains "religious books used by both Jews and Christians which were not included in the collection of inspired writings." Instead, they "were introduced rather late into the collection of the Bible. Catholics call them 'deutero-canonical' (second canon) books" (*St. Joseph Edition of The New American Bible*, 413).

JAMES

JAMES 1:5—Does this verse indicate we should pray about the Book of Mormon to see if it's true?

MISINTERPRETATION: In James 1:5 we read, "If any of you lacks wisdom, let him ask of God, who gives to all men generously and without reproach, and it will be given to him" (NASB). Mormons appeal to this verse in asking people to pray about *The Book of Mormon* to see if it's true (see Moroni 10:4–5, *The Book of Mormon*).

CORRECTING THE MISINTERPRETATION: The Mormon interpretation jerks this verse out of its context. The meaning of James 1:5 is connected to the content of the preceding verses about the purpose of trials (vv. 2–4). He anticipates that some of his readers will say they cannot discover any divine purpose in their trials. In that case, they are to ask God for wisdom.

Even if James were not referring to the purpose of trials, but rather talking about wisdom in general, God's "wisdom" on a matter never contradicts what he has recorded in Scripture. For this reason, one need not pray about matters that God has already given us his verdict on. One does not need to pray about whether to worship another god because the true God has already said it is wrong (Exod. 20:3). One does not need to pray about whether to participate in spiritism. God has already said it is wrong (Deut. 18:9–14). Likewise, we need not pray about the Book of Mormon, because God has already condemned all gospels that contradict that found in the Bible (Gal. 1:6–9).

It should be stressed that prayer is not the test for religious truth. We are instructed by the apostle Paul in 1 Thessalonians 5:21 to objectively "test all things," not pray to receive a subjective feeling that something is true. Though the Bereans believed in prayer, their barometer for truth was not prayer but Scripture (Acts 17:10–12).

JAMES 2:21—Was Abraham justified by works?

MISINTERPRETATION: James declares, "Was not Abraham our father justified by works" (2:21 NASB). Mormons cite this verse in arguing for the necessity of works in attaining salvation (McConkie, 1977, 330). Roman Catholics also use this to show that our ultimate justification before God is not by faith alone (see Ott, 1960, 264).

CORRECTING THE MISINTERPRETATION: James is not talking about justification *before God* but rather justification *before* other people. This is indicated by the fact that James stressed that we should "show" (2:18) our faith. It must be something that can be seen by others in "works" (vv. 18–20). Further, James acknowledged that Abraham was justified before God by faith, not works, when he said, "Abraham believed God, and it was reckoned to him for righteousness" (v. 23). When he adds that Abraham was "justified by works" (v. 21), he is speaking of what Abraham did that could be seen by men, namely, offer his son Isaac on the altar (vv. 21–22).

James wrote at some length about justification before the watching world. The apostle Paul often spoke more frequently about justification before God. Paul declared, "But to him who does not work but believes on Him who justifies the ungodly, his faith is accounted for righteousness" (Rom. 4:5 NKJV). It is "not by works of righteousness which we have done, but according to His mercy He saved us" (Titus 3:5 NKJV). "For by grace you have been saved through faith, and that not of yourselves; it is the gift of God, not of works, lest anyone should boast" (Eph. 2:8–9 NKJV).

While Paul is stressing the *root* of justification (faith), James is stressing the *fruit* of justification (works). But both Paul and James acknowledge both sides of the point. Immediately after affirming that we are "saved by grace through faith" (Eph. 2:8–9), Paul quickly adds, "we are His workmanship, created in Christ Jesus for good works, which God prepared beforehand that we should walk in them" (v. 10). Right after declaring that it is "not by works of righteousness which we have done, but according to His mercy He saved us" (Titus 3:5a), Paul urges that "those who have believed in God should be careful to maintain good works" (v. 8; all NKJV).

We might illustrate the relation between Paul and James on the issue of justification this way:

Paul	James
Justification before God	Justification before humans
The root of justification	The fruit of justification
Justification by faith	Justification for works
Faith as producer of works	Works as the proof of faith

JAMES 3:6—Does the "course of nature" refer to reincarnation?

MISINTERPRETATION: James refers to the "course of nature," which has been translated "wheel of beginning." Some take this to be a reference to reincarnation, since they believe life goes around in cycles of birth, death, and rebirth (into another body), and so forth.

CORRECTING THE MISINTERPRETATION: The subject James is writing about is the power and persuasiveness of the human tongue, with its far-reaching effects. The "course of nature" refers to ongoing of life in general, not the recycling of individual souls.

Beyond this text, James affirmed forgiveness of sins (cf. 5:20) and petitionary prayer (5:15–18), both of which are contrary to the doctrine of karma behind reincarnation, which affirms that whatever is sown in this life must be reaped in the next life (no exceptions).

Finally, even if there were some question as to how this verse should be interpreted, an unclear passage should always be understood in the light of a clear one. And the Bible clearly opposes reincarnation (see John 9:3; Heb. 9:27).

JAMES 5:15—Do James's statements about healing support the claims of the mind science cults?

MISINTERPRETATION: Mind science cults such as Christian Science cite this verse in an attempt to show that we can shape reality by our thoughts. For "a mere request that God will heal the sick has no power to gain more of the divine presence than is always at hand. The beneficial effect of such prayer for the sick is on the human mind, making it act more powerfully on the body through a blind faith in God" (Eddy, 12). Is James referring here to mind cures?

CORRECTING THE MISINTERPRETATION: James says nothing about healing that is like what the mind sciences claim. James does not promise that all will be healed. Indeed, he implies this by saying prayer "can accomplish much." James says such prayer always has great value but he is not saying that it will always be effective to restore health (James 5:16).

It is not the mind but the "prayer of faith" that James declares to be effective (v. 15). This prayer is not uttered by those who are sick, but by the elders who are called in to pray (vv. 15–16). It is not one's mind that heals him but the Lord in whose name the elders pray (v. 14).

Sometimes even the most fervent and effectual prayer of a righteous man or woman does not bring healing, as the apostle Paul discovered when he sought God for his affliction (2 Cor. 12:7–10).

JAMES 5:16—Does the instruction about "confessing sins" in this verse justify the extremist practice of the Boston Church of Christ with its members?

MISINTERPRETATION: Leaders in the Boston Church of Christ have used this verse to justify their practice of having members write down their sins in detail, which can later be used to intimidate them into submission. Is this what the passage in James means?

CORRECTING THE MISINTERPRETATION: There is nothing here or anywhere in Scripture that justifies such an extreme practice. For one thing, we are told to confess our sins to one another and to pray for one another (James 5:16). This would include leaders as well as followers. Further, we are not told to cross-examine one another. Cross-examination of others about their sins is contrary to the spirit of Christ. We are told to bear one another's burdens, not to lay burdens on them (Gal. 6:5). When others do sin, we are to restore them in the spirit of meekness (Gal. 6:1), not inquire about their sins in an authoritarian manner.

1 PETER

1 PETER 1:18–19—Is our redemption based on Christ suffering in hell for three days, as some Word-Faith teachers argue, and not on his shedding of blood at the cross?

MISINTERPRETATION: Word-Faith teachers say that Christ's shed blood on the cross did not atone for our sins. Kenneth Copeland, for example, says, "Jesus went into hell to free mankind from the penalty of Adam's high treason. . . . *When His blood poured out it did not atone.* . . . Jesus spent three horrible days and nights in the bowels of this earth getting back for you and me our rights with God" (personal letter from Kenneth Copeland; cited in McConnell, 1988, 120).

CORRECTING THE MISINTERPRETATION: We were redeemed says 1 Peter 1:19 "with precious blood, as of a lamb unblemished and spotless, the blood of Christ." In keeping with this, Ephesians 1:7 (NASB) states, "In Him we have redemption through His blood, the forgiveness of our trespasses, according to the riches of His grace." Revelation 1:5 affirms that Christ has "released us from our sins by His blood" (all NASB). Even the Old Testament pointed forward to Christ's body being "pierced" (thereby shedding blood) for our iniquities (Isa. 53:5). Clearly our redemption is based on Christ's shed blood. See the discussion of 2 Corinthians 5:21 for the Old Testament background of blood sacrifices.

It is highly significant that right before he died on the cross, Jesus stated, "It is finished" (Greek: *tetelestai*) (John 19:30). This word can also be translated "paid in full." This was not a moan of defeat nor a sigh of patient resignation. Rather it was a triumphant recognition that Jesus had now fully accomplished what he had come into the world to do. The work of redemption was completed at the cross. Nothing further needed to be done. Jesus did not have to complete any work of redemption in hell. He paid in full the price of our redemption on the cross (2 Cor. 5:21).

For scriptural arguments refuting the idea that Jesus went to hell, see the discussion of Ephesians 4:9.

1 PETER 3:15—Are we to use reason in matters of religious faith?

MISINTERPRETATION: New Agers emphasize intuition and mysticism. Mormons speak about a "burning in the bosom" that assures them the Book of Mormon is true. Yet Peter here instructs believers to give a "reason" for their faith. How important is reason in matters of religious faith?

CORRECTING THE MISINTERPRETATION: A person should not believe in something without first enquiring whether it is a worthy object of belief. For example, few people would undergo a serious medical operation by a totally unknown person whom they had no reason to believe was anything but a quack. Likewise, God does not call on us to exercise blind faith.

Since God is a God of reason (Isa. 1:18), and since he has made us rational creatures in his image (Gen. 1:27; Col. 3:10), he wants us to look before we leap. No rational person should step into an elevator without first looking to see if there is a floor. Likewise, God wants us to take a step of faith in the light of the evidence, but not a leap of faith into the dark.

The Bible is filled with exhortations to use our reason. Jesus commanded, "You shall love the Lord . . . with all your mind" (Matt. 22:37). Paul added, "whatsoever things are true . . . think on these things" (Phil. 4:8 KJV). Paul also "reasoned" with the Jews (Acts 17:17) and with the philosophers on Mars Hill (vv. 22–33) winning some to Christ (v. 34). Bishops were instructed to be able "to refute those who contradict" (Titus 1:9 NASB). Paul declares that he was "appointed for the defense of the gospel" (Phil. 1:17). Jude urged us to "contend earnestly for the faith which was once for all delivered to the saints" (Jude 3). And Peter commanded, "be ready to give a defense to everyone who asks you a reason for the hope that is in you" (1 Peter 3:15).

1 PETER 3:18—Was Jesus raised in a spirit body or in a physical body?

MISINTERPRETATION: Peter declares that Christ was "put to death in the flesh but made alive in the spirit." The Jehovah's Witnesses argue from this verse that "at his resurrection from the dead, Jesus was brought forth with a spirit body" (*Reasoning from the Scriptures,* 1989, 334).

CORRECTING THE MISINTERPRETATION: To interpret this as proof of a spiritual, rather than a physical resurrection, is neither necessary nor consistent with the context of this passage and the rest of Scripture.

The passage is best translated, "He was put to death in the body but made alive by the [Holy] Spirit" (NIV). The passage is translated with this same understanding by the New King James Version and others. God did not raise Jesus a spirit but raised him *by* his Spirit.

The parallel between death and being made alive normally refers to the resurrection of the body in the New Testament. For example, Paul declared that Christ died and rose and lived again (Rom. 14:9), and "He was crucified in weakness, yet he lives by the power of God" (2 Cor. 13:4a NIV).

The context of 1 Peter 3:18 refers to the event as "the resurrection of Jesus Christ" (3:21). This is everywhere in the New Testament understood as a bodily resurrection (Acts 4:33; Rom. 1:4; 1 Cor. 15:21; 1 Peter 1:3; Rev. 20:5). Even if "spirit" refers to Jesus' human spirit (not to the Holy Spirit), it cannot mean he had no resurrection body. Otherwise, the reference to his "body" (flesh) before the resurrection would mean he had no human spirit then. It seems better to take "flesh" in this context as a reference to his whole condition of humiliation before the resurrection and "spirit" to refer to his unlimited power and imperishable life after the resurrection.

We must also keep in mind that however we interpret 1 Peter 3:18, it must be consistent with what other verses say about the resurrected Christ. In Luke 24:39 the resurrected Christ said, "See My hands and My feet, that it is I Myself; touch Me and see, for a spirit does not have flesh and bones as you see that I have" (Luke 24:39 NIV). The resurrected Christ testifies in this verse that he is not a spirit and that his resurrection body is made up of flesh and bones. See comments on Luke 24; 1 Corinthians 15:5–8.

The resurrected Christ also ate physical food on four different occasions to prove he had a real physical body (Luke 24:30; 24:42–43; John 21:12–13; Acts 1:4). It would have been deception on Jesus' part to have offered his ability to eat physical food as a proof of his bodily resurrection if he had not been resurrected in a physical body.

1 PETER 3:19—Does Peter support the view that a person has a second chance to be saved after he dies?

MISINTERPRETATION: First Peter 3:19 says that Christ, after his death, "went and preached to the spirits in prison." Mormons believe this verse indicates that people have a second chance to be saved after they have died (Talmage, 1977, 148).

CORRECTING THE MISINTERPRETATION: Difficult passages such as this must be interpreted according to the clearer passages of Scripture. The Bible is clear that there is no second chance after death (Heb. 9:27). The Book of Revelation records the Great White Throne Judgment in which those who are not found in the book of life are sent to the lake of fire (Rev. 20:11–15). Luke informs us that, once a person dies, he goes either to heaven (Abraham's bosom) or to hell and that there is a great gulf fixed "so that those who want to pass" from one to the other cannot (Luke 16:26). The whole urgency of responding to God in this life before we die gives further support to the fact that there is no hope beyond the grave (cf. Prov. 29:1; John 3:36; 5:24). *Now* is the day of salvation (2 Cor. 6:2).

There are ways to understand this passage that do not involve a second chance at salvation after death. Some claim that Jesus offered no hope of salvation to these "spirits in prison." The text does not say Christ *evangelized* them, but simply that he *proclaimed* the victory of his resurrection to them. They insist that there is nothing stated in this passage about preaching the gospel to people in hell. In response to this view, others note that in the very next chapter (4:6) Peter, apparently extending this subject, does say "the gospel was preached also to those who are dead." See comments on 1 Peter 4:6.

Others claim it is not clear that the phrase "spirits in prison" even refers to human beings. Nowhere else is such a phrase used of human beings in hell. They claim these spirits are fallen angels, since the "Sons of God" (fallen angels—see Job 1:6; 2:1; 38:7) were "disobedient . . . in the days of Noah" (1 Peter 3:20; cf. Gen. 6:1–4). Peter may be referring to this in 2 Peter 2:4, where he mentions the angels sinning immediately before he refers to the flood (v. 5). In response, it is argued that angels cannot marry (Matt. 22:30). They certainly could not intermarry with human beings, since angels, being spirits, have no reproductive organs.

Or this passage teaches that Christ preached *through* the person of Noah to those who, because they rejected his message, are *now* spirits in prison. Those who hold to this view note that in this same book we are told that the "Spirit of Christ" spoke through the Old Testament prophets (1 Peter 1:11). In keeping with this, 2 Peter 2:5 informs us that Noah was a "preacher of righteousness." Hence, the Spirit of Christ preached through Noah to the ungodly who now await final judgment.

A final possible interpretation is that this verse refers to Christ's announcement to departed spirits of the triumph of his resurrection, declaring to them the victory he had achieved by his death and resurrection, as pointed out in the previous verse (see 1 Peter 3:18). This view fits the context here, is in accord with the rest of Scripture (cf. Eph. 4:8; Col. 2:15), and avoids the major problems of the other views.

1 PETER 4:6—Is the gospel preached to people after they die?

MISINTERPRETATION: Peter says that "the gospel was preached also to those who are dead." Mormons believe this verse shows there is a second chance to hear the gospel in the spirit world following physical death (Talmage, 1977, 147).

CORRECTING THE MISINTERPRETATION: No hope is held out anywhere in Scripture for salvation after death. Death is final, and there are only two destinies—heaven and hell, between which there is a great gulf that no one can pass over (see comments on 1 Peter 3:19). So, whatever preaching to the "dead" may mean, it does not imply that one can be saved after he or she dies. This is an unclear passage, subject to differing interpretations, and no doctrine should be based on an ambiguous passage. The difficult texts should be interpreted in the light of the more clear.

It is possible that this verse refers to those who are now dead who heard the gospel while they were alive. In favor of this is cited the fact that the gospel "was preached" (in the past) to those who "are dead" (now, in the present). Some believe this might not be a reference to human beings, but to the "spirits in prison" (angels) of 1 Peter 3:19 (cf. 2 Peter 2:4 and Gen. 6:2). Others claim that, although the dead suffer the destruction of their flesh (1 Peter 4:6), yet they still live with God by virtue of what Christ did through his death and resurrection. This victorious message was announced by Christ himself to the spirit world after his resurrection (cf. 1 Peter 3:18).

2 PETER

2 PETER 3:7—Does going into perdition refer to annihilation?

MISINTERPRETATION: Annihilationists who deny an eternal conscious punishment claim that Peter's reference to "perdition" supports their view. Indeed, Judas is called the "son of perdition" (John 17:12). Since the word *perdition* (*apoleia*) simply means to perish, annihilationists such as the Jehovah's Witnesses argue that the lost will perish or go out of existence (e.g., *You Can Live Forever in Paradise on Earth*, 1982, 83).

CORRECTING THE MISINTERPRETATION: The word *perdition* (*apoleia*) simply means to perish or to come to ruin. In 2 Peter 3:7 it is used in the context of *judgment*, a term that implies consciousness.

That the wicked are said to go into "perdition" (2 Peter 3:7) and Judas is called the "son of perdition" (John 17:12) need not mean they will be annihilated. Junk cars perish in the sense of having been ruined. But they are still cars, ruined as they may be, and they are still in the junkyard. In this connection, Jesus spoke of hell as a junkyard or dump where the fire would not cease and where a person's resurrected body would not be consumed (see Mark 9:48).

Jesus spoke repeatedly of people in hell as being in continual agony. He declared that "the subjects of the kingdom will be thrown outside, into the darkness, where there will be weeping and gnashing of teeth" (Matt. 8:12 NIV; cf. 22:13; 24:51; 25:30). But a place of weeping is obviously a place of conscious sorrow. Those who are not conscious do not weep. See comments on 2 Thessalonians 1:9.

1 JOHN

1 JOHN 4:2–3—Does this refer to Jesus being in the flesh before or after his resurrection?

MISINTERPRETATION: John declares that those who deny "Jesus Christ has come in the flesh" are of Antichrist. Orthodox Christians take this to mean Jesus was fully human, with a physical body of flesh, *before* his resurrection. Others contend that Jesus was not raised from the dead in the same body of flesh and bones in which he died, but in a body that was not essentially material. The Jehovah's Witnesses, for example, say Jesus was *spiritually* resurrected (*Aid to Bible Understanding*, 1971, 1396).

CORRECTING THE MISINTERPRETATION: In the Greek, John uses the perfect tense, meaning past action with continuing results in the present. Thus, he affirms that Jesus came in the flesh in the past and continues in the flesh in the present (i.e., when he is writing, which was after the resurrection).

John further clarifies matters a few verses later when he sets that same Greek phrase in the present tense. He declares in verse 7 that many deceivers do not "confess Jesus Christ as coming [present tense] in the flesh." Even after the resurrection when John wrote, he insisted that Jesus was still in the flesh.

Two other New Testament texts explicitly declare Christ's resurrection body to be one of flesh. Referring to the resurrection of Christ, Peter declared, "nor did His flesh see corruption" (Acts 2:30–31 NKJV). Jesus himself said to his disciples in one of his postresurrection appearances, "Handle Me and see, for a spirit does not have flesh and bones as you see I have" (Luke 24:39b NKJV).

1 JOHN 5:7—Does the absence of this verse in modern translations prove that the doctrine of the Trinity is not true?

MISINTERPRETATION: In the King James Version text, 1 John 5:7 declares that "there are three who bear witness in heaven: the Father, the Word, and the Holy Spirit; and these three are one." This is the clearest statement on the Trinity in the Bible. However, most modern translations omit this verse. The Jehovah's Witnesses cite the lack of manuscript evidence for this verse as a proof that the doctrine of the Trinity is unbiblical (*Reasoning from the Scriptures*, 1989, 422–23).

CORRECTING THE MISINTERPRETATION: It is true that this verse has virtually no support among the early Greek manuscripts, though it is found in Latin manuscripts. Its appearance in late Greek manuscripts is based on the fact that Erasmus was placed under ecclesiastical pressure to include it in his Greek New Testament of 1522, having omitted it in his two earlier editions of 1516 and 1519 because he could not find any Greek manuscripts which contained it.

Its inclusion in the Latin Bible probably results from a scribe incorporating a marginal comment (gloss) into the text as he copied the manuscript of 1 John. But including it in the text violates almost every rule of textual criticism. Even the New King James Version, which generally retains the longer readings and disputed passages (see Mark 16:9–20 and John 7:53–8:11), comments in the margin that this is "a passage found in only four or five very late *Greek* mss."

Simply because this one verse has no manuscript support does not mean the doctrine of the Trinity is not true. Numerous other passages that have undeniable places in Scripture manuscript support establish that (1) there is only one true God; (2) there are three persons who are God, and (3) there is three-in-oneness within the Godhead. See comments on Isaiah 9:6; Matthew 28:18–20; 2 Corinthians 13:14.

1 JOHN 5:6–8—Does this verse prove that the Holy Spirit is not a person?

MISINTERPRETATION: This passage indicates that the Spirit, water, and blood are "witnesses" of Jesus Christ. Because water and blood are not persons, the Holy Spirit is not a person either, according to the Jehovah's Witnesses (*Should You Believe in the Trinity?* 1989, 22). Other cult leaders, such as Herbert W. Armstrong, also denied the personality of the Holy Spirit.

CORRECTING THE MISINTERPRETATION: Obviously water and blood are not persons. They are personified as witnesses. But this doesn't mean the Holy Spirit is not a person.

At the time 1 John was written, a group of Gnostics believed that what the New Age movement calls a "cosmic Christ" came upon a human Jesus following his baptism. This Christ departed before his crucifixion. First John 5:6–8, with its three "witnesses," disproves this heretical doctrine. Water (representing Jesus' baptism) and blood (representing his crucifixion) both act as metaphorical witnesses to the fact that Jesus the Christ experienced *both* the baptism *and* death by crucifixion. The Holy Spirit is the third witness testifying to this fact. According to Jewish law, three witnesses were required to establish the truth of a matter (Deut. 19:15).

The Holy Spirit is portrayed as a person throughout Scripture. The Holy Spirit has the attributes of personality—mind (1 Cor. 2:10–11), emotions (Eph. 4:30), and will (1 Cor. 12:11). The Holy Spirit is seen doing many things in Scripture that only a person can do—he teaches believers (John 14:26), testifies (John 15:26), guides (Rom. 8:14), commissions people to service (Acts 13:4), issues commands (Acts 8:29), prays for believers (Rom. 8:26), and speaks to people (2 Peter 1:21). Moreover, certain acts are performed *toward* the Holy Spirit that would not make sense if he did not possess true personality. For example, the Holy Spirit can be lied to (Acts 5:3). One does not lie to a mere power or force.

2 JOHN

2 JOHN 10—Does this verse mean we shouldn't allow cultists into our house?

MISINTERPRETATION: According to John, we are not to receive into our house or even greet anyone who comes to us and does not believe that Christ is come in the flesh. How does this apply to cultists? Should we turn them away?

CORRECTING THE MISINTERPRETATION: Second John 10 does not prohibit Christians from allowing cultists into their home in order to witness to them. Rather it is a prohibition against giving cultists a platform from which to teach false doctrine.

The backdrop to this is that in the early days of Christianity, there was no central church building where believers could congregate. Rather, small house-churches were scattered throughout the city.

After Pentecost early Christians are seen "breaking bread from house to house" (Acts 2:46; 5:42) and gathering to pray in the house of Mary, the mother of Mark (Acts 12:12). Churches often met in houses (see Rom. 16:15; 1 Cor. 16:19; Col. 4:15; Philem. 2). The use of specific church buildings did not appear before the end of the second century.

John is here warning leaders of these housechurches not to allow a false teacher into the church, or give a false teacher a platform from which to teach. Seen in this way, this prohibition guards the purity of the church. To extend hospitality to a false teacher would imply that the church accepted or approved of their teaching. The false teacher would be encouraged in the error.

For similar reasons, John also may be forbidding Christians to allow false teachers to stay in their houses. In the early church, the evangelistic and pastoral ministry of the church was conducted primarily by itinerant individuals who traveled from house-church to house-church, depending on the hospitality of the people. John is directing the church not to extend this kind of hospitality to teachers of false doctrine. Christians are not to let cultists use their homes as a base of operations from which to spread their poison.

In any case, this verse does not prohibit Christians from allowing cultists into the home for evangelistic purposes. When a Jehovah's Witness or a Mormon shows up on the doorstep the Christian should feel free to invite him or her into the living room in order to witness to that person.

3 JOHN

3 JOHN 2—Does this verse indicate that God desires us to be financially prosperous, as Word-Faith teachers argue?

MISINTERPRETATION: Third John 2 says, "Beloved, I pray that in all respects you may prosper and be in good health, just as your soul prospers" (NASB). Word-Faith teachers cite this verse in support of the prosperity gospel.

CORRECTING THE MISINTERPRETATION: The Greek word for "prosper" in this verse does not refer to financial prosperity but simply means "to go well with someone." In fact, the NIV translation correctly reflects this idea in its rendering of the verse: "Dear friend, I pray that you may enjoy good health and that *all may go well with you,* even as your soul is getting along well." In biblical times the wish for "things to go well," along with the wish for "good health," was a standard form of greeting. Financial prosperity is completely foreign to both this ancient greeting and 3 John 2.

REVELATION

REVELATION 1:7—Will Christ's second coming be an invisible event?

MISINTERPRETATION: Revelation 1:7 says, "Behold, He is coming with the clouds, and every eye will see Him, even those who pierced Him; and all the tribes of the earth will mourn over Him. Even so. Amen" (NASB). The Jehovah's Witnesses argue that just as an airplane in the clouds is invisible to people on earth, so Christ's coming "with the clouds" means the event is invisible. Only those with "eyes of understanding" will perceive that his coming has taken place in 1914 (*Reasoning from the Scriptures*, 1989, 343).

CORRECTING THE MISINTERPRETATION: Revelation 1:7 explicitly states that *every eye* on earth will actually (not just spiritually) see Christ coming in glory. The Greek word for "see" *(horao)* literally means "to see with the eyes, bodily vision." There is no possibility that the meaning of this verse is "see with the eyes of one's understanding." A good cross-reference is Matthew 24:30: "And then the sign of the Son of Man *will appear* in the sky, and then all the tribes of the earth will mourn, and they *will see* the Son of Man coming on the clouds of the sky with power and great glory" (NASB; emphasis added). Just as Christ ascended bodily and visibly, so Christ will come again bodily and visibly (Acts 1:9–11).

REVELATION 1:8—Is Jesus the "Alpha and the Omega" mentioned in this verse?

MISINTERPRETATION: The Jehovah's Witnesses argue that all the references to the Alpha and Omega in the Book of Revelation apply to

Almighty God, the Father, and not to the Son (*Reasoning from the Scriptures*, 1989, 412).

CORRECTING THE MISINTERPRETATION: There are two strong reasons for taking this as a reference to Christ and, hence, a proof of his deity. First, Revelation 1:7 speaks of one who was "pierced" and is "coming." Obviously this one who is coming must be Jesus, since he (not the Father) was pierced when he was nailed to the cross. Verse 8 then tells us that it is God who "is coming." The one who is coming in both verses is God, and it is he who was pierced. This can only be Jesus Christ.

Second, John makes an explicit statement of Christ's deity in Revelation 22:12–13: "Behold, I am coming quickly. . . . I am the Alpha and the Omega, the first and the last, the beginning and the end" (NASB). Then in 22:20 (NASB) we read, "'Yes, I am coming quickly.' Amen. Come, Lord Jesus." The one who is coming is God the second person, the "first and the last," Jesus Christ.

REVELATION 3:14—Does this verse indicate that Jesus was a created being?

MISINTERPRETATION: Revelation 3:14 says, "And to the angel of the church in Laodicea write: The Amen, the faithful and true Witness, the Beginning of the creation of God, says this" (NASB). Jehovah's Witnesses say the logical conclusion is that the one spoken of in Revelation 3:14 "is a creation, the first of God's creations, who had a beginning" (*Reasoning from the Scriptures*, 1989, 409).

CORRECTING THE MISINTERPRETATION: The Greek word *archē*, translated "beginning" in this verse, here carries the meaning of "one who begins," "origin," "source," or "first cause." The English word *architect* is derived from *archē*. This verse says that Jesus is the architect of all creation (see John 1:3; Col. 1:16; Heb. 1:2; cf. Isa. 44:24).

Furthermore, the same term, *beginning*, is applied to God the Father in Revelation 21:4–6. It cannot mean a created being, or God the Father is also a creature, which Jehovah's Witnesses reject. Hence, "beginning" should be understood in the absolute sense of Beginner or Source of all things.

REVELATION 5:6–14—Does the Bible's teaching about the Lamb support the Masonic belief in salvation by works?

[305]

MISINTERPRETATION: According to the Masonic Order, "In all ages the lamb has been deemed an emblem of innocence; he, therefore, who wears the Lambskin as a badge of Masonry is continually reminded of that purity of life and conduct which is necessary to obtain admittance into the Celestial Lodge above [heaven], where the Supreme Architect of the Universe [God] presides" (Allen, et al., 1963, 17). Again,

Let its pure and spotless surface be to you an ever present reminder of purity of life and rectitude of conduct, a never ending argument for nobler deeds, for higher thoughts, for greater achievements. And when those weary feet shall come to the end of their toilsome journey, and from your nerveless grasp shall drop forever the working tools of life, may the record of your whole life and actions be as pure and spotless as the fair emblem I have placed in your hands tonight. And when at the last great day your poor, trembling soul stands naked and alone before the great white throne, may it be your portion to hear from Him who sitteth as the Judge Supreme the welcome words, "Well done, good and faithful servant, enter thou into the joy of thy Lord." [Ibid., 60]

Is the teaching about the Lamb of God evidence that salvation is by works?

CORRECTING THE MISINTERPRETATION: Nothing could be farther from the truth than this Masonic Lodge teaching. The "Lamb" in the Book of Revelation is the one slain for our salvation (Rev. 5:6), before we were even born (13:8). He alone is found worthy (5:12) and is worshiped (5:8), not we because of our works. In fact, the saints are clothed in the white robes of his righteousness (7:9). Indeed, believers are washed in the blood of the Lamb (7:14). And he alone is the fountain of salvation (7:17). Any victory the saints have is through his merits (12:11). And the saved are the fruit of his work, not ours (14:4). Thus we are his followers (14:4) and sing his praises (5:8–10; 15:3).

Outside Revelation the Bible is just as emphatic that "it is by grace you have been saved, through faith—and this not from yourselves, it is the gift of God—not by works, so that no one can boast" (Eph. 2:8–9 NIV). For "He saved us, not because of righteous things we had done, but because of his mercy" (Titus 3:5a NIV; cf. vv. 3–6). And "to the man who does not work but trusts God who justifies the wicked, his faith is credited as righteousness" (Rom. 4:5 NIV).

REVELATION 7:2–4—Does this passage prophesy the coming of Reverend Moon, as the Unification Church teaches?

MISINTERPRETATION: Revelation 7:2 makes reference to "another angel ascending from the east, having the seal of the living God" (KJV). The unification church teaches that this verse prophesies the coming of the Lord of the Second Advent from a country in the East. Rev. Sun Myung Moon was born in Korea, and is thus the fulfillment of this verse (DP, 519–20).

CORRECTING THE MISINTERPRETATION: The text is speaking of *an angel,* not the Messiah. This angel is said to come from the *direction* of the east, not from a country in the East. Other references to compass points in Revelation tend to refer to directions, not geographical areas. Even if this reference is to the geographic East, the country would not be Korea. The true Messiah is Jewish (see Matt. 1).

The Scriptures testify that, at the second coming, the *same* Jesus who ascended into heaven will physically come back (Acts 1:11). There will not be a second "Christ" from Korea or anywhere else.

REVELATION 7:4—Are the 144,000 mentioned in this verse the "anointed class" that are destined to live in heaven with God, as opposed to the "earthly class" that will live forever on earth?

MISINTERPRETATION: Revelation 7:4 says, "And I heard the number of those who were sealed, one hundred and forty-four thousand sealed from every tribe of the sons of Israel" (NASB). Jehovah's Witnesses say the 144,000 refers to the anointed class of believers who have a heavenly destiny (cf. Rev. 14:1–3) (*Reasoning from the Scriptures,* 1989, 166–67). These 144,000 are the ones referred to as the "little flock" in Luke 12:32.

CORRECTING THE MISINTERPRETATION: Scripture teaches that *all* who believe in Jesus Christ can look forward to a heavenly destiny, not just some select group of 144,000 (see Eph. 2:19; Phil. 3:20; Col. 3:1; Heb. 3:1; 12:22; 2 Peter 1:10–11). Jesus affirmed that all believers will be together in "one flock" under "one shepherd" (John 10:16). There will not be two "flocks"—one on earth and one in heaven.

Second, there is very good reason to interpret this verse quite literally—as referring to 144,000 Jews, 12,000 from each tribe. Nowhere else in the Bible does a reference to the twelve tribes of Israel mean anything but *twelve tribes of Israel.* The word *tribes* is never used of anything but a literal ethnic group in Scripture.

In support of the literal interpretation is the fact that Jesus spoke of the twelve apostles (whom we know were literal persons) sitting on "twelve thrones, judging the twelve tribes of Israel" in the last day (Matt. 19:28). There is no reason not to take this as a reference to twelve literal tribes of Israelites.

In addition, the last question Jesus answered before his ascension directly implied that he would return and "restore the kingdom to Israel" (Acts 1:6–8). Indeed, the apostle Paul spoke of the restoration of the nation of Israel to its former privileged position in Romans 11 (cf. vv. 11–26).

Many Bible scholars believe in a literal restoration of the nation of Israel, because God's land promises to Abraham's literal descendants (Gen. 12, 14, 15, 17, 26) have never been fulfilled "forever," as they were promised (cf. Gen. 13:15), but at best only for a short period during the time of Joshua (Josh. 11:23).

REVELATION 10:2, 8–9—Is the "little book" of which John spoke the "divine science" of Mary Baker Eddy, as set forth in her book on Christian Science?

MISINTERPRETATION: Mary Baker Eddy claimed that the "little book" that is prophesied in this passage is actually Christian Science (*Science and Health*, 558–59).

CORRECTING THE INTERPRETATION: That this is far from John's intent is evident from the total lack of allusion to teachings of Christian Science. What John clearly does have in mind is the book or scroll *of judgment* to be unleased on the earth in the tribulation period before Christ returns again (cf. Rev. 5:1).

Finally, when ingested this book did not bring physical healing; it made John sick to his stomach. He said, "I took the little scroll from the angel's hand and ate it. It tasted as sweet as honey in my mouth, but when I had eaten it, my stomach turned sour" (Rev. 10:10 NIV).

REVELATION 12:1–6—Does the "woman" being taken into heaven here represent the bodily assumption of Mary?

MISINTERPRETATION: This text speaks of a "woman" who gave birth to "a male child, destined to rule all the nations" (i.e., Christ) who was "caught up to God and his throne." Some noted Roman Catholic scholars claim this refers to the bodily assumption of Mary: "Scholastic theology sees . . . the transfigured mother of Christ" (Ott, 1960, 209).

CORRECTING THE MISINTERPRETATION: The "woman" does not represent Mary but rather the nation of Israel. For this woman there is "a place prepared for her by God, where she might be taken care of for 1260 days" (Rev. 12:6) during the tribulation period before Christ returns to earth (cf. Rev. 11:2–3).

Christ, not the "woman," was "caught up to God and his throne" (Rev. 12:5). It is pure eisegesis (reading a viewpoint into the text), to see Mary's bodily assumption here. Likewise, to argue that Mary, though not being caught up here, is pictured in heaven in the celestial imagery is equally farfetched. Nothing in this text would entail a belief in her bodily assumption before the resurrection of the rest of the saints (1 Thess. 4:13–18).

REVELATION 14:9–12—Does this passage indicate the restoration of the Sabbath?

MISINTERPRETATION: Some Seventh-day Adventist scholars believe John predicts here the restoration of the Sabbath. "We believe that the restoration of the Sabbath is indicated in the Bible prophecy of Revelation 14:9–12. Sincerely believing this, we regard the observance of the Sabbath as a test of our loyalty to Christ as Creator and Redeemer" (*Seventh-day Adventists Answer Questions on Doctrine*, 1957, 153; cited in Martin, 430). For "in the last days the Sabbath test will be made plain. When this time comes anyone who does not keep the Sabbath will receive the mark of the beast and will be kept from heaven" (White, 1911, 449).

CORRECTING THE MISINTERPRETATION: There is no indication of the Sabbath in this or any other text in the New Testament. (See comments on Acts 17:1–3.) The word *Sabbath* does not even occur in the Book of Revelation.

The reference to Jews fleeing on the Sabbath in Matthew 24:20 is descriptive, not prescriptive. It simply refers to the fact that Jews will observe the Sabbath during the future Tribulation period, not that Christians ought to do so.

The day of worship for Christians mentioned in the Book of Revelation is "the Lord's Day" (Rev. 1:10) which in John's day was the "first day of the week" (1 Cor. 16:2) when Christians regularly gathered together (Acts 20:7). According to Paul, the Sabbath passed away with the rest of the Law of Moses as a "shadow" fulfilled in the "substance" of Christ (Col. 2:16–17; cf. Heb. 7:12).

REVELATION 16:14—Can demons perform miracles?

MISINTERPRETATION: The Bible sometimes uses the same words (*sign, wonders, power*) to describe the power of demons as are used to describe miracles of God (2 Thess. 2:9; Rev. 16:14). Can demons perform miracles?

CORRECTING THE MISINTERPRETATION: Although Satan has great spiritual powers, there is a gigantic difference between the power of the devil and the power of God. First, God is infinite in power (omnipotent); the devil (and demons) is finite and limited. Second, only God can create life (Gen. 1:1, 21; Deut. 32:39); the devil cannot (cf. Exod. 8:19). Only God can raise the dead (John 10:18; Rev. 1:18); the devil cannot, though he gave "breath" (animation) to the idolatrous *image* of the Antichrist (Rev. 13:15).

The devil has great power to deceive people (Rev. 12:9), to oppress those who yield to him, and even to possess them (Acts 16:16). He is a master magician and a super scientist. And with his vast knowledge of God, man, and the universe, he is able to perform "lying signs" (2 Thess. 2:9; cf. Rev. 13:13–14). But true miracles can be performed only by God. The devil can do the supernormal but not the supernatural. Only God can control the natural laws he has established, though on one occasion he granted Satan the power to bring a whirlwind on Job's family (Job 1:19). Further, all the power the devil has is given him by God and is carefully limited and monitored (cf. Job 1:10–12). Christ had defeated the devil and triumphed over him and all his host (Col. 2:15; Heb. 2:14–15), thus giving power to his people to be victorious over demonic forces (Eph. 6:10–18). Thus, John informed believers: "He who is in you is greater than he who is in the world" (1 John 4:4 NKJV).

REVELATION 19:8—Do the white robes of the saints represent the "righteous acts of the saints"—an interpretation Roman Catholics offer in support of the doctrine of indulgences?

MISINTERPRETATION: Catholic scholars appeal to Revelation 19:8 to support the idea of a storehouse or collection of the good deeds of the saints. This Treasury of Merit (see comments on Exod. 32:30) is supposedly based on the idea that the white robes of the saints means "the righteous acts of the saints."

CORRECTING THE MISINTERPRETATION: The Roman Catholic use of this passage to support their doctrine of indulgences interprets literally a symbolic picture. This is shown by the facts that the text interprets the symbolism for the reader and that the whole book announces itself as a symbolic presentation, saying they would be "sign-ified" (Gk. *esēmanen*), i.e., made known by symbols (Rev. 1:1). The book proceeds by giving and interpreting many of these symbols for the reader (e.g., 1:20; 17:9, 15).

The text says nothing about there being any such collection of righteous works but simply says that each person's own works follow him or her (Rev. 22:12; cf. Rom. 14:12). Scripture elsewhere makes it clear that "each of us shall give an account of himself [to God]" for *his own* works (2 Cor. 5:10). To claim that saints can contribute to any merit that is granted by God to us for our salvation is an insult to the all-sufficiency of Christ's atoning death on the cross for all of our sins (see John 19:30; Rom. 8:1; Heb. 1:3; 10:14).

Nothing in this passage suggests that righteous acts of the saints are available for others to draw upon for their lives, which is what Roman Catholicism teaches.

REVELATION 19:20—Will everyone be saved in the end, as the Children of God cult claims?

MISINTERPRETATION: The leader of the Children of God cult argued that not all unbelievers will suffer eternal punishment.

> Only the most wicked of all, Satan, the Antichrist, his False Prophet and his most ardent followers who received the Mark of the Beast and worshipped him and his Image will remain in the Lake of Fire to be punished and purged of their diabolical rebelliousness as long as God sees fit, even until such time as they, too, may have learned their lesson sufficiently for God to forgive them and restore His entire creation to its original perfection where all is well! [David, 1974, 3]

CORRECTING THE MISINTERPRETATION: Revelation 19:20 declares that "the beast was captured, and with him the false prophet who had performed the miraculous signs on his behalf. With these signs he had deluded those who had received the mark of the beast and worshiped his image. The two of them were thrown alive into the fiery lake of burning sulphur" (NIV). Revelation 20:10 adds, "And the devil, who deceived them, was thrown into the lake of burning sulphur, where the beast and the false prophet had been thrown. They will be tormented day and night for ever and ever." There is no evidence that *anyone* will be released from punishment in the lake of fire. In fact, there is clear support here for eternal punishment.

Only a few verses later we read that "if *anyone's* name was not found written in the book of life, he was thrown into the lake of fire" (Rev. 20:15 NIV). There is not even an intimation that they will be released from this eternal lake of fire.

The only time for repentance is *before* death. Hebrews 9:27 (NKJV) declares that "it is appointed unto men once to die, but after this the judgment." Luke 16:26 speaks of a "great gulf fixed" between heaven and hell so that no one can pass from one side to the other.

The Bible says that the punishment of all unbelievers will be everlasting. Paul wrote of the "Lord Jesus [who] is revealed from heaven with His mighty angels, in flaming fire taking vengeance on those who do not know God, and on those who do not obey the gospel of our Lord Jesus Christ. These shall be punished with *everlasting destruction* from the presence of the Lord, and from the glory of His power" (2 Thess. 1:7–9 NKJV).

Finally, the duration of suffering in hell will be as long as the duration of bliss in heaven. The same word, *eternal* is used of both heaven and hell in Matt. 25:46.

REVELATION 22:18—Does this verse warn against new "revelations"?

MISINTERPRETATION: Revelation 22:18 says, "I testify to everyone who hears the words of the prophecy of this book: If anyone adds to these things, God will add to him the plagues that are written in this book." Mormons argue they have not added either to the Book of Revelation or to the Bible. Therefore this verse does not apply to them (Richards, 1973, 56).

CORRECTING THE MISINTERPRETATION: The injunction in Revelation 22:18 addresses adding to or subtracting from the Book of Revelation. Joseph Smith blatantly violated this injunction, for he both added to *and* subtracted from the Book of Revelation. Smith made alterations to the (KJV) biblical text and produced the so-called "Inspired Version" of the Bible. An example is Revelation 5:6, where Smith changed the KJV rendering, "having *seven horns* and *seven eyes,* which are the *seven Spirits of God,*" to "having *twelve horns* and *twelve eyes,* which are the *twelve servants of God,* sent forth into all the earth."

BIBLIOGRAPHY

General Cultism

Ahlstrom, Sydney E. *A Religious History of the American People.* New York, NY: Image Books, 1975.

Ankerberg, John and John Weldon, *Cult Watch: What You Need to Know About Spiritual Deception.* Eugene, OR: Harvest House Publishers, 1991.

Boa, Kenneth. *Cults, World Religions, and You.* Wheaton, IL: Victor Books, 1979.

Enroth, Ronald. *A Guide to Cults and New Religions.* Downers Grove, IL: InterVarsity Press, 1983.

———. *The Lure of the Cults.* Downers Grove, IL: InterVarsity Press, 1987.

Gomes, Alan W. *Unmasking the Cults.* Edited by Alan W. Gomes. Grand Rapids, MI: Zondervan Publishing House, 1995.

Hoekema, Anthony A. *The Four Major Cults.* Grand Rapids, MI: Eerdmans, 1978.

Martin, Paul. *Cult-Proofing Your Kids.* Grand Rapids, MI: Zondervan Publishing House, 1993.

Martin, Walter. *Martin Speaks Out on the Cults.* Ventura, CA: Regal Books, 1983.

———. *The Kingdom of the Cults.* Minneapolis, MN: Bethany House Publishers, 1985.

———. *The New Cults.* Ventura, CA: Regan Books, 1980.

———. *The Rise of the Cults.* Ventura, CA: Regal Books, 1983.

Mather, George and Larry Nichols. *Dictionary of Cults, Sects, Religions and the Occult.* Grand Rapids, MI: Zondervan Publishing House, 1993.

McDowell, Josh and Don Stewart. *Understanding the Cults.* San Bernardino, CA: Here's Life Publishers, 1983.

———. *Handbook of Today's Religions.* San Bernardino, CA: Here's Life Publishers, 1989.

Rhodes, Ron. *The Culting of America: The Shocking Implications for Every Concerned Christian.* Eugene, OR: Harvest House Publishers, 1994.

Sire, James. *Scripture Twisting: Twenty Ways the Cults Misread the Bible*. Downers Grove, IL: InterVarsity Press, 1980.

Swenson, Orville. *The Perilous Path of Cultism*. Caronport, Saskatchewan, Canada: Briercrest Books, 1987.

Tucker, Ruth. *Another Gospel: Alternative Religions and the New Age Movement*. Grand Rapids, MI: Zondervan Publishing House, 1989.

Mormonism

Benson, Ezra Taft. *The Teachings of Ezra Taft Benson*. Salt Lake City, UT: Bookcraft, 1988.

Bible Dictionary, in *The Holy Bible*. Salt Lake City, UT: Church of Jesus Christ of Latter-day Saints, 1990.

Book of Mormon. Salt Lake City, UT: The Church of Jesus Christ of Latter-day Saints, 1990.

Cannon, George Q. *Gospel Truth*. Salt Lake City, UT: Deseret Book Company, 1987.

Cares, Mark J. *Speaking the Truth in Love to Mormons*. Milwaukee, WI: Northwestern Publishing House, 1993.

Doctrine and Covenants. Salt Lake City, UT: The Church of Jesus Christ of Latter-day Saints, 1990.

Encyclopedia of Mormonism, ed. Daniel H. Ludlow. New York, NY: Macmillan, 1992.

Farkas, John R. and David A. Reed. *Mormonism: Changes, Contradictions, and Errors*. Grand Rapids, MI: Baker Book House, forthcoming.

Gospel Principles. Salt Lake City, UT: Church of Jesus Christ of Latter-day Saints, 1981.

Hunter, Milton R. *The Gospel Through the Ages*. Salt Lake City, UT: Deseret Book Co., 1958.

Kimball, Edward, ed. *The Teachings of Spencer W. Kimball*. Salt Lake City, UT: Bookcraft, 1982.

Kimball, Spencer W. *Repentance Brings Forgiveness*. Salt Lake City, UT: The Church of Jesus Christ of Latter-day Saints, 1984.

———. *The Miracle of Forgiveness*. Salt Lake City, UT: Bookcraft, 1969.

Martin, Walter. *The Maze of Mormonism*. Ventura, CA: Regal Books, 1978.

Matthews, Robert J. *A Sure Foundation*. Salt Lake City, UT: Deseret, 1988.

McConkie, Bruce. *Doctrinal New Testament Commentary*, Vol. 2. Salt Lake City, UT: Bookcraft, 1976.

———. *Mormon Doctrine*, 2d ed. Salt Lake City, UT: Bookcraft, 1977.

McKay, David O. *Gospel Ideals*. Salt Lake City, UT: Improvement Era, 1953.

McKeever, Bill and Eric Johnson. *Questions to Ask Your Mormon Friend.* Minneapolis, MN: Bethany House Publishers, 1994.

McKeever, Bill. *Answering Mormons' Questions.* Minneapolis, MN: Bethany House Publishers, 1991.

Petersen, Mark E. *As Translated Correctly.* Salt Lake City, UT: Deseret, 1966.

Pratt, Orson. *The Seer.* Washington, DC: n.p., 1853–54.

Reed, David A. and John R. Farkas. *How to Rescue Your Loved One from Mormonism.* Grand Rapids, MI: Baker Book House, 1994.

———. *Mormons Answered Verse by Verse.* Grand Rapids, MI: Baker Book House, 1993.

Rhodes, Ron and Marian Bodine. *Reasoning from the Scriptures with the Mormons.* Eugene, OR: Harvest House Publishers, 1995.

Richards, LeGrand. *A Marvelous Work and a Wonder.* Salt Lake City, UT: Deseret Book Company, 1958.

Smith, Joseph Fielding. *Doctrines of Salvation.* Salt Lake City, UT: Bookcraft, 1975.

———. *Man: His Origin and Destiny.* Salt Lake City, UT.

———. *The Way to Perfection.* Salt Lake City, UT: Deseret, n.d.

Smith, Joseph. *History of the Church of Jesus Christ of Latter-day Saints.* Salt Lake City, UT: Deseret Book Company, 1973.

Talmage, James E. *The Articles of Faith.* Salt Lake City, UT: The Church of Jesus Christ of Latter-day Saints, 1982.

———. *The Great Apostasy.* Salt Lake City, UT: Deseret Book Company, 1975.

Tanner, Jerald and Sandra. *3,913 Changes in the Book of Mormon.* Salt Lake City, UT: Utah Lighthouse Ministry, n.d.

———. *Archaeology and the Book of Mormon.* Salt Lake City, UT: Modern Microfilm Company, 1969.

———. *Major Problems of Mormonism.* Salt Lake City, UT: Utah Lighthouse Ministry, 1989.

———. *The Changing World of Mormonism.* Chicago, IL: Moody Press, 1981.

Tanner, Sandra. *Mormonism, Magic and Masonry.* Salt Lake City, UT: Utah Lighthouse Ministry, 1988.

Widtsoe, John A. *Evidences and Reconciliations.* Salt Lake City, UT: Bookcraft, 1987.

———. *Joseph Smith—Seeker After Truth.* Salt Lake City, UT: Deseret, 1951.

Young, Brigham. *Journal of Discourses.* London: Latter-day Saints' Book Depot, 1854–56.

Jehovah's Witnesses

"Let God Be True." Brooklyn, NY: Watchtower Bible and Tract Society, 1946.

"Let Your Name Be Sanctified." Brooklyn, NY: Watchtower Bible and Tract Society, 1961.

"Make Sure of All Things." Brooklyn, NY: Watchtower Bible and Tract Society, 1953.

"The Kingdom Is At Hand." Brooklyn, NY: Watchtower Bible and Tract Society, 1944.

"Things in Which It Is Impossible for God to Lie." Brooklyn, NY: Watchtower Bible and Tract Society, 1965.

"Your Will Be Done on Earth." Brooklyn, NY: Watchtower Bible and Tract Society, 1958.

1975 Yearbook of Jehovah's Witnesses. Brooklyn, NY: Watchtower Bible and Tract Society, 1975.

Aid to Bible Understanding. Brooklyn, NY: Watchtower Bible and Tract Society, 1971.

Ankerberg, John and John Weldon. The Facts on Jehovah's Witnesses. Eugene, OR: Harvest House Publishers, 1988.

Blood, Medicine and the Law of God. Brooklyn, NY: Watchtower Bible and Tract Society, 1961.

Bodine, Jerry and Marian. Witnessing to the Witnesses. Irvine, CA.: n.p., n.d.

Bowman, Robert M. Understanding Jehovah's Witnesses. Grand Rapids, MI: Baker Book House, 1991.

———. Jehovah's Witnesses, Jesus Christ, and the Gospel of John. Grand Rapids, MI: Baker Book House, 1989.

———. Why You Should Believe in the Trinity. Grand Rapids, MI: Baker Book House, 1989.

Chretien, Leonard and Marjorie. Witnesses of Jehovah. Eugene, OR: Harvest House Publishers, 1988.

Countess, Robert H. The Jehovah's Witnesses' New Testament. Phillipsburg, NJ: Presbyterian and Reformed Publishing Co., 1982.

Creation. Brooklyn, NY: Watchtower Bible and Tract Society, 1927.

Expositor's Bible Commentary. Ed. Frank E. Gaebelein. Grand Rapids, MI: Zondervan Publishing House, 1978.

Franz, Raymond. Crisis of Conscience. Atlanta: Commentary Press, 1984.

God's Kingdom of a Thousand Years Has Approached. Brooklyn, NY: Watchtower Bible and Tract Society, 1973.

Grieshaber, Erich and Jean. Expose of Jehovah's Witnesses. Tyler, TX: Jean Books, 1982.

———. *Redi-Answers on Jehovah's Witnesses' Doctrine.* Tyler, TX: n.p., 1979.

Gruss, Edmond. *We Left Jehovah's Witnesses.* Nutley, NJ: Presbyterian and Reformed, 1974.

Holy Spirit—The Force Behind the Coming New Order! Brooklyn, NY: Watchtower Bible and Tract Society, 1976.

Is This Life All There Is? Brooklyn, NY: Watchtower Bible and Tract Society, 1974.

Life Everlasting—In Freedom of the Sons of God. Brooklyn, NY: Watchtower Bible and Tract Society, 1966.

Light, vols. 1–2. Brooklyn, NY: Watchtower Bible and Tract Society, 1930.

MacGregor, Lorri. *What You Need to Know About Jehovah's Witnesses.* Eugene, OR: Harvest House Publishers, 1992.

Magnani, Duane. *The Watchtower Files.* Minneapolis, MN: Bethany House Publishers, 1985.

Man's Salvation Out of World Distress At Hand! Brooklyn, NY: Watchtower Bible and Tract Society, 1975.

Martin, Walter. *The Kingdom of the Cults.* Minneapolis, MN: Bethany House Publishers, 1982.

Martin, Walter and Norman Klann. *Jehovah of the Watchtower.* Minneapolis, MN: Bethany House Publishers, 1974.

Millions Now Living Will Never Die. Brooklyn, NY: Watchtower Bible and Tract Society, 1920.

New World Translation. Brooklyn, NY: Watchtower Bible and Tract Society, 1981.

Paradise Restored to Mankind—by Theocracy. Brooklyn, NY: Watchtower Bible and Tract Society, 1972.

Prophecy. Brooklyn, NY: Watchtower Bible and Tract Society, 1929.

Qualified to Be Ministers. Brooklyn, NY: Watchtower Bible and Tract Society, 1955.

Reasoning from the Scriptures. Brooklyn, NY: Watchtower Bible and Tract Society, 1989.

Reconciliation. Brooklyn, NY: Watchtower Bible and Tract Society, 1928.

Reed, David. *How to Rescue Your Loved One from the Watch Tower.* Grand Rapids, MI: Baker Book House, 1989.

———. *Index of Watchtower Errors.* Grand Rapids, MI: Baker Book House, 1990.

———. *Jehovah's Witnesses Answered Verse by Verse.* Grand Rapids, MI: Baker Book House, 1992.

Rhodes, Ron. *Reasoning from the Scriptures with the Jehovah's Witnesses.* Eugene, OR: Harvest House Publishers, 1992.

Should You Believe in the Trinity? Brooklyn, NY: Watchtower Bible and Tract Society, 1989.

Studies in the Scriptures, vols. 1–7. Brooklyn, NY: Watchtower Bible and Tract Society, 1886–1917.

The Greatest Man Who Ever Lived. Brooklyn, NY: Watchtower Bible and Tract Society, 1991.

The Harp of God. Brooklyn, NY: Watchtower Bible and Tract Society, 1921.

The Truth That Leads to Eternal Life. Brooklyn, NY: Watchtower Bible and Tract Society, 1968.

Theocratic Aid to Kingdom Publishers. Brooklyn, NY: Watchtower Bible and Tract Society, 1945.

Thomas, E. W. *Masters of Deception.* Grand Rapids, MI: Baker Book House, 1983.

Weathers, Paul G. "Answering the Arguments of Jehovah's Witnesses Against the Trinity." *Contend for the Faith.* Ed. Eric Pement. Chicago, IL: EMNR, 1992.

You Can Live Forever in Paradise on Earth. Brooklyn, NY: Watchtower Bible and Tract Society, 1982.

The New Age Movement

Alnor, William. *UFOs in the New Age.* Grand Rapids, MI: Baker Book House, 1992.

Ankerberg, John and John Weldon. *The Facts on Holistic Health and the New Medicine.* Eugene, OR: Harvest House Publishers, 1992.

Baer, Randall N. *Inside the New Age Nightmare.* Lafayette, LA: Huntington House, 1989.

Bailey, Alice A. *The Reappearance of the Christ.* New York, NY: Lucis Publishing Company, 1948.

Besant, Annie. *Esoteric Christianity.* Wheaton, IL: The Theosophical Publishing House, 1970.

Blavatsky, H. P. *The Key to Theosophy.* Pasadena, CA: Theosophical University Press, 1972.

Brooke, Tal. *When the World Will Be as One.* Eugene, OR: Harvest House Publishers, 1989.

Capra, Fritjof. *The Turning Point: Science, Society, and the Rising Culture.* New York, NY: Simon and Schuster, 1982.

Chandler, Russell. *Understanding the New Age.* Dallas, TX: Word Publishing, 1991.

Creme, Benjamin. *The Reappearance of the Christ and the Masters of Wisdom.* Los Angeles, CA: Tara Center, 1980.

Davis, Lola A. *Toward a World Religion for the New Age.* Farmingdale, NY: Coleman, 1983.

Dowling, Levi. *The Aquarian Gospel of Jesus the Christ.* London: L. N. Fowler, 1947.

Earth's Answer: Explorations of Planetary Culture at the Lindisfarne Conferences. Edited by Michael Katz, William Marsh, and Gail G. Thompson. New York, NY: Harper & Row, 1977.

Ferguson, Marilyn. *The Aquarian Conspiracy: Personal and Social Transformation in the 1980s.* Los Angeles, CA: J. R. Tarcher, 1980.

Fox, Matthew. *The Coming of the Cosmic Christ.* San Francisco, CA: Harper & Row, 1988.

Geisler, Norman L. and J. Yutaka Amano. *Religion of the Force.* Dallas, TX: Quest Publications, 1983.

Geisler, Norman L. and Jeff Amano. *The Infiltration of the New Age.* Wheaton, IL: Tyndale House Publishers, 1990.

Gershon, David and Gail Straub. *Empowerment: The Art of Creating Your Life as You Want It.* New York, NY: Delta, 1989.

Groothuis, Douglas. *Confronting the New Age.* Downers Grove, IL: InterVarsity Press, 1988.

———. *Unmasking the New Age.* Downers Grove, IL: InterVarsity Press, 1986.

Hall, Manly R. *The Mystical Christ: Religion as a Personal Spiritual Experience.* Los Angeles, CA: Philosophical Research Society, Inc., 1951.

Halverson, Dean C. *Crystal Clear.* Colorado Springs, CO: Navpress, 1990.

Hoyt, Karen and the Spiritual Counterfeits Project. *The New Age Rage.* Old Tappan, NJ: Fleming H. Revell, 1987.

Huxley, Aldous. *The Perennial Philosophy.* London: Fontana, 1958.

Keel, John. *UFOs: Operation Trojan Horse.* New York, NY: G. P. Putnam's Sons, 1970.

Keys, Donald. *Earth at Omega.* New York, NY: Branden, 1982.

Kjos, Berit. *Under the Spell of Mother Earth.* Wheaton, IL: Victor Books, 1992.

———. *Your Child and the New Age.* Wheaton, IL: Victor Books, 1990.

Leadbeater, C. W. *A Textbook of Theosophy.* Adyar, Madras, India: The Theosophical Publishing House, 1954.

Levi, *The Aquarian Gospel of Jesus the Christ.* London: L. N. Fowler & Co., 1947.

Lipnack, Jessica and Jeffery Stamps. *Networking.* New York, NY: Doubleday, 1982.

Lovelock, J. E. *Gaia.* New York, NY: Oxford, 1979.

Lutzer, Erwin W. and John F. DeVries. *Satan's "Evangelistic" Strategy for This New Age.* Wheaton, IL: Victor Books, 1991.

MacLaine, Shirley. *Dancing in the Light.* New York, NY: Bantam Books, 1985.

———. *It's All in the Playing.* New York, NY: Bantam Books, 1987.
———. *Out on a Limb.* New York, NY: Bantam, 1984.
Maharishi Mahesh Yogi. *Bhagavad Gita.* Baltimore: Penguin, 1973.
Mangalwadi, Vishal. *When the New Age Gets Old.* Downers Grove, IL: InterVarsity Press, 1993.
Miller, Elliot. *A Crash Course on the New Age Movement.* Grand Rapids, MI: Baker Book House, 1989.
Muller, Robert. *New Genesis: Shaping a Global Spirituality.* New York, NY: Doubleday and Co., 1982.
Mumford, Lewis. *The Transformations of Man.* New York, NY: Harper, 1970.
Needleman, Jacob. *The Heart of Philosophy.* New York, NY: Bantam, 1984.
Not Necessarily the New Age. Ed. Robert Basil. Buffalo, NY: Prometheus Books, 1988.
Pagels, Elaine. *The Gnostic Gospels.* New York, NY: Random House, 1979.
Pollock, Dale. *Skywalking: The Life and Films of George Lucas.* New York, NY: Harmony Books, 1983.
Prophet, Elizabeth Clare. *The Lost Years of Jesus.* Livingston, MT: Summit University Press, 1987.
Prophet, Mark and Elizabeth. *Climb the Highest Mountain.* Los Angeles, CA: Summit University Press, 1974.
———. *The Lost Teachings of Jesus 1: Missing Texts, Karma and Reincarnation.* Livingston, MT: Summit University Press, 1986.
———. *The Lost Teachings of Jesus 2: Mysteries of the Higher Self.* Livingston, MT: Summit University Press, 1988.
———. *The Lost Teachings of Jesus 3: Masters and Disciples on the Path.* Livingston, MT: Summit University Press, 1988.
Purucker, G. de. *Studies in Occult Philosophy.* Pasadena, CA: Theosophical University Press, 1973.
———. *The Esoteric Tradition.* 2 vols. Pasadena, CA: Theosophical University Press, 1973.
Read, Anne. *Edgar Cayce: On Jesus and His Church.* New York, NY: Warner, 1970.
Reisser, Paul C., Teri K. Reisser. and John Weldon. *New Age Medicine.* Chattanooga, TN: Global Publishers, 1988.
Rhodes, Ron. *The Counterfeit Christ of the New Age Movement.* Grand Rapids, MI: Baker Book House, 1990.
———. *The New Age Movement.* Grand Rapids, MI: Zondervan Publishing House, 1995.
Rozman, Deborah. *Meditating with Children.* Boulder Creek, CA: University of the Trees Press, 1975.

Russell, Peter. *The Global Brain: Speculations on the Evolutionary Leap to Planetary Consciousness.* Los Angeles, CA: J. R. Tarcher, 1982.

Ryerson, Kevin and Stephanie Harolde. *Spirit Communication.* New York, NY: Bantam, 1989.

Satin, Mark. *New Age Politics.* New York, NY: Dell, 1978.

Simon, Sidney B., Leland W. Howe, and Howard Kirschenbaum. *Values Clarification.* New York, NY: Hart, 1978.

Spangler, David. *A Vision of Findhorn: Anthology.* Forres, Scotland: Findhorn, 1978.

———. *Emergence: The Rebirth of the Sacred.* New York, NY: Dell, 1984.

———. *Explorations: Emerging Aspects of the New Culture.* Forres, Scotland: Findhorn, 1981.

———. *Reflections on the Christ.* Forres, Scotland: Findhorn, 1981.

———. *Relationship & Identity.* Forres, Scotland: Findhorn Publications, 1978.

———. *Revelation: The Birth of a New Age.* Middleton, WI: Lorian, 1976.

———. *The Laws of Manifestation.* Forres, Scotland: Findhorn, 1983.

———. *Towards a Planetary Vision.* Forres, Scotland: Findhorn, 1977.

Starhawk, Miriam. *The Spiral Dance.* San Francisco, CA: Harper & Row, 1979.

Steiger, Brad. *Gods of Aquarius.* New York, NY: Berkeley Books, 1976.

———. *The Fellowship.* New York, NY: Ballantine, 1989.

Steiner, Rudolf. *Christ in Relation to Lucifer and Ahriman.* Spring Valley, NY: Anthroposophic Press, 1978.

———. *From Buddha to Christ.* Spring Valley, NY: Anthroposophic Press, 1974.

———. *Jesus and Christ.* Spring Valley, NY: Anthroposophic Press, 1976.

———. *Knowledge of the Higher Worlds and Its Attainment.* Spring Valley, NY: Anthroposophic Press, 1947.

———. *The Deed of Christ.* North Vancouver, B.C., Canada: Steiner, 1954.

———. *The Four Sacrifices of Christ.* Spring Valley, NY: Anthroposophic Press, 1944.

———. *The Reappearance of the Christ in the Etheric.* Spring Valley, NY: Anthroposophic Press, 1983.

Strieber, Whitley. *Communion.* New York, NY: Beech Tree, 1987.

———. *Transformation: The Breakthrough.* New York, NY: Avon, 1989.

Teilhard de Chardin, Pierre. *The Phenomenon of Man.* New York, NY: Harper, 1959.

The Findhorn Garden: Pioneering a New Vision of Man and Nature in Cooperation, by the Findhorn Community. San Francisco, CA: Harper & Row, 1975.

The New Age Rage. Ed. Karen Hoyt. Old Tappan, NJ: Revell, 1987.

Thompson, William I. *Passages About Earth: An Exploration of the New Planetary Culture.* New York, NY: Harper & Row, 1973.
Trevelyan, George. *A Vision of the Aquarian Age: The Emerging Spiritual World View.* Walpole, NH: Stillpoint, 1984.
———. *Operation Redemption: A Vision of Hope in an Age of Turmoil.* Walpole, NH: Stillpoint, 1985.
Vallee, Jacques. *Confrontations: A Scientist's Search for Alien Contact.* New York, NY: Ballantine, 1990.
———. *Messengers of Deception: UFO Contacts and Cults.* Berkeley, CA: And Or Press, 1979.
———. *The Invisible College.* New York, NY: Dutton, 1975.
Weldon, John with Zola Levitt. *Ufos: What On Earth Is Happening.* Irvine, CA: Harvest House Publishers, 1975.
Wilber, Ken. *The Atman Project.* Wheaton, IL.: The Theosophical Publishing House, 1980.
———. *Up from Eden.* Boulder, CO: Shambhala, 1983.
Wimbish, David. *Something's Going On Out There.* Old Tappan, NJ: Revell, 1990.
Zukav, Gary. *The Dancing Wu Li Masters.* New York, NY: Morrow, 1979.

Mind Sciences

Bach, Marcus. *They Have Found a Faith.* Indianapolis: Bobbs-Merrill, 1946.
Braden, Charles Samuel. *These Also Believe.* New York, NY: Macmillan, 1949.
Cady, H. Emilie. *Lessons in Truth.* Lees Summitt, MO: Unity School of Christianity, 1962.
Dresser, Horatio W. *History of the New Thought Movement.* New York, NY: Crowell, 1919.
Eddy, Mary Baker. *Christian Science Versus Pantheism.* Boston, MA: Christian Science Publishing Society, 1898.
———. *Miscellaneous Writings.* Boston, MA: Christian Science Publishing Society, 1896.
———. *No and Yes.* Boston, MA: Christian Science Publishing Society, 1891.
———. *Science and Health with Key to the Scriptures.* Boston, MA: Christian Science Publishing Society, n.d.
Fillmore, Charles and Coral. *Teach Us to Pray.* Lees Summit, MO: Unity School of Christianity, 1946.
Fillmore, Charles. *The Metaphysical Dictionary.* Lees Summit, MO: Unity School of Christianity, 1962.

———. *What Practical Christianity Stands For.* Lees Summit, MO: Unity School of Christianity, 1939.

Gottschalk, Stephen. *The Emergence of Christian Science in American Religious Life.* Berkeley, CA: University of California Press, 1973.

Holmes, Ernest. *What Religious Science Teaches.* Los Angeles, CA: Science of Mind Publications, 1975.

Holmes, Fenwicke L. *Ernest Holmes: His Life and Times.* New York, NY: Dodd, Mead, 1970.

Quimby, Phineas P. *The Quimby Manuscripts.* Ed. Horatio W. Dresser. New Hyde Park, NY: University Books, 1961.

Spittler, Russell P. *Cults and Isms: Twenty Alternates to Evangelical Christianity.* Grand Rapids, MI: Baker Book House, 1962.

Trine, Ralph Waldo. *In Tune with the Infinite.* New York, NY: Thomas Y. Crowell, 1897.

Turner, Elizabeth Sand. *What Unity Teaches.* Lees Summit, MO: Unity School of Christianity, n.d.

Unity's Statement of Faith. Lees Summit, MO: Unity School of Christianity, n.d.

Other Cults and Cultic Groups

Allen, Raymond Lee, et al. *Tennessee Craftsmen or Masonic textbook,* 145th edition. Nashville, TN: Tennessee Board of Custodians Members, 1963.

Ankerberg, John and John Weldon. *The Facts on Astrology.* Eugene, OR: Harvest House Publishers, 1988.

———. *The Facts on False Teaching in the Church.* Eugene, OR: Harvest House Publishers, 1988.

———. *The Facts on Spirit Guides.* Eugene, OR: Harvest House Publishers, 1988.

———. *The Facts on the Masonic Lodge.* Eugene, OR: Harvest House Publishers, 1989.

Barron, Bruce. *The Health and Wealth Gospel.* Downers Grove, IL: InterVarsity Press, 1989.

Berg, Moses David. *FFer's Handbook!—Condensed Selected Quotes from More than 50 FF Letters!* Ed. Justus Ashtree. Rome: Children of God, January 1977.

Bernard, David. *The Oneness of God: Series in Pentecostal Theology,* vol. 1. Hazelwood, MO: Pentecostal Publishing House, 1983.

Boyd, Gregory. *Oneness Pentecostals and the Trinity.* Grand Rapids, MI: Zondervan Publishing House, 1992.

Copeland, Kenneth. "Spirit, Soul and Body" (audiotape #01-0601). Fort Worth, TX: Kenneth Copeland Ministries, 1985.

———. "What Happened from the Cross to the Throne" (audiotape #02-0017). Forth Worth, TX: Kenneth Copeland Ministries, 1990.

———. "Why All Are Not Healed" (audiotape #01-4001). Fort Worth, TX: Kenneth Copeland Ministries, 1990.

———. *Laws of Prosperity.* Fort Worth, TX: Kenneth Copeland Publications, 1974.

David, Moses. *Afflictions.* Rome: Children of God, 1976.

———. *Heavenly Homes!* London: Children of God, 1974.

———. *Love vs. Law!* Rome: Children of God, 1977.

———. *Our Message.* London: Children of God, 1974.

———. *The Wrath of God!* Rome: Children of God. 1977.

Davis, Deborah. *The Children of God.* Grand Rapids, MI: Zondervan Publishing House, 1984.

Divine Principle. Washington, DC: The Holy Spirit Association for the Unification of World Christianity, 1973.

Ehrenborg, Todd. *Mind Sciences: Christian Science, Religious Science, Unity School of Christianity.* Edited by Alan W. Gomes. Grand Rapids, MI: Zondervan Publishing House, 1995.

Graves, Robert. *The God of Two Testaments.* USA: Robert Graves and James Turner, 1977.

Hagin, Kenneth E. *Exceedingly Growing Faith,* 2d ed. Tulsa, OK: Kenneth Hagin Ministries, 1988.

———. *I Believe in Visions.* Old Tappan, NJ: Spire Books, 1972.

———. *Right and Wrong Thinking for Christians.* Tulsa, OK: Kenneth Hagin Ministries, 1966.

Mather, George A. and Larry A. Nichols. *Masonic Lodge.* Edited by Alan W. Gomes. Grand Rapids, MI: Zondervan Publishing House, 1995.

McConnell, D. R. *A Different Gospel.* Peabody, MA: Hendrickson Publishers, 1988.

Passantino, Bob and Gretchen. *Satanism.* Edited by Alan W. Gomes. Grand Rapids, MI: Zondervan Publishing House, 1995.

Price, Frederick K. C. *Faith, Foolishness, or Presumption?* Tulsa, OK: Harrison House, 1979.

Sabin, Robert. "The Man Jesus Christ," a Oneness Ministries handout. St. Paul, MN: n.p., n.d.

Savelle, Jerry. "The Authority of the Believer," in *Word Study Bible.* Tulsa, OK: Harrison House, 1990.

Seventh-day Adventists Answer Questions on Doctrine. Washington, DC: Review and Herald, 1957.

White, Ellen G. *The Great Controversy Between Christ and Satan.* Mountain View: Pacific Press, 1911.
Wierwille, Victor Paul. *Jesus Christ Is Not God.* New Knoxville, OH: American Christian Press, 2d ed., 1981.

Issues Related to Death and the Afterlife

Abanes, Richard. *Embraced by the Light and the Bible.* Camp Hill, PA: Horizon Books, 1994.
Ankerberg, John and John Weldon.. *The Facts on Life After Death.* Eugene, OR: Harvest House Publishers, 1992.
Blanchard, John. *Whatever Happened to Hell?* Durham, England: Evangelical Press, 1993.
Connelly, Douglas. *What the Bible Really Says: After Life.* Downers Grove, IL: InterVarsity Press, 1995.
Eadie, Betty. *Embraced by the Light.* Placerville, CA: Gold Leaf Press, 1992.
Groothuis, Doug. *Deceived by the Light.* Eugene, OR: Harvest House Publishers, 1995.
Habermas, Gary R. and J.P. Moreland. *Immortality: The Other Side of Death.* Nashville, TN: Thomas Nelson Publishers, 1992.
Hoekema, Anthony A. *The Bible and the Future.* Grand Rapids, MI: William B. Eerdmans, 1984.
Hoyt, Herman A. *The End Times.* Chicago, IL: Moody Press, 1969.
Kubler-Ross, Elisabeth. *On Death and Dying.* New York, NY: Macmillan Publishing Company, 1969.
Ladd, George Eldon. *The Last Things.* Grand Rapids, MI: William B. Eerdmans, 1982.
Moody, Raymond. *Life After Life.* New York, NY: Bantam Books, 1976.
———. *Reflections on Life After Life.* New York, Bantam Books, 1978.
Pache, Rene. *The Future Life.* Chicago, IL: Moody Press, 1980.
Pentecost, J. Dwight. *Things to Come.* Grand Rapids, MI: Zondervan Publishing House, 1974.
Rawlings, Maurice. *Beyond Death's Door.* New York, NY: Bantam Books, 1979.
Rhodes, Ron. *Heaven: The Undiscovered Country—Exploring the Wonder of the Afterlife.* Eugene, OR: Harvest House Publishers, 1996.
———. *Angels Among Us: Separating Truth from Fiction.* Eugene, OH: Harvest House Publishers, 1995.
Ring, Kenneth. *Life at Death: A Scientific Investigation of the Near-Death Experience.* New York, NY: Coward, McCann, and Geoghegan, 1980.

Smith, Wilbur M. *The Biblical Doctrine of Heaven.* Chicago, IL: Moody Press, 1974.

Wright, Rusty. *The Other Side of Life.* San Bernardino, CA: Here's Life Publishers, 1979.

Zodhiates, Spiros. *Life After Death.* Chattanooga, TN: AMG Publishers, 1989.

General Books

Archer, Gleason. *Encyclopedia of Bible Difficulties.* Grand Rapids, MI: Zondervan Publishing House, 1982.

Arndt, William and Wilbur Gingrich. *A Greek-English Lexicon of the New Testament and Other Early Christian Literature.* Chicago, IL: The University of Chicago Press, 1957.

Brown, Francis, S. R. Driver and Charles A. Briggs. *A Hebrew and English Lexicon of the Old Testament.* Oxford: Clarendon Press, 1980.

Denzinger, Henry. *The Sources of Catholic Dogma.* Translated by Roy J. Deferrari. St. Louis, MO: Herder Book Co., 1957.

Geisler, Norman and Thomas Howe. *When Critics Ask.* Wheaton, IL: Victor Books, 1992.

Geisler, Norman and Ralph MacKenzie. *Roman Catholics and Evangelicals: Agreements and Differences.* Grand Rapids, MI: Baker Book House, 1995.

Geisler, Norman and William Nix. *A General Introduction to the Bible.* Chicago, IL: Moody Press, 1978.

Geisler, Norman. *Ethics: Alternatives and Issues.* Grand Rapids, MI: Zondervan Publishing House, 1979.

Ott, Ludwig. *Fundamentals of Catholic Dogma.* Edited by James Canon Bastible. Translated by Patrick Lynch. Rockford, IL: Tan Books and Publishers, 1960.

Rhodes, Ron. *Angels: What You Need to Know—Quick Reference Guide.* Eugene, OR: Harvest House Publishers, 1997.

———. *Christ Before the Manger: The Life and Times of the Preincarnate Christ.* Grand Rapids, MI: Baker Book House, 1992.

———. *The Heart of Christianity: What It Means to Believe in Jesus.* Eugene, OR: Harvest House Publishers, 1996.

Sire, James. *The Universe Next Door.* Downers Grove, IL: InterVarsity Press, 1992.

St. Joseph Edition of The New American Bible. New York, NY: Catholic Book Publishing Co., 1991.

Sweet, William W. *The Story of Religion in America*. Grand Rapids, MI: Baker Book House, 1979.

Thayer, J. H. *A Greek-English Lexicon of the New Testament*. Grand Rapids, MI: Zondervan Publishing House, 1963.

The New Bible Dictionary, ed. J. D. Douglas. Wheaton, IL: Tyndale House Publishers, 1982.

The New International Dictionary of New Testament Theology. Ed. Colin Brown. Grand Rapids, MI: Zondervan Publishing House, 1979.

The New Treasury of Scripture Knowledge. Ed. Jerome H. Smith. Nashville: Thomas Nelson Publishers, 1992.

The Zondervan Pictorial Encyclopedia of the Bible. Ed. Merrill C. Tenney. Grand Rapids, MI: Zondervan Publishing House, 1978.

Theological Wordbook of the Old Testament. Ed. R. Laird Harris, vol. 2. Chicago, IL: Moody Press, 1981.

Vine's Expository Dictionary of Biblical Words. Eds. W. E. Vine, Merrill F. Unger, and William White. Nashville: Thomas Nelson Publishers, 1985.

Zodhiates, Spiros. *The Complete Word Study Dictionary*. Chattanooga, TN: AMG Publishers, 1992.

Scripture Index

Matthew

1 307
1:23 160
2:2 *93*
2:11 146, 167
2:16 93
3:1–4 147
3:1–6 92
3:11 166
3:2 166
3:15 165, 196
3:16–17 21, *93–95*
3:17 50
4:1–11 150
4:4 271
4:4–10 237
4:7 271
4:8 150
4:10 271
4:16 96
4:17 150
5:1 103
5:5 69
5:13 *95*
5:14 *96*
5:16 18, 96
5:17–18 *96–98*, 104, 264
5:18 113, 147
5:22 271
5:26 *98–99*
5:27–28 186
5:28 271
5:29 *99–100*
5:31 271
5:43–44 97, 123
5:45 101
5:48 *100–101*
6:16–33 101
6:19 136
6:20 136
6:22 *101*
6:30 73
6:33 56, *101–102*, 136
7:6 109, 234
7:9–10 137

7:13–14 244
7:14 18
7:15 42
7:15–23 104
7:20 *103*
7:22 49
7:23 123
7:24–25 104
7:24–27 147
7:24–29 *103–104*
8:2 167
8:3 154
8:4 97
8:12 *104–105*, 128, 140, 269, 297
8:14 163
8:20 *105–106*
9:4 41, 247, 264
9:12 56
9:18 167
10:1 207
10:1–2 231, 254
10:6 175
10:6–7 110
10:7 207
10:8 113, 114, 207
10:15 110, 129, 217, 270
10:16 148
10:22 210
10:28 100
11:11 106
11:14 91, 92, *106–107*
11:20–24 129, 140, 270
11:24 140
11:25 228
11:27 131, 139
11:29 *107*
12:32 *107–108*
12:39–41 110, 217
13:3–9 109
13:10 109
13:10–11 *108–110*, 169
13:10–17 106
13:17 109
13:24–30 109

13:35 110, 217
13:55 147
13:55–56 163
13:58 234
14:6–10 *110*
14:33 284
15:3 272
15:6 97, 272
15:24 *110*, 175
15:25 167
16:13–20 107, 126
16:16–17 105
16:16–18 *111–15*
16:17 242
16:18 111, 199
16:19 *115–17*
16:23 111
16:27 129, 270
17 162
17:1–9 50
17:3 55, 117, 152, 253, 266
17:4 *117–18*
17:5 182
17:10–13 106
17:11 91
17:12 106
17:16 258
17:17–18 258
17:27 139
18:9 100
18:15–18 *118–19*
18:17 *119–20*
18:18 111, 112, 115, 273
18:23–35 *120*
19:4 52, 96, 102, 198
19:5 186
19:8 53
19:9 35
19:11–12 40, 82
19:16–30 *120–21*, 135
19:21 275, 276
19:26 247
19:28 206, 308
20:1–16 *121–22*

11:5 179
11:11 55, 139
11:11–14 *179*
11:20 179
11:24 59, 70
11:25 173
11:25–27 107, 126
11:29 179
11:41–42 131, 177
11:49 237
11:49–52 *179–80*
12:41 160
12:44 181
12:49 44, 46
13:35 188
14:6 22, 173, 189, 200,
 208
14:6–11 *180–81*
14:8–9 *181–82*
14:9 182, 283
14:16 131, *182–83*, 186,
 193, 243
14:16–17 186
14:17 138
14:18 *183–84*
14:26 19, 182, 195, 270,
 272, 273, 300
14:28 176
15:1 169
15:1–5 173
15:7 137, 187
15:8 *184–85*
15:12 122, *185–86*, 197,
 219
15:22 270
15:26 19, 131, 138, 195,
 243, 300
16:7 243
16:12–13 *186*
16:13 138, 183, 226,
 270, 271, 272, 273
16:13–14 131, 243
16:14 183, 186
16:24 *186–87*
16:32 182
17:3 95

17:4 223, 261, 278, 279
17:5 182
17:12 257, 261, 268,
 297
17:17 271
17:20–21 *187–88*
17:21–22 176
17:25 139
18:5 173
18:20 217
19:7 166
19:23–24 155
19:26 188
19:26–27 *188–89*
19:30 38, 223, 249, 254,
 261, 278, 292, 311
19:39 279
20:1 155
20:5–7 238
20:6–8 155
20:11–15 155
20:14–15 155
20:15 141
20:15–16 158
20:17 *190*
20:19 154, *190*, 202
20:21 191
20:22 191
20:22–23 *190–91*
20:23 191
20:24–25 155
20:25 233
20:26 35, 203
20:27 155, 157, 172,
 226, 238
20:28 41, 95, 159, 160,
 161, 167, 171, 184,
 191–92, 228, 247,
 263, 264, 267, 283
20:30 273
20:31 151, 192, 196,
 265
21:4 155
21:6–11 139
21:12–13 158, 294
21:15–19 *192–93*

21:22–23 273
21:25 265, 273

Acts

1:3 157, 233
1:4 158, 294
1:5 183, 186, 191, 252
1:6–8 308
1:8 114, 119
1:9 156
1:9–11 *194*, 304
1:11 125, 307
1:22 113, 206, 272, 273
1:26 231, 254
2 231, 254
2:1 35, 198
2:1–5 119
2:1–8 114
2:4 20, *194–95*
2:5–13 198
2:16–17 275
2:22 114
2:30–31 70, 100, 298
2:31 60, 158, 238, 241
2:31–32 60
2:38 130, 141, 165, 191,
 195–97, 221
2:41 195
2:41–47 135
2:42 231, 254, 273
2:42–47 119
2:44 122, 124, *197–98*
2:44–45 *198*, 200, 276
2:46 301
3 231, 254
3:7 207
3:7–8 154
3:20–21 199
3:21 *198–99*
3:25 199
4 231, 254
4:12 *199–200*, 208
4:33 294
4:34–35 *200*, 275, 276
5 231, 254
5:1–11 114, 207

[335]

2 301
2:3–4 257
2:5 256
2:6 256
2:6–7 256
2:6–8 105, 190, 263
2:7 *256*
2:8 256
2:10 66, 251, 253, *256–57*
2:10–11 78, 220
2:12 211, *257–58*
2:13 211
2:25 81, 137, *258*
2:26 114
3:1–3 257
3:4–6 203
3:18–19 258
3:20 63, 149, 219, 307
3:21 156, 238
3:25–27 81
4:8 73, 293
4:11–12 245
4:12–13 136

Colossians

1:13 164
1:15 80, 159
1:15–16 23, 267
1:15–17 *259–60*
1:15–18 263
1:16 73, 122, 160, 231, 255, 259, 284, 286, 305
1:17 166, 203
1:18 56, *260*
1:19–20 260
1:20 *260–61*
1:24 *261–62*
1:26 109
2 262
2:3 73
2:8 *262–63*
2:8–9 42
2:9 159, 161, 231, 255, *263–64,* 267

2:12 221
2:13 164
2:15 296, 310
2:16 *264*
2:16–17 98, 202, 309
2:16–23 42
2:17 34, 98
2:18 146
3:1 63, 149, 307
3:2 138
3:10 21, 293
3:17 197
3:18–20 229
3:22 282
4:14 56
4:15 301
4:16 *264–65*

1 Thessalonians

1:9 95
4:13 55, 179, *266–67*
4:13–17 24, 150
4:13–18 277, 309
4:16 *267*
5:21 119, 288

2 Thessalonians

1:7 267
1:7–9 251, 261, 312
1:8–9 224
1:9 62, 63, 128, *268–70,* 297
1:12 181
2:9 31, 310
2:9–10 49
2:15 230, *270–73*
5:21 68

1 Timothy

1:3–4 68
1:10 40, 226
1:15 145
1:17 95
1:20 119

2:1–2 *274*
2:2 282
2:4 199
2:5 46, 65, 95, 188, 189, 200, 231, 255
2:5–6 *274–75*
3:2 52
3:12 52
3:15 119
3:16 283
4:1 17, 84, 96, 277
4:1–2 *275*
4:1–5 85
4:3 42
4:3–4 42
4:4 186, 227
4:10 102
4:16 68
5:1–2 135
5:23 56, 81, 114
6:9 136
6:10 136, 276
6:17 276
6:17–18 *275–76*

2 Timothy

1:6 114
1:10 78, 125
1:13–14 68
1:18 274, *277–78*
2:2 *278–79*
2:15 18
3:1–5 136
3:15–17 273
3:16 91, 271
3:16–17 68, 265, 270, 271
4:6 *279*
4:8 223
4:11 56
4:14 119
4:20 81, 114, 137

Titus

1:2 88

TOPICAL INDEX

TOPICAL INDEX

RELIGIOUS GROUPS INDEX

On salvation by works
Revelation 5:6–14   305

HINDUISM
On meditation
Psalms 1:2   61
On miracles
Luke 1:80; 2:52; 4:16   146
On pantheism
Luke 1:80; 2:52; 4:16   147
On salvation
Acts 4:12   199
Vedas
Genesis 3:7   25
Luke 1:80; 2:52; 4:16   147

INTERNATIONAL
("BOSTON") CHURCH
OF CHRIST
(See Boston Church of Christ)

ISLAM
Allah
Genesis 3:7   25
Ishmael
Deuteronomy 18:15–18   43
Mecca and Paran
Habakkuk 3:3   89
On Muhammad
John 14:16   182
Deuteronomy 18:15–18   43
Deuteronomy 33:2   44
On Muhammad's denial of deity
Psalms 45:3–5   64
On Muhammad and God
Habakkuk 3:3   89
On Muhammad receiving
revelation
Deuteronomy 34:10   46
On Muhammad – signs
and wonders
Deuteronomy 34:10   45

On prediction of Muhammad
Deuteronomy 34:10   45
Psalms 45:3–5   64
Isaiah 21:7   79
Habakkuk 3:3   89
Qur'an
Genesis 1:26   20
Genesis 3:7   25
Deuteronomy 18:15–18   43
On visitations of God
Deuteronomy 33:2   45

JUDAISM
On monotheism
Genesis 1:26–27   23

JEHOVAH'S WITNESS
On alpha and omega
Revelation 1:8   304
On annihilationism
Psalms 37:9, 34   62
Psalms 37:20   64
2 Thessalonians 1:9   268
2 Peter 3:7   297
On the "anointed class"
Luke 12:32   148
John 3:5   164
Revelation 7:4   307
On birthdays
Genesis 40:20–22   30
Matthew 14:6–10   110
On blood transfusions
Genesis 9:4   26
Leviticus 7:26–27   39
Leviticus 17:11–12   39
Acts 15:20   201
On Christ as God
John 20:28   192
On Christ – second coming
Acts 1:9–11   194
Revelation 1:7   304
Revelation 1:8   304